THE CHURCH

WHAT THE
BIBLE SAYS
ABOUT
THE CHURCH

Russell Boatman

College Press Publishing Company, Joplin, Missouri

Library of Congress Catalog Card Number: 85-70297
International Standard Book Number: 0-89900-098-3

Scripture quotations, unless otherwise noted, are from the American Standard
Version, 1901. New York: Thomas Nelson and Sons.

DEDICATION

This volume is dedicated to my former students of Minnesota Bible College where I served as president and taught for seventeen years, and to the students of St. Louis Christian College where I have served as academic dean and instructor for the past twenty-two years. Also included in this expression of appreciation and indebtedness is the West Side Christian Church of Wichita, Kansas, with whom the lessons were first shared.

This volume is dedicated also to those who taught me: My beloved parents, Richard Andrew (now deceased) and Verba (Shaddy) Boatman, Bro. Lertis R. Ellett (deceased) who ministered to me with patient understanding in the formative years of my youth, and Evangelist Archie Word, a Christian soldier par excellent still on the firing line for God at ninety years of age.

Appreciation is also expressed for the stenographic contribution of Miss Helen Williams of St. Louis Christian College, whose typing expertise was of great assistance in the preparing of the manuscript for presentation to the publisher.

Table of Contents

              The Church of Our Redeemer
              The Church of Rome
              The Church of the Reformation
              The Church of the Restoration Movement

Section One: Perspectives

              The Church Is the Body of Christ
              The Church Is God's Building
              The Church Is Christ's Bride-elect
              The Church Is the Unveiled Channel of God's Grace
              The Church Is Designed to Glorify God

              Derivation and History of Ekklesia
              Etymology of Kuriakos
              Apostolic Precedent for the Use of Kuriakos
              History of the Transition from Ekklesia to Church
              Fundamental Proposition
              A Modern Parable

Section Two: The Divine Foundation

              Preliminary Considerations
              Time and Place of Founding
              The Foundation Examined
              Identification of the Keys of the Kingdom

              A Living, Life-giving Stone
              Rejected of Men, Exalted of God
              Precious Elect
              Proven, Tried, Sure Foundation
              Conclusions

              Two Illustrative Analogies
              Four Dimensions of the Holy Spirit's Role
              Special Study: Concerning Spiritual Gifts

WHAT THE BIBLE SAYS ABOUT THE CHURCH

TABLE OF CONTENTS

TABLE OF CONTENTS

INTRODUCTION

The contents of this volume have been sifted and tested over the course of forty years. Under the title, *The Church in the Scriptures*, the lessons contained herein have formed a basic course in Christian doctrine. They have been delivered primarily at the collegiate level in Bible college classes over the past four decades. They were first prepared, however, for use in the midweek Bible study program of the West Side Christian Church (Wichita, Kansas) where the author served as minister-evangelist in the early 1940s. The lectures continue to be used effectively in the educational program of local churches and personal evangelism, via students who have been given a free hand in the use of the course outline and supporting teaching materials.

Students through the years, speaking often in retrospect, have appraised the course as one of the most informative and continuing useful studies undertaken in their college years. Many have encouraged the author to put the lectures into printed form. Hesitance to do so has been due in part to the ready availability of one of the perennial best sellers of the College Press textbook series, *The Church in the*

Bible, by editor Don DeWelt. But did not the Holy Spirit inspire the writing of four Gospels?

It is a dictum of Holy Scripture that "by the word of two or three witnesses a thing shall be established," (Num. 35:30; Deut. 17:6; Matt. 18:16; II Cor. 13:1). In view of that Divine principle, and upon the encouragement of many friends, including Don DeWelt, this companion study has been prepared for publication. It is in no sense repetitious. But it will be as supportive of the same truths as the format and text of the Gospel of John prove to be to the synoptic gospels which it supplemented.

Concerning the Preview - Review Questions

The preview - review questions at the close of each lesson are an important aid to this volume. They are intended to serve a dual purpose. When used to preview the lesson material the reader is enabled to read objectively. By approaching each lesson in a question-answer frame of reference specific information will be more readily noted and assessed. When used to review a lesson one's grasp of the contents can be readily tested.

The questions are not intended to be easy, a mere parroting of surface information. They are intended to stimulate thinking. They deal with issues of disputation, basic principles, key scriptures and lines of reasoning.

Throughout the course of study attention will be called repeatedly to the etymology of key words. Etymology may be defined as follows:

Etymology: From the Greek *etymon* (true, real) and *logos* (study of), hence: 1) the literal sense of a word according to its origin, 2) the origin or derivation of a word as shown by an analysis of its elements: the root from which it stems, with such prefixes and suffixes which may be attached, or 3) the process of determining the origin, hence true meaning.

The importance of careful attention to definitions can not be over stressed. Definitions are to words what handles are to tools. One can use a tool without a handle (a saw blade, screwdriver shaft, hammer head, etc.) but not very handily. They can be handled much more efficiently if proper handles are attached. That is why they are called *handles.* One can use words without knowing their precise definition, or the sense in which the word is used in a given context. But communication will ever be impaired unless the hearer or reader understand the words in the sense they are being used by the writer or speaker. This is particularly true in the study of the Scripture, for we are receiving the Word of God through a translation from yet another language.

Unfortunately, many key words of the Bible have not been translated. They have only been transliterated. That is to say, the letters of the original language have been merely replaced by roughly equivalent letters of our English alphabet. The result is a word which has a somewhat similar pronunciation, but is in no sense a translation. This, of course, is the preferred procedure when names of persons and places are brought over from one language to another. The rendering of such names by roughly equivalent letters in our alphabet is helpful in identification. But when the Greek word for messenger is transliterated "angel," or the word for an overseer is transliterated "bishop," or the word for immerse is transliterated "baptize," without so much as a footnote to call attention to what such terms really mean, the uninformed reader will supply in his mind whatever meaning such words have come to have in our own time.

Occasionally the translators follow the lead of the Biblical writers and provide at least an explanatory phrase, or perhaps a footnote. Matthew explained that the angel instructed Joseph to name the son of Mary, *Jesus* (Gr. *Iesous*, "saviour") explaining, "for it is he that shall save his people from their sins," (Matt. 1:21). Again, in Matt. 27:33 it is explained that the name Golgotha means "the place of a skull."

Many words obscured by mere transliteration demand closer scrutiny. The word commonly rendered "church" is one of them. A full lesson (Lesson Two) will deal with that problem. Take note of the preview-review questions. They are not just filler.

PROLOGUE
THE CHURCH THAT JESUS BUILT

The church is a distinctly Christian institution. It is "of Christ" in a sense no other institution is, or can be. The fact is, in the strictest sense of the term, it is open to question whether any other institution may rightly be so called.

The suffix letters *ian* are an adjective-forming suffix. When added to a noun set in a relationship position with another noun, the relationship established thereby denotes the possessive. It denotes the fact that the one is *of* the other. The Philippian jailor, for example, was the jailor of Philippi—Philippi's jailor.

Many and varied institutions and organizations—athletic, benevolent, commercial, educational, political, as well as religious now bear the name Christian. Educational institutions ranging from day-care centers for toddlers to impressive universities, athletic associations for both men and women, commercial institutions ranging from church-related publishing houses to such an anomaly as the Christian Brothers Distillery illustrate the diversity and ambiguity and even the incongruity of the current usage of the name. But the truth is (obvious at least in the instance of the last example cited) Christ never established a one of them.

17

Of the church, and of the church only (or to be more precise, of Christ's *ekklesia* and *His* only) did Jesus say: "I will build it. It will be mine" (Matt. 16:18). He said that of the *ekklesia*, which through a twisted course of circumstances came to be rechristened the church. Of that development we shall take further note, but later. (See Lesson Two).

1. The Church of Our Redeemer

That "the church" (Gr. *ekklesia*) is "of Christ" is a point of specific emphasis in the very first direct reference to the same in the New Testament—Matt. 16:18. The ownership spoken of is that of the founder/builder—a very real and familiar form of ownership. Likewise the last direct mention of His *ekklesia* in Acts, the first (and only Divinely inspired) book of church history, also speaks of the Divine ownership thereof. Paul, in his farewell to the elders of the church at Ephesus, exhorted them to take heed to themselves and to all the flock in which the Holy Spirit had made them overseers, to feed "the church (*ekklesia*) of God which he (Christ) purchased with His own blood" (Acts 20:28). The ownership there spoken of is that of a buyer, another very real and familiar form of ownership.

Throughout the book of Acts, and in the epistles which extend our knowledge of the early history of the church, this fundamental truth concerning the church is underscored—the church (*ekklesia*) which was founded on the day of Pentecost and thereafter built up by adding those who were purchased by Christ's own blood was Christ's church. The congregations formed from city to city were "the churches of Christ" (Rom. 16:16). Paul so spoke of them, and one would have to resort to the language of evasiveness and ambiguity to do otherwise.

Paul's favorite analogy underscores the fact the church is not only "of Christ" but it is His in a very personal sense, and subject to His authority. Repeatedly Paul speaks of the church as the body of Christ and Christ as the head of that body. The analogy is a very fitting one. The body has feelings, appetites, desires, needs, potentialities. But the body has no independent will. It is subject to the processes which emanate from the head. Even of the seemingly involuntary reflexes is this true. Immaturity, infirmity and injury may adversely affect the desired response. This is certainly true of our bodies. Nevertheless we are judged by the deeds which are done in our bodies. Both by our fellow mortals and by God is this so. Ideally, as members of the body of Christ, every word and deed, even our very carriage and visage ought to reflect the mind of Christ.

In Philippians, chapter two, Paul exhorts: "Be of the same mind, having the same love, being of one accord, of one mind" (vs. 2). And to make perfectly clear what (whose) mind he was speaking of he went on to say:

> Have this mind in you which was also in Christ Jesus; who, existing in the form of God, counted not the being on an equality with God a thing to be grasped, but emptied Himself, taking the form of a servant, being made in the likeness of men; and being found in fashion as a man He humbled Himself, becoming obedient even unto death, yea, the death of the cross (vs. 5-8).

Generally speaking, the early Christians understood and accepted this exhortation as the proper behavior for these who profess to be of Christ—Christians. Untold thousands emulated Him in their readiness to die for Him, as He died for them in His body. But still the church grew. Thus Paul said of himself and his fellow Christians:

> We are more than conquerors through Him that loved us. For I am persuaded that neither death, nor life, nor angels, nor principalities, nor things present, nor things to come, nor powers, nor height, nor depth, nor any other creature, shall be able to separate us from the love of God which is in Christ Jesus our Lord (Rom. 8:37-39).

Jesus in one of His paradoxes affirmed: ". . . whosoever shall lose his life for My sake and the Gospel's shall save it" (Mark 8:35b). The early church demonstrated how true that is. From the day Saul set about to lay waste the church, scattering it abroad, the church was destined for world conquest. One can no more destroy the true church of Christ by scattering its members than one can put out a glowing fire by scattering its embers. With hearts aflame for Christ those scattered abroad went everywhere preaching the Word (Acts 8:5). Even Saul, the foremost persecutor, became Paul, an apostle—the most ardent and articulate preacher of them all. He also became the most persecuted of them all. But again the paradox proved true. To the Philippian Christians he wrote of the dire things which had happened unto him that they had "turned out to the furtherance of the Gospel" (Phil. 1:12). His longing to preach the Gospel in Rome was accommodated at government expense. Moreover, though a prisoner in Rome, Paul made inroads into Caesar's own household (Phil. 4:22).

In time the power structure of the empire saw itself as threatened and took the lead in the assault against the church. Beginning with Nero, a succession of Caesars set about to destroy the church. But soon after the third century ended the emperor himself, Constantine the Great, professed conversion to the Christian faith, bringing an end to Rome's fierce persecution of the church.

2. The Church of Rome

The conversion of Constantine was hailed as the crowning victory of the church. But it turned out to be a hollow victory. As one historian so aptly put it: "In conquering the Roman empire the church unwittingly inflicted a near fatal wound upon itself in that the church was induced to restructure her spiritual enterprise after the model of the pagan Roman empire." Out of that restructuring process rose the so-called Holy Roman Empire—obviously more Roman than holy.

The Roman empire was comprised of a coalition of kingdoms with puppet kings appointed to see to it that Caesar's will was done. The kingdoms were comprised of provinces with provincial puppet governors appointed to do the same. The provinces were comprised of supervised districts to which was assigned at least one centurion (captain of a hundred) with military mercenaries at his command—the gestapo of those bygone days. Thus it was when "A decree went out from Caesar Augustus that all the world should be enrolled" (for tax purposes) even in far off Nazareth of Galilee Joseph and Mary, despite her advanced pregnancy, set forth for their ancestral home in Bethlehem of Judea in compliance to the decree.

The restructuring of the church followed strikingly similar lines. The roles of the evangelist and the elders were mingled and merged in the rise of the clerical priesthood, to the demise of the priesthood of believers. The title of bishop, which had already been misappropriated by influential metropolitan churchmen, was given official sanction as the designation of the overseer of the area priests. The next step was the emergence of the office of archbishop (ruler of bishops). Then came the archbishops of the archbishops to whom the title of cardinal was given. All that remained was the appointment of a cardinal of the cardinals, the pope (Lat., papa—"father"), the "big daddy" of the whole unscriptural *schema*.

But that is only part of the tragedy. Having aped the political structure of the Roman empire the church with quickening steps aped the cultural pattern of the empire also. Some one has well said, "People are like rivers, they grow crooked by following the path of least resistance." As streams make their way across the landscape they press against first one embankment and then the other, their direction determined by the degree of resistance encountered from place to place. Moreover, a part of that against which a stream presses is rubbed off and becomes a part of the flowage. Streams merge one with another, and cities empty their sewage and industries their wastes into the streams which serve them. Thus long before a stream reaches its terminus in the sea it may become polluted and vile, the life which it once carried in its flow all but destroyed within it.

The church is like that. Like a sparkling brook the church of Christ began its journey through the centuries and countries of this present world. It gushed forth, as it were, from the side of Christ, the Rock of Ages, as refreshing to a weary civilization as a stream in the desert. But as the extending church encountered the thought systems of the Greco-Roman world part of what it encountered was absorbed into its thought and teaching. Concepts and conduct as foreign to the Christian walk of life and the Gospel as a sewer is to a mountain brook became a part of it. By the time the church had made its way through even the first few centuries it had become corrupt in doctrine and deed.

The paradox of Jesus to which we have alluded was two edged. Not only did He say that whosoever would lose his life for (Christ's) sake and the Gospel's shall save it, He prefaced that promise by warning: "Whosoever would save his life shall lose it" (Mark 8:35a). That is as true of institutions as it is of individuals. The church which sought to preserve its life from persecution and peril by a political alliance with a pagan empire lost its own distinctive life and message and took upon itself the decadent life and perverted doctrines of the world it was sent to salt and illumine and save.

For a thousand years the corrupting of the church continued apace. Historians speak of those years as the Dark Ages. The appellation is applied not to the church's dethronement in terms of power. Never has the church had such power, in the ordinary sense of that term. The appellation refers rather to the church's degradation in deed and doctrine.

The adoration of Mary as "the Mother of God," a phrase borrowed directly from the Magna Mater religions which flourished in the Greco-Roman world, the worship of saints and relics, the sale of indulgences (simony), salvation through deeds of penance, as well as the hierarchial

21

system which divided the church into two classes—a ruling clergy and a hapless laity—these are but a few of the hallmarks of the apostate church which supplanted the apostolic church and the authority of the Holy Scriptures.

3. The Church of the Reformation

This brings us to a third major phase of the church in history, the church of the reformation. It needs to be noted that even in the darkest hours of the Dark Ages there were voices of protest raised—raised but rarely heeded, at least not by the power structure. Reformation voices have been raised in every generation. Even in the apostolic age there were divergent doctrines to be countered and departures from Christian ethics to be corrected. The greater part of the twenty-one New Testament epistles bear witness to that. But with the passing of the apostles and the growing pressures of the Greco-Roman culture the voice of the Spirit was often unheard.

But God, from of old, has promised concerning His Word: "It shall not return unto me void, but it shall accomplish that which I please, and it shall prosper in the thing whereunto I send it" (Isa. 55:11). In time, with the rise of such men as Peter Waldo (12th century, France), John Huss (14th century, Bohemia), Savonarola (15th century, Italy), Martin Luther (16th century, Germany) voices of protest were raised that were heard. Even within the papacy and lesser hierarchy voices of concern, from Innocent III (1215) to Leo X (1512), rocked nine great world councils of the Roman church.

The reformers were not agreed in all they taught and attempted else there would not have followed in their wake such a complexity of divergent denominations, but they were agreed on one thing—the Roman church had to be reformed from top to bottom else it would die of internal rot. A rising wave of atheism was directly attributed to the scandalous lives and wanton cruelties of those professing to be the ministers of Christ. The more vocal and persistent reformers who escaped martyrdom, together with their supporting constituencies, distilled in the diverse and divided sects of Christendom commonly identified as the Reformation Movement.

Reformation is a term befitting the milieu in which the reformers labored. When reason and entreaty fail society has but two recourses when criminals are abroad in the land—incarceration and/or execution. Reformatories and execution chambers are somber testimony to the fact that society has determined to protect itself through lawful and concerted procedures. The rise and relative success of the Reformation Movement in Europe bears witness to the fact that the prevailing religious establishment had become intolerably criminal. The fact that a wave of retaliatory bloodshed rarely followed when Protestant forces came to power witnesses to the fact the reforms sought were primarily spiritual, not political.

On the debit side it needs to be noted that the relative reticence of the escapees from the papal system to seek revenge has been marred by tribal warfare. Not only have the major Protestant parties been sorely divided, each against the others, but successive divisions within the ranks of each of them has all but destroyed at least the visible unity of the body of Christ; if indeed the body of Christ is what they collectively constitute. The movement that purposed to purge the church of the moral, doctrinal and organizational departures of the papal system became the epitome of another monstrous evil—the evil of schismatic bigotry and sectarian division of the body of Christ. That, despite the fervent appeal expressed in the Lord's (own) prayer, John 17, the epitomy of which is recorded in vs. 20-23.

Mead's *Handbook of Denominationalism* lists considerably in excess of two hundred separate sects of Christendom. Not just church splits but splintering is the spectacle exhibited. No segment is unmarred by divisions. Several of the major denominations have suffered as many as a score of formal schisms. Even a sect such as the Latter Day Saints (Mormons), claiming the benefit of additional Scripture and modern apostles and prophets, is split into six different "churches."

4. The Church of the Restoration Movement

The foregoing set the stage for the rise of a fourth, though not successive, phase in the history of the church. Eight score and sixteen years ago (as of this publication date) our fathers brought forth on this continent a renewal movement, conceived in liberty and dedicated to the proposition that "the church of Christ on earth is essentially, intentionally and constitutionally one; consisting of all those in every place who profess their faith in Christ and obey Him in all things according to the Scriptures, and manifest the same by their tempers and conduct."

The year was 1809. In that year Thomas Campbell penned his *Declaration and Address*, from which the first of thirteen propositions has just been cited. The Restoration Movement, as it came to be called, reaches back much further into history than the year 1809, and extended much more widely than the labors of Thomas Campbell. But with the penning of that document, what was aforetime but a wistful longing, or at best but a whispering hope, now found eloquent expression and a movement to restore the church revealed in the Scriptures, in its doctrine, practice, organization and unity became a distinguishable (and one might add, distinguished) phenomenon of the American scene.

At the outset the movement was called the American Reformation, by its promoters as well as others. This was done in candid acknowledgment that those engaged in the effort were standing as it were on the shoulders of others as they took up the task of raising anew the walls of Zion. In a sense they were taking up where the European reformers had left off. What had come to be seen as the unfinished reformation, particularly in the area of Christian unity, now claimed the attention of the American reformers.

The time was ripe, and America was the right place for the restoration of the New Testament order. The war of the revolution had united the colonists politically. But in the aftermath of the war it was soon evident they were by no means "one nation under God" religiously. In fact it was evident they had not really shaken off the shackles of the old world from which they came, many to find religious freedom in America.

The late Franklin H. Marshall, for many years Dean of the Phillips University College of the Bible, often remarked wryly: "When the pilgrim fathers came to America they fell on their knees. But when they arose they seized their muskets and fell on the aborigines." That was his way of pointing out the fact that what they sought for themselves, political and religious freedom, they were slow to extend to others. They colonized according to ethnic and geographical origin, and according to religious persuasion. The churches they founded were in many respects simply transplants of the religious and racial quarrels they had left Europe to escape. The manner in which they named towns and countryside after European counterparts illustrates the old adage, first applied to the Israelite refugees from Pharaoh's brick masonry jobs at non-union hours and pay: "It is hard to leave Egypt, completely."

In the religious realm many citizens of the new republic soon became aware of the fact they were still under the yoke of European hierarchies, religiously.

One of the first to strike for freedom was James O'Kelly. He had fought valiantly against the British in the war of the Revolution only to find that as a preacher he was still subject to British domination

24

in the form of Bishop Asbury. Appeals for redress only worsened the situation. In 1792 O'Kelly revolted. Supported by the congregation he served he severed relationship with the Methodist Episcopal church. Forthwith nearly a dozen fellow ministers did likewise, supported by their congregations. Since it indeed is hard to "leave Egypt" completely, they formed a conference to which they gave the name, Republican Methodist (as distinguished from the Methodist Episcopal). But at the 1794 meeting at Surrey, Rice Haggard proposed they drop the name Methodist and simply be known as Christians. The motion was seconded and carried. Whereupon A. M. Hafferty moved they renounce the *Methodist Book of Discipline* and take the Bible and the Bible only as their rule of faith and practice. That also carried. In the wake of those actions James O'Kelly established at Chapel Hill, North Carolina, a congregation to be known simply as the First Christian Church. To the best of my knowledge that congregation was not only the first Christian church to be established in that community, it was the first church in more than a thousand years to exist anywhere on the face of the earth bearing simply the Messianic title of our Lord and Savior.

The process was destined to be repeated again and again, both far and near. From out of segments of the Baptists, Presbyterian, Congregationalists and others, individuals, congregations (the latter, on occasion, district wide) took up the twin restoration refrain: "No book but the Bible, no name but the name that is above every other name." Christian churches, churches of Christ (the same were used interchangeably, as being synonymous) appeared in all parts of the budding nation, particularly on the frontier. Many of the movements which have been chronicled by historians began without awareness that others from out of different denominational persuasion were doing the same.

At least partly out of the awareness of this phenomenon came the shift of nomenclature from the American Reformation to the Restoration Movement. A significant difference distinguished the American struggle from the European. The European resulted in many and diverse sects of Christendom carved out of the established church. For two reasons this was so: 1) Every effort to reform the established church resulted in the expulsion of the dissidents, and not infrequently the execution of the leaders as heretics. The dissidents therefore found it to be more expedient to give up on the establishment and worship separately with those of kindred mind. This led to the forming of new congregations and eventually new denominations. 2) Each reform movement was

25

generally an effort to achieve reformation in one particular. This led inevitably to exaggerated emphases and polarization.

By way of contrast, on the American scene there was no monolithic religious establishment with which to contend. Instead the contention arose out of the diversity of denominations, the spinoffs and castoffs of the European milieu. The melding of the diversity of colonies into "one nation under God" fostered a climate in which a plea for Christian unity was tenable. Moreover, particularly on the frontier, many concerns were more pressing than the petty quarrels which divided them religiously.

When Thomas Campbell, Presbyterian clergyman lately come from Ireland, was assigned to a church beyond the Alleghanies in Washington, Pennsylvania, he found the issues which were seemingly "set in concrete" in the British Isles of little or no concern on the American frontier. Campbell was of the Three-Seed-in-the-Spirit, Seceder, Anti-burgher segment of the Presbyterian church. In the vicinity of his charge he found Presbyterians representing various admixtures of those and other distinctions, but to whom such distinctions, born and bred in the old world, were irrelevant. But they were deprived benefit of church or clergy because of them. Campbell took a bold step toward correction of the situation. He announced that at the forthcoming communion service all such distinctions would be set aside. It would be an "open communion" service. Public response was gratifying. But the Chartiers Presbytery, upon learning of it, was incensed and sought to effect his ouster. It was out of that traumatic experience that he wrote the *Declaration and Address*. What Campbell expressed struck a responsive chord in the hearts of hundreds who came to learn of it. For this reason he has often been chronicled as the founder of the Christian churches— churches of Christ, along with his son Alexander, whose eloquence of tongue and pen soon catapulted him into national prominence. Though their contribution was significant they arrived on the scene at least a decade and a half too late to be credited as the founders.

With whom, where and when did the Restoration Movement begin? To ask that is somewhat akin to asking where the Mississippi River begins. The answer commonly given to the latter question is Lake Itasca in northern Minnesota. But the truth is there are several score sources which annually contribute more to the flow of the Mississippi River than Lake Itasca.

Where then does the Mississippi begin? One might say, "It begins all over the mid-continent watershed," or "It begins at different places at different times." May we suggest it begins in the heavens above.

26

To return to the original question, similar answers might well be given. The movement of which we speak has no one beginning, neither in time nor space. Certainly it cannot be traced to any one man. Around the turn of the eighteenth century it seemed to begin in America almost everywhere at once. Tiny rivulets formed which merged with others, some larger, some smaller. Streams became rivers and rivers flowed together. And the process still goes on, ofttimes in parts of the world which have never been visited by any one of us. May we suggest it began and still begins with that which has come down from above. If one person above all others deserves to be singled out, and One does, that One is none less than He who prayed one night in an upper room, saying:

> Neither for these only (the twelve disciples) do I pray, but for them also that believe on me through their word; that they may all be one: even as thou, Father, art in me, and I in thee, that they also may be in us; that the world may believe that thou didst send me.
>
> (From the Lord's *own* Prayer, John 17:20, 21)

Postscript

We would be less than candid if we did not take note of the fact that the movement which arose to champion the cause of Christian unity has itself suffered two schisms. The principles and goals brought the movement through the Civil War still united, while many denominations divided and remain so to this day. But the seeds of division were sown.

Every institution, whether religious, fraternal, political or some other, develops a party pulling to the left and a reactionary party pulling to the right (or vice versa). These tend to polarize and in time division results.

The twofold emphasis of the Restoration Movement, 1) restoration of New Testament faith and practice and 2) the unity of all believers (in Christ) were given unequal priority by the two factions which arose in the movement. The more conservative faction, particularly strong in the southern states, began to champion restoration at any cost, even at the cost of unity. Their zeal to "restore the ancient order" crystallized in a mind-set that has been called "patternism," calling for book, chapter, verse authority for every facet of the worship and practice of the church. The opposing faction, championing unity at any cost, resulted in a mind-set in which the authority of Christ and the Scriptures became subservient to "progressive" goals.

27

In 1906 the right-wing conservatives were induced to be listed separately in the forthcoming federal census. They appropriated to themselves the name, Churches of Christ. While many factions existed among them, because of their emphasis on patternism they all shared one common visible feature in their assemblies—the non-use of instrumental music. This became the common denominator that has continued to unite them (at least for census purposes), and the main focus of the division which continues to separate them from others.

In 1966 the left-wing liberals effected a "restructure" of the Christian churches which formalized and finalized a second division, at least fifty years in the making. The restructionist (Disciples of Christ) Christian Churches officially separated themselves from the centrist churches that continue to be known simply as Christian churches, churches of Christ.

Two schisms in two hundred years is two too many, particularly for a movement that has had unity as one of its principal goals. But obviously the principles have borne both merit and fruit, else there would have been more schisms.

Jesus warned His disciples to "beware of the leaven of the Pharisees and the Sadducees" (Matt. 16:6). He warned them not against the Pharisees and Sadducees per se, but the "leaven" (mind-set) which made them what they came to be. Labels change but the leaven continues its insidious work. The church that Jesus built has in no century been unscathed.

1

THE CASE FOR THE CHURCH

The church in recent years has been subjected to fierce criticism, both from some supposedly within and from many of those without. The anti-establishment generation spawned by the Vietnam War years was particularly vocal and vicious. The church was upbraided, downgraded, castigated, flagellated. Not a few of those involved in parachurch "ministries," supported by the church, dependent upon the church for their very living, bad-mouthed with biting words the very hands which fed them.

The assault against the church seems to be somewhat simmering down as new whipping boys come along. Nuclear arms, environmental concerns, and such like, from time to time will be to the forefront. But such concerns come and go. The church remains. One of my college professors, the venerable Claude C. Taylor, likened to dogs barking at the moon those who sought attention for themselves by railing against the things of God. Barking dogs come and go, but the moon sails serenely on, accomplishing the task to which it was assigned from the foundation of the world.

When the apostle Paul arrived belatedly in Rome, still a prisoner in bonds, his accusers were not on hand to take up the case against him.

Not being one to sit waiting for things to happen, Paul took the initiative. Acts 28:17 informs us: "After three days he called together those that were chief among the Jews." When he had briefed them on the circumstances which had brought him to Rome in bonds, their response was: "We neither received letters from Judea concerning you, nor did any of the brethren come hither and report or speak any harm of you" (v. 21). They then informed him they were desirous of hearing firsthand concerning the things he espoused, explaining: "concerning this sect, it is known to us that everywhere it is spoken against" (v. 22).

It likely seemed to them that such was so. But the truth is that Paul was one who had probably come closer than anyone to having been "everywhere" the Christian cause was known. He certainly had not gone everywhere speaking against it. To the contrary. And in the course of his imprisonment in Rome, Paul penned an epistle known to us as the Ephesian letter. The theme of that letter is "The Church Glorious, Universal, Eternal, Sanctified, and Triumphant." That spells *guest;* and the church should be the most welcome guest to ever come and abide in any community.

In a small county seat town in southern Illinois some years ago the resident evangelist of the Christian church asked his wife one Monday morning, "What are we having for breakfast?" She thought for a bit, then answered: "If we had some bacon we could have bacon and eggs; if we had some eggs." Picking up the cue he headed for the butcher shop and found it open. But no one made a move to wait upon him. The butcher and his assistant and some cronies who had dropped in were at the other end of the store swapping tales. The air was blue with obscene and blasphemous language. Like Paul amidst the idolatry that lined the streets of Athens, the evangelist's spirit was provoked within him. Suddenly, in the booming voice so familiar to hundreds who had heard him in revivals, the late G. W. Gibson shouted: "Hallelujah. Praise Jehovah. Blessed be the name of his Son, Jesus, the Christ, my Lord and Savior." Silence hung heavy in the room for several moments. At length, the evangelist broke the tension by remarking cheerily: "I heard the name of my God blasphemed, and the name of my Savior used as a dirty curse word. I thought someone ought to speak a good word for them."

There are many of us who feel the same way about the church, and for much the same reason. It is time the case for the church should be presented against the backdrop of Divine revelation.

30

In the Ephesian letter Paul sets forth five facts concerning the church. Not a one of them could be rightly said of any other institution on the face of the earth. Let us take note of them one by one.

1. The Church Is the Body of Christ

The first of Paul's affirmations with respect to the unique role of the church is set forth in the third and final paragraph-sentence of chapter one. If readers find modern authors sometimes complicated and cumbersome in their composition, let it be noted the entire first chapter of this epistle (in the original language—Greek) is comprised of but three sentences: 1) vs. 1, 2; 2) vs. 3-14; 3) vs. 15-23. Much of what he has written suffers in translation. It suffers more when it is chopped into verse segments, as in the KJV, NASV, NIV, etc. Vs. 15-19 read:

> For this cause (in view of the blessedness of the estate he has described in the preceding paragraph) I also, having heard of the faith in the Lord Jesus which is among you, and the love which you show toward all the saints, cease not to give thanks for you, making mention of you in my prayers; that the God of our Lord Jesus Christ, the Father of glory, may give unto you a spirit of wisdom and revelation in the knowledge of him; having the eyes of the heart enlightened that you may know what is the hope of his calling, what the riches of the glory of his inheritance in the saints, and what the exceeding greatness of his power to us-ward who believe, according to that working of the strength of his might which he wrought in Christ, when he raised him from the dead, and made him to sit at his right hand in the heavenly (places) far above all rule, and authority, and dominion, and every name that is named, not only in this world, but also in that which is to come; and he put all things in subjection under his feet, and gave him to be head over all things to the church, which is his body, the fullness of him that filleth all in all.

Just as your body is the means which your head employs to get about, and accomplishes the myriad things you do, so the church from its inception has constituted the body of Christ, the means to the fulfillment of the purpose of him who fills all in all. It would make little difference how fine a head you have on your shoulders, how noble your goals, how lofty your aspirations, how great your motivation; if you did not have a body which moves as your head commands you would be helpless.

A non-functioning body may be occasioned by any one of three states— immaturity, injury, infirmity. We have all witnessed infants struggling

31

to talk or walk but failing and falling. All have seen injuries incapacitate and illness render helpless those who once were agile and strong. If the glowing portrayal of the church in the verses cited above does not describe one of us, we need to ask ourselves: Are we still babes in Christ? Have we become weak and sickly? Has sin so crippled us spiritually that Christ's will cannot be done in us? Well has an unknown poet written:

> Christ has no hands but our hands to do His work today;
> He has no feet but our feet to lead men in His way;
> He has no tongue but our tongue to tell men how He died;
> He has no help but our help to bring them to His side.

The church is the body of Christ. Of no other institution is this so.

2. The Church Is God's Building

The church is also God's building, even a habitation of God in the Spirit. In Ephesians, chapter two, Paul contrasts the wretched state of sinful man and the blessed state of the redeemed. In the latter half of the chapter he makes a special application of the state of the redeemed by contrasting the plight of the Gentiles before the redeeming work of Christ reconciled both Jews and Gentiles in one body, the church. He closes his rhapsody of reconciliation by noting that the church supersedes the temple, the pride of the Jews, as the habitation of God. Vs. 11-22 read:

Wherefore remember, that once ye, the Gentiles in the flesh who are called Uncircumcision by that which is called Circumcision in the flesh, made by hands; that ye were at that time separated from Christ, alienated from the commonwealth of Israel, and strangers from the covenants of promise, having no hope and without God in the world. But now in Christ Jesus ye that once were far off are made nigh in the blood of Christ, for he is our peace who made both one, and brake down the middle wall of partition, having abolished in his flesh the enmity, even the law of commandments contained in ordinances; that he might create in himself of the two one new man, so making peace; and might reconcile them both in one body unto God, through the cross having slain the enmity thereby; and he came and preached peace to you that were far off and peace to them that were nigh: for through him we both have access in one spirit unto the Father.

So then ye are no more strangers and sojourners, but ye are fellow-citizens with the saints, and of the household of God, being built upon

the foundation of the apostles and prophets, Christ Jesus himself being
the chief cornerstone; on whom each several building, fitly framed together, groweth into a holy temple in the Lord; in whom ye also are
builded together for a habitation of God in the Spirit.

Many buildings dot the landscape. Most of them serve some useful
purpose. Some have endured for centuries. Some are magnificent.
But of one, and one only, can it be said: "This is a habitation of God
in the Spirit." That cannot be said even of our most stately "church"
edifices. "The God that made the world, and all things therein . . . does
not dwell in temples made by hands" (Acts 17:24). Solomon understood that. In his prayer of dedication for the temple he had built he
said: "Behold, neither the heaven nor the heaven of heavens can
contain thee; how much less this house that I have builded" (I Kings 8:27).

Paul has therefore written: "Know ye not that ye are a temple of
God, and that the Spirit of God dwelleth in you?" (I Cor. 3:16). And
again: "We are a temple of God: even as God said, I will dwell in them"
(II Cor. 6:16). Whenever a building, any building, regardless of what
may be chiseled on the cornerstone, is emptied of those who are his
true worshipers, the family of God has left the premises and the Father,
the Son, and the Holy Spirit have also.

Only in the hearts of those whom Christ has "called out"—his *ekklesia*
(the called-out ones) does the Godhead dwell on earth. Only "the
church that Jesus built" is God's habitation. He doesn't remain behind
in solitary confinement when the building is locked and the congregation has dispersed. "Ye are God's building."

3. The Church Is Christ's Bride-elect

To keep "the bees in the same bonnet" we will skip two chapters for
the present as we take note of the fact the church is also Christ's bride-
elect. In Ephesians, chapter five, vs. 22ff., we have Paul's familiar
marriage analogy. The passage opens with an exhortation dear to
the macho male's heart:

Wives, be in subjection unto your own husbands, as unto the Lord. For
the husband is head of the wife, as Christ is the head of the church,
being himself the saviour of the body. But as the church is subject to
Christ, so let the wives be also to their husbands in everything (vs. 22-24).

The next several verses should dispel any notion that Paul was a
male chauvinist.

Husbands, love your wives [No problem? Read on.] even as Christ also loved the church and gave himself up for it; that he might sanctify it, having cleansed it by the washing of water with the word, that he might present the church to himself a glorious church, not having spot or wrinkle or any such thing: but that it should be holy and without blemish. Even so ought husbands to love their own wives as their own bodies. He that loveth his own wife loveth himself; for no man hateth his own flesh but nourisheth and cherisheth it, even as Christ also the church; because we are members of his body. For this cause shall a man leave his father and mother and shall cleave to his wife; and the two shall become one flesh (vs. 25-31).

I do not recall having ever seen an ugly bride. Now with bride-elects that is sometimes a different story. On occasion I have wondered what her suitor saw in her. But at the wedding the bride is always beautiful. I like to watch the groom as his bride makes her grand entry. One could almost reach out a hand and rub off his eyeballs. He has never seen her like that before. The fact is he will never see her like that again. She has been plucked, painted, perfumed, coiffured, contoured, and clothed in a wedding garment white as light. His bride has made herself ready!

What we have just said is not intended to make light of the bride's all out effort to make herself altogether lovely. What a pity it would be if she did not. To do otherwise would be a travesty. For a bride to come to the hour when the groom is presenting her to family and friends as the one he has chosen, and should she come to that hour and that occasion in a soiled frock and tennis shoes, unbathed, and with hair askew; that would disgrace not only herself but also her husband and the institution of marriage.

With Paul we say, "This mystery is great," but we really "speak in regard of Christ and of the church" (v. 32). A vision in the Apocalypse is worthy of note. John has written:

And I heard as it were the voice of a great multitude, and as the voice of many waters, and as the voice of mighty thunders, saying: Hallelujah: for the Lord, our God, the Almighty, reigneth. Let us rejoice and be exceeding glad, and let us give the glory unto him, for the marriage of the Lamb is come, and his wife has made herself ready. And it was given unto her that she should array herself in fine linen, bright and pure: for the fine linen is the righteous acts of the saints (Rev. 19:6-8).

Christ is no polygamist, philandering paramour, or keeper of a harem. He has but one bride-elect, and shall come to claim her, and

34

her only, for his bride. The bridegroom is making ready his house for the church which is to be his bride.

Preliminary Summary

A preliminary summary of the case for the church is in order. We have noted that the church is Christ's body. I have a body. It is hardly of the Mr. America configuration, but it has served me well through three score years and ten, and gives promise of further service. Should someone abuse it or heap scorn upon it, I would regard that as an assault against me, personally. On the road to Damascus Saul of Tarsus learned that Christ feels the same way toward his church, and toward those who do aught against it. (See Acts 9:1-4.)

We have noted the church is God's building, a habitation of God (indeed, of the Godhead) in the Spirit. I have a house of habitation. My wife and I designed it, arranged for its construction, and spent years paying for it. There are larger, more fashionable houses along the avenue. But anything said or done either to deface or to poke fun at our habitation we would take very personally, and both resent and resist it. Jesus was incensed at the manner in which the temple was being desecrated. He is even more concerned when the church is desecrated or ceases to serve the purpose for which he built it.

We noted also the church is Christ's bride-elect. My bride-elect of nearly fifty years ago has long since become my bride. I was never so naive as to believe, even when blinded by romantic love, that my chosen one was (or is) the most beautiful woman ever to walk this earth. But be assured of this, if anyone has any criticism to offer, let such a one keep it to himself. To honor or dishonor my wife is to honor or dishonor me. The two are one. Could we say less about Christ and the church? Beware what one may be inclined to say about the church. Her beloved is near, and hears. He knows even our secret thoughts.

4. The Church Is the Unveiled Channel of God's Grace

The church is the unveiled channel of God's grace, founded in fulfillment of his eternal purpose in Christ. The word "mystery" (Gr. *musterion*), used six times in Ephesians (thrice in the verses we are about to note) was used militarily of a carefully conceived and concealed military strategem. The full plan was known only to the supreme command but was designed to come to light in the course of battle as each subordinate officer set about to carry out the orders assigned each of them. In the first paragraph-sentence of Ephesians, chapter three, it is written:

> For this cause, I Paul, the prisoner of Christ Jesus in behalf of you Gentiles—if so be that ye have heard of the dispensation of that grace of God which was given me to you-ward; how that by revelation was made known to me the mystery, as I wrote before in few words, whereby, when ye read, ye can perceive my understanding of the mystery of Christ; which in other generations was not made known unto the sons of men, as it hath now been revealed unto his holy apostles and prophets in the Spirit, to wit, that the Gentiles are fellow-heirs, and fellow-members of the body, and fellow-partakers of the promise in Christ Jesus through the gospel whereof I was made a minister, according to the gift of that grace of God which was given me according to the working of his power: unto me, who am less than the least of all the saints was this grace given, to preach unto the Gentiles the unsearchable riches of Christ; and to make all men see what is the dispensation of the mystery which for ages hath been hid in God who created all things, *to the intent that now unto the principalities and the powers in the heavenly places might be made known through the church the manifold wisdom of God, according to the eternal purpose which he purposed in Christ Jesus our Lord* . . . (vs. 1-11, italics for emphasis).

The closing lines of the preceding text (vs. 9-11) are remarkable in the light of currently popular concepts of the church. Far from being a stop-gap measure, itself a "mystery parenthesis," an unplanned contingency and hastily devised fill-in for an aborted kingdom sandwiched in between two Jewish eras, God is said to have had the church in mind for the role allotted it, and that from times eternal. It is God's intention (and has been from the beginning) to make known through the church his manifold wisdom according to his eternal purpose which he purposed in Christ Jesus our Lord. That is a fourth thing that is said of the church which cannot be rightly said of any other institution.

5. The Church Is Designed to Glorify God

The closing section of Ephesians, chapter three, informs us that the church is designed to glorify God even as he was (and is) glorified through Jesus Christ. Verse 14-21 record a prayer Paul offered on bended knee on behalf of the saints. It closes with this beautiful benediction:

> Now unto him that is able to do exceeding abundantly above all that we ask or think, according to the power that worketh in us, unto him be the glory in the church and in Christ Jesus unto all generations for ever and ever. Amen.

Jesus came down to the closing days of his earthly ministry able to say to the Father: "I glorified thee on earth, having accomplished the work which thou gavest me to do." Whereupon he prayed: "And now, Father, glorify thou me with thine own self with the glory which I had with thee before the world was" (John 17:4, 5). From the anthems of praise recorded in the Apocalypse we may be assured that has been done. (See Rev. 4:8-11 and 5:9-14.)

The same is said of the church, and on both counts. God is glorified on earth through his saints (Matt. 5:16; John 17:22; Rom. 8:30). Even as the Son glorified the Father on earth and has been received up into glory, so shall it be with the church. In Ephesians 2:4-6 it is written:

> God, being rich in mercy for his great love wherewith he loved us, even when we were dead through our trespasses, made us alive together with Christ (by grace have ye been saved) and raised us up with him, and made us to sit with him in the heavenly places, in Christ Jesus: that in ages to come he might show the exceeding riches of his grace in kindness toward us in Christ Jesus.

Objection Stated and Met

There are some who would counter our appraisal of the church on the ground that what has been said applies only to the mystical church invisible, not to any visible, congregational manifestation thereof. The Ephesian letter has somewhat to say to this point also. We have not overlooked chapter four. Rather we have reserved it for refutation of the point of view just stated. If chapter four does not speak of the church in its visible, congregational manifestation, one wonders what language would be required to do so. The opening verses speak of the church both general and local, replete with appointed offices (functions, functionaries) and their appointed duties. And the place and importance of each and every member is also noted.

Paul begins the chapter with an exhortation to unity in both doctrine and individual accountability. Concerning the latter, he adds to what he has written in vs. 2, 3: "Unto each one of us was the grace given according to the measure of the gift of Christ" (v. 7), then notes: "Wherefore he (David, Ps. 68:18) saith, When he (Jesus) ascended on high he led captivity captive and gave gifts to men." What gifts?

Not apparently the ones so eagerly sought and popularly promoted today, but rather gifts of service, of instruction. Note v. 11: "And he gave some to be apostles; and some, prophets; and some, evangelists; and some, pastors and teachers." Why so? Note what follows:

> For the perfecting of the saints, unto the work of ministering, unto the building up of the body of Christ; till we all attain unto the unity of the faith, and of the knowledge of the Son of God, unto a fullgrown man, unto the measure of the fullness of Christ; that we may be no longer children, tossed to and fro and carried about with every wind of doctrine, by the sleight of men, in craftiness, after the wiles of error; but speaking truth in love, may grow up in all things into him, who is the head, even Christ; *from whom all the body fitly framed and knit together, through that which every joint supplieth, according to the working together in due measure of each several part*, maketh the increase of the body unto the building up of itself in love (vs. 12-16, italics for emphasis).

It would be difficult to ponder what Paul has communicated in the preceding verses and miss the case for the local, visible, and viable church. His dual emphasis upon 1) the Divine provision for offices* with leaders appointed to equip the saints for ministry, and 2) the individual accountability of every member to be fitly framed and knitted together points up the fact that every member of the church needs the church. And the church, in turn, needs every member—present and functioning.

Conclusion

In conclusion, and Paul himself stated it well, the church is worth fighting for: it is worth defending, and worth our contending. In the sixth, and final, chapter of Ephesians Paul has written:

> Finally, be strong in the Lord, and in the strength of his might. Put on the whole armor of God, that ye be able to stand against the wiles of the devil. For our wrestling is not against flesh and blood, but against the principalities, against the powers, against the world-rulers of this darkness, against the spiritual hosts of wickedness in the heavenly places. Wherefore take up the whole armor of God, that ye may be able to stand in the evil day, and having done all to stand. Stand therefore, having girded

---

* The Greek word *praxis*, commonly rendered "office" in the older translations might better be transliterated "practice," in the sense in which we speak of a doctor or lawyer practicing medicine or law. It is best translated "function," as, indeed it is, in the NIV (cf. Rom. 12:4).

your loins with truth, and having put on the breastplate of righteous-ness, and having shod your feet with the preparation of the gospel of peace; withal taking up the shield of faith wherewith ye shall be able to quench all the fiery darts of the evil one. And take the helmet of salva-tion and the sword of the Spirit, which is the word of God; with all prayer and supplication, praying at all seasons in the Spirit, and watching thereunto in all perseverance and supplication for all the saints (vs. 10-18).

The case is closed. The church is the most unique institution on the face of the earth. It is indispensable to the salvation and edification of the human race. It is worth living for, fighting for, dying for. Well has it been written:

> I love Thy kingdom, Lord,
> The house of Thine abode;
> The church our blest Redeemer saved
> With His own precious blood.
>
> I love Thy church, O God!
> Her walls before Thee stand,
> Dear as the apple of Thine eye,
> And graven on Thy hand.
>
> For her my tears shall fall,
> For her my prayers ascend;
> To her my cares and toils be given
> Til toils and cares shall end.
>
> (Timothy Dwight, author)

PREVIEW—REVIEW QUESTIONS

1. What was the prevailing world-view of the church according to the Jewish leaders with whom Paul conferred shortly upon his arrival in Rome? Document your answer (Bk., Ch., Vs.).
2. Does that evaluation differ significantly from the attitude mani-fested by the Jewish leaders in Jerusalem from the outset of the church? Read Acts 4. Document your answer.
3. Does that differ significantly from the stance of the Jewish leaders toward Jesus? What did Peter charge against them on the day of Pentecost? Document your answer.
4. Compare Stephen's charge against them, and their forbears in his martyrdom address. Document your answer.
5. Has the situation changed significantly in modern times? In the world generally? In so-called Christian nations such as the USA?

6. What is the theme of the Ephesian letter?
7. List (identifying the key verses) five affirmations of Paul concerning the worthiness of the church, each of which set it apart from and above every other institution.
8. What evidence can be cited that Paul was speaking of the church in its congregational manifestation, not just the "ideal" church, the so-called "church mystical and invisible"? Document your answer.
9. How did Paul exhort Christians to react in view of the prevailing antagonism manifested against Christ and his church? Document your answer. Document from ch. 6.
10. Does the appraisal of Hebrews 12:1-3 fairly reflect our role in the battle Paul describes in Ephesians 6:10-18?

2

THE LORD'S OWN

The Lord's own—who are they? To which church do they belong? Does anyone know? Paul has affirmed "The Lord knoweth them that are his" (II Tim. 2:19). And Jesus affirmed that those who are his own know him (John 10:14). The apostle John, in his first epistle, repeatedly states that those begotten of God know him. (See I John 2:3-5, 19; 3:14, 19, 24.)

Nearly everyone who professes to belong to a church of some sort, and particularly those who profess the ability to identify the true church, *the Lord's own*, assume the ability to answer the question before us insofar as they themselves are concerned. Of no small consequence is the fact that to profess to be a part of the "church," especially the *true* church, is to profess to be one of *the Lord's own*. That is precisely what the term "church" means.

Does that statement strike you strangely? Likely. It is commonly said that our word "church" comes from the Greek word *ekklesia*. If so, it has come so far from it one would scarcely recognize any connection. Not one letter of *ekklesia* has been carried over into our English word church, much less the meaning of the word *ekklesia*. Our word "church" only replaces the word *ekklesia*. It does not translate it.

Such words as ecclesiastic, ecclesiology, ecclesiasticism stem from the Greek word *ekklesia*. Translated, the term literally means "called out" (ones). Or, when used loosely, as it often was in New Testament times (but only three times so used *in* the New Testament itself), the word might be (and is) translated "assembly." (See Acts 19:32, 39, 41.)

Derivation and History of Ekklesia

Ekklesia is derived from the Greek preposition *ek,* meaning "out" and the verb *kalein,* "to call," hence the noun *ekklesia* originally designated persons who were "called out," or called forth. The pre-Christian history of the term has been carefully traced out by J. C. Lambert. (See *The International Standard Bible Encyclopedia,* Vol. 1, pp. 651, 2.)

Among the earliest experiments with the democratic process were those conducted by the free city states of ancient Greece. Civic business was conducted as follows. Town criers were sent through the streets to call the citizens forth to a designated meeting place. Since all the citizens were by intent "called out," all could in a sense be spoken of as the *ekklesia.* But human nature being then much as it is today, everyone did not respond to the call. Thus in usage the term *ekklesia* came to be applied only to the assemblage of persons who convened at the appointed place. Thus a term which in a general sense referred to all who were called to come forth to the meeting came to be used as a designation only of those who assembled in response to the call.

Once the term *ekklesia* came to have for its settled meaning an assembly, it was inevitable that in time it would come to be applied to gatherings of all kinds. Thus in the text to which we have already alluded (Acts 19:23-41) the word *ekklesia* is used three times, and in each instance is translated "assembly," although a different kind of assembly is alluded to in each case. In verse 32 a rioting mob is called an *ekklesia.* In verse 39 the term is used to designate a "regular" (Greek *ennomos*—"within the law") *ekklesia,* and in verse 41 the spokesman dismissed a then *quieted,* but not legally assembled, *ekklesia.* These three verses of Acts 19 represent the only New Testament usage of *ekklesia* other than its usage to designate those come together in response to the call of the Lord. One hundred and twelve (112) times it is used to designate what the translators of our Scriptures have chosen to call the "church." In one instance the "church" spoken of is not the *ekklesia* of Christ, but Israel (Acts 7:38).

42

It was precisely due to the growing ambiguity of the term that a modifier of some sort was often called for to specify what kind of (or whose) assembly was being spoken of. Jesus, for example, in his first recorded use of *ekklesia*, prefaced the term with a personal possessive pronoun, saying: "I will build *my ekklesia*" (Greek: *mou ten ekklesian*, literally, "the assembly of me"), Matt. 16:18. Bear this in mind. We will have occasion to refer to it again shortly.

Etymology of Kuriakos

Let us now consider the etymology of the Greek word *kuriakos* from which our word "church" actually has been derived. The word has an interesting history. It is derived from a common Greek noun: *kurios* (Lord) plus an adjective ending -*kos* (pertaining to). The specific literal meaning of *kuriakos* is "the Lord's own." In general application it could refer to such things as the Lord's own day, the Lord's own supper, or the Lord's own people. At least by the time of the edict of toleration by Maximin in 313, it was also generally applied to the Lord's own building, a structure where the Christians gathered for worship.

We now have before us two words, each of which has 1) a precise, literal meaning and 2) a general, popular-usage meaning. Neither of the two words could be construed as a synonym or precise translation of the other.

Why the Switch?

How did *kuriakos* come to be linked with *ekklesia*? More important still, how did *ekklesia* come to be replaced by *kuriakos* in a form which is now scarcely recognizable—church? The answer stems from the progressive ambiguity of the word *ekklesia*. As illustrated by Luke's account of the Ephesian riot, an assembly of any kind, for almost any purpose could be called an *ekklesia*, and often was. Thus, if a Christian were wanting to communicate to a casual acquaintance that he was on his way to a meeting of fellow Christians, it would scarcely be enough for him to say he was going to an *ekklesia*. Some further explanation was due. He could scarcely say "*my ekklesia*," as Jesus did. But he might say *kuriake ekklesia* (the Lord's assembly). The time came when that is exactly what they did.

Apostolic Precedent for the Use of Kuriakos

There is apostolic precedent for the use of the term *kuriakos* as a modifier of a noun referring to something that is distinctively "of the Lord, or pertaining to the Lord," as the word *kuriakos* may be properly defined. In I Corinthians 11:20 Paul speaks of that supper which is intrinsically "of the Lord" as the Lord's supper (Gr. *Kuriakon deipnon*, literally, "the Lord's *own* supper"). Likewise the apostle John in Revelation 1:10 speaks of himself as being in the spirit on "the Lord's day" (Gr. *kupiake hemera*, literally, "the Lord's *own* day"). The literature of the sub-apostolic age is replete with examples of the fact that this term was understood as referring to "the first day of the week, the highest of all days, the resurrection day."

This is not to say that the apostles likely coined the expression *kuriake ekklesia*, "the Lord's *own* assembly." It would be pure conjecture to say either that they did or they did not. But they certainly used an expression of equivalent meaning when they referred to the *ekklesia* which Jesus was building through them under the guidance of the Holy Spirit as the *ekklesian tou Theou* (Church of God, Acts 20:28; I Cor. 15:9; Gal. 1:13) and the *ekklesiai tou Christou* (churches of Christ, Rom. 16:16).

History of the Transition from Ekklesia to Church

Historically, the transition from the use of *ekklesia* to *kuriakos* took place in three stages. 1) The phrase *kuriake ekklesia* was coined to designate the kind of, or *whose*, assembly was being spoken of. Then, as now, there were many kinds of assemblies, occasions for assembling. But there was a special occasion which drew Christians together. They met on the *kuriake hemera* (the Lord's day) to observe the *kuriakon deipnon* (the Lord's supper), and in so doing constituted the *kuriake ekklesia* (the Lord's assembly).

2) The second stage in the transition was first chronicled, as of records currently available, at Constantinople where the oldest known "church" building has been identified. Originally, Christians assembled wherever convenient, in homes for example (See Acts 2:46; Rom. 16:5; I Cor. 16:19; Phile. 2.); or wherever necessary, as in the days of persecution Christians found it necessary to go underground, hence met in the catacombs. But in time it seemed expedient for Christians to have an identifiable meeting place on a par with the Jewish synagogue, or shrines and temples of the heathen. When a building was erected or otherwise

44

secured for such purpose, it was inevitable that it should be designated the *kuriakos oikos* (the Lord's house), or simply as the *kuriakos*.

3) The third stage in the transition grew simply out of the fact that the Scriptures speak of Christians as being themselves "the Lord's house." (See Eph. 2:19-22; Heb. 3:4-6; I Peter 2:5.) Thus we not only go to "the Lord's house," we are *the Lord's house*. He dwells in us, not in the buildings where we assemble. Notwithstanding, to this day both the buildings which house congregations and the congregations themselves, whether congregated or otherwise, and among the occasions for assembling, at least "the worship services"—all these are commonly referred to today as "church." We are, so to speak, "stuck" with such usage. We likely cannot change it, but we need to understand how and why it so came about.

Our English word church is a shortened, softened, transliteration of *kuriakos*. It is not a translation of *ekklesia*. It does not communicate the sense and meaning of *ekklesia*. In the old English the word appears as *kyrke*. The harsh "k" sound was later softened to "ch" and the vowel of the original word was restored, resulting in our word church.

Other languages besides our own point up the fact that some form of the Greek word *kuriakos* as a substitute for *ekklesia* is here to stay. See the following list of ethnic transliterations.

Bulgarian - *Cerkova*	German - *Kirche*
Czechslovakian - *Cirkev*	Russian - *Tserkov*
Danish - *Kirke*	Scottish - *Kirk*
Finnish - *Kirkka*	Swedish - *Kirka*

How could a word used more than a hundred times in the New Testament come to be replaced by a relatively obscure word never used in the Greek text in the sense and meaning of ekklesia? A somewhat parallel example may help to explain. The clerical title Reverend came into common usage in much the same way. In Titus 3:5 aged women are urged to be "*reverent* in demeanor." Historically, that adjective came to be applied to churchmen who devoted themselves to "holy things," hence were "reverent(d) in demeanor." But our penchant for shortening has reduced such a title as The Reverend Mr. Jones to the Reverend Jones, or simply The Reverend (when referred to in the third person) or simply Reverend (when used in direct address).

The point we are making is illustrative of the manner in which Christ's *ekklesia* came to be known as the *kuriake ekklesia*, but once the term

HISTORY AND DEVELOPMENT OF OUR ENGLISH WORD "CHURCH"

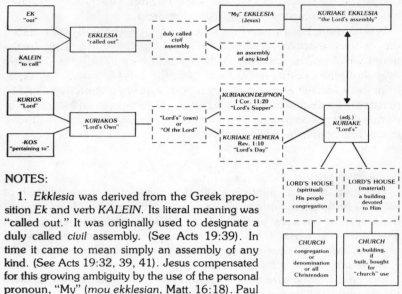

NOTES:

1. *Ekklesia* was derived from the Greek preposition *Ek* and verb *KALEIN*. Its literal meaning was "called out." It was originally used to designate a duly called *civil* assembly. (See Acts 19:39). In time it came to mean simply an assembly of any kind. (See Acts 19:32, 39, 41). Jesus compensated for this growing ambiguity by the use of the personal pronoun, "My" (*mou ekklesian*, Matt. 16:18). Paul compensated by employing a prepositional phrase in the genitive (possessive) case: *ekklesiai tou Christou* (churches of Christ). In the early post-New Testament era this distinction was made by the addition of the Greek adjective, *kuriake*— (*kuriake ekklesia*), "the Lord's (own) assembly."

2. *KURIAKOS* was derived from the Greek noun *KURIOS* and *-KOS*. As a noun *KURIAKOS* meant "Lord's house." As an adjective the word means "Lord's" (own) or "of the Lord." The noun form nowhere appears in the Greek New Testament. The adjective form is used only twice: I Corinthians 11:20; Revelation 1:10. Once joined to *EKKLESIA*, as an application of the principle employed by those two texts, the term in time *revolved* to a *noun* and came ultimately to stand alone as a full fledged substitute (though not an equivalent) of *EKKLESIA*. At the same time it revolved to its original meaning—"Lord's house." As such it lent itself to a dual application. It came to refer to a) Christ's "spiritual house" (I Peter 2:5), "whose house are we" (Heb. 3:6) and b) to such houses (buildings) as Christians devoted to His service. There is, of course, NO NEW TESTAMENT PRECEDENT for this latter application. The custom arose quite naturally, however, when "*ekklesias*" moved from private homes, theaters and other temporary quarters to buildings which they built or bought and dedicated to the Lord. The custom has persisted to our day, and likely will continue. Thus our modern word "church," derived from *KURIAKOS* (not *EKKLESIA*) has dual meaning.

caught on the designation *ekklesia* was jettisoned and the term *kuriakos* modified to produce our English word church.

Who are the Lord's own? As many as have been effectually "called out of darkness into (Christ's) marvelous light" (I Peter 2:9). In the pages which follow we shall focus our attention upon what the Bible says about the *ekklesia* of God and of Christ. In so doing we will likely, from force of habit and common practice (sometimes even intentionally, perhaps), speak of the same as the church. Perhaps, from the foregoing remarks the reader will understand why, and also what is to be understood and hopefully called in mind.

Fundamental Proposition

What we have just noted leads to a fundamental proposition: Christ established but one church, hence only one can be "the Lord's own." Such a proposition leads directly to a fundamental issue, perhaps two: One: if so, which one? Two: is it really so? The basic affirmation expressed is not of itself a point of issue, but the deduction we have drawn from it most certainly is.

One of our generation's most renowned religious leaders has expressed his views on the subject in this fashion:

The New Testament teaches that while there is actually only one church, there can be any number of local churches formed into various denominations or societies or councils. These local churches and denominations may be divided along national and theological lines or according to the temperament of their members.[1]

The foregoing quote calls for some interpretation. Note the author stated the church "may be" so divided, not necessarily that he was approving the fact they indeed are. But a few pages further along, he seems to speak defensively thereof as he writes:

Whenever anyone points a critical finger and demands to know why there have to be so many different churches all serving the same God, I am always tempted to point out how many different styles of hats have been designed for American men and women. We all belong to the same human race, but we have enough differences to make it impossible to wear the same style of hat with equal satisfaction.[2]

---

1. Billy Graham, *Peace with God.*
2. *Ibid.*

At best that is decidedly an oversimplification of a problem the Scriptures nowhere treat that lightly. Against the background of the fierce denominational bigotry of the early 1800's, Thomas Campbell wrote:

> The church of Christ on earth is essentially, intentionally, and constitutionally one, consisting of all those in every age and place that profess their faith in Christ and obedience to Him in all according to the Scriptures, and that manifest the same in their temper and their conduct, and of none else as none else can truly and properly be called Christians.[3]

Obviously the two men are not agreed. To borrow an expression from the apostle Paul, "What saith the answer (oracles) of God?" (Rom. 11:4). Is it a matter of no real concern that Christendom is indeed divided along national and theological lines, and even according to human temperament?

As concerns the first cause and manifestation of division it is highly significant that the name Christian was first called upon an *ekklesia* of Christ, not at Jerusalem where the church began; nor at Samaria, where the first break in the middle wall of partition between Jew and Gentile took place; nor even at Caesarea where the door of the church was opened unto the Gentiles. Rather it took place at Antioch where for the first time since the days of Abraham, Jews and Gentiles came together in one body. See Acts 8:4; 11:19-26.

The verb used in Acts 11:26 (Gr. *chrematisai*) is not a word of uncertain meaning. The translators of the New Testament normally manifest the fact they recognize its special import. The translators of the New King James saw fit to translate the same verb one chapter earlier, "Divinely instructed" in communicating the manner Cornelius is said to have learned he was to send for Peter to preach unto him words whereby he might be saved. (See Acts 10:22; Matt. 2:12, 22; Luke 2:26; Rom. 11:4; Heb. 8:5; 11:7.) Earlier translators insert (in italics) the words *of God* to point up the intrinsic significance of the same Greek verb. The same denotes "the action of God in making known his will." The conditions under which he deigned to first call the name Christian upon an *ekklesia* of Christ clearly shows the church may not be divided along national lines and at the same time be well pleasing unto God.

Such passages as I Corinthians 1:10-13, Galatians 5:19-21, Ephesians 4:1-6 underscore the fact that division along theological lines is a work

---

3. Thomas Campbell, *The Declaration and Address*, Proposition One.

of the flesh, not of the Spirit of God. And the Lord's own prayer for his own, recorded in John 17 (particularly vs. 20-23), certainly make it plain that Christ does not want his disciples divided in any sense. The temperament of the members should give way to the impassioned plea of our Savior that his people might be one that the world might be won.

This brings us back to the fundamental issue. If Christ indeed built only one church, then which one is the Lord's own? Any attempt to answer that question might follow this fundamental procedure: "Search the Scriptures, and see." The Scriptures shall therefore determine the perimeters of this study. This is not a study of contemporary Christendom, nor of comparative denominations. Neither is it intended as an apologetic for the fellowship of churches with which the writer is commonly associated. That fellowship, right down to every congregation, individual member, and form of expression, must be measured by the Scriptures as the only rule of faith and practice for the church.

Jesus once declared "the heavens and the earth shall pass away, but my word shall not pass away," Matt. 24:35. He also warned: "He that rejecteth me, and receiveth not my sayings, hath one that judgeth him: the word that I speak, the same shall judge him in the last day," John 12:48.

It will be better by far for the Word of Christ to judge our religious persuasions, preferences, and prejudices at a time when we can amend our ways and mold our thinking according to his will than that his word should judge us in the last day of these last days and find us wanting and wanton.

A Modern Parable

While I was conducting a revival in Lexington, Kentucky, some years ago, a Christian businessman shared with me this anecdote. His father had come to Lexington at the turn of the century bearing a charter authorizing him to found a bank. While relaxing in the afterglow of a successful grand opening, a stranger carrying a sizable satchel presented his credentials and asked for a few moments of the banker's time. Having introduced himself as an agent of the U.S. Treasury Department and an expert in the detecting of counterfeit currency, he explained that counterfeiters were proliferating in Kentucky and adjoining states, and that bank personnel owed it to their community to safeguard and certify their currency.

From his satchel the agent produced clips of counterfeit bills of various denominations and from a variety of illegal presses, totaling a face value in excess of a million dollars. He offered, for a modest fee, to conduct a seminar to instruct cashiers, tellers, and all who handled monies, to discern readily and accurately the difference between legal tender and counterfeit.

A time was set for the seminar and the schedules of the banker and his staff were cleared for the occasion. When the time came for the seminar to get underway, the agent arrived with only a small attache case in hand. He explained they would not be examining the array of exhibits in his collection. That would not be necessary. Occasionally, for illustrative purposes, they would examine a few representative exhibits. But their attention would be focused on the distinctive marks of the legal tender issued by the Treasury Department.

The agent's premises were these: 1) Even if they were completely aware of the marks of imperfection which characterize and identify each and every counterfeit operation in the land; and if every counterfeiter were apprehended and put behind bars, and every illegal press confiscated, and every bogus bill gathered and burned, the problem would not be ended. Especially would that be true if all they knew to look for were the mistakes of the counterfeiters whose specimens they had learned to recognize. Within a matter of days a new ring of counterfeiters would be operating somewhere. Their work too would be flawed in some respect, but likely in some respect differing from the mistakes of their predecessors. 2) If the bank staff were fully informed as to the marks of identification of legal tender, they would readily recognize counterfeit bills in whatever denomination and whatever form the copying error would appear.

So it is with the church. This work is not intended to serve as a study of contemporary Christendom, nor comparative denominations. Nor is it an attempt to convince the reader that the fellowship of congregations with which the writer is identified is *alone and in toto* the Lord's own.

Time will not permit an assessment of the many and devious ways in which historic and current denominations have failed to conform to the New Testament ideal. Even if we could, and every extant deviation were recognized as such and were eliminated, the problem of division and defection would not be over. Another, and another, and yet others would soon appear, each of them digressing in some way from the apostles' teaching, fellowship, breaking of bread, and prayers. Our concern therefore is: What the Bible Says about the Church.

Does one ask which church in the New Testament is to be regarded as the norm? The church at Corinth, infamous for its licentiousness, abuse of spiritual gifts (real or imaginary), and schism? Or the church at Jerusalem, so slow to break the bonds of racial bigotry? Or the churches of Galatia, among whom at least some are said to have been "severed from Christ" and "fallen from grace"? (See Gal. 5:4, despite the popular preachment in our time that such is impossible.) None of those, nor any other specific congregation *in toto*, but rather that ideal church which Paul described in the Ephesian letter as being the bride-elect of Christ—sanctified and cleansed by the washing of water with the word, that he might present the church to himself a glorious church, not having spot or wrinkle or any such thing, but that it should be holy and without blemish (Eph. 5:25b-27).

The title of this book, and of the college course it represents, determines the perimeters of this study. What the Bible says about the church shall be considered authoritative. The reader may have already noted a conspicuous scarcity of documentation other than the Scriptures. This will continue to be so. In view of the title of this work, if an affirmation cannot be supported and documented Biblically, the affirmation will be deleted. A score of quotations from popular "authorities" must give way to the dictum of Romans 3:4, "Let God be found true; but every man a liar."

PREVIEW—REVIEW QUESTIONS

1. Distinguish between the following terms: a. Translation, b. Transliteration, c. Transcription.
2. In view of the foregoing distinctions, identify each of the following terms: a. Χριστος, b. Christos, c. anointed one (Hebr. Messiah).
3. Identify the Greek word commonly rendered "church" in our English translations (English spelling, transliteration, accepted).
4. Is our English word "church" actually derived from that word? If not, from where does it stem?
5. List at least three English words which obviously stem from the Greek word commonly rendered "church" in our English New Testament. (The name of one book of the Old Testament might well be included.)
6. What is the etymology (linguistic derivation) of the Greek word *ekklesia*? Take note of the root from which it stems, and the meaning of any prefix or suffix attached to it.

7. What would be the literal definition of the term were its verb form under consideration?

8. What would be the literal definition of the noun form which appears repeatedly in the New Testament?

9. How many times does the Greek word appear in the New Testament? How many times is it rendered "church" in our English New Testament?

10. How is it translated in the remaining passages? Where? Book, Chapter, and Verses, please.

11. Cite the chain of circumstances which caused the root meaning to give way to the popular usage meaning reflected in the text(s) just cited.

12. What justification can be cited for Stephen's use of the term with reference to Israel in the wilderness of Mt. Sinai (Acts 7:38)?

13. Identify the Greek word from which our English word "church" has been derived (transliteration accepted).

14. Cite the etymology of the term, as in Question No. 6.

15. Take note of the popular usage sense in which that word came to be used by, during, and subsequent to New Testament times. Why so?

16. Is the word ever used in the Greek New Testament? If so, where and how?

17. How and why, according to secular sources, did the term come to be linked with *ekklesia* when speaking of the *ekklesia* of Christ?

18. How and why did the term come to replace *ekklesia* altogether as a designation of the *ekklesia* of Christ?

19. How does it happen that buildings as well as congregations are referred to as "churches"?

20. Rationale aside, is the place where Christians convened ever called the "church" in the New Testament, rightly translated or otherwise?

21. Is our word "church" a translation or a transliteration, or both? If so, or of either, of what? The question is not intended to be tricky, but it is technical.

22. Does putting the name "Church," or even "Christian Church/ Church of Christ" on a building mislead the public into believing the building is actually the church? Does a farmer's name printed on a country mail box alongside the road lead those who pass by to believe it is actually that farmer standing there on one leg, with one foot resting on the knee of the leg he is standing on, and the box is his upper torso resting on his thigh?

23. Is it possible that a knowledge of the Biblical usage of a term can lead to an over-reaction which could cause more confusion than good?
24. The ultimate question: Must an increase in Biblical knowledge lead inevitably to legalistic judgmentalism? Or can one grow in both the grace and the knowledge of our Lord Jesus Christ? Read II Peter 3:18.
25. What is the profit of *The Modern Parable* appended to the chapter? How does it relate to the title of the chapter, and of the book?

3

THE DIVINE FOUNDATION IDENTIFIED

Preliminary Considerations: Time and Place of Founding

The founding of the church was obviously a future event at the time Jesus made his announcement to the disciples at their approach to the city of Caesarea Philippi. Since Jesus equated the church with his kingdom by linking the two together in his response to Simon Peter's confession, it is also obvious the founding of the church was yet future at the time of his ascension. The disciples impatiently asked, "Lord, dost thou at this time restore the kingdom to Israel?" Rather than upbraid them for their continuing failure to grasp the true nature of his kingdom, he informed them it was not theirs to know times and seasons which the Father has set in his own authority (Acts 1:6, 7). But before he parted from them he gave them a clue.

In responding to their question as to when he would be setting up his *kingdom,* he set forth the mission and mandate of the *church,* commissioning them to carry it out in due season. He then added, "but tarry ye in Jerusalem until you are endued with power from on high" (Luke 24:49). In Luke's flashback upon the scene in Acts, chapter one, the promised endowment of power is identified with the coming of the Holy Spirit (v. 5). And when the Holy Spirit came upon them, in that very hour they began the task enjoined upon them in the Great Commission. From that time forth the church is spoken of in the book of Acts, the epistles, and the apocalypse as a present reality. Moreover the kingdom of Christ is spoken of in the same fashion (Acts 8:12; 14:22, 23; 19:8; 20:25; 28:23-31; Col. 1:13; I Thess. 2:12; Rev. 1:9).

Logic as well as Scripture leads to the certainty that the day of Pentecost, following the ascension of Christ marks the birth of the church. Two lines of reason and revelation converge. 1) References to the church prior to Pentecost speak of it as in the future. All references from that day onward speak of it as a present reality. 2) Logically, we must conclude:

If the church were established

before)	(Pentecost, 30 AD)	(Stillborn, a corpse
on)	(the result would)	(A LIVING ORGANISM
after)	(have then been)	(A bodiless "ghost"

As to the place where the church began that too is readily identified. If I knew (and I now do) where my mother was at the time she gave birth to me, I would know exactly where I was born. Since we definitely know where the Holy Spirit descended upon the apostles, credentializing, empowering, and directing them in the task of laying the foundation of the church, we know thereby where the church began. Both Isaiah and Micah, in identical words, predicted the birth and birthplace of the church, writing in the bold imagery typical of the prophets.

> And it shall come to pass in the latter days, that the mountain of Jehovah's house shall be established upon the top of the mountains, and shall be exalted above the hills; and all nations shall flow unto it. And many peoples shall go and say, Come ye, let us go up to the mountain of Jehovah, to the house of the God of Jacob: and he will teach us of his ways, and we will walk in his paths: for out of Zion shall go forth the law, and the word of Jehovah from Jerusalem (Isa. 2:2, 3; Mic. 4:1, 2).

The Foundation Examined

Of prime importance to a study of the true nature of the church is the identification of the foundation. This inquiry brings us to an area of conflict between the Word of Truth and papal tradition. The primary text of this point of discussion is Matthew 16:13-19. What did Jesus actually say to Simon Peter at their approach to Caesarea Philippi?

Matthew informs us that Jesus first elicited from the disciples the appraisal of the populace concerning him. He then asked them directly their own estimate of him. It is worthy of note that though the appraisal of the populace was neither united, nor were they yet convinced he was the Messiah, the opinions of those who heard him and saw his miracles were by no means as diverse as we encounter today. No one thought that he was an ordinary person. And apparently no one regarded him as some kind of imposter. Some were saying he was John the Baptist (whether recapitated and resurrected, or reincarnated in the person of Jesus of Nazareth, is not stated). Others thought him to be the Elijah of Old Testament prediction (Mal. 4:5). Others suggested Jeremiah, or some one of the prophets. Again, whether he was regarded as a resurrectee or a reincarnation, or simply one coming in the spirit of such men, is not said, nor does it matter. Jesus wanted to know who the disciples believed him to be.

Peter's confession of the Divine sonship and messiahship of Jesus is remarkable for its profundity and its brevity. Jesus commended him for it, and it was in that context that he said: "I also say unto thee that thou art Peter (Gr. *petros,* a rock), and upon this rock (Gr. *petra,* bedrock), I will build my church, and the gates of hades will not prevail against it."

At first glance it would appear that papal tradition has the edge in our inquiry. But an indepth study of the passage harmonizes with the rest of the Scriptures which bear on the subject. We need to note precisely what Jesus said, and what he did not say. Jesus did *not* say:

epi	soi	to	Petro
upon	you	the	Rock

In the stead of using a personal pronoun, Jesus used the demonstrative pronoun. He also used a different noun from the one represented by the name he had earlier bestowed upon Simon. What Jesus did say was:

epi	taute	te	petra
upon	this	the	rock

The key to the inquiry is twofold, linguistic and contextual. Linguistically, Jesus artfully used two different words for rock. (See accompanying diagram.) *Petra,* the rock Jesus said he would build upon, is the Greek word for what we call bedrock, or the massive outcroppings of rock such as the site of Caesarea Philippi. From such sources rock fragments are being continually produced. The Greeks called rock fragments *petroi* (pl.). A single fragment was called *petros*.

When viewed contextually, particularly in the larger context of the Scripture, it is even more evident that Peter was by no means the rock on which Jesus proposed to build his church. To appreciate the immediate context one needs to remember two things: the Jewish penchant for imagery, and Jesus' alertness to the illustrative value of things at hand.

As a teacher, Jesus was an opportunist. The happenings about him, even mundane nature, became teaching vehicles. In the instance of the site of Caesarea Philippi he had at hand an especially dramatic object lesson. Mt. Herman is a towering uplift of *petra*, a massive extrusion of rock. At the foot of the mountain an extended ledge of the same massive rock outcropping constituted the site of the city. Inevitably rock fragments, both great and small, would be scattered about the landscape.

One can imagine Jesus taking up one of the rocks strewn about. As he responded to Peter's confession, he may very well have held out before him the specimen he had taken in hand, saying, "and I also say unto you that you are *petros*." Then, with a sweep of his other hand toward the massive uplift of Mt. Herman, he may well have made his historic announcement: "and upon this rock (*petra*) I will build my church."

Fortunately, what has just been said has much more to support it than the supposition we have just shared. The larger context of the Scriptures underscores the fact that Jesus did not build the church upon Peter. Had he done so, Peter, of all people, would surely have known it, and made the most of it. Instead he pointed the minds of his hearers to Christ as the only sure foundation for their faith. On the day of Pentecost, as the church was being founded, he said of Jesus, "Let all the house of Israel know assuredly that God hath made him both Lord and Christ, this Jesus whom you crucified" (Acts 2:36).

In Acts 4:11, 12, Peter alludes to a prediction of David, saying of Jesus:

He is the stone set at nought of you the builders, which was made the head of the corner. And in none other is there salvation: for neither is there any other name under heaven that is given among men wherein we must be saved.

Again, in his first epistle, he repeats the citation from Psalm 118:22 and links it to a prophecy of Isaiah (Isa. 28:16) saying:

58

Behold, I lay in Zion a chief cornerstone, elect, precious, and he that believeth on him shall not be put to shame.

For you therefore that believe is the preciousness: but such as disbelieve,

The stone which the builders rejected, the same was made the head of the corner (I Peter 2:6, 7).

Were that not plain enough, Paul in the plainest language possible has written:

According to the grace of God that was given me, as a wise masterbuilder, I laid a foundation and another buildeth thereon. Let each man take heed how he buildeth. *For other foundation can no man lay than that which is laid, which is Jesus Christ* (I Cor. 3:10, 11).

In any building operation the first thing that is done, constructively speaking (once the site has been cleared), is the laying of the foundation. Beginning with the founding of the church on Pentecost one facet was a constant. Whether it were an apostle, a deacon turned evangelist (such as Stephen and Philip) or any other; all laid a foundation of faith in Christ, not in Petrine supremacy. Even those who were moved by jealousy at Paul's success and labored apparently to outdo him, found it expedient to preach Christ. (See Phil. 1:15-18.)

The church's one foundation
Is Jesus Christ her Lord.

It needs perhaps to be noted that a papist objection to the linguistic analysis included in the foregoing discussion points out the fact that the Aramaic dialect in which Jesus likely spoke does not make the distinction between rocks and bedrock which is made in the Greek language. Our response is twofold: 1) Gestures, vocal inflections, or an object lesson such as we have suggested could easily have made up the deficiency. 2) Fortunately, the preciseness of the Greek language became the vehicle of New Testament revelation under the guidance of the Holy Spirit. Equally fortunate is the fact that the Greek language, as though by Divine providence, was read and spoken throughout the Mediterranean world.

There is still another question that is often raised in connection with Matthew 16:18. Is the church built upon Christ, or upon the truth embodied in Peter's confession of Christ? Or upon both? A case can be made for either of the two; hence, a case may be made for considering both to be true. Taking Matthew 16:18 out of the larger context which has already been noted, it may be affirmed that the truth to which Peter bore witness is that upon which Jesus said he would build his church. But since that truth depends for its verity upon him who is the embodiment thereof, it is ill advised to press too far the premise that the confession is the rock. Practically speaking, there is a sense in which it is true. For example, the hilltop on which St. Louis Christian College is situated existed long before the founders of the college chose the location as a suitable place to build. Though it did not become the site of the campus until 1958, it had the potentiality of being the campus site. As the buildings which now grace the site began to be erected, the site became in fact what it had aforetime been only potentially.

So it was with Christ. He was born the Christ, the Son of the Living God. He was born the King of the Jews, even the King of Kings and Lord of Lords, intentionally, intrinsically. But he had no kingdom subjects, no church, until faith, arising in response to the truths and demonstrations which provided ground for faith, became manifest in humankind. If Simon Peter had never made the confession for which he is noted, if no one ever did, there would have been no church founded. The same is true today throughout the world. Potential "living stones" for a "spiritual house" exist wherever man is found. But there is no church found, nor can one be founded, until persons are found who are moved by faith to confess that Jesus is the Christ, the Son of the Living God. Is that not our experience? As Gentiles, we were once of wretched estate. But in Christ that was wondrously changed. Thus it is written:

> So then ye are no more strangers and sojourners, but ye are fellow-citizens with the saints, and of the household of God: being built upon the foundation of the apostles and prophets, Christ Jesus himself being the chief cornerstone, in whom each several building (structured segment) fitly framed together, groweth into a holy temple in the Lord in whom (we) are builded together for a habitation of God in the Spirit (Eph. 2:19-22).

Identification of the Keys of the Kingdom

Closely linked to the question of the identity of the church's foundation is another question wherein the Word of truth and papal tradition differ sharply. What did Jesus mean when he said to Peter, "I will give thee the keys of the kingdom. Whatsoever you loose on earth shall be loosed in heaven" (Matt. 16:19, as commonly translated)? Is there more truth than humor to the jokes which represent Peter as standing at heaven's gate deciding on the spot whom he shall admit and whom he shall refuse admission?

The popular parody aside, did Jesus give to Peter (and his successors) the power and the prerogative to make decisions, assign conditions which would be binding in heaven, appointing him thereby the first pope?

The fact that Jesus later (Matt. 18:18; John 20:23) extended to the rest of the twelve the prerogatives postulated to have been given to Peter is no problem to those of the papal tradition. To the contrary, they find in that support for their college of cardinals. But if Peter was accorded such a role, and others of the twelve were appointed to the role postulated for them, they never acted the part, or ever made mention even of the possibility, or their right to do so.

On the day of Pentecost, when the guilt-stricken multitude inquired as to what they should do, Peter's answer was precisely what Jesus had commissioned the apostles to declare. Moreover, it cannot be demonstrated that a one of them ever bound upon anyone anything that Jesus had not already bound, nor did they loose anything that Jesus had not already loosed.

When Jesus, at his ascension, took leave of his disciples, he declared that all authority had been given in heaven and on earth (Matt. 28:18). He did not then say, but since I am leaving the earth, I now bequeath at least my earthly power to one of you, and you know who. Instead, he exercised his authority in commanding them to take up the work of the great commission, placing them under orders as to what to preach, to whom, and the conditions to announce as the basis on which their hearers might be saved. It is worthy of note that protestants (so called because of the historic protests of their forebears to the arrogance of the papists in setting aside the authority of Christ) commonly rewrite the terms of salvation laid down in the great commission. As stated above, Peter assumed no such prerogatives, neither in addressing Jews nor Gentiles. He bound on earth only what Christ had already bound and continues to bind through his Word from his place of enthronement at the right hand of God. (See Rev. 3:21.)

The assumption that Peter was appointed Christ's successor is seriously flawed. At no time did Peter, brash as he often was, attempt to fill that role. In criticism of the papal claims for Peter the following facts are offered:

1. In the context of the disputed passage Jesus saw fit to rebuke Peter, calling him "Satan" and a "stumbling block" (Matt. 16:23).

61

This is hardly a good beginning for one supposed to be exalted to the realm of infallibility.

2. If Jesus indeed appointed Peter his right hand man that day, we would have to conclude that he was less than honest shortly afterwards in his response to the mother of James and John. When she asked that her two sons should sit, one on his right hand and the other on the left, instead of telling her the left-hand position was the only one then open, he stated that such decisions were not his to make. (See Matt. 20:20-23.)

3. In Acts 8:15 we find Peter was sent to Samaria to check out a report that the Samaritans had received the Word of God. Should not the head of the church be the sender rather than one of the persons sent?

4. At the Jerusalem conference concerning circumcision Peter was only one of several reporting to the conference. It was James who presided, and it was James' judgment that was adopted and circulated among the churches (Acts 15:19-21, 28, 29).

5. If Peter as the reigning pope was not the subject of veneration such as the pontiffs receive and delight in, Peter acted quite unlike a pope. He refused the prostration and worship of Cornelius: "I am but a man," he said (Acts 10:25, 26).

6. Peter's behavior at Antioch was out of character with one supposedly infallible. When he gave in to pressure from Jewish segregationists and withdrew from fellowshiping with the Gentiles, and in the process even drew Barnabas away also, Paul rebuked him openly, and indicted him as a hypocrite (So the Greek text reads; see also the New KJV.) and as a coward (Gal. 2:11-14).

7. At least weeks after the Caesarea Philippi episode, Jesus announced that the Father would send the Holy Spirit in his name; and it was he (not Peter) who would lead them into all the truth (John 14:16, 17; 15:26; 16:13-15).

8. According to Peter's own testimony, salvation is in the name of no man, himself being no exception (Acts 4:11, 12). This is in keeping with Paul's indictment as divisive any partyist who would say, I am of Peter, Paul, Apollos, etc. (I Cor. 1:10-13).

9. In several places the New Testament lists various offices conspicuous in the church. Never is such an office as that of Pope, nor his associates in the papal hierarchy mentioned. The fact is that the mind set which produced the hierarchy is severely condemned. (See Rom. 12:3-8; I Cor. 12:28, 29; Eph. 4:11; I Tim. 3:1-13. Cp. III John 9; I Peter 5:1-6.)

10. In Romans 1:10, 11 Paul expressed the desire to visit the church at Rome that he might impart to them some spiritual gifts. Would not that have been uncharacteristically audacious of Paul if Peter were ensconsed in Rome as the head and benefactor of the church?

11. Peter was definitely a married man, as indeed were the rest of the apostles, contrary to papal tradition and custom. (See Mark 1:30; I Cor. 9:5; I Tim. 3:2, 4:3.)

12. Peter, in addressing the elders of the church, identified himself simply as a fellow-elder (Gr. *sun-presbuteros*) identifying Christ as the chief Shepherd, and urged a posture of humility upon one and all. What an opportunity for him to have declared his high office, were he now reigning on earth in Christ's stead (I Peter 5:1-6).

13. In any building operation, once the site has been cleared, the foundation laying is the first construction task undertaken. Never did the apostolic messengers lay a foundation of faith in Petrine supremacy, but rather the preeminence of Christ (Col. 1:18).

14. An exegesis of the crucial passage mitigates against the papal pretension. The following analysis of Matthew 16:19b is not the work of the author. Its origin in the form presented is not known. The author has conferred with authorities in New Testament Greek and has been assured the analysis is correct:

MATTHEW 16:19b ANALYZED

The Greek construction of the latter half of Matthew 16:19 (cf. 18:18) makes it clear that Jesus never intended to give to Peter (or to the apostles, much less their so-called "successors") the power to "bind heaven" by such rulings as they might devise relative to the forgiveness of sins and other spiritual matters. The fact is that when correctly translated the passage binds the apostles to the principles and policies already determined in heaven.

Were the intended meaning that which is suggested by our common English versions, a simple future passive verb would have sufficed. The awkward construction in the Greek text, using the future verb with the perfect participle would have been uncalled for. The grammatical construction chosen by the inspired penman to record Jesus' words expressly guards against the very translation (and contingent error of interpretation) which has become so familiar to English readers.

Christ *gave* "the keys." Peter and the apostles were not to manufacture them. At his ascension Jesus affirmed that *all authority* resided in Himself. As sole authority He told them then and there the basis on which forgiveness of sins is to be offered. (Matt. 28:18, 19; Mark 16:15, 16; Luke 24:45-48).

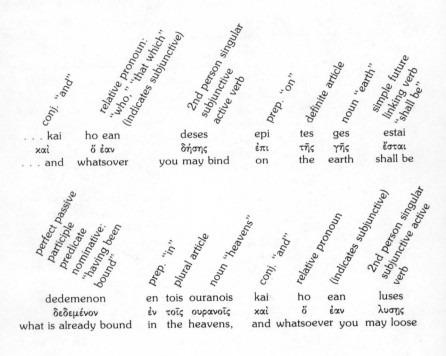

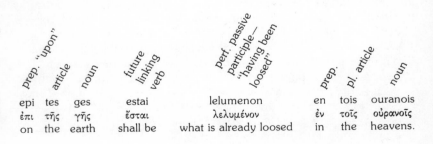

PREVIEW—REVIEW QUESTIONS

1. Aside from the role of the Holy Spirit in the founding of the church, state other lines of Biblical data which pinpoint the time the church began.
2. In view of the role of the Holy Spirit, how does the descent of the Holy Spirit on the day of Pentecost relate logically to the inquiry as to the birthdate of the church?
3. Cite at least one prediction in each of the testaments which pinpoint the place where the church began.
4. Prophecies aside, how might one logically determine the place the church began?
5. State the papist tradition which is supposedly supported by what Jesus said to Peter in Matthew 16:18.
6. What should Jesus have said had he meant to say what the papists claim that he said?
7. Identify the two Greek words for rock used in the disputed text and distinguish between them.
8. Identify, and distinguish between the two, the pronouns Jesus used in his prediction.
9. Did Peter indicate at any time that he understood Jesus was founding the church upon him? Support your answer Biblically.
10. Cite and locate the text which most clearly identifies the foundation of the church.
11. State the papist tradition concerning "the keys to the kingdom."
12. Locate (Bk., Ch., Vs.) and cite the evidence contained therein that Peter was far from infallible.
13. Cite, and locate textually, an occasion in which Peter, quite unpope-like refused homage.
14. Cite, and locate textually, an occasion in which Peter took pains to present himself as a fellow-servant, urging all to be likeminded.
15. Cite texts which list Biblical offices, none of which conform to the papal or even modified protestant hierarchies.
16. What did Jesus actually say with respect to binding and loosing?

4

THE DIVINE FOUNDATION DESCRIBED

Having identified the Divine foundation of the church, with particular attention given to the chief cornerstone, we would do well to note the description thereof as set forth in prophecy, and artfully restated by Peter in his first epistle:

> If ye have tasted that the Lord is gracious: unto whom coming, a living stone, rejected indeed of men, but with God elect, precious, ye also, as living stones, are built up a spiritual house, to be a holy priesthood, to offer up spiritual sacrifices, acceptable to God through Jesus Christ. Because it is contained in Scripture:
>
> > Behold, I lay in Zion a chief cornerstone, elect, precious: and he that believeth on him shall not be put to shame.[1]
>
> For you therefore that believe is the preciousness: but for such as disbelieve,
>
> > The stone which the builders rejected,
> > The same was made the head of the corner;[2]

---

1. I Peter 2:3-8; Isa. 28:16.
2. Psalm 118:22.

and,

A stone of stumbling, and a rock of offence.[3]

A Living, Life-giving Stone

It would be pressing the words of Peter beyond our power to prove, were we to assume that the expression *living stone,* as used today as a synonym for bedrock (Gr. *petra* from which stone fragments (petroi) are generated, was in Peter's mind as he wrote this text. But what he said nevertheless lends itself to the analogy. Stone is not alive in the ordinary sense of the term. For Peter to speak of Jesus as the living stone represents a deliberate mixing of metaphors.

To liken Jesus to the chief cornerstone of the temple of itself serves a dual purpose. Stone is a symbol of strength and permanence, and thus the proper basis of any structure which is by intent to be capable of withstanding the onslaught of storms and floods and to be extensive in height and dimension. In the parable of the two builders with which Jesus closes the Sermon on the Mount that fact is dramatically set forth.

The Jefferson Memorial Gateway Arch which graces the Mississippi River waterfront of downtown St. Louis, Missouri, is reckoned as one of the wonders of the modern world. In preparing for the foundation core drills were used to test the underlying rock for any semblance of structural weakness. Not until a depth had been established that was fissure free did the construction begin. The footings for the 635-foot parabolic arch were embedded in the underlying rock at a level that had been tested and proved to be "faultless." The church of Christ is builded on the only rock that is in a dual sense of the word, faultless—the Holy One of Israel, the sinless Christ.

To speak of him in the same phrase as the *living* stone is to emphasize the fact the foundation of the church is singular also in that he alone can give life, and indeed imparts life to those who are builded together in him. "Because I live, ye shall live also" is his promise as recorded in John 14:19b. (See also John 1:4; 6:57; 14:6; I John 5:12.)

The illustration of a magnet and metal particles attracted to it would serve as a modern analogy. The closer the pieces or particles are linked to the magnet, the greater their strength to attract others. The words of Jesus come to mind in this context: "And I, if I be lifted up from the earth, will draw all men unto myself" (John 12:32).

---

3. Isaiah 8:14.

Rejected of Men, Exalted of God

The quotation from Psalm 118:22 which Peter cited also in his defense before the Jewish council (see Acts 4:8-12) is particularly intriguing to contemplate. The quotation is first recorded in Scripture in Psalm 118:22. The verse is an allusion to an incident which is believed to have occurred during the building of Solomon's temple.

I Kings 6:7 informs us that the temple, "when it was in building, was built of stones made ready at the quarry, and there was neither hammer, nor axe, nor any tool of iron heard in the house when it was built"; so perfectly were the stones cut to measure and smoothed aforehand. Tradition states that the builders rejected[4] one stone sent from the quarry as unsuited to any place they considered it might be intended. But they soon found themselves at a standstill. They were ready to lay the chief cornerstone, and they had no stone suited to the purpose. It was then that the rejected stone was remembered, retrieved, and hoisted into place. And lo, it fitted perfectly. Thus the incident became a proverb. Peter, in Acts 4:11, 12, indicts the Jewish leaders of doing the same with the chief cornerstone of the spiritual temple. *The International Standard Bible Encyclopedia,* Vol. II, p. 722, documents the foregoing interpretation of Psalm 118:22 as traceable to the *Midrash,* an exposition of the Hebrew Scriptures, quoted by De Lira. E. B. Pusey, author of the *Commentary on the Minor Prophets* (Baker Book House), published as a part of the *Barnes Notes* series, does likewise. Pusey (see pages 361, 362), provides some perceptive insights on the origin and interpretation of the incident.

Pusey's comments are found in connection with the prediction of Zechariah where it is written of Zerubbabel, "He shall bring forth the *headstone* with shoutings of grace, grace, unto it" (Zech. 4:7). Pusey then notes that the foundations of the post-exilic temple had been laid long before, but work had come to a stop, and it was questionable whether it could be brought to completion. The prophecy of Zechariah was to the effect it would be, and under the leadership of Zerubbabel who would set the summit cornerstone.

There were two cornerstones of the temple, one at the foundation level, the other at the summit. Both were cornerstones in the sense they tied adjoining walls together. In the prophecy of Zechariah the emphasis is upon the summit. Psalm 118:22, possibly, and Peter's use of his sources quite certainly combine the two, and fittingly so. Christ is both the beginning and the end, the author and finisher of our

---

4. Heb. *maas,* loathed despised. Cp. Gr. *exoutheneo* (see Acts 4:11).

faith, the foundation and the summit. He is indeed the chief (head) cornerstone and the foundation of the church; and even the corner-stone thereof also.

That which is true of Christ is in a sense true of the whole church. Consider the example of the apostles, and of the prophets which were before them. The cornerstone analogy is used in the Scriptures to emphasize the fact that Christ is not the sole author or object of our faith. The church is indeed "builded upon the foundation of the apostles and the prophets, Christ Jesus being the chief cornerstone" (Eph. 2:20).

Even as Christ the cornerstone was rejected, so it was with the prophets and the apostles. Recall Stephen's stinging challenge: "Which of the prophets did not your fathers persecute?" (Acts 7:52). Recall too, Jesus' warning to the apostles: "They shall put you out of their synagogues: yea, the hour cometh that whosoever killeth you shall think that he offereth service to God" (John 16:2). And recall as well Peter's warning to the church: "Beloved, think it not strange concerning the fiery trial among you, which cometh upon you to prove you, as though some strange thing happened unto you" (I Peter 4:12).

The late Sam Lappin told of a congregation in Lawrence County, Indiana, near the quarry from which comes the well known Bedford limestone used so often in construction throughout the midwest. When their meeting house burned to the ground, the congregation took stock of its resources. The time was in the bottom days of the Great Depression. Many were out of work. Almost all were hurting financially. Having lost a frame building in a fire, some thought they should erect a stone structure, but the costs seemed prohibitive. One of their members suggested they appeal to the owners of the quarry to permit them to salvage the stone which had been discarded as un-suited for construction. Their appeal was granted. One man, well advanced in years, used a dilapidated truck to haul several hundred loads of the rejected stone. The limited funds of the congregation were used to buy the sash work, roofing, flooring, and such like. When the building was readied for dedication it proved to be, and remains to this day, a beautiful structure, gracing the community it serves, yet built of rejected stone. 'Tis a parable of the church.

REJECTED!

(of men, but exalted of God)

Psalms 118:22

Isaiah 53:3

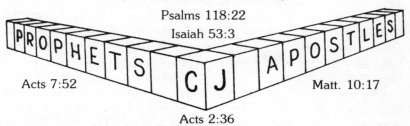

Acts 7:52

Matt. 10:17

Acts 2:36

HOW THE APOSTLES DIED

Matthew - Slain with a sword in Ethiopia

James, the son of Zebedee - Beheaded by Herod in Jerusalem

James, the son of Alpheus - Thrown from a pinnacle of the temple

Philip - Hanged on a pillar in Hieropolis

Bartholomew - Flayed (skinned alive with whips) in Armenia

Andrew - Crucified in Persia

Thomas - Thrust through with lances in the East Indies

Simon, the Zealot - Crucified in Persia

Peter - Crucified upside down (RC tradition says in Rome)

Thaddeus - Stoned, beheaded

Matthias - Shot to death with arrows

Judas - Hanged himself in despair following his act of betrayal

Paul - Beheaded in Rome

John - He alone died a natural death, but died in exile on the Isle of
Patmos, see John 21:21-23

Precious, Elect

Peter also speaks of the foundation as precious, elect (KJV, chosen, Gr. *eklekton*) of God. Recall the mockery of rulers at the cross: "He saved others, let him save himself if *this* is the Christ of God, his *chosen*" (Luke 23:35). That he indeed was the Christ in whom God was well pleased was demonstrated by his resurrection and ascension to the right hand of God. (See Acts 2:30-36, Heb. 1:3-9.)

He is certainly a foundation most precious. The foundation of the New Jerusalem is said to be adorned with precious stones. The description in Rev. 21:19, 20 staggers the imagination.

71

Repeatedly, Jesus is called the *monogenes* Son of God. The word, translated literally, reads: "only begotten." As used in the Scriptures, however, it has a deeper meaning. Isaac, for example, is called Abraham's *monogenes* son (Heb. 11:17) when in fact he was neither Abraham's firstborn son (Gen. 16) nor his last (Gen. 25:1, 2). But he was, as Thayer defines the term, "the only one of his kind"; the child of promise, and even more—a miracle child.

Sarah	unnatural		
conceived		time by super-	
		natural means,	of Divine
in an / a		and bore a son	promise !
Mary	natural		

Some things are considered precious, some almost priceless, by reason of their intrinsic worth; others by reason of their scarcity, rarity. In every sense Jesus is "the only one of his kind."

Sir Thomas Lipton, famed English yachtsman, was once showing a friend the many racing trophies he had amassed through the years. His friend was effusive in his compliments. Suddenly Lipton's face flushed and his voice filled with emotion as he replied, "I would gladly give them all up for one I have not attained—the American Cup." What a tragedy it would be for one of us to have come down to life's closing, having amassed all the tinseled trophies of this world, only to find we have missed the prize of the high calling of God in Christ Jesus. Ah yes, "to such as believe is the preciousness!" (I Peter 2:7).

Proven, Tried, Sure Foundation

The medicines, the miracle drugs, and other products we buy are promoted as having been proved before placed on the market. Virtually every drug carries the possibility of some baneful side effects. And despite the advanced engineering techniques and professed extensive testing before marketing, scarcely any line of cars has been released for long to the buyers ere thousands are recalled for the correction of defects. Only Christ is without flaw. Only he could fling this challenge to his enemies: "Which of you convicteth me of sin?" (John 8:46).

For such a high priest became us, holy, guileless, separated from sinners, and made higher than the heavens; who needeth not daily like those priests (the Levitical priesthood), to offer up sacrifices, first for his own sins, and then for the sins of the people: for this he did once for all, when he offered up himself (Heb. 7:26, 27).

Conclusions

A building is no more secure than the foundation on which it rests, even as a chain is no stronger than its weakest link. In Jesus' parable of the two builders the inference is that the two houses spoken of differed in only one respect. They may have followed the same blueprints. But however that may have been, there was one important difference, and what a difference that made. One was built on the rock, the other upon the sand. Year after year our newspapers carry the pictures and stories of people who build houses costing even hundreds of thousands of dollars upon mud banks overlooking the ocean, in order to gain an unobstructed view of the sea. Again and again it may well be said, "And great is the fall thereof" (Matt. 7:27).

We may also draw another conclusion from observation. The shape, size, and strength of a foundation predetermines what can be built on it. As the college grows where the writer has been privileged to serve for more than a score of years, it has been necessary for the buildings to grow apace. We have reached a point where it would be very desirable and advantageous financially were we able to add a story or two to some of the present buildings. That cannot be done. The foundations of the present buildings are only strong enough to support the buildings they already bear. Thanks be unto God, "The Church's One Foundation is Jesus Christ Her Lord."

> Rock of Ages, cleft for me
> Let me build my life on Thee.

PREVIEW—REVIEW QUESTIONS

1. List as many qualities of rock, and other factors such as availability and distribution, which make rock especially suitable for foundations.
2. Underscore those which are especially illustrative of Christ.
3. Granted that every analogy, even Jesus' parable subjects, breaks down if pressed too far, note certain aspects of rock which do not compare to Christ.
4. Note an adjective Peter introduced into his analogy to compensate for at least one vital difference between Christ and a rock, and for that matter, between Christians and rocks.

5. Note how the power of a magnet might well illustrate that aspect of Christ's relationship to Christians which rock cannot in any way supply.
6. What further lesson can be inferred from the power of a magnet, as transmitted to particles drawn to it?
7. Identify precisely the illustrative prediction upon which Peter furthered the analogy suggested by the prophecy of Isaiah declaring the Messiah to be the cornerstone.
8. Briefly state the tradition which relates to the building of the temple which illustrates the following of the Jews in their rejection of Jesus as their Messiah.
9. Identify the location of the two "cornerstones" of the temple, and identify the one called the chief (head) cornerstone.
10. Since Jesus is indeed the one through whom God has elected to save us, must we look for another if he does not come through on our terms and according to our timetable? Read Matt. 11:2, 3, and apply.
11. Identify the Greek word commonly translated "only begotten." State the special sense in which it is used in the Scriptures.
12. How does the use of the term in Hebrews 11:17 help us to understand the special sense in which the Scriptures use the term?
13. How does that use of the term help us to understand why the "sacrifice" of *Isaac* was such a severe test for Abraham?
14. Note both the parallel and the contrast in the circumstances of the birth of Isaac, and of Jesus of whom the "sacrifice" of Isaac was a type.
15. State two conclusions which may be drawn concerning the special importance of a foundation.

5

THE LAYING OF THE FOUNDATION: THE ROLE OF THE HOLY SPIRIT

"Behold, I lay in Zion for a foundation a chief cornerstone"
(Isa. 28:16, I Peter 2:6).

From the bold affirmation of Paul in verse eleven, chapter three, of First Corinthians we may confidently affirm the foundation of the church had already been laid when he penned that epistle. The evidence has already been cited which pinpoints the day of Pentecost (following the climactic events of Jesus' ministry) as the precise day the church was founded. That noted, the important role of the Holy Spirit in the founding of the church moves to the front and center. However, the words of Jesus in Matthew 16:16-18; 18:18; and John 20:23, plus his commission to the apostles (See Matt. 28:18-20; Mark 16:15, 16; Luke 24:46-49; cp. Acts 1:6-8) combine to underscore the fact that the apostles also had an important role in that significant event; and, we may add, in the subsequent history of the church in the course of their lifetime.

The context in which the Great Commission given to the apostles is couched in Luke's gospel makes it equally plain the Holy Spirit had an important role also in the founding of the church. In fact, the apostles carried out their role under the direct superintendency and empowerment of the Holy Spirit.

Luke 24:49 is an especially pertinent text. To the commission given the apostles, Jesus added this directive: "Behold, I send forth the promise of the Father upon you; but tarry ye in Jerusalem until you are endued with power from on high." Vs. 52, 53 inform us that following his ascension, and the worship that awe-inspiring event elicited from them, "they returned to Jerusalem with joy, and were continually in the temple, blessing God."

The promise of Luke 24:49 recalls the series of promises and predictions relevant to the office and work of the Holy Spirit enunciated at the Last Supper. Note especially these:

> These things have I spoken unto you, while yet abiding with you. But the Comforter, even the Holy Spirit, whom the Father will send in my name, he shall teach you all things, and bring to your remembrance all things that I said unto you (John 14:25, 26).

and again:

> But when the Comforter is come, whom I will send unto you from the Father, even the Spirit of truth which proceedeth from the Father, he shall bear witness of me. And ye also shall bear witness because ye have been with me from the beginning (John 15:26, 27).

and yet again:

> I have yet many things to say unto you, but ye cannot bear them now. Howbeit when he, the Spirit of truth is come, he shall guide you into all the truth: for he shall not speak from himself: but what things he shall hear, these shall he speak: and he shall declare unto you the things that are to come. He shall glorify me: for he shall take of mine, and shall declare it unto you. All things whatsoever the Father hath are mine, and shall declare it unto you (John 16:12-15).

Two Illustrative Analogies

To understand the role of the Holy Spirit in the laying of the foundation of the church, two illustrations or analogies may help us visualize a work which was spiritual in effect, not physical or material.

1. The Holy Spirit *himself* (that is, the Holy Spirit acting in his role as a Divine being sent from God), functioned in the role of a construction foreman. Though the site where the church was to begin was

long since predetermined, and the workmen trained by none other than Jesus himself, and personally commissioned by him for the work which was about to begin, they acted in accordance to his command, as instructed (Luke 24:49).

When the plans I had drawn for the home we occupy had been approved by the city building commission, the site having already been selected and secured, and necessary financial arrangements for a building loan approved; it remained only for the contractor we had selected to assemble a crew and "get with it." Our family could hardly wait.

It was a high day in our lives when the work of construction was promised to begin. I arranged for a substitute teacher in each of my morning classes that day. At 6:30 a.m. I was at the site. (The day before some forms and machinery had been brought there.) The next hour was one of the longest in my life. It was at least an hour before anyone else appeared. Then four men in two cars appeared at the scene, but they made no move to evacuate their vehicles. In response to my impatient inquiry they explained that my contractor personally supervised and directed every building operation he contracts. I knew him to be a dedicated Christian and a man of his word, and was aware of the fact he would be the construction foreman. But the men who worked under him were skilled and practiced workmen. Nonetheless they were waiting for their foreman to appear. It was his responsibility to see to it that the foundations were laid at the precise place, at the proper grade, and that they be of the exact dimensions, configuration, and strength.

Shortly before 8:00 a.m. the foreman appeared. Immediately he took charge and by noon the excavations for the footings and foundation were completed, forms in place, and cement ordered for pouring that afternoon.

The laying of the foundation of the church proceeded in much the same manner. The apostles, the chosen workmen, had been trained for the task by none less than Jesus Christ, the builder of the church that was to be his own "house"; as the tabernacle in the wilderness was in a sense the house of Moses (Heb. 3:1-6). But they tarried nonetheless, as he had commanded them, till the Holy Spirit should come to direct them. And when he, the Holy Spirit, came upon them, immediately "they spake as the Spirit gave them utterance."

It was well that it was planned to be that way. Peter would never have said some of the things he said that day as foundations were being laid in Jerusalem for the long-planned "house of prayer for all people" (Isa. 56:7; Mark 11:17). Peter actually announced that the blessings of the Spirit of God being poured out upon them were to be extended to the Gentiles also, "even to them that are afar off, as many as the Lord our God shall call unto Him" (Acts 2:39). His behavior at Antioch some years later (Gal. 2:11-14) indicates that even after what he was directed by the Holy Spirit to say on Pentecost, and the oversight of the Holy Spirit which he had experienced in connection with the conversion of the Gentile house of Cornelius, Peter was a slow learner, or else had a poor memory when left on his own. No wonder it was Divinely arranged that the apostles should wait until the Holy Spirit was sent to guide them into all the truth.

The temple in Jerusalem had a court of the Gentiles, which undoubtedly was to them a generous concession on behalf of the proselytes drawn from among the Gentiles to the worship of the one true God. But the Gentiles were barred from the temple proper. Had the Holy Spirit not directed the laying of the foundation of the church, a Gentile annex would have had to be added when the time came for the opening of the doors to the Gentiles. It will be recalled that the Holy Spirit again appeared on the scene in a signal manner, indeed in much the same manner as he did on Pentecost, at the conversion of the Gentile house of Cornelius. Once again Peter spoke out of keeping with his inborn prejudice.

The words of Paul in Ephesians 2:11-22 are of special import at this point. The passage which deserves to be read in its entirety closes with the text that is so very relevant to the topic at hand:

> So then ye (Gentiles) are no more strangers and sojourners, but ye are fellow-citizens with the saints, and of the household of God, being built upon the foundation of the apostles and prophets, Christ Jesus himself being the chief cornerstone (Eph. 2:19, 20).

2. The second analogy to which attention needs to be called relates to the specialized gifts of the Holy Spirit. The specialized gifts of the Holy Spirit served as the forms and scaffolding employed in the laying of the foundation for the church. The forms into which the footings and the foundation walls of my house were poured, and the scaffolding which both supported the workmen at certain stages of the construction and provided access to building materials and tools also—these were removed when the foundations were firmly set. And when scaffolding was no longer needed to support the walls, workmen, or supplies, these were removed also. The fact is the house would be an eyesore in the community if everything needed in building it were left in place to this day.

78

Such Scriptures as I Corinthians 13:8-11 and Hebrews 2:1-4 (among others) should make this plain to all. The fact is the further one reads in the New Testament, chronologically speaking, the less emphasis is placed upon supporting signs and wonders, and the more emphasis is placed upon the role of the Scriptures, and the role of those whose office it is to be ministers of the Word. (See "Excursus on Mark 16:17, 18", appendix to Lesson Six.)

Four Dimensions of the Holy Spirit's Role

Let us now turn our attention specifically to the founding work of the Holy Spirit. That work had four important dimensions.

1. The first function of the Holy Spirit was the empowerment and credentializing of the apostles. a) The apostles definitely spoke, not according to their own inclinations or ability, but "as the Spirit gave them utterance" (Acts 2:4). They spoke, as chosen ones among them also wrote, by Divine inspiration. b) They were also credentialized, certified by the Holy Spirit, both audibly and visually, for the sake of the hearers. There came a sound as of a rushing mighty wind. (Note what is said—not a wind itself, but the sound "as of a mighty rushing wind," Acts 2:3.) Were it the sound of a mighty rushing wind the people would have fled for safety rather than moving in the direction from where the sound was coming. How long they huddled in fright before they realized there was no storm bearing down upon them is not stated, only that they came together where the sound was emanating. And as they did so, the second facet of the phenomena was noted. The visual aspect took the form of tongues of fire, but was not fire. Nothing burned.

The visual manifestation of the Holy Spirit was adroitly designed to suit the purpose served by the outpouring of the Holy Spirit that day. It is worth our reflection that when the Holy Spirit was sent to publicly anoint Jesus as the Messiah at his baptism, the manifestation took the form of a dove settling down upon him. The Holy Spirit had come upon chosen vessels in times past, to empower them for special tasks, but was not promised to any as an abiding presence. John the immerser relates that he had been informed that: "Upon whomsoever thou shalt see the Spirit descending, and abiding upon him, the same is he that baptizes in the Holy Spirit. And I have seen, and have borne witness that this is the Son of God" (John 1:33, 34).

At the founding of the church the special role of the Holy Spirit was to supply and credentialize not only the chosen messengers but also the redemptive message, which, unlike the Law of Moses, was to be unto all people. Thus he appeared that day "like as of fire" (as a *visual* manifestation); and then to the multitudes who had been called together by the sound, he manifested himself *audibly* and *verbally* by the miracle of the tongues—tongues which were heard by those present as though the speakers were their next-door neighbor back home. The record reports that despite the fact the audience was composed of celebrants from more than a dozen different countries, whereas all the apostles were Galileans, yet everyone heard the message in their own *language* (Gr. *dialect*) wherein they were born (Acts 2:6, 8).

Tongue speaking then and tongue speaking now have little in common beyond the fact both employ the vocal apparatus. To understand the purpose of the gift, one needs to study it against the backdrop of the historical situation described in Acts, versus the hysterical situation which prevailed in Corinth. On Pentecost everyone heard in his own dialect "and got the message" in a twofold sense. They understood what was spoken, and the phenomenon was a convincing sign to the unbelievers (I Cor. 14:22). Tongues(?) as practiced today fulfill neither function.

2. The second function fulfilled by the Holy Spirit in the founding of the church relates to the extension of the gospel to the Gentiles. This too consisted of two facets: a) The Holy Spirit credentialized the initial household of Gentiles, especially chosen by God. In this process Cornelius was, first of all, "Divinely instructed" to send for Peter (Acts 10:22, NKJV, Gr. *echrematisthe*. Cp. Matt. 2:12, 22; Luke 2:26; Heb. 8:5, 11:7; and Acts 11:26). Secondly, with the same Divinely arranged timing that moved Philip from Samaria in time to intercept the Ethiopian eunuch on the Gaza road, Peter's thrice-given vision was concluded just in time for him to receive, with that mystifying series of visions as a background, the messengers from Cornelius. Peter put the two happenings together and concluded that God was showing him he should make no distinction between himself and his brethren and them (Acts 15:7-10).

Were there any doubt about it at the first, those doubts were soon erased when he arrived in Caesarea. While Peter was speaking the Holy Spirit fell upon Cornelius and his household even as upon the apostles on Pentecost. They too spoke with tongues and glorified God. Whereupon Peter commanded them to be baptized in water, seeing God had shown his choice in the matter by baptizing them in the Holy Spirit (Acts 10:44-48). Somehow word of it got back to Jerusalem before Peter did. When called before an inquisition of the die-hard segregationists at Jerusalem, Peter rehearsed the whole story. And then asked: "If God gave them the like gift as he did also unto us . . . who was I that I could withstand God?" (Acts 11:17). One can almost see the die-hard racists' minds fairly explode at the revelation. Whereupon they reversed their judgment, saying, "then to the Gentiles also God hath granted repentance unto Life" (Acts 11:18).

Note that at Pentecost, the miraculous manifestation of the baptism of the Holy Spirit credentialized the preachers for the sake of their hearts. But to effect a turnaround of the prejudice against the Gentiles, in the second instance the hearers were credentialized by the same sign to convince the preacher.

b) Having demonstrated by a sign that was incontestable that the Gentiles were to be received into the church without distinction, the Holy Spirit was thereby readied to implement the next forward step in the extension of the Gospel to the Gentile world. It is of special interest to note the congregation chosen to serve as the launching pad, so to speak, was the church at Antioch where the first time since the human race was divided, beginning with Abraham, Jew and Gentile came together in one body.

It is significant also that the integrated church at Antioch became the first great missionary church. Acts 13:1-3 relates the visitation of the Holy Spirit at Antioch, and the charge: "Separate unto me Barnabas and Saul for the work unto which I have called them." With the compliance of the church to that command, and the apparent willingness of the two chosen vessels to be so used of God, the great missionary expansion of the church began, and proceeded, under the direction of the Holy Spirit.

How wisely and understandingly the Holy Spirit works. Had he used Saul, the latecomer to the apostolic office, to lead in the conversion of Cornelius, the admittance of the Gentiles into the church would have ever been suspect by the Jewish establishment within the church at Jerusalem. Thus Peter was used as the channel of certification for the Gentiles. But despite the commission given them at the ascension, the apostolic band showed little disposition to leave Jerusalem, seeming to prefer to wait there for the several annual homecoming pilgrimages to bring their own kinsmen to them, rather than themselves going into all the world. This worked to a degree to spread the Gospel, especially when persecution scattered the church. Witness the case of Philip's ministry to Samaria. (See Acts 8:4 and 11:18-26.) But it only partially fulfilled the plan outlined so graphically in Luke's restatement of the Great Commission in Acts 1:8.

Incidentally, Acts 1:8 serves as the outline for the book of Acts. Chapters 1 through 7 are devoted to the church in Jerusalem and Judea, Chapters 8 through 12 are devoted to the church in Samaria, and chapters 13ff. to the church unto the uttermost parts of the earth. The name, Acts of the Apostles, often ascribed to the book is a misnomer. It only records some of the acts of some of the apostles, plus some acts of some who were not apostles. The acts Luke sees fit to chronicle are those acts which, under the supervision of, and in response to the call of, the Holy Spirit, extended the Gospel throughout the then known world.

3. The third function of the Holy Spirit was that of supplying to chosen vessels the extraordinary gifts of the Holy Spirit which served as the forms and/or scaffolding, illustratively speaking, for the early stages of the building of the church. These gifts served in lieu of the New Testament which now furnishes the church unto every good work (II Tim. 3:16). They are catalogued thrice in I Corinthians, chapter twelve. It needs to be noted that the gifts were distributed by the Holy Spirit, not on demand, nor for ego expansion, but "according to his own will" (I Cor. 12:11). Not one of the gifts was given to everyone as the one sure evidence one was baptized into the Holy Spirit. And apparently some in the church had none of the "showy" gifts in which some exulted and disparaged unto their discouragement the non-endowed. But on the other hand, the moral gifts which had to be "growed," rather than having been bestowed, are said to be greater and more to be sought after than the more conspicuously exhibited specialized gifts. (See I Cor. 12:31, and the explanation which follows in the text, I Cor. 13.) Incidentally, the gift of tongues, the most sought after and most publicized "spiritual gift" today, is nowhere spoken of in the Scriptures as a *charismatic* gift, nor included under the Greek term, *charismata* (gifts of grace). Romans 6:23 informs us that the *charisma* (*free* gift) of God is eternal life in Christ Jesus. That makes the whole church a charismatic fellowship! Romans 12:5ff. informs us that the church is like a body, it has many members, but they all do not have the same function (else they would not constitute a body, as explained by Paul in I Cor. 12). Paul then continues on to say, "having *charismata* (gifts of grace) differing according to the grace that was given us" (Rom. 12:6), we should use whatever gift we have to the glory of God, whether it be teaching, exhorting, giving, or

consoling. And the whole discussion is predicated on the warning that whatever our gift or role, we should "not think of ourselves more highly than we ought to think," v. 3.

The specialized, functional gifts which served as temporary devices may be classified under three heads: 1) gifts of knowledge, providing information, 2) gifts of power, providing confirmation, and 3) gifts of labor, providing administration. These supplied a critical need as evangelists passed through cities and provinces and left behind infant churches without a single book of the New Testament as yet written to be left in the hands of anyone. Congregations needing administration often had not a single experienced mature Christian in their midst. Witness the plight that would have befallen the church at Philippi, a new congregation made up of an unenviably small and diverse nucleus. To the best of our knowledge, that church stood alone in all the land of Greece as Paul left them the day after he converted the only man mentioned among them, the Philippian jailer. Were it not that "through the laying on of apostle's hands the Holy Spirit was given" (Acts 8:18) in the form of specialized gifts of ministry, such a church as the Philippian congregation would likely have not survived.

4. The fourth special ministry of the Holy Spirit, needed as much from the beginning as now, is the one facet of his work that remains a constant factor wherever the church exists, and necessarily so even to the end of the age. The Holy Spirit indwells the church, 1) strengthening our inward man, Ephesians 3:16; 2) assuring, sealing our sonship, Ephesians 1:13; Romans 8:16; I John 3:24; 4:13; and 3) producing in us the fruit of the Spirit, Galatians 5:22, 23.

With the Holy Spirit living within us, our spirits which were aforetime buffeted and often beaten by the lusts of the flesh are made strong, giving us the power to overcome. He is said to be the earnest of our inheritance (Eph. 1:13). Earnest money is money advanced as a surety to bind a contract, and to serve as a guarantee we will carry out the contract according to the terms thereof. In giving us the Holy Spirit as the earnest of our inheritance, God has provided an advance token of his promises to see us through to the end, and thereafter throughout eternity. Note that Paul speaks of the fruit (singular) of the Spirit. We are not an exotic "fruit cocktail" tree, a la Stark's Nursery catalog offering. Just as an apple at its best combines many qualities—crispness, tanginess, sweetness, juiciness, fragrance, etc., so the fruit of the Spirit ideally expresses itself in such qualities as love, joy, peace, longsuffering, goodness, faithfulness, meekness, self-control, and such like. Those are not optional qualities to be born selectively by different Christians. All should characterize the life of every professing Spirit-filled Christian. Note: Supplementing the "Preview—Review Questions" at the close of this chapter are exhibits containing catalogued Scriptures and some guidelines for study related to the work of the Holy Spirit. Note also the "Excursus on Mark 16:17, 18" appended to Lesson Six.

PREVIEW—REVIEW QUESTIONS

1. Where does the Scripture plainly state the foundation of the church had already been laid when Paul began his work as a "wise master builder"?
2. State the analogy which illustrates the Holy Spirit's personal role in the founding of the church.
3. Why did the Holy Spirit so take charge that the apostles spoke "as the Spirit gave them utterance"? Had Jesus not adequately trained them?
4. State the analogy which illustrates the function of the specialized gifts as they relate to the founding of the church.
5. Cite the threefold classification of those gifts, and the purpose served by each class.
6. How were such gifts ordinarily bestowed? Cite supporting texts.
7. Does the New Testament record any exception to that rule (principle)? Why so? Identify and explain.
8. Who determined which of such gifts was bestowed upon the recipient? Cite proof.
9. Were tongues ever received by every Christian? How would you support your answer from the Scriptures?
10. Was any *bestowed* gift the one ever-identifying proof of the baptism of the Holy Spirit?
11. Cite the reaction of the Jerusalem church when they learned what happened at the house of Cornelius during Peter's visit.
12. How do we know it was the baptismal gift that was received by Cornelius and his household? Acts, Ch. 10, which describes the happening, does not say so.
13. How do we know the apostles were baptized with the Holy Spirit on the day of Pentecost? Acts, Ch. 2, does not say so.
14. How does the metaphorical meaning of the word "baptize" differ from its literal meaning? Illustrate.
15. Why did God give the gift of the Holy Spirit to Cornelius and his household before they were baptized in water?

16. Is the baptism of the Holy Spirit available today? Or was the promise fulfilled in the two classic episodes, Acts 2, 10?
17. Define the term "charismatic." List some gifts the Greek New Testament speaks of as charismatic gifts.
18. Are tongues ever actually so spoken of in the Scriptures?
19. What was the difference in the purpose for which the gift of tongues was given on Pentecost and at Caesarea?
20. How did the Holy Spirit initiate the missionary expansion of the church?
21. Why was the Antioch church chosen to be the first church upon which the name Christian was Divinely called, and to be the first truly missionary congregation?
22. What "gifts" (benefits) do we receive through the Holy Spirit as believers today?
23. Are such benefits (gifts) inferior to tongues, healings, etc.?
24. Incidentally, why does Paul, when including healing in the three listings of specialized gifts (I Cor. 12), speak of "healings" (pl.), and why are they prefixed with the term "charismata"?
25. What about the fruit (fruits?) of the Spirit? May we choose according to our taste, as when we go shopping?

SPECIAL STUDY: CONCERNING SPIRITUAL GIFTS

Three chapters of I Corinthians (12-14) were written that we be not "ignorant" concerning spiritual (gifts). From these chapters we can establish certain guidelines.
1. We may know what the "spiritual gifts" were, or at least what they were called.
    a. It is obvious there were two classes, or levels of spiritual gifts.
        1) Some were apparently "showy"—enough so they tended to make those possessed with them vain and non-possessors depressed and jealous (listed, 12:8-11).
        2) Others were less spectacular, yet are said to be "greater" and more to be desired than the others. See I Corinthians 12:31ff.
    b. We note that except for the word "greater" there are no other potentially "classifying" terms used in the Scriptures (terms like "miraculous, special, ordinary, etc."). All such are of human origin and interpretation.
2. Concerning the more showy gifts we know (at least within limits) what these included, though there is some confusion as to terminology within the several found in Ch. 12. Note the same:

Vs. 8-10 "to one is given . . .	V. 28 "God hath set . . .	Vs. 29, 30 "are all . . ."
1. the word of wisdom	firstly, apostles	apostles
2. the word of knowledge	secondly, prophets	prophets
3. faith	thirdly, teachers	teachers
4. gifts of healing	then miracles	(workers of) miracles
5. miracles	then gifts of healing	gifts of healing
6. prophecy	helps	. . . .
7. discerning of spirits	governments	. . . .
8. kinds of tongues	kinds of tongues	tongues
9. interpretation of tongues	. . . .	interpret

3. Concerning the less showy gifts we know they were not readily regarded THEN NOR NOW as superior to the others, though Paul plainly says they are, and this is the point or occasion for the whole discussion.

4. We know from 12:7-11 everyone did not receive each and every gift listed, and apparently none of them was received by everyone.

5. It is evident some did not receive any of the showy gifts, and felt cheated, but should not have done so. They possibly had even superior gifts.

6. From the greater amount of attention devoted to the gift of tongues (and from the record in Acts) we may conclude that tongues was either the most commonly bestowed (and/or exercised) or pretended —the latter is at least a possibility.

7. We note that tongues and its counterpart, the interpretation of tongues, was placed LAST in all three listings, but receives the most attention in the discussion and is treated as the one most likely to cause confusion and discord. (From Acts we may note that more than one person in a given group could possess the gift of tongues. This might be true of the prophetic and teaching gift also.)

8. It is obvious all persons did not possess the less showy gifts either, but they were encouraged to do so, for these belong to the more mature state (13:8-13). Apparently these cannot be "bestowed." Being MORAL in character, they must be "grown."

9. We know the gift of tongues especially could be misused and abused. This would be true of any gift which made the professors or possessor vain and arrogant.
10. We know there was a terminus anticipated for at least a few of the showy gifts (tongues, for example) but not the greater (character trait) gifts.

THERE ARE CERTAIN MATTERS OF WHICH WE REMAIN IGNORANT FOR ALL THAT HAS BEEN SAID:

1. We do not know if the spectacular gifts could be received (normally) other than through the laying on of the apostles' hands. (The case of Cornelius is obviously special.)
2. We do not know for sure what some of the gifts actually consisted of, who had them, or how they were exercised.
3. We do not know that there were non-language "devotional" tongues, or whether utterances were sometimes counterfeited, as variously induced ecstatic vocalizations can be.

FURTHER ASSESSMENT OF SPIRITUAL GIFTS

1. Traditionally, the gifts of the Holy Spirit have been classified as: 1) the baptismal gift, 2) the specialized, or miraculous gifts, and 3) the ordinary, or indwelling gift. To these three a fourth classification has been added: 4) the charismatic gifts. Certain of the gifts aforetime listed under the second classification are selectively chosen for inclusion under the term charismatic; generally, a) tongues, b) healing, and c) prophecies. The traditional assessment, a kind of "trickle-down" theory, has been diagrammed as shown on page 88.

2. This concept is open to challenge. I Corinthians 12:31 through ch. 13, consummates Paul's challenge to a similar concept he reviewed critically in vs. 1-30. Moreover the Greek text of Romans 6:23 informs us "the gift of eternal life in Christ Jesus" is the *charisma*, "gracious gift" (KJV, "free gift") of God. Romans 12:6-8 and I Peter 4:10 affirm the service gifts of the church, and even liberal giving and showing mercy are "charismatic" gifts. Thus the whole church, not just a favored few are so endowed.

3. A reclassification is in order. As an alternate to the traditional terms we suggest: 1) the apostolic (unique) gift, 2) assisting (utilitarian), and 3) abiding (universal). The latter, viewed in the light of I Corinthians

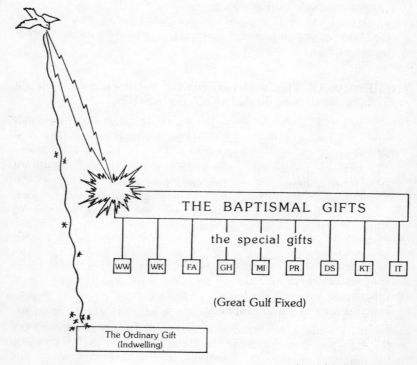

THE BAPTISMAL GIFTS

the special gifts

| WW | WK | FA | GH | MI | PR | DS | KT | IT |

(Great Gulf Fixed)

The Ordinary Gift
(Indwelling)

Art work by David Boatman

12:13 and context in which the baptism of the Holy Spirit was announced (particularly the fuller accounts in Matthew and Luke), make it clear that between the two baptisms predicated of Christ, the baptism of the Holy Spirit and of fire, the whole of the human race is to be encompassed. Those lacking the one will fall under the judgment of the other—not just representatively (in neither case is this true), but universally. *A Third Look at the Baptism of the Holy Spirit* is in order. The author's essay under that title is included in the appendices at the close of this volume.

4. The distinction between the abiding and assisting gifts of the Holy Spirit are noted in the following comparison:

Abiding	Assisting
a) Moral in essence	a) Miraculous in expression
b) Grown	b) Bestowed
c) Internal	c) External
d) Achieved effortly	d) Acquired instantaneously
e) Constantly valid	e) Of intermittent value
f) Eternal	f) Transitory

Note: The "fruit of the Spirit" represents the end (Gr. *teleos*) toward which the entire ministry of the Holy Spirit is directed.

The abiding gifts, those qualities spoken of as the fruit of the Spirit represent the perfect blending of human nature with the Divine. The assisting gifts (while temporarily utilitarian) were imposed (at times, at least) upon human spirits for an immediate, emergency, temporary service, and are not of true and lasting value. They certainly will be no part of the age to come.

5. Concerning Corinthian and Neo-Corinthian Tongues: Observations deduced from I Corinthians, chapters 12-14.

a) Tongues are not the confirming sign of the Spirit, 12:10, 28-30.
b) Tongues belong to the lower rank of spiritual gifts, 12:31.
c) Tongues are only noisome clamor apart from (agape) love, 13:1.
d) Tongues belong to an order of gifts that shall cease, 13:8.
e) Tongues do not profit our fellows, at best they are "unto God," 14:2.
f) Tongues are inferior to prophecy, which edifies, exhorts, consoles, v. 3.
g) Tongues may build up the speaker in his own sight, but not hearers, v. 4.
h) Tongues are inferior to senseless harps and pipes, vs. 7-9.
i) Tongues are inferior to all kinds of voices, v. 10.
j) Tongues are comparable to the chatter of barbarians, v. 11.

(Note: None of the foregoing could be said of tongues in Acts.)

k) Tonguers, zealous for spiritual gifts, should set sights higher, v. 12.
l) Tonguers should be concerned with communication, not babbling, v. 13.
m) Tonguers need to get "their understanding in gear," v. 14.
n) Tonguers should follow the example of Paul who preferred understanding, vs. 15, 16.
o) Tongues (a la Corinthian) provoked sarcasm even from Paul, v. 17.
p) Tongues are a poor communication bargain (odds: 5 to 10,000), vs. 18, 19.

q) Tongues (a la Corinthian) reminiscent of babes and barbarians, vs. 20, 21.
r) Tongues of the historical sort (cp. Acts) were convincing, v. 22.
s) Tongues (a la Corinthian) were they universalized in the church, a la neo-pentecostalism, produce the opposite effect, v. 23.
t) Tongues, at best, should be subject to rules of decorum, vs. 26-29.

> 1) should be limited to three, at the most 2) each should take his turn, 3) if no interpreter present, desist.

Conclusion: To understand the "gift of tongues" it should be studied in an historical setting (Cp. Acts, not an hysterical setting—Corinth).

6

THE LAYING OF THE FOUNDATION: THE ROLE OF THE APOSTLES

The apostles were given an important role in the laying of the foundation of the church. For that work they were carefully prepared. Yet, that notwithstanding, they were told to wait for the "power from on high," the Holy Spirit, before they began. We have taken note of the importance of a foundation. Christ therefore took every precautionary measure to see to it that the church he had promised to build would have a sure foundation, perfectly laid.

We have noted the role of the Holy Spirit, acting as the construction foreman, and the special powers he provided serving as scaffolding and/or forms. Let us now turn our attention to the work performed by the apostles.

The Preparation of the Apostles

1. In preparation for their task, the apostles had received better than three years of training in the school of Christ. The proverbial ideal school, with "Mark Hopkins on one end of a log and a student on the other" cannot begin to compare with the privilege extended the twelve

apostles. Though it was not "one on one," it was "the incomparable one," the master teacher, and twelve chosen men. And there were no extended breaks, nor free weekends. And the daily schedule was not a few hours, sixteen or so, scattered over the course of a week.

A four-year Bible college degree program consists of approximately sixteen classroom hours, in the course of eight semesters. The average semester schedule calls for approximately fifteen class sessions per semester. When chapel services are included, a student receives only about twenty-three hundred fifty-minute instructional sessions. Compared to an eight-hour working day that figures out at approximately nine months. Even if the ideal of two hours of preparation for every classroom hour were attained, the time spent in learning (including chapel services) would barely top six thousand hours, or seven hundred and fifty eight-hour working days. That is barely over two years' work. The apostles spent nearly three and one-half years in the school of Christ. That is preparation!

2. They were further qualified for their work in that they were eyewitnesses of the fact they were to proclaim. The importance of this dimension of preparation is heavily stressed in the Scriptures. It is that important. When Jesus was taking his leave of them, he said:

> Thus it is written, and thus it behooved the Christ to suffer, and to rise from the dead the third day, and that repentance and remission of sins should be preached in his name unto all the nations, beginning from Jerusalem. *Ye are witnesses of these things* (Luke 24:46-48).

Moreover, he said to them:

> And ye shall be my witnesses both in Jerusalem, and in all Judea and Samaria, and unto the uttermost parts of the earth (Acts 1:8).

Were we to go into a courtroom and watch the trial proceedings, we would be witnesses of a sort. We would be spectators viewing the scene and hearing the testimony. But near the judge's bench there is a seat which is called the witness chair. Those who occupy that seat are witnesses in a different sense. They are not just witnesses of the trial, but witnesses to the trial. But to qualify for that performance of duty in the search for truth, those called upon to occupy that chair for testimony and cross examination must be eyewitnesses of that to which they testify. The apostles were that kind of witnesses. Thus John writes in his first epistle, in contradiction to the gnostic heretics:

> That which we have heard, that which we have seen with our eyes, that which we beheld and our hands handled concerning the Word of life (and

we have seen, and bear witness, and declare unto you the life, the eternal life, which was with the Father, and was manifested unto us; that which we have seen and heard declare we unto you (I John 1:1b-3a).

Now hear it from Peter:

We did not follow cunningly devised fables when we made known unto you the power and coming of our Lord Jesus Christ, but we were eye-witnesses of his majesty. For he received from God the Father honor and glory, when there was borne to him the voice of Majestic Glory, This is my beloved Son, in whom I am well pleased: and this voice we ourselves heard borne out of heaven, when we were with him in the holy mount (II Peter 1:16-18).

That is witnessing at its best. So important to the founding of the church was witnessing at that level the same was reckoned to be a fundamental qualification for the apostleship. Note the criteria laid down when a selection was made to fill the gap left by the defector and suicidist, Judas:

Of the men therefore that have companied with us all the time that the Lord Jesus went in and went out among us, beginning from the baptism of John unto the day that he was received up from us, of these must one become a witness with us of his resurrection (Acts 1:20, 21).

That quickly narrowed the field. Two were put forward, and the lot fell upon Matthias, and he was numbered with the eleven apostles (v. 26).

To qualify Saul of Tarsus for the apostleship as a special vessel, he was given a special revelation of the risen, ascended Christ. But it is of interest that in Paul's first recorded address, he emphasized that the witness to the resurrection was given in a more tangible form to the original witnesses, saying:

God raised him from the dead: and he was seen for many days of them that came up with him from Galilee to Jerusalem who are now his witnesses unto the people (Acts 13:30, 31).

The testimony of Peter to Cornelius is especially pertinent. Though Cornelius had already been "divinely instructed" (Acts 10:22) to send for Peter, it is worthy of note that Peter further set forth his credentials as follows:

We are witnesses of all things which he did both in the country of the Jews and at Jerusalem: whom also they slew, hanging him on a tree. Him God raised up the third day, and gave him to be manifest, not to all the people, but unto witnesses that were chosen before of God, even to us who ate and drank with him after he arose from the dead (Acts 10:39-41).

The surety of the apostolic witness was emphasized also by calling upon those who were not Christians to acknowledge what they too had witnessed: Note Peter's words on the day of Pentecost:

Ye men of Israel, hear these words: Jesus of Nazareth, a man approved of God unto you by mighty works and wonders and signs which God did by him in the midst of you, even as ye yourselves know (Acts 2:22).

The apostle Paul likewise challenged King Agrippa, as Paul made his defense before him, saying:

The king knoweth of these things, unto whom I also speak freely: for I am persuaded that none of these things is hidden from him: for this was not done in a corner (Acts 26:26).

3. The apostles were also especially equipped by a unique endowment of the Holy Spirit. This had already been touched upon from the perspective of the Holy Spirit's role in the founding of the church. But it deserves to be reemphasized here. The apostles were indisputably provided an unparalleled endowment of the Holy Spirit, functionally speaking. To none other was the promise given that when the Holy Spirit was come, he would guide them into all the truth and bring to their remembrance all things Jesus had said to them (John 14:26; 15:26). For one thing, Jesus had not said all the things they were to remember to others besides themselves. Many were the things he taught them when they were alone. The upper room discourse is an example.

The writer has heard persons lay claim to such high standing, begging the question by quoting out of context Hebrews 13:8, "Jesus Christ, the same, yesterday, today, and forever." But their faulty memories as to what Jesus is recorded as having said witnesses against them.

Not only did the apostles have special revelatory powers, they also had the power through the laying on of hands to impart specialized gifts of the Holy Spirit, subject to the selective will of the Holy Spirit (Acts 8:18, I Cor. 12:11, Heb. 2:4). These powers too are claimed by modern pretenders, but again the observable facts witness against them. In Biblical times miracles were acknowledged, though grudgingly (which grudging admission further testified to the verity thereof) by enemies and unbelievers. When see we such miracles today?

The specialized spiritual gifts, those I prefer to call the assisting (utilitarian) gifts of the Spirit, filled a void in the founding congregations until such time as the New Covenant Scriptures could provide the teaching, reproof, correction, and instruction in righteousness whereby men of God are made mature (Gr. *teleios*), thoroughly furnished unto every good work (II Tim. 3:16). There is a sense in which I Corinthians 13:10 might be added here. But "that which is perfect" (Gr. *teleios*) there spoken of is not a direct reference to the completion of the New Covenant Scriptures, much less the second coming of Christ (who, of course, is not a "that which" but he who). In the previous chapter we took note of the fact that miraculous gifts began to wane long before the New Testament books were all written. As individual congregations *matured* (the sense in which *teleios* is used in the New Testament), congregations were less and less dependent on such gifts. As Paul explained it, "when I became a man, I put away childish things." As the church matured it did the same. (See the "Excursus on Mark 16:17, 18" appended to the close of the lesson.)

By way of summary, the endowment of the Holy Spirit did three things for the apostles: 1) It provided for them immediate inspiration, revealing Divine truth, as needed; 2) it gave them, from the very outset, powers—signs to credentialize their apostleship and confirm their message; and 3) it empowered them to impart needed utilitarian (assisting) spiritual gifts within the will of the Holy Spirit.

The Founding Work of the Apostles

The work of the apostles was authorized and set forth in the Great Commission, particularly as stated in Matthew 28:18-20 (epitomized in Mark 16:15, 16), and supplemented in Luke 24:44-49 (epitomized in Acts 1:8). John's gospel, written much later, assumes the commission without directly restating it. However, his statement of his purpose in writing is in keeping with the very heart of the Great Commission:

> Many other signs did Jesus in the presence of the disciples, which are not written in this book; but these are written that ye may believe that Jesus is the Christ, the Son of God; and *that* believing ye may have life in his name (John 20:30, 31).

The work of the apostles had several facets, all of which, directly or indirectly, grow out of their commission from Christ. Early in the life of the church the apostles had to make a decision as to whether they should "forsake the Word of God, and serve tables," or whether they should entrust matters of humanitarian considerations to deacons

95

(servants) who might well be set over that sort of business. They opted to do that which they were commissioned and trained to do and committed mundane, though humanitarian, matters to others who could do those things as well, or perhaps better. Their commission led them to attend the following responsibilities:

1. The apostles bore their witness of Christ. This was their first obligation, and the task in which they had no peers or successors, and certainly no superiors. Luke reports concerning them: "With great power gave the apostles their witness of the resurrection, and great grace was upon them all" (Acts 4:33). The aged apostle John, the lone survivor of the apostolic band, explained his exile to the Isle of Patmos, saying: "I John, your brother and partaker with you in the tribulation and kingdom and patience which are in Jesus, was in the isle that is called Patmos for the word of God and the testimony of Jesus" (Rev. 1:9).

2. The apostles "made disciples." There are two different Greek words rendered "teach" in the KJV of Matthew's account of the Great Commission—*matheteusate* and *didaskontes*. The New King James Version has joined the ranks of virtually every other translation in rendering the first of the two verbs, "make disciples."

A disciple is much more than a learner, someone who has been *taught* something. A disciple is someone who has also been *caught*—captivated, in a sense, by the teaching received, or by the teacher, or both. In the case of "the twelve," the disciple-apostles, it is difficult to say which came first, "the chicken or the egg." Was it the person of Christ which drew them to his teaching, or his teaching which drew them to his person? His masterful manner of teaching and matchless teachings along with his personal magnetism caused them quickly to call him Master.

A disciple is more than a follower. Many followed him, for a time at least, who were slow to learn—if indeed they ever did come to learn who he was, and the nature of the kingdom he came to establish in the hearts of men. Consequently there were multitudes whom he taught that did not become his followers, at least not for long. Whether they were lacking in courage or were simply disenchanted with him when they finally understood what kind of kingdom he had in mind, or both, the episode described in John, chapter six, was not an isolated one. Recall that following his discourse on the bread of life it is written: "Upon this, many of his disciples went back, and walked no more with with him" (John 6:66). That is when their discipleship ended, if indeed they were truly disciples in the first place. They had been caught up in the excitement that he generated, but were really not that much "taken" by his concept of the kingdom and its demands upon its citizens.

3. They baptized the disciples they made. In doing so they were following both the example of Christ and the commandment of Christ. A much neglected textual tidbit is found in John 4:1, 2 where we are told that Jesus was "making and baptizing more disciples than John!" There was, however, one difference. Actually Jesus did not do the baptizing. His disciples did, but obviously at his command. Jesus was perceptive. If he had done the actual baptizing, there would have likely developed a "Jesuit Baptist Alliance" and a "Johanine Baptist Alliance," with each group counting themselves superior to the other because of whose hands it was that baptized them.

Neither under the Old Covenant or the New is there such a thing as a person entering into a redemptive state without some appropriate act of obedience. Even Jesus, who could read the inmost thought, required some tangible, manifest token of obedience. And such a token is indeed incorporated in the Great Commission. Christ's disciples understood that well even if modern interpreters do not.

When the guilt-stricken multitude on Pentecost asked: "What must we do?" (Acts 2:37), Peter missed a golden opportunity to set the record straight and explain they were to do nothing, if such were the proper answer to be forthcoming from one "speaking as the Spirit gave him utterance." But instead of assuring them they need "only believe and they would receive," or instead of telling them to remember how it was with the dying thief (all he did was to look to Jesus in faith), Peter answered their question in keeping with Christ's commission. "Repentance and remission of sins" was definitely preached in his name, in keeping with Jesus' express will (Luke 24:47). Peter's answer was: "Repent ye, and be baptized, every one of you in the name of Jesus Christ, for the remission of your sins." Where do we hear such an answer today in the mass evangelism circuit, or even from the pulpits of local congregations today?

But such was the way it continued to be proclaimed throughout the apostolic age. Even Cornelius was commanded to be baptized though he already was visibly, manifestly baptized in the Holy Spirit, like unto the apostles "at the beginning" (Acts 10:44-48, cp. 11:15-17). And even Saul of Tarsus, to whom Jesus appeared in a vision on the road to Damascus, and was informed by Christ that he was a chosen vessel; when he asked of Christ, "Lord, what shall I do?"—not even he was

97

given the stock answer of the currently popular faith-only circuit. Did the Lord Jesus somehow miss an opportunity to explain that one need not do anything but believe, lest he might be led to think he has worked out his own salvation? Instead Saul was instructed to go into Damascus where he would be told what to do. So he went into Damascus. For three days he awaited the answer, in fasting and prayer even. But that was not the answer. At length a disciple named Ananias was directed by the Lord to go and minister to Saul. According to Saul's own testimony this was the answer he received: "Why tarriest thou? Arise and be baptized and wash away thy sins, calling on the name of the Lord" (Acts 22:16). Once again, "repentance and remission of sins was preached in Jesus' name," and the latter was accomplished through obedience in baptism.

There can be no gainsaying the fact. The apostles baptized the disciples they made. And their disciples in turn did the same to those whom they discipled. Witness the case of Philip at Samaria (Acts 8:12, 13), and on the Gaza road (Acts 8:35-39). The witness of Ananias in his ministry to Saul further underscores the point. Baptism is an integral part of the Gospel, and the redemptive response thereto.

4. The apostles taught the disciples they made to do likewise. The preceding paragraph documents the fact that they did. But it deserves to be noted that the examples cited are not the exception but the rule, in keeping with the genius of the Great Commission. By divine design a built-in chain reaction process was set in order when the apostles took up the task for which they were prepared and commissioned by Christ.

II Timothy 2:2 reflects the pattern noted. In writing to his favorite son in the Gospel, Paul exhorted Timothy, "The things thou hast heard from me among many witnesses the same commit thou to faithful men, who shall be able to teach others also." The series of questions Paul asked in Romans 10:14, 15a relate to a facet of this Divinely instituted process, tracing the chain of reaction backwards:

How then shall they call on him in whom they have not believed? and how shall they believe in him of whom they have not heard? and how shall they hear without a preacher? and how shall they preach except they be sent?

Our denominational neighbors, hung up on the dogma of salvation by faith only, balk at teaching baptism for remission of sins on the premise that one's salvation would then be dependent upon what someone else does for us. Big deal! So what? When has it not been so? There is an old hymn which asks the question: "Will the circle be unbroken, by and by?" If the built-in chain reaction Christ set in motion through the Great Commission is broken, or if the terms for the remission of sins which he made implicit in that commission are broken, the answer is yes. Many a family circle, and many a circle of friends will indeed be broken, by and by.

5. The apostles established congregations, "churches of Christ" (Rom. 16:16), which saluted, cared for, and fellowshipped one another. Paul Benjamin, professor at large of Lincoln Christian Seminary, has wisely observed that every movement which fails to organize its constituents into congregations dies, often with the first generation. How true that is. Where are the "street Christians" of yesterday? The "Jesus People" and the "Children of God"? The two movements flourished in the latter half of the decade of the sixties and the early seventies. Several from the two movements found their way into St. Louis Christian College. They were amazing in several respects. They had been delivered from deep involvement in the drug scene. Generally they had aforetime received little or no Bible instruction. But in the short time they had become involved with the "street Christian" movements, they had gained a greater familiarity with the Scriptures than most of the sons and daughters of the parsonages, and the homes of elders, deacons, and Bible school teachers. But few finished even a year in Bible college. None graduated. Few are known to be active for Christ anywhere or in any way. Why? Because they were victims of systems of indoctrination which taught them to be anti-establishment, anti-institution. Separated from their authority figure who was their personal stand-in for Christ, programmed to regard the church as an enemy camp, they have all but disappeared from the religious scene in America.

The apostles, under the direction of the Holy Spirit established and organized congregations. They led them in selecting elders, deacons, and deaconesses (overseers and male and female servants). (Cf. I Tim. 3:1-7, 8-10, 11; Rom. 16:1.) They confirmed the churches (Acts 14:23, 15:32) and instructed evangelists to "set the churches in order" by guiding them in the selection of elders from city to city (Tit. 1:5).

6. The apostles served as channels through which the Holy Spirit imparted, selectively, "according to his own will," specialized spiritual gifts (Acts 8:18; I Cor. 12:11). This, and the reason for the same, has already been noted as the preparation of the apostles for their work was considered. It deserves to be emphasized that in lieu of the New

99

Testament which was still in the making, the impartation of specialized gifts through the laying on of the apostles' hands—gifts of knowledge (for information), of power (for confirmation), and service (for administration) were essential to neophyte congregations, some of which (like the church at Philippi) were far removed from other congregations and lacking in mature, experienced leadership.

7. The apostles served as the channels through which the inspiration of the Holy Spirit provided the New Covenant Scriptures. Every book of the New Testament was written either by an apostle or an understudy of an apostle. Matthew and John, apostles of Christ, wrote the first and the fourth Gospels. Mark and Luke, companions of Peter and Paul, wrote the two which bear their names.

Thirteen epistles bear Peter's autograph. The writer chooses to speak of them as the *Pauline Autographs*. To call them the Pauline epistles is to say in effect that Paul did not author Hebrews. Personally, I no longer think that he did, but that is a question with which the church has wrestled for centuries and any judgment pronounced either pro or con can neither be substantiated nor disproved. To call the group of Pauline Autographs the Special Letters is to overlook the fact they are not all "all that special." Galatians, for example, was written to the Christians of a whole province, not to a community of believers in a certain city. And Ephesians is obviously a cyclical letter written to that circle of churches in Asia of which Ephesus was chief, and likely the first recipient and its custodian.

The eight remaining epistles this author sees fit to designate: *Miscellaneous Authorship*. Why? The designation fits. The common designations, Non-Pauline or General (Catholic), are flawed. The parenthesized designation, even when spelled with a small "c" is confusing to those unacquainted with the fact that the term is simply a general term for *general*, or *universal*. And the eight epistles commonly so designated are really not all "all that general." Hebrews is entitled in all manuscripts, *Pros Hebraious* (for the Hebrews). James and I Peter are addressed to the tribes of the dispersion. If a letter to the Galatians is a special letter, then so are those three. II John is addressed "to the elect lady." Those locked in on the traditional designations explain this is a figurative term and refers to the universal church as the bride of Christ. Interesting. Then who is her "elect sister, and her children" (II John 13)? And how general is a letter written to the "beloved Gaius" (III John 1)? Is that more general than a letter addressed to Philemon, or Titus, or Timothy? *Pauline Autographs* and *Miscellaneous Author-ship* ("Pa and Ma," for those who look for memory pegs) fitly describe the two groups of epistles.

The Apocalypse, The Revelation of Jesus Christ (not of St. John, the Divine, as the title often is in the KJV, and commentaries based on the text thereof), completes the New Covenant Scriptures. Accord-ing to the warning near the close, Revelation 22:18, 19, we should expect no more. We should accept no more. In penning the book at the command (Rev. 1:11, 19) of the angel of the apocalypse by which Christ sent and signified to John the visions recorded (Rev. 1:1), John becomes unique among the New Testament writers. All three classes of New Testament literature: 1) historical reporting, the fourth Gospel, 2) epistles, of which we have three, and 3) prophecy have all come to us through his pen.

The Holy Spirit and the apostles did their assigned work well. It is said of the first community of believers that "they continued steadfastly in the apostles' teaching, and fellowship, in the breaking of bread and the prayers. Would that the same could be said to this day of the spiritual heirs of "the faith once and for all delivered to the saints" (Jude 3).

Reflection

Jesus said: "I will build my church" (Matt. 16:18). We now see how the foundations were laid and the superstructure started. We see how the work continues to this day. The writer is often asked, "Did you build your house, or did you buy it?" The answer is: "I built it." In a sense I did, though I did not lay one brick in place nor nail one board to another, nor put in place one piece of sheeting, or even one shingle. I did not even do the painting. But I built it—in dream. I drew the plans, complete to the last detail. In collaboration with my wife, being sensitive to the things she desired in the home we hope to share to-gether for years to come; I drew the plans, secured an architect, and arranged for the financing. The contractor and the workmen took no liberties with our plans. When their work was done the house looked exactly as I had pictured it in my mind. They used the specified materials, and even the painting of the trim and of the inside walls, room by room, was according to our choice. The workmen finished; we moved in; and a house became our home.

God and Christ collaborated in the grand design for the church. It is therefore also called the church of God (Acts 20:28; I Cor. 1:2;

101

11:22; II Cor. 1:1; Gal. 1:13). The church was not an afterthought, a contingency that came to Christ's mind when the purpose of his coming failed. It was in the planning stage from times eternal (Eph. 3:8-11). What a privilege it is that to this day we are privileged both to have a part in building Christ's church and to be a part of the building.

PREVIEW—REVIEW QUESTIONS

1. Cite the threefold preparation the apostles received for their appointed task.
2. Compare the three years' schooling the apostles received from Christ to a four-year Bible college degree program amid many instructors—in terms of time and quality of instructors.
3. Do students today have any advantages Christ's disciples did not have? Be objective. How were some advantages we have today compensated for through the work of the Holy Spirit?
4. What importance is placed today upon eyewitness reporting when matters of life and death are at stake? Any spinoffs or applications of this to present circumstances?
5. What basic qualification was established for the apostleship when a replacement for Judas was undertaken?
6. What compensation in that regard was made for Saul of Tarsus?
7. In what respect may we speak of the apostles' endowment of the Holy Spirit as unique?
8. State the one thing they could do for those they discipled which could not be passed to the third generation.
9. Cite two texts which support the preceding inquiry.
10. What was the first task of the apostles; the task for which they had no peers, successors, or superiors?
11. Fully defined, what is a disciple? When does a pupil become a disciple in the fullest sense of the term?
12. Whom did the apostles baptize? On what conditions? For what purpose?
13. Did they have either precedent or command to so baptize?
14. What did they instruct their baptized disciples to do?
15. State two texts which make it clear the format was to continue to the end of the world.
16. Did the apostles form believers into congregations with a plurality of leadership? Or did each community of believers form a loosely knit group with a kind of prototype guru?

17. For what class of spiritual gifts did the apostles serve as a channel? Why were such gifts so important then? But not now?
18. In what other important respect did the apostles serve as channels for the Holy Spirit?

EXCURSUS ON MARK 16:17, 18

Following Mark's statement of the Great Commission we have one of the most controversial passages of Scripture in the Bible. The text continues on to record Jesus as saying:

> And these signs shall accompany them that believe: In my name 1) they shall cast out demons, 2) they shall speak with new tongues, 3) they shall take up serpents, and 4) if they drink any deadly thing it shall in no wise harm them; 5) they shall lay hands on the sick, and they shall recover.

The introductory announcement (these signs shall accompany them that believe), and four of the five specific promises which follow, employ the future indicative form of the verbs used. The actions (accomplishments) predicted are thereby said to be things which shall surely come to pass. The one variance is the reference to the drinking of some deadly thing. In this instance the verb form is the aorist subjunctive. The subjunctive accounts for the word "if" which appears in connection with that particular prediction.

How are we to understand what is said in Mark 16:17, 18? What are our options? There are three possibilities:

OPTION ONE: WE CAN REJECT THE PASSAGE AS SPURIOUS

Many have taken this option. The passage, including vs. 9 through 20 (that is v. 9 to the end of the chapter), is wanting in some of the oldest and most reliable manuscripts of the New Testament. For example, a footnote in the *New King James* version reads:

> Verses 9-20 are bracketed in the NU texts as not original. They are lacking in the Codex Sinaiticus and Codex Vaticanus, although nearly all other manuscripts of Mark contain them.

NU is an acronym for the Nestle-Aland Greek New Testament and the United Bible Society Third Edition of the Greek text.

Questioning the authenticity of the text does not solve the difficulty. Aside from the drinking of deadly poison all the other signs listed in the text are recorded in Acts as miracles which actually materialized

103

in the history of the early church. Personally, I consider the first option as a cop-out, and no solution to the problem presented.

OPTION TWO:
THE PREDICTION WAS RESTRICTIVE, NOT GENERAL

Those who take this option assume the predictions applied only to the apostles, and such persons as may have been especially endowed through the laying on of the apostles' hands. For example, Philip and the Samaritans. (See Acts 6:5, 6, cp. 8:5-7, 13, 17, 18.)

The chief difficulty with this view is that it is not the conclusion to which one would be readily drawn in reading Mark 16:17, 18 in context. Taken in context the passage says nothing to the effect that the signs would be visited upon believers selectively. The inference seems to be that the signs (plural) are accompaniments of the state of believing. This brings us to the third option.

OPTION THREE: THE PROMISE IS TO ALL WHO BELIEVE.

This option is really beset with problems. Not the least of which is that which is both stated and elaborated upon in I Corinthians, chapters 12 through 14, particularly chapter 12. The one point that Paul drives home is that such gifts as tongues and healings were *not* possessed by all that believed, nor were any of the other specialized gifts catalogued therein. The gifts were very selectively distributed. Moreover, it was the Holy Spirit who did the selecting and the distributing. (See I Cor. 12:11, cp. Heb. 2:4.) Lest anyone should miss the point he was making, he introduced an analogy which he painstakingly explained. The inference that is to be drawn, and which is then reinforced by chapter 13, is that some of the b lievers who made up the Corinthian church did not have any of the specialized gifts with which some were endowed. Nonetheless, they were in no wise less spiritual than those who did. In fact, if they were loving, they had a greater gift of the Holy Spirit than those who gloried in the signs they could display or simulate. The latter possibility cannot be disallowed.

The record in Acts plainly attests the fact that the signs listed in Mark 16:17, 18 did not automatically accompany or "follow" all who believed. Witness the case of the Samaritans. They are definitely identified as believers. (See Acts 8:12, 13.) But though Philip had wrought such signs among them that even Simon the sorcerer "*believed*: and being baptized, he continued with Philip" (v. 12), the fact remains that neither the signs listed in Mark 16:17, 18 nor any other visible or audible manifestation of special spiritual endowment "followed" as an inevitable accompaniment of faith. Despite the fact that Philip had received the laying on of the apostles' hands (Acts 6:6) and exhibited miraculous powers, not until the apostles Peter and John came to Samaria and laid their hands upon the believers did the Holy Spirit "fall upon" them (v. 16).

Simon Magus saw the connection, even if modern interpreters with the record before them do not. Vs. 18 states that when "Simon saw that through the laying on of the apostles' hands the Holy Spirit was given" (in the form or miraculous endowment, obviously) Simon sought to "buy into the system."

The case of the twelve believers who had received the Baptist's baptism out of dispensation provides another example. (See Acts 19:1-7.) Note Paul did not question their faith, only their baptism (vs. 2-4). Upon their submission to Christ's (Christian) baptism Paul laid his hands upon them, and the Holy Spirit then "*came upon* them, and they spake with tongues and prophesied," (v. 7).

The expressions, "fallen upon them" (Acts 8:16) and "came upon them" (Acts 19:7) are reminiscent of Old Testament references to the special spiritual endowment of Old Testament persons who were thereby endued with miraculous powers. Judges 6:34 informs us that "the Spirit of Jehovah came upon Gideon" prior to his miraculous defeat of the Midianites. The same expression appears in Judges 11:29 with reference to Jephthah. In Judges 14:6 we read that "the Spirit of Jehovah came mightily upon Samson" and immediately he was endowed with superhuman strength.

On the surface it might seem that the language used in Acts 8 and 19 with reference to the Samaritans and the twelve Baptist disciples is at variance with the promise of Acts 2:38. The key to the seeming variance is in the language we have just noted. The "Spirit of adoption" which "bears witness with our spirits that we are children of God" (Rom. 8:15, 16) is the gift promised in Acts 2:38 to baptized believers (cp. Acts 5:32). Miraculous endowment of the Holy Spirit is described with other language, as we have noted in the examples cited above.

The case of Cornelius and his household, at first glance, seems to provide a proof text for those committed to the third option. They received the gift of tongues apart from the laying on of the apostles' hands, and even prior to water baptism. But there is an obvious reason for that. For one thing, they were obviously a special case. They were the first strictly Gentile converts, and were providentially selected to be so, and providentially put in touch with Peter, and Peter with them.

Notwithstanding, Peter would likely have never laid his hands on them, even to baptize them, much less to bestow a special spiritual gift, if God had not baptized them in the Holy Spirit before Peter's very eyes, and manifested the same by "giving them the like gift" which he had poured out upon the apostles "at the beginning." (See Acts 10:45-47; 11:15-17.) On the day of Pentecost (at the beginning of the church), the apostles were thusly credentialized for the sake of the audience. At Caesarea, the Gentiles were credentialized for the sake of the apostle, and the six Jewish brethren Peter had discreetly taken with him.

This seems the appropriate time to inquire as to what happened at the first ingathering of believers "at the beginning." It is recorded about three thousand "received the Word and were baptized" (Acts 2:41). But nothing is said to the effect that the signs catalogued in Mark 16:17, 18 followed that group of believers. To the contrary, v. 43 reports that it was through the apostles that "many wonders and signs were done." Chapter three reports a healing (the lame man at the temple gate) but it was Peter, an apostle, who healed him. Chapter four informs us that the multitude of them that believed were of one heart and soul (v. 32), but it was the apostles who "with great power gave their witness of the resurrection" (v. 33).

Chapter five continues in the same vein. Vs. 12 informs us: "By the hands of the apostles were *many* signs and wonders wrought among the people," but there is no mention of *any* signs and wonders being wrought by the people.

Chapter six relates the choosing of seven men who were "full of the Holy Spirit" but not until the apostles had laid their hands upon them are even they said to have wrought wonders and signs among the people. (See Acts 6:3-8; 8:6-8, 18.) And so it goes throughout the book of Acts.

OPTION TWO: RECONSIDERED

This brings us back to option two as our only viable option. This is not to limit God's power or his promises. It is simply to observe the limitations which according to his inspired Word he himself saw fit to place upon the predictions under consideration. In the Epistle to the Hebrews it is written:

> The word . . . which was first spoken by the Lord, was confirmed unto us by them that heard, God bearing witness with them both by signs

106

and wonders and manifold powers, and gifts of the Holy Spirit according to his own will (Heb. 2:3, 4).

Read it again, carefully. It has something to say to us.

Let us now return to the text in question and consider our options from a different perspective. Again several options may be considered.

One: The things predicted either did or did not happen. We should have no difficulty in choosing between those two considerations. Except for the drinking of deadly poison, the one sign spoken of as "iffy," the book of Acts chronicles the fact the other signs predicted were definitely manifested.

Two: The things predicted accompanied the state of believing in every instance, or they did not. If one takes the affirmative position in this case, one has the apostle Paul to combat in I Corinthians, chapter 12. There, as we have already noted, he expounds the point that such was not the case, and were it so the church as the body of Christ would be ludicrous, even freakish.

Three: The things predicted still happen or they do not. The negative position is supported, both in the Scriptures, as we have already shown, and in the history of the church through the ages, and in observable human experience today. We say this for several reasons:

1) Hebrews 2:3, 4, cited above, contains a strong indication that confirming signs and wonders, even at that point in history, were no longer extant. He speaks of the confirmation for which they were given as already accomplished "through them that heard the Lord speak," rather than "us" (himself, perhaps, and certainly those to whom the epistle was directed).

2) Following through with the inference of that passage, it deserves to be noted that the further we advance in both New Testament history and literature, the less emphasis is placed upon confirming signs. For example, Paul, near the end of his life, left Trophimus "sick" at Miletus (II Tim. 4:20). And Timothy, his most beloved child in the Gospel, he admonished to take a little wine for his stomach's sake, and oft infirmities (I Tim. 5:23). At the time, Timothy was residing in Ephesus where once "handkerchiefs" carried from Paul's body healed the sick and even exorcised demons (Acts 19:11, 12). Can you imagine the healing ministry Paul might have carried on if they had Kleenex in that day? If miracle healing were intended to be an ongoing part of the confirmation of the faith, why did Paul not wrap the epistle in a handkerchief?

3) That is only the beginning of the problem, if this third option is taken. The text reads: "These signs shall follow them that believe." If

that means all who believe, and for all time, we have the following conundrums to be considered.

a) Take the case of the beacon lights of the Reformation: John Hus, Martin Luther, John Calvin, the Wesleys, the Campbells (to name but a few). Were all these men unbelievers? Did God bypass the believers to use unbelievers to usher in and extend the reformation? The signs of Mark 16:17, 18 not a part of the repertoire of any one of them.

b) Take the case of the evangelists who ushered in the Great Awakening of the 19th century: George Whitfield, John Knox, Jonathan Edwards, Barton W. Stone, Charles Spurgeon, D. L. Moody, and Billy Sunday. I would not for a moment endorse Billy Graham's professed "faith only" stance, but I could hardly call him an unbeliever. The man who has undoubtedly preached to more millions than any other person in all history has never spoken in tongues, exorcised a demon, or resorted to snake handling or healing shows to credentialize his message.

c) And what shall we say of the renowned missionaries? William Carey, the father of modern missions, Judson, Taylor, Livingston, Shelton, and I hesitate not for a moment to add the name of Max Ward Randall? The men God has used to carry the Gospel of enlightenment and salvation to the four corners of the earth have done so without exercising a one of the powers listed in Mark 16:17, 18. Were they, and scores of others like them, unbelievers?

d) And that is not all. What shall we say of the translators of the Bible? Men who faced death to give us the Bible in our own language? And men who still brave death to bring the Word of God to people who have never heard of Christ: Wycliffe, Tyndale, Coverdale, the translators of renown, and the translators and missionaries of modern Bible societies who invade malaria-infested jungles facing headhunters, jealous witchdoctors, and tribal chieftains to bring the Word of God to savages dwelling in ignorance, darkness, and superstition? Think what the gift of tongues could mean to them. And think what the gift of tongues as manifested on Pentecost would mean to score upon scores of primitive tribes without even a written language, if every one of them could hear the Word of God in his own language, yea, even in his own dialect. Are the Bible translators, both at home and abroad, unbelievers? Why does the gift of tongues not follow those who could really use it to God's glory (not their own ego) and to bring the light of salvation to people in darkness? How do we explain these things if we opt for option three?

Is it not strange those who often show the greatest evidence of being believers do not exhibit the signs of Mark 16:17, 18? But men who grow rich hustling the select signs which turn out to be moneymakers— simulated tongues and psychosomatic healings—these, if Mark 16:17, 18 is the test, are the true believers!

To our neo-Corinthian friends of the peasant class, those who are the "rope holders" and bank account bulgers of those who like Simon the sorcerer see in certain signs a way to make gain; to those (I say) whose "love offerings" not only pay the fare for the big timers who ride the proverbial "gravy train," but who also have elevated them to the place where they criss cross the continent in private jets; let me ask you a few questions:

1) When did you last exorcise a demon, really? I mean when has anything happened that was visible, audible, and convincing even to unbelievers?

2) What new tongue has God given you lately? Or are you still mouthing the same mumbo-jumbo you started with? Have you edified anybody thereby besides yourself? (If indeed you yourself are really edified, informed, or enlightened?) Or do you just do your thing to get attention, to assure yourself (and maybe others) that you are a part of the "in" group?

3) Have you taken up any deadly serpents lately? Oral Roberts, in his book on *The Baptism of the Holy Spirit,* confesses backhandedly that he does not. In fact he avers that promise is not to be taken literally. It only means that you can deal effectively with the Devil, the old serpent who is our adversary, Satan. I guess Oral Roberts does not care too much about that "snake bit."

4) When have you drunk some deadly poison, or even eaten some tainted food, without it in any wise harming you? Oral Roberts, in the same publication, also disallows that promise is to be taken literally. It only means missionaries will not get sick from eating tainted food. Ah, but they do. Are they then unbelievers?

5) And what is your box score on miracle healings? Does your power work best on simple things such as headaches, stomachaches, and the like? Have you lengthened and strenthened any withered limbs lately? Or is the best that you have done so far been to have convinced someone they can hear a little better, or do not need their prescription on their eye glasses updated?

So, the wheel has come full circle. We have reviewed three options. The only one that meets the 1) test of time, 2) the test of sound exegesis, and 3) the test of human experience is the one that squares with Acts 8:18 and Hebrews 2:3, 4. The word which was spoken first by the Lord was confirmed unto us by them that heard, God bearing witness with them both by signs and wonders, and by gifts of the Holy Spirit *according to his* own will. Personally, I am *willing* to leave it that way.

7

THE SUPERSTRUCTURE DESCRIBED IN SPECIFIC TERMS

The term superstructure does not appear in our English New Testaments, but it is readily suggested by a number of texts. Not the least of these is the key verse to the course of study in which we are engaged—Matthew 16:18. Ephesians 2:20 and I Peter 2:5 likewise provide a sound Biblical basis for designating all that is "built upon" the Divine foundation, the "superstructure."

Our word superstructure is of Latin derivation. It is formed from 1) the prepositional prefix *supra,* "above, upon" (cp. Gr. *huper,* and such words as hyperactive, hypercritical, and 2) the verb *structus,* "to build" (lit., "to heap up"). Thus a superstructure is something built upon something else, such as a basement (substructure) or foundation. Hence when Jesus said: "Upon this rock I will build my church," the text might have been translated: "Upon this rock I will superstructure my church." However the term is more commonly used as a noun to designate the completed work.

In Ephesians 2:19-21 Paul addressed his words to Gentile Christians who were at long last being included in the building of the church, saying:

You are no more strangers and sojourners, but fellow-citizens with the saints and of the household of God, being *built upon* the foundation of the apostles and prophets, Christ Jesus himself being the chief corner-stone.

The Divinely designed superstructure is defined, identified, illustrated, and otherwise described in many ways. Often it is spoken of under specific terms. At other times it is spoken of under illustrative terms. Specific terms tell us precisely what something is, or at least the class or category to which persons, places, or things belong. Illustrative terms compare one thing with another, the less familiar to that which is better known. For example, we might say of an apple that it is a fruit. But to someone who has never seen an apple, that classification or categorization might not bring to mind anything which in any way resembles an apple. Suppose the only fruits one had ever seen were bananas and watermelons. Then it would be helpful to speak of an apple as an edible ball or globular fruit with flesh about the consistency of a potato, but much sweeter, and produced by trees rather than growing underground. But a person would still have to see one and eat a choice specimen before a perfect knowledge of what an apple is would be gained.

Apparently the Biblical writers would have us gain a full knowledge and appreciation of what the church is, and its purpose for existing, for it is defined and described in the Scriptures in a variety of ways. Moreover, it is the intent of the Scriptures to bring us to know what the church is like, within and without, experientially. In this chapter we shall consider the specific terms used in the Scriptures to define and identify the superstructure.

1. *The Ekklesia*

The Greek word *ekklesia*, from which our word ecclesia, and derivations thereof is drawn, is used in the New Testament in nine different ways. Normally it is used with reference to what translators have led us to call the church. Four times, however, the word ekklesia is used with references to assemblies other than "the church." Altogether, the word appears in the Greek New Testament 115 times. Only three times is it actually translated in the sense in which it was commonly used in New Testament times. The following is an effort to set the record straight.

A. *Ekklesia: Used of "Christ's Own"*

1) Used of the whole church—that is, of all who in every age and place are called by the Gospel into the fellowship of those "called out of darkness into Christ's marvelous light" (I Peter 2:9). Note these texts:

(Matt. 16:18) Upon this rock I will build my church, and the gates of hades shall not prevail against it. [Obviously, Jesus is referring to the whole of his "called out" ones, throughout the whole of the Christian era, not just to the *ekklesia* which was soon to be formed in Jerusalem.]

(Eph. 1:22, 23) And he put all things in subjection under his feet, and gave him to be head over all things to the church, which is his body, the fulness of him that filleth all in all." [Again, it is obvious the *ekklesia* of Christ is being spoken of in a larger context than its manifestation in any one age or place.]

(Heb. 12:22, 23) But ye are come unto Mount Zion, and unto the city of the living God, the heavenly Jerusalem, and to innumerable hosts of angels, to the *general assembly*, [Gr., *panegyria*—*Ekklesia* is not the word used here, but it appears in the next phrase] and church [*ekklesia*] of the first born (pl.) who are enrolled in heaven. [The whole of the redeemed, all who are enrolled in heaven, are the *ekklesia* of Christ.]

2) *Ekklesia* is used of the whole of Christ's own at a given point in history. For example, it is said in Acts 9:31 that following the conversion of Saul of Tarsus, the spearhead of the persecution against the Christians, "Then had the church(es) (*ekklesia*—sing.) rest throughout all Judea and Galilee and Samaria" (the extent of the expansion of the church to that time). In Romans 16:16 the plural form of the word (*ekklesia*) is used and the whole of the church implied in the words: "All the churches of Christ salute you." In Galatians 1:13 wherein Paul says: "I persecuted the church of God, and made havoc of it," he is speaking of the church as an entity, not merely of the individual congregations he had managed to assault. It was the church as an institution, as the extension of the person of Christ beyond his earthly life—that is what Paul had been set to destroy.

3) *Ekklesia* is used of Christians assembled in the name of Christ at a given place. For example, Acts 11:26 reads: "It came to pass that for a whole year they (Barnabas and Saul) were gathered together with the church (*ekklesia*) and taught much people, and that the disciples were called Christians first at Antioch." In Philemon 2, we find Paul sending greetings to his friend Philemon, along with two others who receive personal mention, and then Paul adds categorically, "and to the church in thy house." (See also Rom. 16:5.)

4) *Ekklesia* is used of Christians of a given geographical subdivision, whether assembled or not (I Cor. 1:1, 2; II Cor. 1:1; II Thess. 1:1; Acts 13:1). A church of Christ does not disintegrate or fall apart like a rope of sand when the benediction has been spoken at a worship service. On the other hand, any number of scattered Christians may live in a given community, but there will not be a church in that community until the individual members become aware of one another and begin to assemble themselves together. This observation is not a contradiction of the foregoing one.

5) *Ekklesia* is used of a particular ethnic group, as in Romans 16:3 and II Corinthians 8:1. Once again, as noted above, Christians of a certain racial stock do not cease to be a church between their times of assembling together, nor does one cease to be a part of the church if deprived of the privilege of worship. Witness the case of John exiled on the Isle of Patmos. There is such a thing as the church universal, the *panegyria*, as well as the church manifest in local congregations and area fellowships.

B. *Ekklesia Used of Israel at Mt. Sinai*

Stephen in his martyr address spoke of Israel at Mt. Sinai as "that church (*ekklesia*) in the wilderness" (Acts 7:36). This usage of the term forms a bridge between the foregoing usages of *ekklesia* and those to follow. Some find it difficult to believe that James was speaking of the church when he used the term synagogue in James 2:2, but the term is in keeping with the usage we have already noted in Hebrews 12:23 where the term *panegyria* (lit., general synagogue) is used. The term synagogue, of itself, simply denoted a gathering together, and could be used as a synonym for *ekklesia* in view of its general application which we shall note next.

C. *Ekklesia Used of Secular Assemblies*

Ekklesia is used even in the New Testament of secular assemblies— unruly, ruled, and semi-ruled—as witnessed by the account of the Ephesian riot (Acts 19:23-41).

1) In v. 32 it is used with reference to a rioting mob. The mob, for the most part, was "called" together by the tumult. It is said of them that "they knew not why they were come together," but that did not keep them screaming as one voice for the space of two hours.

2) In v. 39 *ekklesia* is used of the same people, but of a different kind of "assembly." At this point in the narrative the town clerk has

managed to quiet the mob, and explains that the matter could have been settled in an *ennomo ekklesia*, that is, an assembly "within the (*nomos*) law."

3) In v. 41 Alexander is reported to have dismissed the *ekklesia*. The term now refers to an orderly crowd, no longer a rioting mob, but neither was it a duly called out group of citizens called together according to the due process of law.

It was this growing generalization of the meaning of *ekklesia* which prompted Christians to start prefacing the term *ekklesia* with a descriptive adjective as Alexander did in v. 39. The adjective Christians chose was *kuriokos*, meaning "The Lord's (own)." In lesson one, we took note of the fact that in time the adjective superceded the noun it was used to describe, and itself became a noun and evolved into our word church.

In all that has been said about *ekklesia* the chief point is that its root meaning is "the called out." In early Christian usage that fact was kept constantly before them. They were called out of sin, out of paganism, out of spiritual darkness and bondage into the light and freedom of Christ's redeeming love.

There is a twofold emphasis in the word *ekklesia* when used in a Christian sense. It expresses: 1) our Divine calling and 2) our devout congregating. The latter is both a natural and essential corollary of the other. The adage states the principle aptly: "Birds of a feather flock together." Their kind would soon cease to exist if they did not. It is no different with the church. But the gathering together must be for the devout expression of their love for Christ and for one another to be an *ekklesia* of Christ.

Undoubtedly, thousands of church members make up the throngs that fill the bowls for the baseball and football playoffs, but the dedication whereby they are called out of their comfortable living rooms, and often away from their air-conditioned and comfortably heated "churches" to huddle in the rain or shiver in the cold could hardly be called Christian devotion. Neither could those assembled in that context be called the *kuriake ekklesia*—an assembly of the Lord's own.

In every community of considerable size, at least in America, there are likely enough erstwhile adherents of the standard brands of American churches to start a congregation of any one of them. But until they become aware of one another, and care enough about one another and about the will of Christ, such chance meetings as may occur will lack that express devotion to the will of God that will result in their assembling together as an *ekklesia* of Christ.

2. Disciples

The term disciple(s) is used in the New Testament 267 times, 236 times in the four Gospels, otherwise in Acts. It is a curious thing that not even once is it used in the twenty-one Epistles or the Apocalypse. In the Gospels it is used both of the followers of John the immerser and of Jesus. Once (John 9:28) it is used, as a self-designation, of those who opposed Jesus, calling themselves "disciples of Moses."

In Acts the term is used thirty-one times. Except for the first instance (1:15), a transitional passage, it is used as a synonym for those who otherwise are commonly called the *ekklesia*, the church.

In the preceding lesson, we took note of the fact that a disciple is primarily a learner, but yet more. A disciple is also a follower. The term stems from a root (*math*) which denoted learning accompanied by endeavor. Thus it designated something more than one who was merely taught something. Unless the teaching caught hold, unless the learner exemplified a commitment, to call one a disciple would be to use the term loosely. Jesus said, for example, "Whosoever does not bear his own cross, and come after me, cannot be my disciple" (Luke 14:27). Crossbearing is a vivid symbol for commitment.

It also needs to be noted that the New Testament calls "disciples" those instructed in the doctrines of Christ both before and after baptism. Howbeit in the case of the former, the usage is provisional, anticipatory. Discipling is a process that is calculated to lead to baptism, but one does not cease to learn thereafter. At least one should not, though some do. A shortcoming of many evangelistic outreach endeavors is that the neophyte converts suddenly cease to be the focus of the attention of those who led them to Christ and feel abandoned. The second half of the teaching program inculcated in the Great Commission (as stated in Matthew) is as important as the first.

The other side of the coin is that some expose themselves to Christian teaching throughout their lifetime and submit to the perfunctory outward preformances which are associated with being a member of the church, but never commit themselves to Christ as an obedient responsible believer. II Timothy 3:7 speaks of some who are "ever learning but never come to the knowledge of the truth."

The term disciple (Gr. *mathetes*) has a dual emphasis: 1) It relates to the learning process, and emphasizes also 2) the disciplinary demands of Christ, the Lord. It is well to note that the terms Lord and Saviour, as used in the Scripture, appear in that order—never conversely. (See II Peter 1:1, 11; 2:20; 3:2, 18.) He himself said: "Why call me Lord, Lord, and do not the things I say?" (Luke 6:46).

116

3. *Christians*

For the present we shall consider this descriptive designation only in the context of its New Testament usage, exclusive of denominational overtones—real or imaginary. There is a sense in which the first usage of the name, as of record, did in fact set one congregation apart from all its contemporaries. But it was not given to initiate an elitist sect of the church exclusively entitled to be so named, and to wear that name exclusive of all others. In a day when the church has been so long fractionized and factionized, with exclusivist brand names carefully chosen or contrived to set themselves apart from all others, it is difficult to fully appreciate the sense in which the terms under consideration were used in the New Testament era. All the terms we will be discussing, both specific and illustrative, were intended to be applied to all the congregations. None was intended to set the pattern for denominationalizing the *ekklesia* of Christ.

At the same time, it is worthy of note that the Scriptures distinctly inform us that God called the name Christian upon an *ekklesia* of disciples "first at Antioch" (Acts 11:26). We have previously taken note of the fact that the verb used in Acts 11:26 denotes the action of God in making known his will. That fact is quite uniformly noted, and expressed by the translators, except in the instance of this text. And yet this text, more than any other, demands that the true sense of the verb *chrematisai* be made explicit. The occasion for its use was that of the fulfillment of an important Messianic age prophecy. In Isaiah 62:2, 5, it is written:

> The nations (Gentiles) shall see thy righteousness, and all kings thy glory, and thou shalt be called by a new name, *which the mouth of Jehovah shall name* . . . for as a young man marrieth a virgin, so shall thy sons marry thee.

If the name Christian is not that new name, what name given the people of the Messiah is new? And if the circumstances which are cited in the instance of the church at Antioch do not fit the conditions of the prophecy, then what situation does fit?

Beginning with Abraham God divided the human race in two streams which flowed separately for two thousand years. Israel (the princes of God) were separated from the Gentiles and made God's covenant people through whom the Messiah would come. The Law was added at Mt. Sinai which widened the gap betwixt the two. The Gentiles were "alienated from the commonwealth of Israel, the strangers from the covenants of promise" (Eph. 2:12). But in Christ Jesus those that were once far off were "made nigh in the blood of Christ. For he is our peace who made both one, and brake down the middle wall of partition" (vs. 13, 14). While the provision for the inclusion of the Gentiles in the same body was provided through the cross, and an important step toward the reception of the Gentiles was taken at Caesarea, it was not until those that were scattered abroad upon the tribulation that arose over Stephen came to Antioch that "they preached unto the Gentiles also." (See Acts 11:20, cp. v. 19.)

Acts 8:5 through 11:19 is an extended parenthesis. The events described in the parenthesis were all designed to help us understand the significance of what took place at Antioch. Even the same verb used

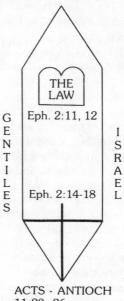

GENESIS - ABRAHAM
12:1-3

THE LAW

G E N T I L E S — Eph. 2:11, 12

I S R A E L

Eph. 2:14-18

ACTS - ANTIOCH
11:20, 26

in Acts 10:22 is repeated in Acts 11:26. Incidentally, it was first introduced to denote the providence of God in the instruction which provided guidance to Joseph in behalf of the Messianic child. (See Matt. 2:12, 22; cp. Luke 2:26; Heb. 8:5; 11:7.)

The name Christian is derived from the Greek *Christianos*—"a *new* name" if ever there was one. It is coined from the Greek translation of the Hebrew word for Messiah (the Anointed one), to which translation was added the Latin possessive suffix, *ian*. Thus the three principle languages of the Mediterranean world (the same three used to inscribe upon his cross the charge against him) combined to give us the name Christian. The Greek word *Christos* was spread to accommodate the suffix *ian*, becoming *Christianos*. The last syllable in Greek denotes number and gender, and has been dropped in English translations to conform to English usage.

Literally translated, the name Christian denotes those "belonging to the Messiah," those who are "of Christ." Obviously, all who are "in Christ" (II Cor. 5:17; Rom. 6:7), "baptized into his name" (Acts 19:5),

118

"baptized into his death" (Rom. 6:4), "baptized into the remission of sins" (Acts 2:38), "baptized in one Spirit into his body" (I Cor. 12:13); all such are assuredly Christians—those who "belong to Christ."

Note: For an indepth study of the name Christian, and how it came to be given, the reader is directed to lesson twenty-two in which the Divinely Given Names by which congregations were designated are treated.

PREVIEW—REVIEW QUESTIONS

1. Define Superstructure. What is the linguistic basis of the word?
2. Locate (Bk., Ch., Vs.) and cite the gist of two texts which suggest the use of the term in the context of this study.
3. What is the distinction between specific and illustrative terms used, for example, to describe the church?
4. What is the literal meaning of *ekklesia*?
5. What is the general meaning of the term, as it was commonly used in the New Testament times?
6. State at least two ways in which the word was used in the New Testament with reference to congregations and/or the church in general.
7. In what respect could Israel at Mt. Sinai be called an *ekklesia* (church)? Where so called?
8. Note some ways in which *ekklesia* was used in a secular sense. Identify the setting of the usage.
9. In addition to the literal meaning of the term, note the dual emphasis attached to the word when used in a Christian context.
10. When do those called out of sin by the Gospel become a part of "the general assembly and church of the first born"?
11. From whence is that quotation taken? What is the word rendered "general assembly"? To what does it compare?
12. When do those redeemed in Christ become members of a local congregation? Note implications of Acts 9:26.
13. Define discipleship. Note the two facets that should be reflected in the definition to conform to Biblical usage.
14. Note two lines of evidence that the name Christian was Divinely given.
15. Locate (Bk., Ch., Vs.) supporting texts.
16. What was significant about the church at Antioch that it should be chosen of God to be the first recipients of the name Christian?

17. Explain the diagram intended to show the beginning and ending of the separation of Jews and Gentiles.
18. Identify and explain the extended parenthesis in Acts which climaxed with giving of the name Christian.
19. What does the name Christian literally mean?
20. What is the derivation of the name, linguistically?
21. Cite several resultants of conversion, particularly as it finds expression in Christian baptism, which makes the name Christian appropriate as a designation for all who are in a saving relationship with Christ.

8

THE SUPERSTRUCTURE DESCRIBED IN SPECIFIC TERMS, CONCLUDED

4. Saints

A term which ranks second only to *ekklesia* in the frequency with which it appears in the Scriptures as a description of Christ's own is one of the least so used today. That is true even of those who pride themselves on the fact they "speak where the Bible speaks, and as the Bible speaks, calling Bible things by Bible names."

Christians are called saints in the New Testament no less than sixty-three times. And when such expressions as "holy brethren" (saintly brethren) and kindred expressions are included, the number approaches three score and ten.

Our word saint is derived from the Latin *sanctus*, which gives us a hint as to why it is so widely misunderstood as to its meaning, and so avoided outside of Romanist circles. In the New Testament, saint is used to translate the Greek word *hagios*. The same word is also translated "holy." In fact, it is so translated 166 times. When the two renderings are combined, and such expressions as "holy brethren" and "holy women" are added, we find the Greek word *hagios* being used in the

121

New Testament 240 times. Obviously, God is trying to tell us something. But what?

The root from which the word *hagios* stems has to do primarily with separation, particularly when the separation is for a special purpose. Thus:

1) a person set apart is a saint.

2) the act of setting apart is to sanctify.

3) the state of being set apart is sanctification.

4) a place set apart is a sanctuary.

No doubt you have noted, if passing by or through a wilderness preserve, a sign reading: Game Sanctuary. One is recalled which read: Bird Sanctuary. That one was "for the birds." Seriously, it really was. It was set apart for their habitation and preservation.

Unfortunately, popular usage reflects the Romanist corruption of the term. A mentor of mine observed that in the popular mind a saint is either someone who is too old to get into mischief, or those dead so long all the mischief they got into has been forgotten. That is almost too true to be funny, or better stated, it is too sad to be funny. Address a brother or sister in Christ as a saint and note the response. You will be thought being playful, not serious. We sometimes speak of a dear little old lady as a saint, but we would hesitate to address her as such, nor anyone else for that matter. But Paul did. (Cp. Rom. 1:7; I Cor. 1:2; Eph. 1:1; Phil. 1:1; Col. 1:2; I Thess. 3:13; II Thess. 1:10; I Tim. 5:10; Philem. 5, plus multiplied uses throughout the text of his epistles.)

Jude did so, twice in his short epistle (vs. 3, 14). The Hebrew writer did so (Heb. 6:10, 13:24). John, in the Apocalypse, uses the expression thirteen times, in passages ranging from Revelation 5:8 through 20:9.

The Biblical usage of the term serves a dual purpose. 1) It emphasizes the distinctive character—the mind-set that should mark those called by the Gospel, and hence the lifestyle which "becometh saints" (Eph. 5:3).

Abraham, whom Paul uses in Romans, chapter four, as a prototype of those who believe in Christ, illustrates what we have just said. As Abraham moved about, he did two things which should instruct us. The verbs are instructive and the order is also. Abraham *builded* an altar (Gen. 12:7). Then he *pitched* his tent (Gen. 12:8). Abraham's sojourning in Canaan could scarcely be traced from the accommodations whereby he provided for his bodily comfort, but that which was for his spiritual good became landmarks in Canaan.

Abraham's response to Lot when it was reported to him there was strife twixt Lot's herdsmen and Abraham's ought not to surprise us. Most men in similar circumstances would have reminded Lot whose land it really was, and that by Divine promise. Abraham did not say, however, "If your herdsmen cannot get along with mine, then get out." Instead he offered to divide the land with Lot. Moreover, he gave Lot first choice. Should Lot choose to go to the right, Abraham would take what was left. Or vice versa. The record is that "Lot lifted up his eyes" (Gen. 13:10) and saw "all the plain of the Jordan that it was well watered everywhere." And Lot's eyes got as green as the valley. Verse 11 informs us that "Lot chose all the plain of the Jordan." At that point most men would have said, "Nephew, you have blown it. Your greed is more than I will bear. Get out of the country, now!"

Abraham let Lot get away with his greedy grasp for this world's wealth. But God did not. Lot soon lost it all. And Abraham? Abraham lifted up his eyes also, but higher. One has to turn to Hebrews 11:10-16 to see how it turned out for him, and why. There we read: "He (Abraham) looked for the city which hath the foundations, whose builder and maker is God" (v. 10). "Wherefore God was not ashamed of (him) to be called (his) God: for he hath prepared for (him, and them that are likeminded) a city" (v. 16).

2) The term saints not only serves to emphasize the distinctive character which becomes us as Christians, it also holds forth a Divine challenge. As we have already noted, the repeated use of this term is obviously intended to tell us something, and lead to something.

In the Genesis record there is an account of the birth of Jacob—the cheat, the tripster, by name and by nature (Gen. 25:24-26). What a baleful name he was given. True, it was descriptive. He indeed came into this world as one who "takes by the heel." He lived up to the name that was given him. But God gave him a new name, Israel—prince of God. It did not fit him; not when it was given him. But in time it did. In time his new name began to reflect in Jacob's thought and life. The tripster became a prince of God!

The New Testament carries a similar story. The name Simon is by no means a pernicious name, like Jacob. In Hebrew it means famous. But that could lead to cockiness. And at times it seems to have done so in the life of Simon, the fisherman. Jesus renamed him Cephas (Aramaic for rock; cp. Gr., *petros*, rock). One wonders what the reaction of the other disciples was when Jesus called Simon a rock. Rock? How about straw in the wind? That would fit him better.

123

But wait. See him after the resurrection, and after Pentecost, as he faced the Jewish council which sought to still him and John: "Whether it is right in the sight of God to hearken unto men, rather than unto God, judge ye: for we cannot but speak the things we saw and heard" (Acts 4:19, 20). Now, we are beginning to see a rock.

John Chrysostom, famed fourth century Christian orator, counseled Christian parents to bestow upon their children an ennobling name, the name of one before them perhaps who had borne it nobly, and then keep its meaning and challenge before them. What a challenge there is for us in this: We are called (to be) saints (I Cor. 1:2, and elsewhere); or to be more precise, "We are called saints!" (the words "to be" are added by the translators). We are separated from the world, called into the *ekklesia* of Christ.

5. *Children of God*

"Behold, what manner of love the Father hath bestowed upon us, that we should be called the children of God" (I John 3:1). It is amazing, is it not? But that is not the half of it. *Called* children of God, only called such? Now hear this: "Beloved, *now* are we children of God" (v. 2a). Nor is that all. Hear the rest of it:

> It is not yet made manifest what we shall be. We know that (when) he shall be manifested, we shall be like him, for we shall see him even as he is. And every one that hath this hope set on him purifieth himself, even as he is pure (I John 3:2b, 3).

1) This descriptive term speaks first of our Divinely bestowed filial relationship to God, the Father. We are "begotten" (KJV, "born," Gr. *gennao*) of God.

This relationship is not to be equated with that of Christ. He is again and again referred to as *the* son of God, and "the only begotten from the Father" (John 1:14; 3:16, etc.). If he is the only begotten (Gr. *monogenes*), then how are we said to be begotten of him? The answer is found in James 1:18: "Of his own will he brought us forth (KJV, begat us) by the word of truth, that we should be a kind of first fruits of his creatures." Cp. I Peter 1:23: "Having been begotten again (KJV, being born again, Gr., *ana-gegennemenoi*), not of corruptible seed, but of incorruptible, which liveth and abideth for ever." Does this begin to sound a bit like "paper work"? Do not let the suggestion panic you. Let us see how Paul explains it:

124

For as many as are led by the Spirit of God, these are the sons of God. For ye received not the spirit of bondage again unto fear: but ye received *the spirit of adoption,* whereby we cry, Abba, Father. The Spirit himself beareth witness with our spirit that we are children of God: and if children, then heirs; heirs of God, and joint heirs with Christ; *if so be that we suffer with him* that we may be also glorified with him (Rom. 8:14-17).

But when the fullness of time came, God sent forth his son, born of a woman, born under the law, that he might redeem them that are under the law, *that we might receive the adoption of sons,* and because ye are sons, God sent forth the Spirit of his Son into our hearts, crying, Abba, Father (Gal. 4:4-6).

Those whose creeds demand that the Scriptures be forced into the mold of the dogma of eternal security find the texts just cited conveying an idea which to them is disconcerting, and to be explained away somehow. The shibboleth, "once a son, always a son" (Text? None!) is not so comforting when the adoptive process is brought into the picture. Adoption papers can be rescinded. The genetic code cannot. But even children by birth can be, and many have been, cast out, disinherited—utterly. Remember Adam? (See Luke 3:38.)

Paul's emphasis is upon the fact that though we are adopted, we are heirs of God, and made joint heirs even with his only begotten son—if so be that we suffer with him, that we may be glorified with him.

Actually the doctrine of adoption introduces an element in the story of God's love that is beautiful to contemplate. You have no doubt received at some time an announcement which read: "I was not expected. I was selected." There is a sense in which sonship by adoption more fully demonstrates the wonder of love, both human and Divine. It is not difficult to love our own flesh and blood. Not to do so is to be guilty of one of the blackest sins in the catalog of human iniquity, the want of "natural affection." (See Rom. 1:21-32; note v. 31.)

To love a child not our own, perchance of a different race, even one with obvious birth defects, and to bring that child into our home, and make of the child an heir, and joint heir with our own flesh and blood offspring—that is akin to the love of God toward us. Let us not presume upon his love as though he has trapped himself in a relationship which he cannot terminate, "no matter what!"

2) Our sonship with God also emphasizes our Divine inheritance. This has already been noted, but it deserves to be underscored. We are in fact heirs of God. Christ, his only begotten son, is at this time preparing for us a place in his Father's house.

6. *A Royal Priesthood*

In I Peter 2:9, we are told that we are an elect race, a royal priesthood, a holy nation, a people for God's own possession." In the prologue to the Apocalypse John says of Jesus, "He made us to be a kingdom, to be priests unto his God and Father" (Rev. 1:6). The announcement is repeated in the heavenly chorus recorded in Revelation 5:9, 10.

There is a significant difference between the priestly institution under the Law and Gospel. Under the Law there were four distinct levels. 1) There was Jehovah God, the Almighty; 2) the High Priest, inaugurated with the appointment of Aaron; 3) the Priesthood (the order of Aaron's sons) and 4) the Congregation (the people). Only the High Priest could pass through the second veil into the Holy of Holies, there to appear before the face of God for the people. And he could do so but once a year, and then only after he had offered a sacrifice, first for his own sins, and then the sins of the people (Heb. 9:7).

Under the New Covenant that changed drastically. There are now but two levels. Deity and the High Priest are merged into the person of Christ, and the Priesthood and the Congregation are merged in the Persons of the Church.

Old Covenant	New Covenant
DEITY: JEHOVAH) The High Priest) — Christ	
The Priesthood) The Congregation) — The Church	

When Christ died on the cross, the veil of the temple was rent from top to bottom, signifying the way into the presence of God has now been opened for us. Read Hebrews 10:19-25, and rejoice and be exceeding glad we live under the New Covenant, and we are all priests, and even kings, through Christ.

In Christ, the whole church is a priesthood. There is no one, no office to whom, or to which office the privilege of presiding at the Lord's table, or baptizing, or aught else is restricted. That is scarcely demonstrated even in churches which once eschewed all forms of hierarchy to restore the priesthood of believers. The one-man pastor system is once again bringing even the elect into bondage.

2) The doctrine of the priesthood of believers not only emphasizes the *mediatorial role* of the whole church under one great High Priest, the one mediator between God and man, himself man, Christ Jesus (I Tim. 2:5) it emphasizes also our *royal mission.*

126

The series of contingent questions asked in Romans 10:14-17 illustrates the role of the church in a sinful world. Those who balk at baptism for remission of sins on the ground it makes one's salvation depend on something someone else does for us need to ask themselves how they came to *believe* on Christ. Did they come to that state alone? Did they receive no help from anyone along the way?

S. G. Gordon, in a devotional book long out of print, *Prayer Changes Things*, relates an imaginary conversation between Jesus and the angel Gabriel upon Christ's return to heaven. It goes something like this:

Gabriel: "Jesus, you died for all men, did you not?"
Christ: "Yes, I died for everyone."
Gabriel: "Do they all know that? How many do?"
Christ: "Only a handful of disciples whom I left behind."
Gabriel: "Well, how are the others to learn of it?"
Christ: "I asked Peter, James, and John and the rest of my disciples to make it their business to tell others, and to instruct them to make it their business to tell others, and so on until the whole world knows."
Gabriel: "But Lord Jesus, what if they neglect, what then?"
Christ: "I have no other plan."

And indeed, he does not. He has *no other plan*. As an unknown poet once put it:

> He's counting on you,
> On a love that will share
> In his burden of prayer
> For the souls he has bought
> With his life's blood, and sought
> Through sorrow and pain
> To bring home yet again
> He's counting on *you*.
> If you fail him, what then?
>   He has no other plan.

7. Kingdom

With this term we are back where we started, with the pace-setting words of Jesus himself: "I will build my church (*ekklesia*), and I will give unto you the keys of the kingdom" (Matt. 16:18, 19). Is Jesus talking in the same breath of two different institutions he would head, the first to be established shortly, but the second to be delayed for nearly two thousand years, if not longer?

It is almost beyond comprehension that Bible scholars today, in large numbers, refuse to believe that Christ is king and the church is his kingdom. But then it was the scholars of Jesus' own day, the doctors of the Law, who were likewise so hung up on an earthly, material Messianic kingdom that they chose to reject him as Messiah, despite his obvious credentials, rather than accept a kingdom that is within one's heart. Strangely, Pilate, the Roman governor, was able to grasp the concept. When he asked Jesus: "Art thou a king?" Jesus answered: "My kingdom is not of this world. If my kingdom were of this world, then would my servants fight. But now my kingdom is not from thence" (John 18:36). At that Pilate began to understand. He knew full well already what kind of kingdom the Jews wanted, and he could readily see why they did not want Jesus for their king. His next question therefore was intriguing, but no more than Jesus' reply: "Art thou then a king?" Jesus answered: "You've said it!" (to put it in the common vernacular). "To this end have I been born, and to this end came I into the world, that I should bear witness of the truth" (John 18:37).

Is Christ then King?

1. He was born king of the Jews. At least the wise men from the east following the heralding star thought so, and paid him homage as king. If they were mistaken, Matthew had plenty of time to find it out and correct their false assumption. Instead he recorded the incident as entirely fitting and proper. Why so?

2. If Christ is not king, he acted out an interesting charade on the occasion of the triumphal entry. Or was he not sufficiently prescient at this point to know he could not pull it off? How is it then that in the wake of his announcement in Matthew 16:18, 19, Jesus (it is said) "from that time began to show unto his disciples that he must go into Jerusalem, and suffer many things of the elders and chief priests and scribes, and be killed, and the third day be raised up" (v. 21)? That notwithstanding, when he announced he would build his *ekklesia* he announced he would give them the keys to the kingdom. If the two terms do not refer to the same institution, he must truly have confused the twelve.

3. Moreover, he concluded the discourse by saying, "Verily, I say unto you, there are some of them standing *here*, who shall in no wise taste death, till they see the Son of man coming in his kingdom" (Matt. 16:28). If the church and the kingdom are not in some real sense to be

equated, where are those who were standing there that day, who are still alive to this day, and will be alive (with beards reaching from Dan to Beersheba) when he comes at long last to do what he hoped to do the first time?

4) If Christ is not king, and his church is not therefore "the kingdom that is within you" (Luke 17:21), then why did Peter quote the kingdom prophecy of David (Ps. 110:1), and, "speaking as the Holy Spirit gave him utterance," declare the prophecy to be fulfilled, saying (in the light of the resurrection of Christ):

> Being therefore by the right hand of God exalted, and having received of the Father the promise of the Holy Spirit, he hath poured forth this which ye see and hear. For David ascended not into the heavens: but he saith himself:
>
>> The Lord (Jehovah) said unto my Lord,
>> Sit thou on my right hand,
>> Till I make thine enemies the footstool of thy feet.
>
> Acts 2:33-35   (Ps. 110:1, 2)

5) If Christ is not king, and we who have entered the church are not in his kingdom, then why did Paul write in Philippians 3:20, 21:

> Our citizenship is in heaven, whence also we await the Saviour, the Lord Jesus Christ: who shall fashion anew this body of our humiliation that it may be conformed unto the body of his glory according to the working whereby he is able to subject all things unto himself.

The term kingdom has a dual emphasis. 1) It testifies to our heavenly citizenship, but it reminds us also, as Paul has just done of 2) our earthly pilgrimage. Like Abraham, we are sojourning here, looking for a better country in that time to come. The term kingdom grows out of the fact that the church is a heavenly society, a royal priesthood over which Christ reigns as king and high priest of our confession having all authority in heaven and on earth. The church of Christ is not a federation of sovereign states, a democracy, or a league of separate sects, nor a world council of ecclesiastical hierarchies. It is a society over which Christ is king.

Summary of Lessons Seven and Eight

The church has been described under several specific terms. While we have not exhausted the list, we have taken note of these things:

1. We are an elect race, a chosen generation, called out of the world into the kingdom of the son of God's love, hence we are called the *ekklesia*.

2. We are learners, and followers of the Master teacher and Lord, being disciplined by his precepts and example, hence we are called disciples.

3. We belong to Christ, having been bought with a price, redeemed by his blood, and baptized into his death, burial, and resurrection, yea, even into him. Hence we are called Christians.

4. We have been set apart from the world, and set apart for this service. We are therefore called saints.

5. We have been adopted into the Divine family, and made heirs of God and joint heirs with Jesus Christ. Hence we are called the children of God, and such we are.

6. We are those through whom Jesus seeks to bridge the gap which yawns between sinful man and the holy and righteous God and maker of all mankind. Hence we are called a royal priesthood.

7. Our citizenship is in heaven where our king sits enthroned at the right hand of God, there to reign until his enemies are made the footstool of his feet. Meanwhile we are his kingdom subjects on earth, pilgrims in a weary land. We are therefore called a kingdom.

PREVIEW—REVIEW QUESTIONS

1. Define the term saint. Note meaning of the root.
2. Define three other terms which stem from the same root.
3. What is the popular concept of a saint? Note the sects of Christendom which misuse the term.
4. How does the life story of Abraham illustrate the true meaning of sainthood?
5. State the dual emphasis of the term.
6. Are we called "to be" children of God, or are we now children of God?
7. If Christ is the only begotten Son of God, then what kind of children of God are we?
8. Does the Bible teach that once we become God's child he is stuck with us forevermore? Illustrate.
9. State the dual emphasis of the term children of God.
10. Define the term priest.
11. Note the difference between the priesthood in the two covenants.

12. Does the growing dominance of the church, even at the congregational level, by elitist clergyman, obscure the Biblical doctrine of the priesthood of believers? How so?
13. State the dual emphasis of the term priest.
14. Is Christ king, his church his kingdom, or is he to be likened to "presidential hopefuls" who never made it?
15. Support your answer from the Scriptures.
16. State the intrinsic nature of the kingdom of Christ. Where is its territory, really?
17. State the dual emphasis of the term kingdom.

9

THE SUPERSTRUCTURE DESCRIBED
BY ILLUSTRATIVE TERMS

A minister asked an aged saint what her favorite word in the Bible might be. Her answer was surprising. He expected her to say "heaven," or "hope," or one of the other words which epitomize our Christian faith. But she answered, "like."

"Why did you pick that word?" he asked.

"Because," said she, "Jesus said the kingdom of heaven is like a woman making bread, or searching the house for a mislaid coin, and like a sower sowing seed, or a fisherman casting a net into the sea. I know something about all those things, and the many others Jesus spoke of. If the kingdom of heaven is like those things, then I know a lot about the kingdom of heaven."

That is precisely the purpose served by the illustrative terms used in the Bible, whether contained in a metaphor, simile, or parable. Each helps to bridge the gap between the known and the unknown, or to make the familiar more familiar. Knowing something about the one helps to understand the other.

A word of caution is due, however. Comparisons should not be pressed too far. Generally speaking, only the point of discussion which called forth the parable or simile or metaphor is to be made a point of doctrine. Recall, for example, the parable of the persistent widow and the unrighteous judge (Luke 18:1-8). We are told that Jesus spoke the parable "to the end that (we) ought always to pray, and not to faint" (that is, lose heart, give up). The judge finally complied with her request, not in the interest of justice (he was not that kind of judge (cp. v. 6), nor out of compassion for her (cp. v. 2). In the vernacular of our time, he did so to "get her off his back."

The point of the parable is not to teach us that God is like that unrighteous judge; if we will keep the pressure on, he will buckle, or knuckle down, and give in to us. The point is that we should be like that widow who did not give up at the first "faint" effort which did not avail. God is not a genie in a lamp, nor is prayer a sort of "alakazam tomato can" hocus-pocus phrase that produces amazing results on a moment's notice.

Parables and metaphors are like crooked sticks laid alongside of a rail. Each may touch the rail at a point or two. No parable is to be pressed out of shape so as to parallel the rail inch by inch. It requires many parables and metaphors to touch upon every truth concerning the kingdom of God. Consider, for example, the basic metaphor which is the basis of this immediate series of lessons—the superstructure. A congregation is to be compared to the superstructure atop a foundation. Do you know of any building that is dismantled every week and scattered far and wide across the town and countryside, then hastily put back together (in part, at least) for an hour or so, and the process then repeated?

The illustrative terms we are about to consider readily kindle the imagination. Many practical lessons may be drawn from each of them. There is one core comparison which is common to them all.

1. The Church Is God's Building, I Cor. 3:9

Specifically, the church is a holy temple in the Lord (Eph. 2:21), a temple of God (I Cor. 3:16, 17), a temple of the Holy Spirit (I Cor. 6:19), and, combining the two into one saying, a habitation of God in the Spirit (Eph. 2:22). As Christ's church we are likened in one sense to the tabernacle in the wilderness built by Moses, "according to the pattern that was shown in the mount" (Heb. 3:3-5; 8:5) through the labors of "wise-hearted men" (Exod. 28:3; 31:6; 35:10, 25; 36:1, 2, 8). Thus we are called Christ's house, having been built by him

(Heb. 3:6) through the labors of (hopefully) wise-hearted and Spirit-led men.

Moses, "as a servant," built but one house. Christ, "as a Son," built but one house. As Moses built "according to the pattern" God showed to him, so Christ built the church "through the manifold wisdom of God, according to his eternal purpose which he purposed in Christ" (Eph. 3:10, 11).

In the house that Jesus built each of us is spoken of as "a living stone" (I Peter 2:5), undergirded by the foundation which is Christ. The adjective chosen emphasizes the fact that the relationship between the founder and the superstructure is both vital and vitalizing.

Note the church is described as a temple, not a mall; as a house, not a metropolis replete with everything from mansions on snob hill to tenement slums. In our Father's house above, there are many mansions, but no hovels. Christ, his Son, has designed but one church.

Singularity, in the sense of both oneness and uniqueness is the hallmark of the church that Jesus built. If everything that is called the church in the world today is indeed the house of God, it would be unique in quite a different sense—a building following no unifying design, conforming to no master plan, with sections upon section closed off, even separate from and inaccessible to other sections.

All that we behold today cannot be the house that Jesus built, or would have us build. We repeat the fundamental proposition of this course of study: Christ built only one church, hence only one can be "the Lord's own."

2. The Church Is the Body of Christ, Eph. 1:23

This figure of speech, even more than the other, emphasizes the vital link which exists between Christ and those who are the "Lord's own." The analogy is especially meaningful. The body has appetites, feelings, sensitivities, functions, and needs; but the members have no independent will. The whole of the body is subject to the head. Were one's hand to suddenly clench into a fist and come crashing into someone's jaw, no one could be convinced the hand was acting independently of the head, and to be more precise, the will. If we want to know what kind of person one is, we need only to observe what the body does amid various circumstances. Every word and deed reflect the mind from whence such proceed. Even so, the church ought to reflect the mind of Christ. If it does not, it is open to question as to whether what is called the church is indeed what it is being called.

135

There are three circumstances which may preclude a body from functioning as a perfect reflection of the mind: 1) infancy or immaturity, 2) injury, and 3) infirmity. If we do not reflect the mind of Christ, we should ask ourselves: 1) Are we yet babes in Christ though by reason of the time we ought to be behaving ourselves with a much greater manifestation of spiritual maturity? (cp. Heb. 5:12-14, I Cor. 3:1-7). It should be of interest that in the latter passage Paul addresses himself to the problem of immaturity in the context of the divisions which were manifest in the Corinthian church. 2) If immaturity is not our problem, are we spiritual cripples? Has sin maimed or incapacitated us? Do we go limping between the Lord's side and the side of Satan? 3) Or is our problem spiritual sickness? Paul lays that charge against the Corinthians in connection with his rebuke against them for the manner in which they were conducting themselves at the Lord's supper. (Cp. I Cor. 11:20-34. See v. 30.)

Taking our cue from Paul's specific application of the analogy before us to the problem of division, we do well to ask: Is everything that is called the church indeed the body of Christ? If so, we have a dual incongruity. If Christ is head over every religious body of so-called Christendom, we have a freakish spectacle without parallel in the natural world—a head with scores of bodies, each behaving somewhat at variance with the others, if not in actual conflict.

Conversely, 1) if all the sects of Christendom are really one body, despite the contradictions in their behavior and obvious conflicts of interest, and 2) if the heads of state, so to speak, which control the various denominations are indeed the heads of the sections of the body each controls, then we have again a freak unlike anything ever seen in a sideshow—a body with scores of heads. "Ye did not so learn Christ" (Eph. 4:20).

3. The Church Is the Father's Family, Eph. 3:15

The third chapter of Ephesians contains a beautiful prayer from the heart of the apostle Paul which opens with these words:

> For this cause I bow my knees unto the Father, from whom every family (Gr., pasa patria—all the fatherhood, or father's own) in heaven and on earth is named (Eph. 3:15).

That Paul was speaking of the church is evident from the fact that Paul closes the prayer with these words of benediction:

136

> Now unto him that is able to do exceeding abundantly above all that we
> ask or think, according to the power that worketh in us, unto him be the
> glory *in the church* and in Christ Jesus unto all generations, for ever
> and ever. Amen (Eph. 3:20, 21).

Elsewhere Paul speaks of the church in such kindred expression as,
"the household (*oikeios*) of God" (Eph. 2:19), and "the household
of faith" (Gal. 6:10).

Note that all these expressions are in the singular. The suggestion
of different families, of different faiths, reflecting differing interests and
behavior, and particularly families of different names, alienated, and
antagonistic, each against the other—such conjecture would make a
mockery of this prayer.

It has been suggested that denominational names are like first names
(given names) which are bestowed upon children to enable each to
have his or her own identity while yet being a part of the family. The
fact is, aside from the utterly baseless conjecture, it does not work
that way. For one thing, a close family relationship is always weakened,
and unity of thought and act is broken by the usage of denominational
names. Moreover, though a father may give one son his own given
name as a prefix to the family name, all his descendants through that
son do not become Russellites, or whatever the given name might
be. But denominational names become the name of all the members
which accrue to any given denomination. And when additional "given"
names are given or appropriated by schisms within a denomination
(Northern, Southern, Free, United, Evangelical, etc.), that extends
the schism, deepens the rift.

To denominate is "to name from." That may be taken two ways.
A baby receives a name from its family to identify the child as belonging
to that family. A bride takes the name of her husband to mark her
separation from all others and her exclusive partnership with him.
Paul views the family of God denominated 1) in a manner which identifies us with his son, Jesus Christ, and 2) in a manner that distinguishes
us from those who are not a part of the household of faith, the faith
which is in Christ our Lord. The name Christian so denominates
Christ's own.

Again let it be noted that if all that is called the church is that indeed,
God has a strange family—a family that will not live together, work together, nay, that cannot even share a single meal together in honor
of his beloved Son, though to do so would be to honor his "death wish,"
so to speak. How could we call rival clans conducting feudal war a
"family," much less the family of God?

137

God has only one family, hence only those who come to him in Christ (John 14:6) are the *patria*—the fatherhood, the Father's own.

4. The Church Is Christ's Bride-Elect, Eph. 5:25-32

The imagery of the church as the bride-elect of Christ stems from Old Testament analogy in which Israel is represented as betrothed to Jehovah. The prophet Isaiah, foreseeing the light of the Gospel going forth from Jerusalem even unto the Gentiles, wrote:

> For Zion's sake will I not withhold my peace, and for Jerusalem's sake I will not rest, until her righteousness goeth forth as brightness, and her *salvation* as a lamp that burneth. And the nations shall see thy righteousness and all kings thy glory, *and thou shalt be called by a new name, which the mouth of Jehovah shall name.* Thou shalt also be a crown of beauty in the hand of Jehovah, and a royal diadem in the hand of thy God. Thou shalt no more be termed Forsaken; neither shall thy land any more be termed Desolate: but thou shalt be called *Hephzibah* (that is, my delight is in her); and thy land *Beulah* (that is, *married*): for Jehovah delighteth in thee, and thy land shall be married. For as a young man marrieth a virgin, so shall thy sons marry thee: and as a bridegroom rejoiceth over the bride, so shall thy God rejoice over thee (Isa. 62:1-5).

At Antioch, with the Divine bestowal of the new name (Christians) upon the disciples in the first church to fulfill the implications of the foregoing prophecy, the *ekklesia* of Christ became manifest as the new "Israel of God" (Gal. 6:16).

Several kindred texts are worthy of note. John, in the Apocalypse, closes the third major cycle of visions with these words:

> Let us rejoice and be exceeding glad, and let us give glory unto him; for the marriage of the Lamb is come, and his wife hath made herself ready (Rev. 19:7).

And again, in the Grand Finale, the vision of the age to come:

> And I saw the holy city, New Jerusalem, coming down out of heaven from God, made ready as a bride (Gr., *numphe*—"nymph") adorned for her husband (Rev. 21:2).

And these words from near the closing Amen:

> The Spirit and the bride say, come (Rev. 22:16).

Particularly significant are these words from Paul: "I espoused you to one husband, that I might present you as a pure virgin unto Christ" (II Cor. 11:2).

Two things may be drawn from this analogy. The first was discussed in lesson one, under the third main sub-topic of that lesson. There attention was given to the pains to which a bride goes to prepare herself for the hour of her wedding. To the passage alluded to above (Rev. 19:7) John added: "And it was given unto her (the bride of the Lamb) that she should array herself in fine linen, bright and pure; *for the fine linen is the righteous acts of the saints*" (v. 8).

The second lesson grows out of the fact that all the references cited are in the singular, in respect both to the bride and the groom. They all point to the church, not denominations, as the bride of Christ. Christ, you will recall, taught a rigorous monogamy (Matt. 19:3-9). Of this we may be sure, the church is not a harem. Christ is not a second Solomon. He has no bevy of wives. He keeps no concubines. He is not a paramour or polygamist. He is not a spiritual adulterer without parallel. Christ has chosen only one bride, hence only one can be the "Lord's own."

5. *The Church Is Christ's Flock, John 10:16*

A striking commentary on this figure of speech is found in Jesus' "I am the good shepherd" discourse (John 10:1-16), a discourse which closes with the startling announcement that the Gentiles will be gathered into Christ's fold, and there shall be "one flock, one shepherd" (v. 16). An even more provocative chapter, one that ought to be read at every service of ordination or installation, whether of minister-evangelist, associate, elders, deacons, teachers, or whoever else it may be, is Ezekiel, chapter 34. (Note particularly vs. 1, 2, 7-10, 17-19, 31, and all the verses in between!)

Note the words of Peter in his first epistle, and make a special note of how he represents himself, and who he declares the "head pastor" to be, (I Peter 5:4). Note also the words of Paul, as he addresses the elders of the church at Ephesus. Notice whom he elects to summon to meet him as he has a brief stopover nearby, and note whom he identifies as the pastors of the church, and the bishops, and how they came to that responsible office, (Acts 20:28-31).

One of the most beautiful benedictions of the Bible is built around the imagery under consideration. It reads:

> Now the God of peace who brought again from the dead the great shepherd of the sheep with the blood of an eternal covenant, even our Lord Jesus, make you perfect in every good thing to do his will, working

in us that which is well pleasing in his sight, through Jesus Christ, to whom be the glory for ever and ever. Amen (Heb. 13:20, 21).

Once again, the singularity of the metaphor, everywhere it is used in the Scriptures. The church is not a menagerie, a zoo, or an animal farm. It is Christ's flock. He is the chief shepherd. Hence the proposition of this course of study presses its way to the forefront again: Christ has only one flock, hence only one can be the "Lord's own."

6. The Church Is God's Husbandry, I Cor. 3:9

This is one of the least familiar of the illustrative terms applied to the church, and understandably so. The Greek word so translated, *georgion*, appears only this one time in the Scriptures. But the idea it communicates is by no means limited to this text. *Georgion* is formed from *geos* (earth, ground) and *ergo* (to work). Hence a husbandman (Gr. *georgos*), a word which is used nineteen times in the New Testament, is a worker of the ground, a tiller of the soil. Husbandry is an archaic word for the tillage, that is, the tilled or cultivated field, including what is grown thereon.

Such Scriptures as the parable of the sower (Matt. 13:3-23), Isaiah's song of the vineyard (Isa. 5:1-7), and Jesus' parable of the vine and the branches (John 15:1-8) provide a commentary on this figure of speech. Vineyard would be a meaningful synonym for *georgion* in the context of the latter two texts cited. Vineyard relates to both the tilled field and the vines which grow thereon.

Isaiah's song of the vineyard (Isa. 5:1-7) was addressed to Israel and speaks of the inexcusable failure of the Hebrew nation to produce the "fruit of righteousness" God had every right to expect of them. Hebrews 6:7, 8 updates the complaint. The same charge can be, and in the epistle to the Hebrews is, laid against apostate and fruitless Christians. The writer says concerning those whom he describes as: 1) once enlightened, 2) who tasted of the heavenly gift, 3) were made partakers of the Holy Spirit, 4) tasted the good word of God and powers of the age to come (vs. 4, 5); if such as they fall away, they "crucify to themselves the son of God afresh and put him to an open shame" (v. 6). What then? The writer charges that such persons are akin to fleshly Israel whom even Christ, God's Son and their Messiah, could not renew unto repentance. Thus he concludes that they too, like the vineyard Isaiah described, shall be trodden down, burned, and destroyed. Vs. 7, 8 tell us why:

140

For the land which hath drunk the rain that cometh oft upon it, and bringeth forth herbs meet for them for whose sake it is also tilled (Gr. *georgetai*), receiveth blessing from God: but if it beareth thorns and thistles, it is rejected and nigh unto a curse; whose end is to be burned.

The thrust of all this is twofold: 1) One rightly expects far more of land that has been tilled, fenced, and planted with the choicest vine (or grain, trees, etc.) than a field that has received no such care. 2) The church is the only *georgion* God has to bear for him the fruit of the Spirit. We have been sown with the choicest of seed and have been extended the labor of love. If found fruitless, we are nigh to a curse, whose end is to be burned.

We weed our gardens, our lawns, and our fields. We need to weed our lives also. Weeds grow without planting or cultivation. Fruit, choice fruit, requires both.

With this figure of speech also let it be noted that denominationalism corrupts the imagery. It makes of God's field at best a diversified farm, growing something to everyone's liking. God's husbandry is not a truck garden, a tobacco plantation, a stock ranch. We are to be the garden of God, bringing forth the fruit of righteousness. God has only one field, the church. If we do not produce the fruitage of the Gospel seed, are we the "Lord's own"?

7. *The Church Is Christ's Corps of Soldiers, Eph. 6:10-20*

The weapons of our Christian warfare are not carnal (II Cor. 10:4). Our only offensive weapon (Eph. 6:17) is only offensive to those who are offended by the truth. It is nonetheless "mighty before God to the casting down of strongholds; casting down imaginations, and every high thing that is exalted against the knowledge of God, and bringing every thought into captivity to the obedience of Christ" (II Cor. 10:5).

Paul, in whose writings militant imagery is often found, spoke of himself as "set for the defense of the Gospel" (Phil. 1:16). Translated, he was saying he was prepared to fill the role of a Christian apologist. The Greek word he used is *apologian*. It is derived from *apo* (from) and *logeo* (to speak). It carries the idea of speaking from a fixed (set) position, as from a position of strength. And so it was with him. Whenever Paul was called upon to defend himself, whether among the philosophers on Mars Hill, or before rulers such as King Agrippa, Paul's use of the sword of the Spirit almost immediately put his hearers and/or accusers on the defensive—they in the popular sense of the term.

141

As Christian soldiers we may liken ourselves to the national guard, not soldiers of fortune or mercenaries. Or we may liken ourselves to a peace-keeping force in a land not our own. Others come, like thieves, to steal, kill, and destroy. But like our Lord, "we are come that they may have life and that they may have it more abundantly" (John 10:10). Ours should be the 1) discipline of soldiers, 2) the readiness even to die in the proclamation and defense of the Gospel, and 3) allegiance to him who called us as soldiers. Beyond that, comparison ceases.

Christ has none other than the church to fight the good fight of the faith. If we are fighting one another, or if we shrink from the foe, are we the "Lord's own"?

Summary

Every picture of the church which is given in the New Testament has been perverted or defaced or otherwise marred either by denominationalism or disunity among brethren, or our failure in some way to live up to our God-given opportunities and responsibilities.

1. Jesus, Peter, and Paul likened the church to a building. Unfortunately, many who profess to be Christ's builders have ignored the blueprints, and used inferior materials, or failed to properly prepare the materials that would be suitable. The house that Moses built, though he was but a servant, was built according to the pattern God showed him in the mount. Christ's workmen, unlike the servants of Moses, have seen fit to make alterations.

2. Paul described the church as the body of Christ. But the body has undergone mutilation, dismembering, and desecration; often self-inflicted, or so it seems. Would Christ, the head really direct membersof his body to maim, lop off, and even sever themselves from the body?

3. Paul speaks of the church as God's family. Denominationalism makes it appear as almost anything else but one big happy family. It often appears as feuding clans.

4. Paul and John speak of the church as Christ's bride-elect. Today he appears as a polygamist and philanderer, the keeper of a harem instead of the husband of one pure bride.

5. Peter and Paul speak of the church as God's flock. But it often appears as a zoo, where animals of diverse nature must be kept in separate pens to keep them from devouring one another.

6. Isaiah and Paul speak of God's people as his cultivated field.

142

Does it not often appear today as a wilderness, with thorns and thistles infesting the ground?

7. Paul likened the church to a corps of soldiers set for the defense of the Gospel. Denominationalism would make it appear that we have forgotten who our enemy is and whom we ought to be fighting.

What a sordid and distorted picture of the church is drawn by a divided Christendom. What a far cry from the church revealed in the Scriptures. Note again the singularity of the figures of speech contained in the Scriptures:

1) Not buildings of many kinds: casinos, shanties, roadhouses, dwellings, chapels, etc., but God's building, a habitation of God in the Spirit.

2) Not bodies of every kind: beasts, fish, fowl, and creeping things, but the body of Christ.

3) Not families of various names, lifestyles, conflicting interests, but the family of God.

4) Not wives, concubines, mistresses, live-ins, call girls, but Christ's own pure bride-elect.

5) Not a menagerie or zoo, in separate enclosures to keep some from devouring others, but God's flock.

6) Not a diversified farm or an untamed wilderness, but God's tilled ground, planted with the choicest vine.

7) Not mercenaries, guerillas, insurrectionists, and rebels, but soldiers of the cross set for the defense of the Gospel.

Hence the proposition of this course of study: Christ built only one church, therefore only one can be the "Lord's own."

PREVIEW—REVIEW QUESTIONS

1. State an inherent danger that befalls us in the interpreting of parables and figures of speech generally.
2. As a builder, how does the epistle to the Hebrews compare and also contrast Christ and Moses?
3. State three circumstances which may hinder the body from carrying out the purposes determined by the head.
4. Note the spiritual implications of the foregoing conditions.
5. How does denominationalism make Christ appear to be a freak of nature?
6. Are denominational names to be compared to our given names, thus we are after all one big happy family?

7. Is there a sense in which God's family is itself denominated, hence a denomination? Explain.
8. Is the church Christ's bride, or bride-elect? Explain.
9. Wherein does denominationalism make Christ to appear to teach one thing about love, courtship, and marriage, but himself to live by a different standard?
10. Who is the chief shepherd of the church (according to the Scriptures)?
11. Who are the pastors of the flock, according to the Scriptures?
12. What does the word husbandry mean? Identify God's husbandry.
13. Cite a text in Isaiah, echoed in Hebrews, which bears on the issue: once saved, always saved.
14. In what sense are we, and are we not, compared to soldiers?
15. Take note of how denominationalism and dissension among brethren destroys every picture the New Testament writers have drawn of the church.

EXCURSUS
BUILDING CHRIST'S INTERNATIONAL MANOR
(Vs. Our Little "White House")
Ephesians 2:19-22

A man who commanded a world-wide enterprise determined to build a house that would become equally renowned. Calling in his agents, he charged them to seek out and secure the choicest of building materials and house furnishings: exotic stone for beauty and durability, the rarest of woods for paneling and trim, oriental rugs and tapestries, art and sculpture. "Spare no cost!"

Soon materials began to come in from around the world: exquisite marble for facade and colonades, the choicest of European quarries, ebony and sandalwood from deepest Africa and Indonesia, Persian carpets, furniture from the hands of Bavarian craftsmen plying generations-old family trades, art work and sculpture such as grace galleries of renown. Course upon course, the great house rose, overlooking the Riviera. When completed, friends from every nation were invited to participate in the housewarming festivities of International Manor.

Such a builder is Christ. "Is it not written?" he once asked, "My house shall be a house of prayer for all nations" (Matt. 11:17). He thus commissioned his envoys: "Go ye therefore and make disciples of all the nations" (Matt. 28:19).

Christ's church is frequently referred to in the New Testament in figure as a building. Christians are spoken of both individually and collectively as "the temple of God" and "the temple of the Holy Spirit" (I Cor. 3:16; 6:19; II Cor. 6:16; Eph. 2:21). In Hebrews 3:6 we are spoken of as Christ's "house." Peter speaks of us as "living stones" built up (to be) a "spiritual house" (I Peter 2:5).

I. *INSTRUCTION CONCERNING THE PROCURING AND PROCESSING OF THE MATERIALS*

The full implication of the international character of the church, planned by its Divine architect and set forth in the Great Commission, has not always been recognized. This is no new problem, as witnessed by the context of the text before us. The Holy Spirit (see Eph. 3:3-7) directed Paul to write certain instruction concerning the building of Christ's church.

A. *The Gathering of the Materials.* The materials are to be gathered from all over the world. This is the chief point of the two chapters of which Ephesians 2:19-22 is the apex. The "elect race" is no longer any one "nation." Spiritual antecedents now supersede any and all fleshly ancestry. (Cp. Rom. 2:28, 29; 4:11; 9:6-8; Gal. 3:7-9, 26-29; Phil. 3:3.)

Beginning with the first verse of Ephesians, chapter two, Paul lays the foundation for the pinnacle of the temple of truth concerning race roles in the Christian church. Vs. 1, 2 describe the state of the un-evangelized Gentiles. Vs. 3, 4 are a candid acknowledgment that the Jews shared their debasement. Vs. 5-10 delineate the twin facts that 1) apart from God's mercy and grace neither would be saved. 2) By his grace both Jews and Gentiles "sit with him in heavenly places in Christ Jesus."

Vs. 11-18 detail the implications of the foregoing. Paul's conclusion is that "through him (Christ) we both (Jew and Gentile) have our access in one Spirit unto the Father" (v. 18). That conclusion leads to another, even more far-reaching in its implications and intended effect: Jews and Gentiles are not two churches "equal (perhaps in his sight) but separate"; but one church. They are to be "fitly framed together" and are to grow into "a (one) holy temple in the Lord, in whom (said he) ye also are builded together for a (one) habitation of God in the Spirit" (2:19-22). This is the apex of the two chapters.

Chapter three underscores what has just been said. Note particularly v. 6. Gentiles are fellow members of the (one) body and fellow partakers of the promise of Christ through the Gospel. Note too vs. 14, 15.

There is no basis for the notion that *a few* of the Gentiles—our class, our color, our culture group—now occupy the exclusive and privileged role once accorded fleshly Israel. The word "gentile" translated the Hebrew *goi* and the Greek *ethnos*, both of which are also rendered "heathen" and "nations." The text before us is wrested out of context and its truth contorted, if the chief and overriding application of it does not take into account the twin facts: 1) the building materials which go into the church are to be gathered from every ethnic group, and 2) all races are to be builded together into one church—united and equal.

B. *The Processing of the Materials.* Rarely are building materials of any kind found in a state immediately usable. One does not cut down a tree and use it "as is" anywhere—not even for a joist or a rafter. Stone must be quarried and cut. Other materials such as mortar, plaster, paint, nails, and hardware require considerable processing. The Great Commission instructs us to teach (disciple) the nations by the Gospel. Whatever their color, class, or economic condition, none are suitable "as is" for the building of Christ's church. Our very thoughts, our purposes, must be shaped by the Gospel. Much about us must be cut away by the sword of the Spirit. Some, like rock, have to be blasted out, so to speak, by the power (Gr. *dunamis*) of God, the Gospel. We are to occupy a new environment, serve a different purpose, take on new relationships. We must be altered to fit the change of state.

There is an old saying, "Gold is where you find it." No less precious in God's sight are the materials which are to go into Christ's church. There is no race that cannot be refined by the Word of God. Too often we want to find building materials all shaped and sized, like the materials racked and shelved in a building mart. The frontiersmen "started from scratch." We need to recover the pioneer spirit.

II. *INSTRUCTION CONCERNING THE FITTING TOGETHER AND FINISHING OF THE MATERIALS*

Chapters 4 through 6 of the Ephesian letter relate to phase two of the building process, the actual work of construction. Bringing men to faith, repentance, confession, and baptism avails little unless converts are "fitly framed together." Only so do they "grow into a holy temple unto the Lord, for a habitation of God in the Spirit."

A. *The Arranging of the Materials.* Not every piece of building material is interchangeable. Christ gave some to be apostles, some prophets, some evangelists, and some pastors and teachers (4:11). The list leaves many without mention. Yet the most common are essential to completeness (cp. 4:16). Moreover, the more ordinary a piece of building material is, the more significance and purpose it accrues when made an integral part of a building. A cement block left to itself is an eyesore and stumbling block. Given a place in a building, it contributes to the strength and beauty of the finished work.

In a day when the "established" church is under attack, we do well to note that no movement ever made a lasting contribution to the progress of the Gospel which failed to form its adherents into congregations. The church the Ephesian letter speaks of is a structured church, replete with appointed offices and the injunction that each several part contribute to the functioning of the whole.

B. *The Finishing of the Materials.* A building is by no means complete when every board, panel, and shingle are secured, every brick and stone mortared in place, every fixture, conduit, etc., installed. Floors must be sanded, sealed, and varnished, or tiled or carpeted. Walls and ceilings must be painted, woodwork finished, etc. Neither is the building of Christ's church complete, not even a local congregation thereof, when the name of the last member has been added to the roll, nor even when each member has been assigned a specific task.

Paul deals with this specifically in 4:12-16, but to do so he is obliged to employ a different figure, likening the church to a body. Churches, like bodies (but unlike buildings) grow in two ways: 1) in mass (both in size and numerically) and 2) in maturity. The first, however extensive, is incomplete without the other; but the second is equally incomplete if the first is not effectuated.

This then is our task. We are no more to establish mutual admiration societies, after our liking and likeness—little "white houses," than were the Jewish converts of the first century to build "Christian" versions of their synagogues to perpetuate their culture under a veneer of Christianity. Christ's house (Heb. 3:6) must be "a house of prayer for all people" (Isa. 5:7; Matt. 21:13), and "a habitation of God in the Spirit" (Eph. 2:22). To make the first our goal is to achieve the other also.

SECTION FOUR: THE GREAT SALVATION

10

SALVATION DEFINED AND DESCRIBED

The title which embraces the subject matter of the next several lessons is taken from Hebrews 2:3, wherein it is asked: "How shall we escape if we neglect so great a salvation?" In that the writer includes himself in the question raised, it should be obvious that he is not speaking to alien sinners. Were we to fail to note that fact in the question set before us, it should become unquestionably clear from the context in which we find it.

The writer has just finished admonishing his readers to give the more earnest heed to the things they have learned lest haply they drift away from them. As though anticipating the error so common to our time, that we really have nothing of any great consequence to fear, ("we may lose a little reward maybe, but not our salvation"), he proceeds to remind his readers it has already happened, and it could happen again, *to us!* Thus it is written:

> For if the word spoken through angels proved steadfast, and every transgression and disobedience received a just recompense of reward; how shall we escape if we neglect so great salvation?

149

Did you note we dropped a syllable, actually a word—the indefinite article, "a"? It is not in the text as composed by the author. It is a translator's gloss to smooth the reading. But what it gains in euphony, it loses in force, in vigor of expression, and in precision. The writer speaks not of *a great* salvation, as though it were to be compared to others and found to be a great one. That it is. But the truth is, it is the only one. Peter expressly declared this to be so when he said of Jesus: "In none other is there salvation, for neither is there any other name under heaven that is given among men, wherein we must be saved" (Acts 4:12).

Salvation Defined

How is salvation to be defined? It is exemplified in God's gift of his only begotten Son to be our atoning sacrifice. But the defining of salvation must extend far beyond an analysis of the term salvation, and the root from which it stems.

Salvation, like love, "is a many splendored thing." It takes not only the word itself, but at least ten other terms used in the New Testament, to set forth the richness, fullness, comprehensiveness of salvation—the "state of being saved." The Greek word so translated is *soteria*. The term refers primarily to wholeness, health. Etymologically, to be saved is to be made whole, to regain health. That definition fits well into the social gospel concept of the mission of Jesus, but it is an over-simplification. It is like defining salvation as "the state of being saved."

What is that state? What is to be whole? Or to have health? Webster correctly notes that, theologically, the word refers to the state or process of recovery from a lost state, or to be delivered from a perilous situation. Such a definition approximates the Biblical usage of the term.

The coin Jesus spoke of in the second of the three companion parables (Luke 15) was saved through the process of recovery from a lost state. And so it was also with the lost sheep. But with the lost boy, it was somewhat different. He too was lost to the presence and control of the father. But the fact is he was likely lost in the latter sense even before he left home. The fact that the father did not go out looking for him testifies to that. The shepherd went out and found the lost sheep, and brought it to the fold. The sheep had no choice in the matter. The woman found the lost coin and restored it to a place of safekeeping. The coin was neither responsible for its lost state nor its recovery. But the son was responsible, in part at least, for both. Had the father gone forth and found him, and brought him home against his will, he would not have been saved in the truest sense of the term. It would not have been a *healthy* situation. The relationship in the home would not have been *wholesome.*

FACETS OF THE "DIAMOND" OF SALVATION

"SO GREAT SALVATION"
HEBREWS 2:3

Regeneration

Sanctification

Justification

Reconciliation

Conversion

Adoption

Forgiveness
of Sins

Remission
of Sins

Redemption

Everlasting
Life

Art work by David Boatman

SALVATION - WHOLENESS - HEALTH - DELIVERANCE

1. ***EVERLASTING LIFE*** - GIVEN "THE RIGHT TO EAT OF *THE TREE OF LIFE*"

2. ***FORGIVENESS OF SINS*** - SINS GOD FORGIVES ARE *FORGOTTEN* EVERMORE

3. ***REMISSION OF SINS*** - "AS FAR AS THE EAST IS FROM THE WEST"

4. ***CONVERSION*** - WE HAVE *TURNED* FROM "IDOLS" TO THE LIVING GOD

5. ***SANCTIFICATION*** - WE HAVE BEEN *SET APART* IN LIFE AND SERVICE

151

6. **JUSTIFICATION** - *SET IN RIGHT RELATIONSHIP* TO GOD *JUST AS IF* NEVER SINNED
7. **RECONCILIATION** - RECONCILED TO GOD BY THE DEATH OF HIS SON. SAVED BY HIS LIFE
8. **REGENERATION** - *BEGOTTEN AGAIN* THRU "BATH OF BEGINNING AGAIN," RENEWING OF HOLY SPIRIT
9. **REDEMPTION** - RANSOMED BY A GREAT PRICE
10. **ADOPTION** - ADOPTED INTO GOD'S FAMILY - JOINT HEIRS WITH CHRIST

1. Rev. 2:7; 22:14. 2. Heb. 8:12. 3. Acts 2:38; Ps. 103:12. 4. Acts 3:19; I Thess. 1:9. 5. I Thess. 4:7, 8. 6. Rom. 5:1, 2. 7. Rom. 5:10. 8. Titus 3:5. 9. I Peter 1:18, 19. 10. Rom. 8:15-17.

Does the picture begin to take shape? It will take many illustrative terms, many synonyms for salvation to make the picture complete. The New Testament provides at least ten such terms.

Salvation Described Under Sundry Terms

Much controversy rages over the means of our salvation, and what salvation means. When is one saved? And how? Is salvation an affair of a moment? Or is it a process? If the latter, is there a point at which one can be said to be saved? There is no simplistic answer to such questions; not even in the more secular sense and meaning of the term.

When is a lost child saved? When it realizes it is lost? When it starts crying for its mother? When the mother realizes the child is lost and starts looking for it? When she espies it afar off, perhaps in a state of jeopardy? When she calls her child by name and starts running toward it? Or when the child is gathered safely in her arms?

When is a drowning man saved? When he realizes he cannot make it to shore? When he calls for help? When the lifeguard hears his cry? When the lifeguard sees him bobbing perilously in the billowing waves? When the lifeguard reaches his side? Or when he is safe on shore, still very much alive?

When is a cancer victim saved? When she realizes she is seriously in need of medical attention? When she calls a reputable doctor and makes an appointment for examination? When a biopsy is taken and diagnosed as cancer? When the operation is performed and the malignancy removed? Or when the wounds are healed and periodic examination indicates the operation was completely successful?

When is a man saved from sin? When he realizes he is a sinner? When he becomes concerned about his sinful condition? When he acknowledges he cannot save himself? When he believes Christ can save him? When he asks the Great Physician to save him? When he submits himself to the Great Physician, complying to what he is told is necessary for him to do? Or what if he should insist on being saved on his own terms? Or by some easy convenient way some quack doctor of divinity assures him that thousands are being saved daily? Is there a sense in which salvation is not complete until this world of sin and of death has passed away and we have awakened in the new heavens and the new earth wherein dwelleth righteousness, and that forevermore!

In a day of instant coffee, instant pudding, instant potatoes, instant replay; must the eternal God conform to our hurried ways? "What saith the answer (Gr. *chrematismos*, Divine response) of God?" (Rom. 11:4).

1. *The Gift of Eternal Life*

The most common synonym for salvation is what Paul in Romans 6:23 calls the charismatic gift of God (Gr. *charisma*, lit., "gift of grace"), or as it is commonly translated, the "free gift" of God, which is *eternal life* in Christ Jesus our Lord. This gift is set in apposition to "the wages of sin (what the sinner has earned, deserved), which is death."

The phrase eternal life, or everlasting life, depending on the translation used, appears in the New Testament over forty times; and when such phrases as eternal redemption, eternal salvation, and eternal glory, are added, the count rises to fifty times that this redolent hope of the redeemed is set forth in the New Covenant Scriptures. John 3:16 is, of course, the most familiar.

There is a pressing need for sound exegesis and for what Paul calls "the whole counsel of God" (Acts 20:27) with respect to this expression. It is not uncommon to hear someone contend that, since the present tense of the verb "have" is used in John 3:16, the "once saved, always saved" dogma needs no further support. The reasoning(?) is on this wise: If the life we have in Christ could for any cause ever cease or be taken from us, then it would not really be *eternal* life that we have, would it? But Jesus says we *have* eternal life. Sounds like a foolproof argument, does it not?

There is fault with such an oversimplification. The Biblical words which are translated eternal, or everlasting, both the Hebrew word, *olam*, and its Greek counterpart *aion* (from which we get our word *eon*) no more mean everlasting than an evergreen will be forever green. Fifteen minutes spent with an analytical concordance looking up references using the words *olam* and *aion* should be enough to convince all but the most tradition and creed-bound dogmatists that they have been reading into the Scriptures something the texts do not demand, or else they are breaking laws of God which carry intertwined with their enactment the penalty of certain death for any transgression thereof.

For example, which of you spend Saturdays, the seventh day of the week, resting at home from any form of labor, and virtually no travel, except perhaps going to the nearest synagogue where you can join others in remembering how God delivered your ancestors from Egypt? Anyone? Perhaps you have not read the Sabbath enactment lately. Turn to Exod. 31:12ff.

> And Jehovah spake unto Moses, saying, Speak thou unto the children of Israel, saying: Verily ye shall keep my sabbaths: for it is a sign between me and you throughout your generations: that ye may know that I am Jehovah your God who sanctifieth you.
>
> You shall keep the sabbath therefore; for it is holy unto you: *everyone that profaneth it shall surely be put to death; for whosoever doeth any work therein, that soul shall be cut off from among his people.*
>
> Six days shall work be done; but on the seventh day is a sabbath of solemn rest, holy to Jehovah: *whosoever doeth any work on the sabbath day, he shall surely be put to death.* Wherefore the children of Israel shall keep the sabbath, to observe the sabbath *throughout their generations,* for a *perpetual* (Hebr. *olam,* Gr. LXX, *aion*) covenant. It is a sign between me and the children of Israel *for ever* (*olam/aion*).

Do not try to weasel out of this obligation by saying the sabbath commandment is plainly stated to have been given to the Jews. That it was. But are we not told that in the Christian era "there is no distinction between Jew and Greek for the same Lord is Lord of all" (Rom. 10:12)? If *olam/aion* mean forever, everlasting, in perpetuity, the Jew is still bound by the sabbath law, and will continue to be bound throughout all eternity. And if in Christ there is no distinction between Jew and Gentile, then we are obligated under the penalty of death to keep the sabbath also.

154

SALVATION DEFINED AND DESCRIBED

Ah, then why do we not join the Seventh Day Adventists, or perhaps the Armstrong empire? If *olam/aion* mean what the translators have translated them to imply, we had better do so. But on second thought, we would then be little better off than we are now. For the fact is, that not only the sabbath law, but virtually every ritual of the Mosaic covenant, was likewise enacted by the same solemn decree, and for the same time frame. For example, in your leisure time check out the following:

1) The passover, "an ordinance forever," Exod. 12:14, 17.
2) The feast of unleavened bread, "an ordinance forever," Exod. 12:15-17; 13:6-10.
3) The feast of the tabernacles, "appointed forever," Lev. 23:41-43.
4) The table of shew bread, "an everlasting covenant, a perpetual statute," Lev. 24:5-9.
5) The day of atonement ritual, "an everlasting statute," Lev. 16:34.
6) The Aaronic priesthood, "an everlasting priesthood," Exod. 40:15 (but cp. Heb. 7:11-17, 26-28, etc.).

7) Even circumcision, "an everlasting covenant," Gen. 17:13, 14, cp. Exod. 12:42, and Gal. 3:28. The plot thickens!

Now what shall we do to be right with God? What if *olam* and *aion* do not mean forever, everlasting, perpetual? What if they denote an indefinite period of time subject to God's decree? That ought to make a difference. But do they? Read on. Note, for example, the following:

1) In Joshua 8:28 we are told that Ai is to be a heap forever, even unto this day. That does not sound too long lasting, certainly not when we are told that even the earth itself shall pass away.

2) In Isaiah 34:9, 10 it was predicted of Edom that "the smoke of her destruction would go up forever, and none shall ever again pass through the land." Yet, for centuries pilgrims have visited the land, walked all through it, and see neither fire nor smoke. Did the prophet make a miscue, or have the translators thrown us a curve?

3) Deuteronomy 23:3 informs us that the Ammonites and Moabites were barred from the assembly of Jehovah "for ever, even unto the tenth generation." That forever had a dateline of about three hundred years.

4) Jonah 2:6 records the reluctant prophet as reporting that when he was swallowed by the great fish "the bars of the earth closed over me for ever." It probably seemed like it at the time, but the truth is it lasted three days and nights.

5) Jude 7 reports that Sodom and Gomorrah suffered the vengeance of eternal (*aion*) fire. But the waters of the Dead Sea are believed by

155

Christian archeologists to now cover the area where the destroying fires once raged. Incidentally, the Greek word *aion* uniformly replaces the Hebrew *olam* whenever Old Testament passages using *olam* are quoted in the New Testment. This is in keeping with the pattern set by the Greek Septuagint (LXX). It is to be regretted that English translations, for doctrinarian considerations, failed to follow the example set by the New Testament writers who followed the lead of the Septuagint translators, using the Greek word *aion* (age-lasting), instead of the Latin *eternalis* from whence the word *eternal* crept into the King James Version.

What then does this do to our hope of endless life in the age to come? Nothing. Remember that *olam* and *aion* refer to "an indefinite period of time, the duration of which is determined by the decree and purpose of God." Remember also three things: 1) Of the redeemed in glory it is said, "They shall live and reign with him (not just forever, for an age, but) for ever and ever" (Lit. unto the ages of the ages! Endlessly.), Revelation 22:5. 2) It is said also of the redeemed that they shall be given the right to eat of the tree of life which is in the paradise of God, Revelation 2:7; 22:2, 14. 3) Thus it is written that "this mortal shall put on immortality, and this corruptible shall put on incorruption . . . then shall come to pass the saying that is written, death is swallowed up in victory! . . . Thanks be unto God who giveth *us* the victory through our Lord Jesus Christ" (I Cor. 15:50-57).

What does it mean to be saved? Let Paul spell it out once again, "The *wages* of sin is *death*, but the gracious gift of God is *age-lasting life* in Christ Jesus our Lord. The security of believers rests in our relationship to God and Christ of whom it is said: "who only hath immortality" (is immortal, NIV), I Tim. 6:16. It is promised us that we shall *put on* immortality (Gr. *endusasthai*, lit., *enclothe* oneself). Cp. Gal. 3:37 where the same word is used to inform us that in baptism we "put on Christ." We do not become Christ any more than we become a suit of clothes which we put on; but in this life we put on Christ that we may be enclothed with immortality in that life to come.

Taking a cue from Jesus (John 15:1-8), an excursion into the illustrative realm of botany may help. Traditionally, the flora of this world has been grouped into two phyla: annuals and perennials. 1) Annuals constitute those plants which have a life span limited to the growing season of a single year. 2) Perennials are those plants, shrubs, and trees which live *through* the years.

A tomato vine is an annual. A branch of such a vine has the potential of living as long as the plant which produced and sustains it. But if severed, its life is ended, and, like a lifeless corpse, will soon be evident. Then it does not have the quality of life called *annual* life. Of course it does, but not of itself. The vine which produces it imparts its life quality to it. But the relationship must be sustained to be a vital one.

An oak tree is a perennial. What is true of a tomato vine is true of an oak tree. A severed limb of an oak tree is dead, and will soon show it; not as quickly as a severed tendril of a tomato vine, for it was imbued with a higher quality of life. But it has no life of itself. Yet, when joined to the tree, it has the life quality of an oak tree.

A new classification for one segment of plant life is needed. There are trees which actually have millennial life. They are capable of living a thousand years or more. Many of the hoary giants of the Pacific coast, the Sequoia redwoods, have done so. Some tower nearly four hundred feet into the air and are estimated to be upwards of two thousand years old. But the repute as the oldest living things on earth is now ascribed to the bristlecone pines along the seascape of central California. Some of these are estimated to have already lived upwards of three thousand years, and are still virile. But a limb lopped off of a bristlecone pine cannot survive that excision. Then does the limb not really have millennial life, as does the tree? Nonsense. Of course it does. The tree imparts its life quality to every branch and twig. But the life is inherent in the stock. It is transmitted to the branches provisionally, the provision being obvious. At least it should be.

But is this not sophistry? Perchance the analogy is being carried too far. We have warned that one should guard against this danger. What saith the oracles of God? (Rom. 11:4). Lo, it is Jesus who both introduced the analogy and developed it along these very lines. Read John 15:1-8, noting what Jesus said and also what he did not say.

V. 1. "I am the *true* vine, and my Father is the husbandman" (Gr. *georgos,* ground keeper, worker).

V. 2. "Every branch *in* me (Note he did not say every tacked on branch, or everyone who thinks himself to be one of my branches. He is speaking of the real thing.) that beareth not fruit, he (the Father, not some misguided hireling) taketh it away; and every branch that beareth fruit, he cleanseth it that it may bear more fruit."

V. 3. "Already ye are clean because of the word which I have spoken unto you" (cp. Eph. 5:26).

V. 4. "Abide in me, and I in you. As the branch cannot bear fruit, except it abide in the vine; so neither can ye, except ye abide in me."

V. 5. "I am the vine, ye are the branches: He that abideth in me, and I in him (note not *every* branch that was ever joined to him, but those that abide in him), the same beareth much fruit: for apart from me ye can do nothing."

V. 6. Watch this one! "IF A MAN ABIDE NOT IN ME, HE IS CAST FORTH AS A BRANCH, AND IS WITHERED; AND THEY GATHER THEM, AND CAST THEM INTO THE FIRE, AND THEY ARE BURNED."

Need one read any further? Once in Christ, always in Christ? Is he stuck with you, no matter what? Once in grace, always in grace? Once a branch, always a branch? You did not so learn Christ! A fruit-bearing branch or fuel for the burning! God, the owner-husbandman, is not in the foliage business. Note v. 8, "Herein is my father glorified that ye bear much fruit, and so shall ye be my disciples."

Our great salvation is too great a thing to trifle with it, or to assume we can name our own terms. In the words of Paul, as he answered those of his day who thought to exploit the arrangement: "What, shall we continue in sin that grace may abound? Certainly not!" (Rom. 6:1, 2a, New KJV, Gr. *me genoito,* an expression of abhorrence). The profane "God forbid," here and elsewhere in the traditional versions, is an unwarranted corruption of the text.

2. *The Forgiveness of Sins*

There are two Greek words which are translated forgive or forgiveness. 1) *Charizomai,* a derivative of *charis* (grace), means "to be gracious." That is what forgiveness really entails. *Charizomai* is used twenty-three times in the New Testament. Ten times it is rendered "forgive" or "forgave": Luke 7:42, 43; II Cor. 2:7, *10; 12:13, *Eph. 4:32; Col. 2:13, 3:13 (*used twice in these verses). 2) *Aphiemi* is used 57 times in the New Testament. It means literally, to send away. Ten times it is translated in the traditional versions, "remission" (of sins) in keeping with its fundamental meaning. Otherwise it is also translated forgive, forgiveness, as the form of the word (verb or noun) may require.

The terms forgiveness of sins and remission of sins are commonly regarded as synonymous. They have much in common, but forgiveness is a much more personal word. The two expressions have a cause and effect relationship. One is not forgiven because one's sins have been remitted. The law can do that. Our sins are remitted because we

SALVATION DEFINED AND DESCRIBED

have been forgiven. President Gerald Ford pardoned Richard Nixon. It is questionable whether he forgave him, or that Nixon considered himself forgiven. But one could say his part in the Watergate debacle was legally remitted. Could he have been forgiven, he could have continued as president. The law cannot forgive. It can absolve penalty. It cannot blot out the transgression. The fact is, in the final analysis, this is something only God can do. And this is what he has promised to do. Consider these texts:

Isaiah 43:25, "I am he that blotteth out thy transgression for my own sake, and I will not remember thy sins." Jeremiah 41:34 (recorded in the context of the promise of the New Covenant): "I will be merciful to thy iniquities, and your sins will I remember no more" (cp. Heb. 8:12; 10:17). See also Micah 7:19 "Thou wilt cast all our sins into the depths of the sea," and Psalm 103:12 "As far as the east is from the west, so far hath he removed our transgressions from us." The first two texts cited focused on forgiveness of sins, and the second on the effect, the remission thereof.

Alexander Pope (*Essays on Criticism*, Part II, line 325) has said: "To err is human, to forgive is Divine." How true that is. To err is human. It is the one thing we are prone to do. To forgive is Divine. That is God's specialty. Presidents and governors may pardon, the courts may acquit, we may excuse. But we rarely meet the full demands of forgiveness because we find it difficult to forget. To forgive is to restore fellowship, extend love, be gracious.

3. *The Remission of Sins*

We have noted the motivating factor that results in the remission of our sins. Forgiveness of sins takes place in God's heart and mind. Remission of sins takes place in our own. Whenever one sins against another, the only one who really knows the offender is forgiven is the one doing the forgiving. Often an offender considers himself forgiven simply because the person he has wronged, and may still be wronging, takes no reprisals against him. This is certainly so in man's relationship to God. "Why repent? God has not cracked down on us. We are evidently forgiven." Yet we have neither repented of or confessed our sins, nor ceased from our sinning.

The offender may very well know his sins have been remitted when he is restored to the full fellowship of the person he has wronged, and restrictions and penalties against him have been taken away.

The annual day of atonement (Lev. 16) illustrates the remission of sins. Two goats, chosen to represent the nation, were brought to the door of the tent of meeting. By lot, one was chosen to be slain, dramatically pointing up the fact that sin demands punishment, even death for its atonement. The other was then placed before the high priest who laid both his hands upon the head thereof (actually, he leaned upon the head of the animal, with the animal supporting him lest he fall). Symbolically, the sins of the people were thereby transferred to the "scape (going away) goat" that was driven into the wilderness, carrying their sins with him. The ceremony was scarcely designed to focus attention on God's forgiveness. The slain animal testified to the fact that guilt must be atoned. But the scape goat dramatized the fact that their sins were remitted.

Under the New Covenant the forgiveness (*charizomai*) of our sins is dramatically underscored by the supreme act of Divine grace. God gave his own son to provide atonement for our sins. The remission (removal) of our sins is something God calls upon us to dramatize by manifesting our "faith in the operation of God through baptism" (Col. 2:12). Thus Peter's answer to the guilt-stricken multitude on Pentecost was: "Repent ye, and be baptized, every one of you, in the name of Jesus Christ, *for the remission of your sins.*" Note too the command given by the Divinely directed messenger to Saul of Tarsus. What three days and nights of fasting and prayer could not do was readily accomplished as Ananias commands: "And now why tarriest thou? Arise and be baptized, and wash away thy sins, calling on the name of the Lord" (Acts 22:16).

PREVIEW—REVIEW QUESTIONS

1. State the basic definition of our English word salvation.
2. State the primary definition of the Greek word so translated.
3. State two other facets of salvation commonly associated with this concept.
4. Why does the New Testament use so many different terms to describe it?
5. Does salvation come like "a bolt out of the blue"? Or is it a process with a climax? Explain.
6. What is the actual root meaning of the Hebrew and Greek words commonly translated forever, everlasting, eternal?
7. What evidence can be cited that they obviously are rarely used in the Scriptures in that fashion?

8. From what language does our English word eternal derive? Technically, what does the source word really mean?

9. What basis have we for our hope of endless life with Christ in glory, in the light of the foregoing word study?

10. According to the Scriptures, how do we become immortal?
( ) By birth ( ) By rebirth ( ) By resurrection
Document, Biblically.

11. Granting, for the sake of the argument, that the phrase "have eternal life" means we really do, right now; how then would you reason with those committed to eternal security dogma?

12. What parable of Jesus clarifies the issue? Explain.

13. What is the basic difference between forgiveness and remission of sins?

14. Identify and distinguish between the two words translated forgiveness.

15. Identify the Old Testament ritual which dramatized remission of sins.

16. Identify the New Testament ordinance which does the same.

17. When and how did Paul receive the remission of sins?
( ) By his Damascus road vision and experience ( ) Three days of fasting and prayer ( ) By confessing Jesus as Lord
( ) _____

11

DESCRIPTIONS OF SALVATION, CONTINUED

The fact that our great salvation, like the love of God from which it flows, is a many splendored thing is further illustrated by such terms as justification, regeneration, and adoption. Having considered the terms: 1) Eternal Life, 2) Forgiveness of Sins, and 3) Remission of Sins, let us now note other facets of the precious diamond of "so great salvation."

4. Justification

Justification is primarily a legal term. In the Scriptures it is used only in Paul's contrast between the Law (of Moses) and the Gospel in his epistle to the Romans. There it appears three times: Romans 4:25; 5:16, 18. The noun, justifier (one who justifies), is used once. In Romans 3:26 Paul speaks of God as "the justifier of him that has faith in Jesus."

The verbs, justify and justified, appear more extensively. They appear seven times in the Gospels (Matt. 11:19; 12:37; Luke 7:29, 35; 10:29; 16:15; 18:14), twice in Acts 13:39, three times in James (2:21, 24, 25), and as might be expected, quite extensively in the Pauline epistles, particularly Romans and Galatians. Incidentally, the passage in Acts is a quote from the apostle Paul. Romans, chapters 3 through 5, and Galatians, chapters 2 and 3, are extended discourses on the subject of justification. James, chapter 2, provides a necessary balance. Paul is not discounting "the obedience of faith" (Rom. 1:5; 6:16-18; 16:26), but rather "the works of the law"—the insufficient and now abrogated rites of the Law of Moses.

Technically, justification is "the state of being declared righteous before the law." It does not declare us to be actually righteous, else none could be justified, save one—the Lord Jesus Christ. Except for him, "all have sinned and fall short of the glory of God" (Rom. 3:23).

A simple, working definition may be drawn from a play on the word justification: "just-as-if." In the judicial act of justification, we are dealt with just as if we had not sinned. For example, a soldier who takes the life of another in the course of a military encounter is not reckoned as a murderer. Neither is one reckoned as a murderer who kills in self-defense when his own life, or perhaps that of a family member, was at stake. One is not counted guilty before the law though a life is taken in an auto accident, if the driver is innocent of any traffic violation and is not chargeable for negligence in the maintenance of his vehicle or the exercise of due caution. The courts do not deny a life was taken, perhaps even the life of a child, but the courts set forth the accused as righteous, subject to neither reproof nor penalty.

A predecessor in one of my preaching ministries underwent such an experience. On his way to church, almost to the door thereof, a child darted from behind a parked car, leaving him neither time nor space to maneuver. The traffic court and even the family of the child acquitted him on all counts. Nevertheless, he resigned from that ministry at the height of his career, and moved miles away. Though "justified" by the law he could not pass the spot day after day without reliving that terrible scene. He was justified, even forgiven, but he could not accept the remission of the blame. It is for this reason many, many terms are used to describe our great salvation. To be justified or forgiven is not enough. As previously stated, forgiveness takes place in the heart of the one offended. Remission of sins takes place in our own. When God forgives our sins, he reckons us justified. It is our responsibility to accept the remission of our sins.

Unfortunately, the Biblical doctrine of justification has been perverted by extremists on either side of this currently divisive, and ofttimes explosive, issue. On the one hand are those who believe certain acts:

164

baptism, church activities, and such like, save us. Others hold that nothing we do as an outward expression of faith has aught to do with our salvation. As is generally the case, the truth is found somewhere between the two extremes.

As of the present, the "faith only" protagonists are they who are pressing the issue. We do well therefore to consider what they are saying, and what they are actually doing. The latter is often incongruous in view of what they are saying.

That which the contenders for the faith-only model practice is not justification by faith alone, but justification by faith, *minus* baptism, *plus* works of righteousness(?) which they do themselves; but which have no counterpart in the salvation models recorded in the Acts of the Apostles.

The only place in all the Bible which adjoin the words *justified, faith,* and *only* states just the opposite of what the "faith only" protagonists proclaim. Climaxing an illustration drawn from the life of Abraham (incidentally drawn even from the same historical setting to which Paul alludes in both Romans and Galatians), James concludes by saying: "You see then that by works is a man justified, *and not by faith only.*" Perhaps James' readers could see that, and those not blinded by Calvinism may see that, but others cannot even see that verse, much less what Paul wrote as his conclusion to the lesson to be learned from Abraham (Rom. 6:1-18; Gal. 3:27). In no way can the faith-only model be reconciled with such "therefore" texts as these:

> Are you ignorant that all we who were *baptized into Christ Jesus were baptized into his death? We were buried therefore with him through baptism into death:* that like as Christ was raised from the dead through the glory of the Father, *so we also might rise to walk in newness of life.* For if we have become united with him in the likeness of his death we shall be with him also in the likeness of his resurrection (Rom. 6:3-5).

> Know ye not that to whom ye present yourselves as *servants unto obedience, his servants ye are whom ye obey;* whether of sin unto death, or of *obedience unto righteousness.* But thanks be to God, that whereas ye were servants of sin, *ye became obedient from the heart to that form* (Gr. *tupon:* type, pattern, example) *of teaching whereunto ye were delivered,* and being made free from sin, ye became servants of righteousness (Rom. 6:16-18).

Moreover, as though Paul's extensive remarks in the ten chapters which follow might cause some to forget the basis on which the epistle is built, he closes the book of Romans by restating its prevailing theme:

not salvation by faith only, apart even from obedience to Christ, but the obedience of faith in Christ as opposed to the works of the Mosaic Law. Note how the epistle closes:

> Now to him that is able to establish you, according to my gospel and the preaching of Jesus Christ, according to the revelation of the mystery which hath been kept in silence through times eternal, but now is manifested, and by the scriptures of the prophets, according to the commandment of the eternal God, is made known unto all the nations *unto obedience of faith:* to the only wise God, through Jesus Christ, to whom be the glory for ever. Amen.

It should be obvious that Paul is not correcting James, nor was James correcting Paul. Both are saying the same thing, each writing from a different perspective, and handling thus a different facet of the same problem. Their treatises combine to underscore the fact we are not given a fielder's choice. We can neither be justified by faith alone, nor by works alone. We are justified rather through the obedience of faith.

Down deep in the subconsciousness of those who press the salvation by faith only dogma is an awareness that something tangible needs to be elicited, else how can they fill out their scorecards, and tally the points they have scored? So, the Gospel of "salvation apart from works" which is, being translated, "apart from baptism for remission of sins," turns out to be "salvation *plus* works of righteousness(?) which they do themselves." For example, having respondees 1) raise their hands to ask the evangelist to pray for them, and 2) ask Jesus to come into their hearts. And when the climate seems to be ripe for more tangible expression, 3) asking those who raised their hands to "show they mean business" by coming to the altar, and 4) by then "praying through."

Somehow, all that is reckoned as less work than submitting to Christ in Christian baptism—not that baptism of a sort is not going to be required before the process is completed. Baptism as a predicate for church membership is generally required, but entrance into the kingdom of heaven presumably is attained more easily. Speaking from experience, I found it harder to die to sin than to submit to Christian baptism. The latter was the least of all the things I did the day that I was "washed, sanctified, and justified in the name of Jesus Christ, and in the Spirit of our God" (I Cor. 6:11).

The key to this inquiry is found in the simple fact that the bankrupt cannot pay their debts, nor can others who are bankrupt pay their debts for them. The problem with which God was dealing at Calvary is that "*all* have sinned and fall short of the glory of God" (Rom. 3:23).

How then can anyone be saved? How can a just God be both "just and the justifier of them that believe in Christ" (Rom. 3:26)? God's solution was for sin to be punished in him "who knew no sin, that we might be made the righteousness of God in him" (II Cor. 5:21).

If the Christ died for all, why are not all saved: the impenitent, ignorant, and unbelieving and disobedient? Because God who justifies has ordained otherwise. He has established the obedience of faith in the atoning death of his son as the condition of justification. Bear in mind that justification is an act of God and a state of man. It is God who is said to justify (active voice). Man is said to "be justified" (passive voice). One may justify himself in his own sight, as many do in various circumstances of life. But only the courts, through due process of law within the scope of their jurisdiction, or the offended can justify the guilty. Even when the offenders do all things required of them—confess their guilt, seek forgiveness, attempt restitution, or whatever—nothing the offender does actually justifies him or her. Justification is an act of mercy on the part of the offended toward the guilty. Thus it is written:

> Not by works of righteousness (Gr. *dikaiosune*) which we did ourselves, but according to his mercy he saved us, through *the washing of regeneration* (baptism, cp. John 3:5, Acts 2:38) *and the renewing of the Holy Spirit* through Jesus Christ our Saviour, that, *being justified* (Gr. *dikaiothentes*) by his grace we might be heirs according to the hope of eternal life (Titus 3:5-7).

5. *Regeneration*

The passage just cited contains another of the sundry terms used in the Scriptures to describe our great salvation. Surprisingly, regeneration is a term which only appears twice in the King James and American Standard versions of the Bible. In Matt. 19:28 it is used in quite a different sense than its use in Titus 3:5. In Matthew the term appears in an eschatalogical setting in which Jesus speaks of himself as the Son of Man sitting on the throne of his glory in the regeneration (new creation, or consummation). In Titus 3:5 its use is in a soteriological setting, and has direct reference to our personal participation in the experience commonly called the new birth.

Titus 3:5 provides a perceptive commentary on John 3:3, 5—"Except one be born anew (Gr. *gennethe anothen*, lit., born from above) he cannot see the kingdom of God" (v. 3) and "Except one be born of water and Spirit he cannot enter the kingdom of God" (v. 5).

The cherished expression "born again" has its best textual support from Titus 3:5 and I Peter 1:23. A literal rendering of the key phrase in Titus would read: "bath of beginning again" (Gr. *loutrou palingenesias*). The passage in I Peter 1:23 is rendered "being born again" in both the KJV and the NIV. The ASV renders the verse "begotten again," identifying the Word of God as the begetting agent. At this point then a problem arises. The same word that obviously means "beget," just as obviously means to "give birth, to bring forth." For example, in the genealogy of Jesus in Matthew 1:2-16, gennao is translated "begat" forty times, consecutively. But in the middle of the sixteenth verse the translators of necessity switch to the expression "was born" with the introduction of Mary into the lineage "of whom (indeed) was born Jesus, who is called the Christ." From that point the term "born" appears consecutively thirty times in the translation which follows.

At the outset the foregoing information may appear somewhat confusing. Normally the Greek lanugage is very precise and exacting, but in the area under discussion we have an exception. They were aware, of course, as we are that there are two overt phases of the generation process—begetting and bringing forth. The first requires a male as the primarily active agent. The other requires a female as a very much involved agent. The Greeks assuredly knew that also. But they understood also that a birth requires both the seed of man and the seed of the woman. Thus both the male and the female are begetters and progenitors of the child that is brought forth. It is now known that both the male and female contribute an equal number of chromosomes to the offspring which they beget.

But there is one important difference. Whereas with the male the begetting may be but an affair of a moment, after which the male may never again so much as see the female he has impregnated, much less the offspring; the female is involved in the procreational process throughout the whole of the long drawn-out gestation period, and up into recent times, involved for weeks and months to come in suckling the infant. The Greeks therefore were being quite perceptive when they used the word for beget to apply to the role of the female also.

Technicalities aside, how are we (as children of God) regenerated? By the water and the Spirit, according to John 3:5 and Titus 3:5. The role of the Spirit is both comparable and nonconformable to the role of a father in begetting a child. The Spirit most certainly does not invade the mind and heart for but a few moments, implant the seed which is the Word of God, and then depart. The role of the water, baptism,

168

is somewhat conformable to the role of a mother in bringing forth a child. In baptism there is bringing forth to public view a new life which has been forming from the moment the Word of God was received in a fertile heart.

There is a facet or two of the analogy before us that deserves further notice. In the preceding paragraph we touched briefly upon one of them. Both James (1:18) and Peter, in his first epistle (1:23), spoke of the Word of God as the seed through which we are begotten from above. In the natural world there is, without exception, some passage of time between the begetting of life and birth. Generally speaking, natural law determines the duration of the interim twixt the two. In the spiritual realm the gestation period, so to speak, has no comparable norm. The receptivity of the human heart, not natural law, determines the interim twixt begetting and baptism. In several classic cases of conversion recorded in Acts the process from begetting to baptism was but a matter of hours at the most. But take note of two things: 1) Baptism followed belief, always. There is no record in Acts of believers who refused or were excused from baptism. 2) And there is no record in Acts of baptizing anyone who was not a believer.

It is at least worthy of consideration that a mother is aware of life in her womb long before the child is born. And it is also coming to light that the unborn child is mentally alive and responsive to stimuli and the rhythm of its mother's heartbeat long before it is born. This is called to attention in response to some who are inclined to believe, and some who teach, we are not quickened by the Holy Spirit until we are baptized and receive then the gift of the Holy Spirit. If so, there is nothing in all nature that corresponds to spiritual birth. No embryo that has ever died in the womb has ever been quickened by birth. Baptism does not give life, it brings forth life that has already been quickened. On the other hand many an embryo that was very much alive has died because it was not brought forth in due season. Fortunately in the spiritual realm, birth is not as regimented as physical birth, else few would enter the kingdom of God. Whether or not there is, in the spiritual realm, aught that is comparable to Caesarean-section birth in the physical world cannot be said with certainty. But I find myself wondering if the Great Physician is not as ingenius and able to save a life that has been begotten but obstructed from birth as are physicians here below, and as concerned for those begotten of the Spirit as we are for those we have begotten.

Such a suggestion no more negates the teaching of the Scriptures than Caesarean-section birth violates natural law which God ordained, and results in stillborn babies. No mother capable of natural birth opts for Caesarean-section delivery. Nor does a mother refuse such an option if a life can be saved in that manner. And no parent has ever refused to accept a child because it was not born in a natural manner. And no physician would be tolerated on a hospital staff who would refuse to assist birth in the natural manner even under ordinary circumstances on the ground that babies have been known to be delivered and live through delivery in a different manner.

Such speculation as that in which I have just indulged proves nothing. At best it offers only a "whispering hope" for some who have died without benefit of our knowledge or opportunity. For something sure, underscored by the sure word of one having all authority both in heaven and on earth, now hear this: "He that believeth and is baptized shall be saved!" (Mark 16:16).

5. *Adoption*

The Biblical doctrine of adoption, when considered against the backdrop of regeneration, presents a theological problem. If we are "begotten of God," and/or "of his Spirit," as we are certainly said to be (John 3:3-8; I John 3:9; 4:7; 5:4, 18), how then and why are we spoken of as adopted? And such we are (Rom. 8:15; Gal. 4:5; Eph. 1:5).

The key to our inquiry is in the golden text of the Bible, likewise found in John, chapter 3, and in John's first epistle (John 3:16; I John 4:9). Technically speaking, Jesus is God's "only begotten Son." The Greek word *monogenes* is thusly literally translated. It is also used in the New Testament, however, in a still stricter sense, namely: "the only one of the kind." Hebrews 11:17 applies the term to Isaac. He was not Abraham's only begotten son in the common sense of the term. In fact, he was not even his first nor his last. But as a miracle child, a child of promise, he was the only one of his kind. Such a son as Ishmael was obtainable to Abraham throughout his adult life. After the death of Sarah, Abraham remarried and begat both sons and daughters. But a child of a barren woman, and well beyond child-bearing years also, such a child was Isaac, of whom there was to be no other.

John's use of the term "begotten of God," with reference to us, is not to be taken literally. However, inasmuch as God is the genesis, the originator and instigator of the total process which brings us into a

170

filial relationship with him, he is in a figurative sense our procreator. This is accomplished not in the sense that Jesus was begotten of him, nor in the sense that Adam "the son of God" (Luke 3:38) was begotten of God. We are begotten by an accessory means—the Gospel, and that through fellow human beings. (See I Cor. 4:15; Philem. 10; James 1:18; I Peter 1:23.)

Beside angelic beings (called sons of God, Job 1:6), God has brought persons into being and into filial relationship with himself in three ways: 1) Some were simply created. Adam and Eve were brought into being by an act of creation. Apparently this was so of angels also. Since angels do not procreate (Matt. 22:30) yet are multitudinous in number, and are called sons of God (Job 38:7), God has evidently used his creative power to bring "many sons into glory." 2) Jesus of Nazareth was procreated through the instrumentality of a virgin birth. Though Jesus pre-existed, antedating all creation, he emptied himself of those qualities of godness which God sustains with reference to the universe— omnipotence, omniscience, and omnipresence, and became a man, yet uniquely the Son of God.

3) In contrast to the foregoing, we are said to be regenerated and/or recreated (Titus 3:5, II Cor. 5:17). Obviously this is sonship of a different kind. This has bearing on the popular dogma of eternal security. Proponents of the same often parrot the phrase: "Once a son, always a son." Biologically speaking, this is so. But even they can be, and many have been, disinherited. Adam is called in Luke 3:38 "the son of God." But he was driven from the Garden of Eden, barred from the tree of life, and died for his sin. Is it different with sons by adoption?

Does the doctrine of adoption take away something precious? Does it dull one facet of our great salvation? Paul certainly did not think so. One can sense a thrill of exultation as Galatians 4:4-7 and Romans 8:14-17 are read. It is significant that only in those two texts that Paul lapses into the intimacies of his native tongue and calls God "Abba Father." This is akin to a burst of tenderness that oft came over me long after I had grown into manhood. As a boy I called my father "papa." As I grew older, I underscored my maturation by dropping the name I used in childhood. But what I gained in a demonstration of maturity, I lost in terms of filial affection. The time came when I once again threw my arms about him and called him, "papa father."

There is a sense in which greater love is required and expressed in the process of adoption than in procreation. Not every procreated child is wanted. But every adopted child is wanted, that is, by those who

171

adopt them. "Behold, what manner of love the Father has bestowed upon us, that we should be called 'the children of God'" (I John 3:1). And if children (though adopted) then heirs, heirs of God and joint heirs with Jesus Christ.

PREVIEW—REVIEW QUESTIONS

Justification

1. State the technical definition of justification, in the legal aspect of the term.
2. State a popular definition based upon a play on the word.
3. Where in the Scriptures do we find the words: 1) "justified," 2) "faith," and 3) "only" adjoined in a single sentence?
4. What does that text say? Does it echo or clash with popular theology?
5. What did Paul announce to be the theme of the letter he proceeded to pen to the church at Rome? Cite pertinent texts.
6. Evaluate the profession and the performance of those who preach "salvation by faith only."
7. As the Scriptures use the terms, who is said to justify and who is said to be justified?
8. What bearing does that have on Paul's affirmation that we are not saved by works of righteousness which we do ourselves?
9. Is baptism such a work? Is it ever spoken of as a work? State some popular practices which do fit that category.

Regeneration

1. Cite the text where the word regeneration is used in the context of the process of salvation.
2. How might the phrase "washing of regeneration" be better translated?
3. Relate Titus 3:5 and John 3:5. Do they harmonize or contradict?
4. State a popular phrase which is closely allied with the topic of regeneration. How might the pertinent texts be more literally translated?
5. State the technical problem which arises from the dual meaning of the Greek word for procreation.
6. Cite texts and textual data which illustrate the dual meaning.
7. How might the analogy of procreation justify the dual meaning of the term, and relate the same to the process of salvation?

8. State how the analogy of the begetting, bearing, and bringing forth process illustrates the fact we are begotten of the Spirit before we are baptized. He is not a stranger we meet as we emerge from the water.

Adoption

1. Identify the seeming theological dilemma which arises from the fact Paul states we are adopted children of God.
2. How do you explain the fact we are said to be both begotten and adopted?
3. Does the phrase "once a son, always a son" provide a viable basis for the "once saved, always saved" dogma? Explain.
4. Cite evidence that Paul did not consider our filial relationship with God is depreciated by the fact we are children by adoption.
5. Note the technical and literal definition of *monogenes*. Illustrate the fact they can and do differ.
6. How does that difference help resolve the seeming problem under discussion?

12

DESCRIPTIONS OF SALVATION, CONCLUDED

There are three terms which to various degrees relate directly to man's response to what God does in effectuating our salvation. This is not to say man is altogether passive with respect to those discussed in the two previous lessons. But certainly, such terms as the (gracious) gift of everlasting life, forgiveness of sins, and adoption speak of the out-pouring and overflowing of God's love and mercy.

Other terms, such as justification and remission of sins, imply some response upon the part of the sinner. Even the advocates of the justification by faith alone dogma recognize that the sinner at least must believe (although hyper-Calvinism would have us understand that faith is something with which God zaps his elect, and that man cannot even believe unless God wills it and gives faith as a gift of grace).

Such terms as conversion, reconciliation, and sanctification call for some overt response on the part of the sinner. That response deserves and demands attention.

7. Conversion

Conversion is a term which appears only once in the KJV and ASV of our New Testaments. Paul and Barnabas, enroute to the Jerusalem conference, are said to have passed through Phoenicia and Samaria, "declaring the conversion (Gr. *epistrophen*) of the Gentiles," (Acts 15:3). The verb form (*epistrepho*) is used thirty-nine times in the New Testament, and signifies to *turn* (*strepho*) upon (*epi*); that is, to turn in response to some stimulus or attraction. The root, *strepho* (unprefixed), is used an additional eighteen times and is uniformly translated "turn," so there is no question as to its meaning.

Our words convert and conversion are derived from the Latin, via the Vulgate, and are laden with theological overtones when used in the context of our great salvation. Otherwise our power of understanding is unimpaired. For example, to the Latin root, *vertere*, we add familiar prefixes and come up with such readily understandable terms as these:

re-vert,	turn back	a-vert,	turn from
di-vert,	turn aside	per-vert,	turn wrongly
in-vert,	turn inward	extro-vert,	turn outward

Convert, derived from the Latin *convertere*, means literally to "turn with," that is, "turn together." The KJV translators normally experienced no difficulty with the word *epistrepho* except when it is used in the context of salvation. Five times it is so used, and in each case they translated as though it were used in the passive voice. Thus Acts 3:19 which reads in the ASV, RSV, NIV, etc., "repent and turn . . . that your sins may be blotted out," is made to read, "repent and be converted." So it is also with the prophecy of Isaiah 6:9, 10 which is quoted four times in the New Testament: Matthew 13:15; Mark 4:12; John 12:40; and Acts 28:27. The passage in Isaiah is primarily an indictment of rebellious Israel, of whom it is said they hardened their hearts, stopped their ears, and closed their eyes lest they should see, hear, understand, and *convert* (note that), *and be healed*.

But when the text appears in the New Testament, and comes closer to home, as it is used in the context of the preaching of the Gospel, the translators have rendered the phrase, "and *be* converted," as though conversion or nonconversion is something which happens to us, not something we are to do. Curiously, the translators of the KJV have uniformly rendered the verb "turn" in the passages cited above, except in the crucial text, Acts 3:19.

Elsewhere, throughout the New Testament, when theology is not threatened (as for example, such texts as Matt. 9:22; Mark 8:33;

John 21:20; Acts 9:40; Rev. 1:12), the true sense of the word is communicated clearly: the subjects of the verb *turned*. They were not acted upon, they were not passive, they turned.

8. *Reconciliation*

A companion word to conversion is that of reconciliation. The classic expression of the doctrine of reconciliation is found in II Corinthians 5:18—6:2.

18, All things are of God, who reconciled us to himself through Christ, and gave unto us the ministry of reconciliation, 19, to wit, God was in Christ reconciling the world unto himself, not reckoning unto them their trespasses, and having committed unto us the word of reconciliation.

20, We are ambassadors therefore on behalf of Christ, as though God were entreating by us: We beseech you, on behalf of Christ, be ye reconciled to God. Him who knew no sin, he made to be sin in our behalf, that we might become the righteousness of God in him.

6:1, And working together with him we entreat also that ye receive not the grace of God in vain, 2, (for he saith)

> At an acceptable hour, I hearkened
>   unto thee,
> In a day of salvation
>   did I succor thee.

Behold, now is the acceptable time, behold, now is the day of salvation.

Romans 5:6-10 should also be read. In both passages cited, Paul is emphasizing (through a different term) what has just been discussed in some detail. Conversion is our response to the overtures of God's grace through the preaching of the Gospel. God does not need to be reconciled to man. Man needs to be reconciled to God. A verse from an old hymn states it thusly:

> He called me long before I heard,
> Before my sinful heart was stirred;
> But when I took him *at his word,*
> Forgiven, he lifted me.

The mourner's bench mode of seeking salvation has nothing in the Scriptures to compare with it, save the futile exercises of the priests of Baal in the contest which Elijah waged against them on Mt. Carmel (I Kings 18:25-29). It would often appear that God may be dead, or at least deaf, or perhaps hardened of heart, not just of hearing; or he is off on a journey, or in a deep sleep; or perhaps he delights in toying with the anxious sinner until he is beside himself with anxiety before he will answer his fervent prayer.

It is a curious phenomenon that those who are the most insistent that salvation is by faith alone, are often those who make the process of conversion, reconciliation, and the assurance of salvation the most difficult, drawn out, and laborious. (The reader's attention is directed to the exhibit at the close of this lesson, documenting the origin of the mourner's bench/altar call as a confessed and deliberate substitute for the commandment of Christ and the practice of the apostolic church. See "The Mourner's Bench," appended to this lesson.)

In setting aside an open confession of Christ as Lord and Saviour, and submission to him in baptism, a void was created which (experience soon disclosed) had to be filled in some way. Expedience dictated against returning to the Biblical norm. In big-time evangelism numbers is the name of the game. Unfortunately, small-time operators tend to imitate the methods of the "biggies," and so the malignancy spreads. The irony of it all is that in order to justify the setting aside of a Divine commandment, it has been necessary to represent obedience thereto as a "work of righteousness which we do ourselves." Supposedly to follow the pattern demonstrated in the book of Acts and commanded in the Great Commission is to "add to the finished work on Calvary," deny the grace of God, and to replace saving faith with dead works.

9. *Sanctification*

The basis for an understanding of the Biblical doctrine of sanctification was laid in Lesson Eight as attention was called to the description of the church as the fellowship of saints. The doctrine of sanctification informs us as to how we become saints.

Contrary to prevailing notions, sainthood is not reserved for an elitist, or antiquated or antedated class of churchmen. In the New Testament all Christians are called saints, and "called to be saints." We are so called in contra-distinction to the unsaved who are, frankly, called sinners.

Both the Hebrew *gadash* and the Greek *hagios* translated saints stem from root words which mean to separate in the sense of setting one apart for special service. The act of setting apart is to sanctify, the state of being set apart is sanctification.

The Greek word for this ninth synonym for salvation is *hagiasmos*. It is also translated "holiness." In Hebrews 12:14 we are exhorted:

"Follow after peace with all men, and the sanctification (KJV, holiness) without which no man shall see the Lord." Such a verse makes of sanctification an imperative.

Holiness is a no more popular word in modern Christendom than is sanctification. Both are often encrusted with cultists overtones. An aggressive segment of the church teaches that sanctification is a "second work of grace," posterior to our entrance in upon salvation, through which one is so endowed with the Holy Spirit as to no longer be capable of sinning. It is of interest that those who so teach find their chief support for the dogma in John's first epistle wherein John openly warns that one making such a claim is not only a liar, but actually makes God out to be a liar. (See I John 1:6-8.)

The translators of the NASV, and to a lesser degree, the NIV, have eased the confusion perpetuated through the KJV by giving special attention to the verb forms used in the key passages. The verbs involved are generally present active participles denoting continuous, habitual activity. The NASV underscores this by including the words "practice, practices" in the rendition of the Greek construction. For example:

> Little children, let no one deceive you: the one who *practices* righteousness (makes right doing one's practice) is righteous, just as He is righteous. The one who practices sin is of the devil; for the devil has sinned from the beginning (I John 3:7, 8).

The following texts are germaine to this area of controversy: I John 1:6, 7, 8; 2:5, 29; 3:4, 6, 7, 8, 9, 10, 24; 5:2, 3, 4, 18. For example, the phrase in I John 1:7, "the blood of Jesus His Son *cleanseth* us from all unrighteousness" actually affirms that the blood of Jesus *is cleansing* us. The verb *katharizéi*, from which comes our word cathartic (a purgative), is a present active indicative form of *katharizo*.

I John 3:9, which reads in the KJV, "Whosoever is born of God *doth not commit* (Gr. *poiei*) sin" uses the present active indicative form of *poieo*, signifying one who is begotten of God does not make sin his lifestyle. He does not practice sin. To translate it as though to say he cannot sin, contradicts the warning of John already forcefully expressed in 1:6-8. It is one thing to say something contrary to what we observe daily. It is equally folly to say something contrary to what God has spoken over and over again, and even within the same document.

For one to claim for himself a state of sinless perfection is to claim something even such a one as Paul never claimed for himself. Quite

179

the contrary. In Romans 7:15-25 he described himself as a man undergoing a constant struggle with what he calls "the body of this death." He admits at times to losing a skirmish or two in the ongoing struggle. In I Corinthians 9:26, 27 he affirms it necessary to buffet his body, to keep it in bondage, lest after he had preached to others, he himself should be rejected.

Moreover, in Philippians 3:12-16, as he nears his life's closing, he announced he had not yet become perfect. He had not attained any righteousness of his own of which he could boast. He was still pressing on if so be that he might lay hold on that for which he was laid hold on by Christ. How audacious for one who exhibits nothing of such discipline and daring and selfless service and sacrifice manifest in Christ to profess to be without sin.

In the New Testament sanctification is set forth as the work of a joint undertaking in which the redeemed and the Holy Spirit work together. II Corinthians 6:14—7:1; I Peter 3:15; and Romans 6:19 combine with Hebrews 12:14, already noted, in urging us to do our part, apart from which we shall not see the Lord.

10. *Redemption*

This term might properly have been introduced much earlier, since it has to do with what God has done to bring us to salvation. It has been placed last by way of serving as a reminder of something we should never forget: the cost of our salvation.

One of the most traumatic words of the Bible relates to the cost of our great salvation. It is sometimes translated ransom, sometimes redemption. The Greek word most commonly so translated is *lutron*, from the verb *lutroo* meaning "to loose." In the ancient world the term had reference to loosing in a very special sense. It has its roots in the institution of human bondage—both slavery and imprisonment. Prisoners of war and persons impounded for crime or non-payment of debts were often forced into chattel slavery. It was not uncommon for prisoners to be rented or even sold to wanton taskmasters who often worked them with less consideration than was accorded an ox or an ass. The slave labor camps of communist regimes provide a modern example.

By reason of greed few taskmasters were found willing to release a prisoner even when the convicted man's sentence was complete. Thus it was not uncommon for family or friends to buy a man's freedom. The institution of paying ransom to loose one from imprisonment and from bonds became a pattern in the ancient world. The poor wretch in bondage was rarely paid; and even were he paid, rarely could a bondman save enough from his meager pay to buy his own freedom.

In the Old Testament the word ransom appears thirteen times. Normally it translates the Hebrew word *kopher* (covering), and refers to a sum-covering the value of a man's labor. The Hebrew word *gaal* (free) is also so translated, but is more commonly rendered redeem.

In the New Testament also there are two words used somewhat interchangeably, *lutron* (verb, *lutroo*) and *agorazo*. The first is translated both ransom and redeem. In Matthew 20:28 Jesus speaks of himself as giving his life "as a ransom for many." In Titus 2:14 Paul speaks of Jesus as the one "who gave himself up to redeem us from all iniquity, and purify unto himself a people for his own possession, zealous of good works." The words of Peter in his first epistle are especially provocative as he writes concerning Jesus against the backdrop of both the slave market and the Old Testament sacrificial system:

> Knowing that ye were redeemed, not with silver or gold, from your vain manner of life handed down from your fathers; but with precious blood, as of a lamb without blemish and without spot, even the blood of Christ (I Peter 1:18, 19).

The message is plain. As sinners we are like chattel slaves. We have not the price to purchase our redemption, and Satan is of no mind to set us free. But that is only half the story. We are sinners in desperate need of atonement. We have robbed our maker of the honor and service that is due him, and we cannot make it up. If we served him faultlessly from this day forward, we would only be doing what we ought to have been doing all the while. We are in double jeopardy. How shall we escape if we neglect so great salvation as is proffered us through Christ our Lord and our redeemer?

During the slavery era that once blighted our nation, a black was placed upon the auction block. The cruelest slave owner of the southland was there and took note of the youth—the physique and bearing of the young black—and determined he would own him whatever the cost. His opening bid made that plain. But to his surprise, a stranger entered the bidding with obvious equal determination. The shrewd auctioneer quickly sized up the situation and made the most of it. Higher and higher the bids rose. At length, the stranger bid an unheard-of sum, and the black became his possession. In fear and wonderment, the young black fell to his knees before his new master. What awesome toil would be laid upon him to justify such a price as was paid?

181

The stranger reached down and took the black by the shoulder and gently urged him to his feet. "My friend," said he, "I did not buy you to enslave you. I bought you to set you free." Overwhelmed, the black stood in awe and wonder, wrestling with unbelief. When at last he gained his composure, he said: "Master, I cannot be free in this land. Someone will someday figure out some way to get possession of me. Let me be your servant till I die."

> Know ye not that your body is a temple of the Holy Spirit, which is in you, which you have from God? And ye are not your own: for ye have been bought with a price. Glorify God therefore in your body (I Cor. 6:19, 20).

The word redeemed has a firm place in the vocabulary of the church. Many of our most beautiful hymns ring with the rapturous joys evoked by the message of wondrous love that it has long conveyed. Ransom, its approximate synonym, rarely appears in the hymnology of the church, and is used only three times in the text of the New Testament. In Matthew 20:28 and Mark 10:45 Jesus is recorded as saying, "The Son of Man came to give his life a ransom for many." In I Timothy 2:5, 6 we are reminded that there is one God, and one mediator between God and man, himself man, Christ Jesus, who gave himself a ransom for all.

Unfortunately such words as redeem and redemption have been cheapened in our day. About the only things spoken of as redeemed are such trivia as trading stamps and coupons, or, at the most, something that has been hocked at a pawn shop. Thus the word ransom probably communicates more clearly in our time what redemption communicated in times past. Ransom demands generally are shrewdly and diabolically calculated to virtually exhaust the resources of the family whose loved one's life is in the gravest jeopardy until the ransom demand has been paid.

> There's a sweet and blessed story
> Of the Christ who came from glory
> Just to rescue me, from sin and misery.
> He in loving kindness sought me
> And from sin and shame has brought me,
> Hallelujah! Jesus ransomed me.

Summary

Salvation is indeed a many splendored thing. Each facet of the jewel of salvation shines with Divine luster. And in addition to the several facets of salvation which have been examined, salvation has three phases. The Greek verb *sozo* is used in the New Testament to speak of salvation as an accomplished fact, as a continuing process, and as something which is yet to be realized.

Salvation is a past event. Ephesians 2:8 states that "by grace (we) have been saved" (Gr. *sesosmenoi*, lit., you are *having been* saved). Titus 3:5 states that "by his mercy he saved us (Gr. *esosen)* through the washing of regeneration and the renewing of the Holy Spirit." Here the aorist tense is used, and the basis of our confidence stated: We have undergone the bath of beginning again (Gr. *palingenesis*) and received the seal of our redemption (cp. Eph. 1:13), the Holy Spirit. (See Acts 2:38.) Thus when asked, "Are you saved?" one can answer, "I have been saved."

Salvation is a present, progressive state. Acts 2:47 says that in addition to those who were added to the church on Pentecost "The Lord added day by day those who were *being saved*," Gr. *sozomenous* (present passive participle). See also I Corinthians 1:18 for a similar construction of the verb. I Corinthians 15:2 contains an interesting notation. Paul informs his reader that the Gospel he preached, which they had received, is the Gospel by which they were *being saved,* Gr. *sozesthe* (present passive indicative), adding, "if ye hold fast the word which I preached to you, except you believed in vain." Thus when asked, "Are you saved? One can appropriately respond, "I am being saved."

Salvation is also a future event and a future hope. Romans 5:9, 10 states that "Now, having been justified by his blood, much more then shall we be saved from the wrath to come," Gr. *sothesometha* (future passive indicative). See also I Corinthians 3:15 and 5:5 where the future tense of the verb is used to convey the fact there is a finalizing of the process of salvation, in which we shall be saved from the fire of destruction in the day of the Lord Jesus Christ. Thus we may answer the question in terms of our future hope, "I trust I shall be saved in that time to come when Jesus shall have his day."

II Corinthians 1:10 sums this all up in a single verse. Paul, in the preceding verse, reminds us of our past state in which we were under sentence of death, hence we should not put our trust in ourselves but in God, who "*hath delivered* (past tense), and *doth deliver* (present tense) and in whom we have *set our hope* that *he will deliver us*." That verse pretty well wraps it up.

PREVIEW—REVIEW QUESTIONS

Conversion

1. State the root meaning of the words convert, conversion.
2. What is the literal meaning of the verb "convert"?
3. In what way does the KJV rendering of Acts 3:19 mislead?
4. In the context of grammatical construction, what is meant by "voice"? Should conversion be considered active or passive?
5. How does the mourner's bench, altar call invitation exercise of modern revivalism relate to all this?

Reconciliation

1. Aside from the fact both are synonyms of salvation, what else do the terms conversion and reconciliation have in common?
2. State the basic idea communicated by the word reconciliation.
3. Who is the enemy of whom in the alienation between God and man? Who has the greater right to be offended?
4. How does Elijah's Mt. Carmel contest with the priests of Baal compare to the mourner's bench exercise?
5. Relate the faith-only revival practice to question number 3. Note the contradiction.

Sanctification

1. State the root meaning of the words from which are derived such terms as saint, sanctify, and sanctification.
2. State the difference, if any, between holiness and sanctification.
3. What is the popular conception of sanctification?
4. How does the KJV, among others, contribute to the dogma of the so-called holiness groups, especially in I John?
5. How does the "holiness" (so called) doctrine compare with Paul's estimate of his own spiritual attainment?

Redemption

1. State the root meaning of the principal Greek word translated redemption, sometimes ransom.
2. What social institution gave rise to the use of such a term in a monetary sense?
3. State the root meaning of the Hebrew word *kopher*, commonly translated ransom.

4. How does the root meaning of *kopher* relate to our salvation? State the application.
5. What change in the manner in which redemption has come to be used makes the word ransom more readily understandable and apt as descriptive of the cost of our salvation?
6. Precisely what does the New Testament have to say about the cost of our salvation?

Summary

1. Locate the verse of Scripture which speaks of the three phases of salvation.
2. What is the sense in which salvation is involved in each?

THE MOURNER'S BENCH

What is it? Is it of God, or of man?

Charles G. Finney, celebrated evangelist of the early 19th century and president of Oberlin College, delivered a series of lectures on evangelism in 1838 which, by popular demand, were made available to the general public in book form. Fleming H. Revell & Co. secured publishing rights. A copy of the second edition, entitled *Revivals of Religion,* dated October 22, 1868, is before me.

Evangelist Finney, probably more than any other man, popularized the mourner's bench (or anxious seat, as he preferred to call it) as he led the vanguard of revivalists in the Great Religious Awakening that swept Europe and America a century ago. On pages 254-256 of the 1868 edition, Mr. Finney wrote in defense of the anxious seat. The following quotation is taken verbatim from page 254, including the italics Mr. Finney used for emphasis. Speaking of an "awakened sinner," Mr. Finney wrote:

> If you say to him, "There is the anxious seat, come out and avow your determination to be on the Lord's side," if he is not willing to do so small a thing as that, then he is not willing to do *anything*, and there he is, brought out before his own conscience. It uncovers the delusion of the human heart, and prevents a great many spurious conversions, by showing those who might otherwise imagine themselves willing to do anything for Christ, that in fact they are willing to do *nothing*.
>
> The church has always felt it necessary to have something of the kind to answer this very purpose. In the days of the apostles *baptism* answered

185

this purpose. The Gospel was preached and those who were willing to be on the side of Christ were called on to be *baptized*. It (baptism) held the precise place that the anxious seat does now, as a public manifestation of their determination to be a Christian.

Mr. Finney goes on to state that there were those who opposed the "anxious seats," but countered by saying, "in modern times those who have been violently opposed to the anxious seat have been obliged to adopt some substitute, or they could not get along in promoting a revival." Note, there is no appeal for evangelists to return to the apostolic practice of baptism, only a defense of the premise that some kind of substitute is necessary "in modern times" to the promotion of a revival. Who is it that has so much to say about not being "saved by works of righteousness which we do ourselves"? What they do speaks so loudly, it is difficult to hear what they say.

13

THE PROCESS OF SALVATION: THE WHOLE COUNSEL OF GOD

The apostle Paul, in his farewell address to the elders of the church at Ephesus, had this to say (among other things), "I shrank not from declaring unto you *the whole counsel of God*," (Acts 20:27). In the context of the great salvation of which he was speaking, and of which we are now declaring, that is a profound statement of a pressing obligation.

How does one arrive at thé whole counsel of God on this vital subject? Is the process of salvation set forth somewhere step by step, in every detail from the first step to the last? If not, why not? And if not, how can we arrive at the whole counsel of God, and be sure we have done so? These are vital questions, and they have no quick and easy answers.

How does one arrive at the full counsel of God on any subject of the Bible? Faith? Spiritual gifts? Love? Baptism? Or any other? None is discussed comprehensively, that is, in fullness in any one chapter or even in any one book of the Bible. True, we have a faith chapter (Heb. 11); and three chapters "concerning spiritual gifts" (I Cor. 12 through 14), with what is called "the love chapter" (13) in the midst of those three; and an excursus on baptism (Rom. 6). But to gain the whole counsel of God on any of those topics, or any other, one must read all that God has caused to be written concerning those matters, and then draw such deductions as are in harmony with all that God has caused to be written, not only on that subject but others which are interrelated.

To gain the whole truth on any subject one needs to be somewhat familiar with at least three things: 1) the basic principles of hermeneutics, the laws of interpretation; 2) the principles of inductive reasoning; and 3) the extent to which a manner of speaking called a synecdoche is used in both oral and written communication, the Bible being no exception.

Obviously there are thousands of individuals who have been brought to a saving knowledge and submission to Christ who may have never even heard of a one of the three terms just mentioned (at least not by name). But they are at least somewhat aware of the principles so called, and may have been fortunate to be taught by one who faithfully applied the principles in interpreting the Scripture with regard to the question: "What must one do to be saved?"

Hermeneutics

Take the first, heremeneutics. The rules are simple: 1) Who spoke? 2) To whom spoken? 3) Why spoken? 4) When spoken? and 5) Under what circumstances (dispensation) spoken? For example, it is written: "By faith Noah *being warned of God* (Gr. *chrematistheis*) concerning things not seen as yet, moved with godly fear, prepared an ark to the saving of his house" (household) (Heb. 11:7). That hardly is what is expected of us today, except by way of type (Gr. *tupos,* example). (See I Peter 3:20, 21.)

Who spoke? God. To whom spoken? Noah. Why spoken? To enable him to save himself and others from the impending flood. When spoken? In time for Noah to render the obedience of faith necessary to his salvation. Under what circumstances (dispensation) spoken? In the patriarchial age, with a view to God's announced intention to purge the earth by water.

Obviously the salvation Noah secured by building a mammoth boat is not the same kind of salvation we secure by being baptized (see I Peter 3:20, 21). Consider also the salvation gained by a penitent thief dying (actually, not just symbolically) with Christ on Calvary. The circumstances of his conversion were hardly normative, to say nothing of the fact that he died under a different dispensation. He was offered pardon personally by Christ before the ratification of what Jesus called "the new covenant/testament in (his) blood" (Luke 22:20) was ratified either 1) by his death (see Heb. 9:16, 17) or 2) by the descent of the Holy Spirit on the day of Pentecost.

Certainly the circumstances of the dying thief were not considered by the Holy Spirit and Peter to be parallel to the guilt-stricken crowd on Pentecost. To their question, "What shall we do?" Peter, moved by the Holy Spirit (Acts 2:4), did not tell them to remember the dying thief. He told them to do what Jesus prescribed should be done in the Great Commission. (See Acts 2:38, cp. Luke 24:47; Mark 16:16.) But when hear we such an answer in mass evangelism situations today?

Someone needs to know and respect the principles of hermeneutics. The inquiring sinner may have never heard the term, but blessed are they who receive the answer to their question either from direct study of the conversion episodes recorded in the book of Acts, or who hear the Gospel from someone who obeys God and not man.

Closely associated with hermeneutics are two other terms important to this study: *exegesis* and *eisegesis*. The root of the two words is the Greek word *hegeisthai,* meaning to lead or guide. Exegesis is an attempt to draw out the meaning of a text. Eisegesis is an attempt to read something into a text. The first seeks to determine what the text is actually saying when analyzed. The second seeks to make a text say what the reader or teacher wants it to say. Commentaries are replete with examples of both.

Inductive Reasoning

Some attention needs to be given to the process of inductive reasoning. The root of this word is a Latin verb, *ducere,* meaning to lead or carry, the latter being more common in its usage. From this root we get many familiar terms besides induct, inductive, and induction. Many nouns come to mind, such as viaduct, aquaduct, and tear duct. All have to do with carrying something, whether traffic or truth, water or tears.

Inductive reasoning may be defined as the process of carrying into the mind all the data which is known to relate to a given subject, with a view to deducing, drawing out, a conclusion which is in harmony with all the facts. Such a process quickly makes a person chary of any dogmatic assertion which incorporates the word "only." The dogma

189

of salvation (or justification) by faith only is a notable example. Martin Luther, in reacting to the Romanist credo of salvation through works of penance and such like, added the word *sola* to the text of Romans 1:17b. That is a classic example of eisegesis. Later, in reading the epistle of James he came to a text which says just the opposite of what he had altered Romans 1:17 to say. Instead of deleting the word he had added to the book of Romans, he found it easier to delete the whole book of James. He declared it to be an epistle of straw. Deleting the epistle of James is not an exercise in exegesis. The meaning of the problem passage (James 2:24, in the context of 2:14-26) was not unclear. In fact that was the problem. It was altogether too clear. It required no exegetical study to "draw out" its meaning. The Lutheran church has since learned to live with the book of James by applying eisegesis to the passage which contradicts the dogma of justification by faith only.

Inductive reasoning may be illustrated thusly. A passenger on a sea-going vessel espied a man floundering in the open sea. He sounded an alarm and the pilot began to maneuver the vessel in such a manner as not to awash the desperate man. A lifeboat was quickly lowered and strong rowers sped to his rescue. As they drew near, he began to sink away. One of the seamen flung a life preserver with a line attached. It settled providentially acircle an upraised arm. Instinctively the man clutched it and drew his head to the surface for a much needed gasp of air. Strong arms began to draw him to the lifeboat taking care not to overtax his enfeebled grasp. Soon he was being lifted into the lifeboat and escorted to the ship. They were to learn the man had fallen overboard unnoticed from another vessel and had treaded water for hours, praying desperately that he would be missed or another ship would come along in time to save him.

It so happened a newsman was aboard the rescue ship. He readily sensed the making of a human interest story. "Rescue at Sea" would be the headline. Of course, he would want a picture of the saved man and his saviour, or saviours. Who should be in the picture? The man who espied him and sounded the alarm? The skillful pilot? The captain who took charge of the rescue operation? The men who lowered the lifeboat? The oarsmen? The man who so precisely threw the lifebuoy in the nick of time? The men who drew him to the boat and then from the water? Or should the man insist he saved himself? After all, he treaded water for hours, and prayed, and grasped the lifebuoy that was thrown to him, and hung on with his last measure of strength. If he had not wanted to be rescued, if he had not done all he was humanly able to do, and much more than he ever thought he could do; he would not have been saved. Right?

Fortunately the man was not at the mercy of theologians. He would have drowned while they were arguing over the proper means of his salvation. They might have asked him not to do anything but pray, and trust God.

The truth is obvious. All the factors mentioned, perhaps some over-looked, combined to save him. The various factors mentioned were all part of one total interrelated process. *That is inductive reasoning.* Such reason applied to the doctrine of Christian salvation would greatly alter the preaching and practice of creed-bound and blinded would-be rescuers of untold millions adrift on life's sea.

Synecdoche

Closely allied to inductive reasoning, in fact often the factor that calls for inductive reasoning, is the extensive usage in the Scriptures of a rhetorical device called synecdoche (Gr. *sunekdesthai,* "to receive jointly."). The word itself is not used in the Scriptures, but it describes a literary style that abounds in the Scriptures. Webster properly defines synecdoche as "a rhetorical device in which 1) a part stands for the whole, or 2) the whole for one of its parts."

Take the first, a part standing for the whole. Ask a rancher how many cattle he has, and he might reply, "Well, I reckon I have about a thousand head." Cattle heads are all he has? No one would so interpret his words. A farmer may inform you he has two hired hands. Does he mean to say his hired man has use of both his hands, and the farmer has contracted for him to use both of them? "How many are present today? Let's have a show of hands; or shall we just count noses?" Another synecdoche! The ancients reported the volume of traffic in the harbor by counting the sails in the harbor. By now it should be obvious why they counted the sails instead of the hulls. The most forward part of a thing, the part the most readily seen, or the part most involved in the process being spoken of is singled out, and that part stands for the whole. In secular affairs the rational mind "receives jointly" with the mention of the specific item, the *whole picture.* Well has God invited, "Come, let us reason together" (Isa. 1:18).

Now for the other side of this manner of speaking: the whole stand-ing for one of its parts. The lad who very much wants to be accepted by his peer group may ask his parents for permission to do the thing that is "in" at the time. His appeal will likely be, "Everbody's doing it." Of course, it is not so. He knows it. His parents know it. But they get the message. Everybody their son regards as really somebody is doing it, and he does not want to be a nobody in their sight.

The Scriptures use synecdoches of both kinds. When the Philippian jailer asked Paul, "What must I do to be saved?" Paul answered synecdochically: "Believe on the Lord Jesus and thou shalt be saved, thou and all thy house." (Note there is actually a double synecdoche in that answer.) Now, be it noted that Paul did not say, "Only believe." But neither did he recite to him all the facets of the redemptive process in his initial response. That would have been confusing, perhaps overwhelming. Paul began with the most forward part of the process, the part without which no other part has any validity. Repentance that is not an act of faith is really just reformation (and that likely only temporarily). Confession that is not a confession of personal faith is only the mouthing of a ritualistic formula. Baptism that is not an act of faith is only "the putting away of the filth of the flesh," to borrow an expression from Peter (I Peter 3:21), that is, a bath, and not even a good way to take a bath. So Paul led the jailer step by step to repentance, baptism, and the joy of salvation (Acts 16:30-34). Read the account and make a list of all the things it is said the jailer did, "having believed in God."

Note: Appended to the "Preview—Review Questions" is a study entitled: "The Synecdoche and Salvation." What a far cry such a compendium presents as compared to dogmatic theology. Only a denominational bias would lead one to reject the inclusion of a certain factor (or factors) in God's redemptive system because God in some other place has mentioned another factor (the dogmatist's favorite) as being the means of his redeeming grace.

Proof-text Theology

The failure to note synecdochical language, and the failure to use inductive reasoning coupled with the substitution of eisegesis for exegesis, and the ignoring of sound hermeneutics have combined to produce what is called "grasshopper" exegesis or proof-text theology. One such example has long been a standing joke. It is written: "Judas went out and hanged himself." Jesus has commanded, "Go thou and do likewise." In fact he said: "What thou doest, do quickly."

Consider another example: "It is not good for man to live alone" (Gen. 2:18). "He that knoweth to do good, and doeth it not, to him

192

it is sin" (James 4:17). From these two texts taken out of context, it could be proved that it is sinful for a man to be single.

A similar example is this one: "Wives be in subjection to your husbands" (Eph. 5:22). "Husbands love your wives as your own bodies" (Eph. 5:28). The same apostle who wrote these two commandments stated, "I buffet my body and keep it in bondage, lest I should be a castaway" (I Cor. 9:27). Thus one could use the Scriptures not only to defend but encourage wife beating. Untold harm is done the body of the bride-elect of Christ because many doctrines have been contrived in much the same manner.

The whole counsel of God is to be deduced from all of its parts, exegeted according to sound hermeneutics, employing the common sense principles of inductive reasoning. Let us be giants for God in Biblical study, and be done forever with grasshopper exegesis, particularly in responding to the question of everlasting consequence: What must one do to be saved?

A Word of Warning about Words

A word of warning about words is in order in view of the technical discussion in which we have engaged in this lesson. In II Timothy 2:14 Paul commands that one "strive not about words, to no profit, to the subverting of them that hear." In doing so, he was by no means suggesting we make no use of dictionaries and lexicons, or that we are free to speak loosely. He did not do so. In I Corinthains 2:13 he affirmed that he was speaking, "Not in words which man's wisdom teaches, but which the Spirit teaches, combining spiritual things with spiritual words." If we are to speak and write in the manner that Paul did, it behooves us to use words in our language which parallel as closely as possible the thoughts conveyed by the words used by the Biblical writers. Such is the avowed goal of the translators of the Scriptures.

At times, however, we find the need of expressing a thought which is not directly expressed in the Scriptures. The title of this lesson is an example. Before the rise of conflicting teaching as to how and when one is saved, converted, justified, etc., such an expression as the plan or steps of salvation, or the scheme of redemption, or the process of salvation would not likely be used. The question, "What must I do to be saved?" would be answered in the light of where the person asking the question had arrived along the way that leads to salvation. The Philippian jailer who raised the question (Acts 16:30) was by no means as advanced in the process of salvation as the guilt-stricken multitude on Pentecost who asked "What shall we do?" (Acts 2:37). And they were not as far advanced as the twelve disciples Paul encountered at Ephesus (Acts 19:1-5). Unlike the Philippian jailer those twelve men had already "heard the word of the Lord," and had believed what they heard (v. 2). They had obviously already repented, for it turns out they had been baptized with the baptism of John, which was "baptism of repentance" (vs. 3, 4). Their only shortcoming was that, like so many in our times, they had been improperly taught concerning baptism. Neither their sincerity nor their willingness to render the obedience of faith was a problem. Witness the fact that when Paul explained to them the difference between John's baptism and the baptism Christ commanded, it is written, "Now when they heard this they were baptized in the name of the Lord Jesus" (v. 5).

How shall we express what we must do to be saved? Those who insist that salvation is by faith alone find fault with any other manner of speaking, despite the fact their form of expression is nowhere so stated in the Scriptures. In fact the contrary is stated in James 2:24.

To speak of the steps of salvation is not the best of phrasing. When we progress from hearing the Word of God to believing it, we do not leave the "first step of salvation" behind as we do the first step of a stairway or ladder. Nor do we leave faith behind when we move on to repentance, confession, and baptism. The use of the expression, the steps of salvation, was never intended to imply such but rather to note the fact there is a logical progression in the process of salvation.

To speak of the scheme of redemption is to suggest to some that there is something secret or furtive about the way of salvation. To use the expression, the laws of pardon, is to be charged with legalism. To speak of the terms of salvation is thought by some to smack of bargaining. To speak of the plan of salvation is thought by some to make the matter too routine. Would they care to defend the proposition that God has left something as important as our salvation unplanned?

The Pauline expression, "the obedience of faith" has much to commend it. It is Biblical, and it diminishes the dichotomy some read into the emphasis of Paul as opposed to James. But the phrase is not all inclusive. The hearing of the Gospel necessarily precedes faith. (See Rom. 10:14-17.) Hearing, in the sense of receiving the information which leads to faith, is an essential element in man's response to God's proffered salvation. I have elected therefore to speak of those things which we are "to do to be saved" as man's response to God's proffered salvation.

PREVIEW—REVIEW QUESTIONS

1. Locate the text which contains the expression, "the whole counsel of God." Note its context. Do you believe all evangelists are like-minded?
2. Can we find the whole counsel of God on a given subject if we are familiar with the topic headings of the great chapters of the Bible? Explain.
3. Define hermeneutics. State the 5 principles of hermeneutics.
4. Illustrate the need for hermeneutics in the context of the general topic of the Great Salvation.
5. Define and explain exegesis.
6. Define and explain eisegesis.
7. Define and explain inductive reasoning.
8. Illustrate the process of inductive reasoning.
9. Define synecdoche.
10. State the two forms of synecdochical language.
11. Illustrate, Biblically and secularly, one of the two forms.
12. Do the same with the other form.
13. Complete the quotation: "Only a denominational bias . . . "
14. Give an example of such a bias.
15. Why was the Philippian jailer not given the same answer to his question that Peter gave on the day of Pentecost?
16. Why is the familiar expression, the steps of salvation, somewhat faulty if the analogy is pressed too far?

THE SYNECDOCHE AND SALVATION

The synecdoche appears many times in the New Testament in connection with the presentation of the means whereby we are brought to the state of salvation, to wit:

References	Key Phrases	Who or What Saves
Matt. 1:21	He (Christ) shall save His people . . .	Christ
Matt. 18:11	The Son of Man is come to seek and to save . . .	Christ
John 12:47	I came not to judge . . . but to save the world.	Christ

THE SYNECDOCHE AND SALVATION (continued)

References	Key Phrases	Who or What Saves
I Tim. 1:15	Christ came to save sinners . . .	Christ
Matt. 16:25	Whosoever shall lose his life shall save it	Losing one's life for Jesus' sake
Luke 18:24-30	(Story of the Rich Young Ruler)	
Matt. 10:22	He that endureth to the end	Endurance, Faithfulness
Cp. Matt. 24:13,	Rev. 2:10, 2:17, Heb. 3:14, I Cor. 15:22	to end
Luke 7:50	Thy faith hath saved thee	Faith
Acts 16:31	Believe on the Lord Jesus Christ . . . be saved	Faith
Eph. 2:8	. . . ye are saved, through faith	Faith
Acts 2:21	Whosoever shall call on the name of the Lord . . .	Calling on Name
Acts 2:40	Save yourselves	One's self
Phil. 2:12	Work out your own salvation	One's self
Acts 11:14	Who shall speak words . . . whereby . . . be saved	Preached Word
Rom. 1:16	The Gospel is the power of God unto salvation	The Gospel
I Cor. 1:21	. . . thru the foolishness of preaching to save . . .	Preaching
II Tim. 3:15	The Scriptures . . . make you wise unto salvation	The Scriptures
James 1:21	The ingrafted word . . . able to save your souls	The Word
Rom. 10:10	Confession is made unto salvation	Confession
Rom. 8:24	In hope are we saved	Hope
Rom. 11:14	That I may provoke . . . and save some	We save others
I Cor. 9:22	I am become all things . . . to save some	We save others
James 5:20	He that converteth a sinner . . . shall save a soul	We save others
I Cor. 3:11-15	(Analogy of proper foundation)	Right Foundation
II Cor. 7:10	Sorrow worketh repentance unto salvation	Repentance

196

THE SYNECDOCHE AND SALVATION (continued)

References	Key Phrases	Who or What Saves
Eph. 2:5, 8	By grace are ye saved, through faith . . .	Grace
II Thess. 2:10	They receive not the love of the truth . . .	Love of Truth
II Thess. 2:13	. . . chose you to salvation . . . in sanctification	Sanctification
I Tim. 4:16	In doing these things . . . shall save . . .	Doing right
Titus 3:5	By his mercy he saved us . . .	God's Mercy
Titus 3:5	. . . thru the washing of regeneration . . .	New Birth
Heb. 7:25	He is able to save . . . them that draw nigh	Draw near to God
James 2:14-22	(Faith vs. or & Works Discussion	Works of Faith
I Peter 3:21; Mark 16:16	Baptism now saves us	Baptism

SHALL WE RECEIVE THESE THINGS JOINTLY? OR SHALL WE REJECT THE "WHOLE COUNSEL OF GOD" AND HOLD ON TO ONLY THAT WHICH WILL FIT OUR PARTICULAR THEORY OF SALVATION?

Only a denominational bias would lead one to reject the proper place of certain factors in God's redemptive system because he has in another place spoken of some other factor as being the means of his redeeming grace.

14

MAN'S RESPONSE INITIATED: HEARING, BELIEVING THE GOSPEL

Lessons 10 through 12 focused on our great salvation, viewed from the perspective of what God has done to make it so. Man's response to God's gracious proffer of salvation was occasionally touched upon. In Lessons 14 through 16 the focus will be on man's response, as set forth in the Scriptures. Lesson 13 serves as a bridge between the two emphases.

The question of the Philippian jailer needs to be answered in the light of the whole counsel of God. "What must I do to be saved?" is the most important question that any man could ever ask. To give less than the full answer to such a question is to deceive and defraud the inquirer, and to court danger and disaster. "What saith the oracles (answer) of God?" (Rom. 11:4).

1. *Hearing the Gospel*

The importance of hearing the Gospel cannot be over emphasized. The classic expression of this fact is found in Romans 10:14-17 where Paul asks: "How shall they call on him in whom they have not believed?

and how can they believe in him whom they have not heard? . . . So belief cometh by hearing and hearing by the word of Christ."

The book of Acts is replete with examples of this process at work. Of the day of Pentecost, the day the church began, it is written: "Now when they heard this (the message Peter had just preached, proving from the Scriptures of the prophets that Jesus is the Christ) they were pricked in their hearts and cried out, Men and brethren, what shall we do?" (Acts 2:37).

The answer of God, channeled through the Holy Spirit, and through Peter speaking as the Spirit gave him utterance, was also something they needed to hear. The answer given was not the answer penitent believers are accustomed to hearing today. Peter did not tell them there was nothing they could do, except believe; that to do something more would be to fail to trust God's grace. Instead he instructed them to do two things: "Repent, and be baptized in the name of Jesus Christ for (Gr. *eis*, into) the remission of sins" (v. 38). And they did so. V. 41 reads: "They then that gladly received the word were baptized." And about three thousand so responded and were added that day to the church.

So it was also with the next conversion episode recorded in Acts. In Acts 8:5, 6 we read that "Philip went down into Samaria and proclaimed unto them the Christ, and the multitude *gave heed* to the things that were spoken by Philip." Mark the expression, "gave heed." It shows up again in v. 10 but with a different application. V. 9 introduces Simon the sorcerer of whom it is said: "Who beforetime in the city used sorcery, and amazed the people of Samaria, giving out that he himself was some great one." V. 10 then reports that to him "they all *gave heed*."

Webster defines hearing as "auditory perception." Primarily that is what hearing is. But as used in the Scriptures it may very well be defined in the sense in which Luke has used it in vs. 6 and 10. Hearing profits little unless one *gives heed* to what is heard. More than once my mother rebuked me, saying "What you hear goes in one ear and out the other." Not so with the Samaritans. V. 12 reads: "But when they believed Philip preaching good tidings (the Gospel) concerning the kingdom of God and the name of Jesus Christ, they were baptized, both men and women." Apparently Philip gave the same answer to the question, "What must I do to be saved?" that Peter gave on Pentecost, and they too gave heed to what they heard.

The pattern set on Pentecost continued to be the norm throughout the apostolic age. Dramatic as was the conversion of Saul of Tarsus, though a "chosen vessel unto Christ," he was not received into the kingdom of Christ any differently than were the Jews on Pentecost nor the Samaritans to whom Philip preached. In response to his question, "Lord, what shall I do?" (Acts 22:10) he was simply told to go into Damascus and it would be told him what he should do. He heeded what he heard and went into Damascus. For three days he fasted and prayed, neither of which he was told to do, though neither was inappropriate. But neither of the two effectuated the remission of his sins, modern preachments notwithstanding. Meanwhile Christ directed an evangelist, Ananias, to go to him. And when he did so, Ananias said to him, "And now why tarriest thou, arise and be baptized, and wash away thy sins, calling on the name of the Lord" (Acts 22:16).

The case of the Gentile household of Cornelius exhibits the same pattern. Though his "prayers and alms ascended as a memorial before God" (Acts 10:4), neither brought him into a saving relationship with Christ. In v. 5 we read he was instructed to send for Peter, and in v. 22 it is explained that the instruction was given through a holy angel to the intent Cornelius would "hear words" from Peter. In chapter 11, v. 14, Peter amplifies a bit on that, reporting that the promise was that he (Peter) would "speak words whereby he (Cornelius, and his household also) shall be saved." That Peter did, and despite the baptism of the Holy Spirit that was visited upon Cornelius and his household, they too were commanded to be baptized in water.

Acts 18:8 is a sort of one verse summary of the pattern reported in Acts: "And Crispus, the ruler of the synagogue, believed in the Lord with all his house, and many of the Corinthians hearing, believed, and were baptized."

The New Testament closes with the emphasis upon the importance of hearing the Word of God unabated. The opening paragraph of the book of Revelation contains this promise: "Blessed is he that *readeth*, and they that *hear* the words of the prophecy, and *keep* the things that are written therein" (v. 3). Note the italicized words. If hearing is so important, can a deaf person be saved? Of course. Those that read the Word of God are assured of the same blessing as those who hear, provided that both *give heed* to the Word of God, or, as it is phrased in the verse just cited, provided they *keep* the things that are written therein.

Each of the letters to the seven churches of Asia close with the admonition, "He that hath ears to hear, let him hear what the Spirit saith to the churches" (2:7, 11, 17, 29; 3:6, 13, 22). Note the message they were to hear (heed) was contained in a letter suited to the special need of each congregation. God's Word is to be heeded, not just perceived via the auditory apparatus.

The warning of Isaiah, oft repeated in the New Testament, is still very much to the point:

> This people's heart is waxed gross, and their ears are dull of hearing, and their eyes they have closed, lest haply they should see with their eyes, and hear with their ears, and understand with their hearts, and should turn again (convert) and I should heal them (Isa. 6:9, 10, cp. Matt. 13:15; Acts 28:27, etc.).

Seeing therefore how important it is that unsaved peoples of every race should hear the Gospel we do well to note once again the text with which this lesson began:

> How then shall they call on him in whom they have not believed? and how shall they believe in him whom they have not heard? and how shall they hear without a preacher? and how shall they preach except they be sent? . . . So then faith cometh by hearing and hearing by the word of Christ (Rom. 10:14, 15, 17).

What has just been noted was underscored by Alexander Campbell in his classic debate with N. L. Rice, a champion of Calvinism. Campbell confronted Rice with fourteen propositions, each one challenging Rice's thesis that the Holy Spirit operates directly upon the minds of the elect, apart even from the Word (though not always) to "quicken" them and bring them to faith and hence to salvation.

In his second proposition, Campbell challenged Rice with the fact that no one can be found with any concept of the Christian faith where the Bible, or the teaching thereof, has not preceded. In his next proposition he challenged him with the fact that no one professing to have been enlightened is possessed of a single distinctive Christian concept not derived from the Word of God. Rice was challenged to produce one certified case of any man anywhere who had come into a saving relationship with Christ apart from the Word of God. He closed his challenge with this proposition:

> Nowhere has God operated apart from his word, neither in creation or regeneration. God has always operated through his word. 1) He operated on nonentity through his word. (The worlds were framed by the Word

of God, so that the things which are have not been made out of things which appear.) God spake the worlds into existence, and is this not remarkable, he did so through him whom John speaks of as the eternal "logos" (Word). 2) Having created the heavens and the earth through his word, God is said to have operated upon inert matter, bringing forth living creatures out of both the earth and the sea from non-living, inert matter, by his word. Now that he has an entity in nature (man) capable of receiving instruction and responding to his word, how illogical that he would now bypass the use of words, and operate upon the mind and heart of man apart from words.

Note: The foregoing argument has been condensed and paraphrased by the author. Campbell's challenge yet awaits a certified example to the contrary. "So then (Christian) faith cometh by hearing, and hearing by the Word of Christ" (Rom. 10:17).

2. Faith

To be saved one most certainly must "believe the Gospel" (I Cor. 15:1-4) and "believe in the name (bow to the authority) of Jesus Christ" (John 1:12). When faith (belief) is rightly understood, to believe in the one (the Gospel) is to believe in the other (the authority of Christ) and bow thereto. One who does not bow to the authority of Christ does not really believe what the Word of God teaches concerning him. One may mentally assent to the four propositions which comprise Paul's definition of the Gospel of salvation, but faith consists of much more than a mere mental acquiescence to statements one is not prepared, or for the time being, not minded to deny. Just as there is "an evil heart of unbelief" (Heb. 3:12) that is to be distinguished from honest doubt, or unbelief stemming from a lack of knowledge, there is also a faith that is to be distinguished from a passive acceptance of the things one may have heard or read.

a. *Faith (belief) defined.* It is a vagary of our English language that whereas the word belief has both verbal and noun forms the word faith is used only as a noun. One never speaks of *faithing* someone, or of having *faithed* something one has heard.

A practical definition of faith may be deduced from Romans 10:17, "So then faith cometh by hearing." *Faith is the belief of testimony.* In the context of Romans 10:17, Christian faith may be defined as believing the testimony concerning Christ. Mormon testimony is calculated to produce Mormon faith. Buddhist testimony is calculated to produce

Buddhist faith. Testimony of politicians is intended to produce faith in the party lines which distinguish one from another. The word faith is not of itself a sacred word. Faith takes on sacredness only as it is based on things thought to be sacred.

1) Technically, faith that is rightly so called needs to be distinguished from knowledge. Knowledge is based upon firsthand experience. Knowledge is information directly received through one of the five senses. It is true that when a matter has been reported from several sources, investigated, and duly confirmed, such information is taken as common knowledge. Many things in the realm of history are accepted as fact though we were not in a position to personally observe the reported happenings. But, technically speaking, faith is belief of testimony whereas knowledge is based upon experience.

As I write these lines I am seated in my study at home rather than in my office at the college. Twice in the last hour I have been called from my study to respond to a phone call. As a reader, you will have to take my word for that—not that the matter is of importance of itself, but it illustrates the point that is being made. I know it is so. You do not. In fact you can never know. You can only believe what is being written.

Since it is a dictum of Scripture that by the word of two or three witnesses a thing shall be established (Deut. 17:6) I might ask my wife to read the preceding paragraph and verify what I have reported, were it that important. But even were she to sign an affidavit to that effect, duly certified with a notary seal, and a photostatic copy thereof printed on this page, you will still not know what I have said to be so.

2) The foregoing leads to another important distinction. Faith, if it is to conform to the dictum cited above, must be based upon *adequate testimony. Faith therefore needs to be distinguished from credulity,* "the state of being full of faith," too full in fact. Another word for that is gullibility, "the state of being able to swallow (gullet) anything." Is it not significant that four writers, not just one, or even two, were moved by the Holy Spirit to chronicle the facts of the Gospel? (Cp. II Peter 1:21.) Three writers provided a synoptic account, a kind of three-in-one testimony, and John wrote from a different perspective providing a second line of apostolic witness.

The kind of superstructure our minds build depends on the foundation or support thereof. The house of faith requires adequate, duly authenticated testimony. Gullibility teeters on the sand of hearsay and rumor. Knowledge is built upon verifiable experience.

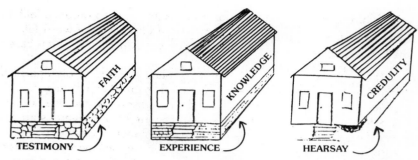

Only a faith based upon reliable testimonies is worthy of the name. In Romans 1:4 Paul says of Jesus that he was "declared the Son of God with power, according to the spirit of holiness by the resurrection from the dead." Suppose the doctrine of the resurrection were based on a testimony kindred to Joseph Smith's account of his nocturnal jaunt to a desolate hillside where he alleged that he dug up the golden plates from whence came the "revelation" upon which the Mormon faith is founded. Suppose that no one saw the resurrected Christ but two teary-eyed women who reported they came to the tomb early one morning and found it empty, but a man whom they at first thought was the gardener identified himself as the one they were seeking, but who forbade them from touching him, and commanded that they hurry away and tell his disciples they had seen him alive. Instead the New Testament chronicles ten separate appearances—indoors, in the open, daytime and nighttime, to individuals and groups, eating with them, talking with them, inviting the doubter to examine his wounds. The resurrection Gospel is summarized by Luke in this fashion, "He showed himself alive after his passion by many proofs, appearing unto them by the space of forty days, speaking the things concerning the kindgom of God" (Acts 1:3).

b) *The function of faith.* Hebrews 11:1 contains a statement which is often cited as a definition of faith. Actually, it describes the function of faith. Faith is there described as "the assurance (Gr. *hupostasis*, cp. Lat. *substantis*) of things hoped for, a conviction (Gr. *elenchos*, proof) of things not seen." The first of the two phrases affirms that faith undergirds, substantiates, serves as a foundation for the things hoped for. The ASV translation, assurance, represents an intensified form of the root word for surety. The second phrase affirms that faith provides the kind of conviction which proof accords. Faith that is based on

205

adequate testimony is counted as proof in courts of law. Juries regularly convict the accused on the basis of their confidence in the testimony of credible witnesses who solemnly swear to the things they affirm they have seen and heard. Faith serves a similar function in our daily lives, as it is written, "for we walk by faith, and not by sight" (II Cor. 5:7). That is not just limited to the area of our Christian walk of life. We could not function in the present social order were it not that our faith functions in the manner described in Hebrews 11:1.

c. *The source of Christian faith.* How is Christian faith received? From whence does it stem? Two answers are commonly given. In a sense both are true, but not in the popular sense that one is commonly articulated. 1) Some lift two texts out of context and through an eisegetical exercise teach that "faith is the gift of God" in the sense that God by his sovereign will elects some to be saved, some to be damned, and to such as he elects to be saved he gives the gift of faith, *saving faith.* Others may believe the same testimony, but without an assuring subjective experience theirs is not a saving faith but rather "a working of error" (likewise sent from God, II Thess. 2:11). The two "proof texts" alluded to are Ephesians 2:8; I Corinthians 12:9.

A text taken out of context is a pretext. This is readily demonstrated in the case of I Corinthians 12:9. Beginning with v. 8 the passage reads:

> For to one is given through the Spirit the word of wisdom: and to another the word of knowledge, according to the same Spirit; (9) *to another faith,* in the same Spirit: and to another gifts (pl.) of healings (pl.), in the one Spirit.

V. 10 continues to list five other specialized gifts of the Spirit said to be given to one or to another (not all) in the church, including miracles, tongues, and interpretation of tongues. V. 11 then explains: "But these all worketh the one and the same Spirit dividing to each one severally even as he will." In the verses which follow, Paul points out how ludicrous it would be if all members of the body of Christ were given the same endowment. For example, suppose all the body were an eye, ear, or nose, or tongue. There would be no body but rather one overgrown organ. He concludes by saying:

> Now ye are the body of Christ, and severally members thereof. And God hath set *some* in the church, first apostles, secondly prophets, thirdly teachers, and then miracles, then gifts of healings, helps, governments, (divers) kinds of tongues. Are all apostles? are all prophets? are all teachers? etc. (vs. 27-30).

206

When the three catalogues of the specialized gifts are compared: 1) vs. 8-10, 2) v. 28, 3) vs. 29, 30, it is evident that the term is used in a restrictive sense, and compares to the teaching office through which faith is disseminated (cp. Rom. 10:17). To conclude otherwise is to be forced to conclude that there was but *one* (see v. 9), or at the most but a few "members of the body" in the Corinthian church that had faith; the others (though unbelieving!) had such gifts as the apostolic, prophetical and teaching offices, and other such goodies as the power to work miracles, perform various healings, and speak with tongues. How ridiculous can one get? Likely this exercise in absurdity would never have been entered upon were there not sought a "second witness" to support a mistaken interpretation of Ephesians 2:8.

Ephesians 2:8, as it is translated into our language, could be construed to support the "*gift* of faith to the *elect*" dogma. But the grammatical construction in the Greek cannot be so construed. The key to the interpretation is to identify the antecedent of the demonstrative pronoun, *that*. The verse as commonly translated reads: "for by grace are ye saved through faith: and that not of yourselves; *it is* the gift of God" (KJV). Paraphrased, the text might more properly be rendered: "By grace are ye saved, and *that* salvation is not of yourselves, by God's grace it is a gift, *through* faith."

The demonstrative pronoun, *that*, cannot refer to faith, as though faith is the gift spoken of. *Touto* (that) is a *neuter* pronoun, not feminine. But faith is a *feminine* noun. It is a fundamental rule of grammar that a pronoun (a word which stands *for a noun*) agrees with its noun antecedent in number and gender.

By way of illustration, take note of what is wrong with this sentence, clipped from a news item: "Three men miraculously escaped death as the car crashed through the guardrail into Devil's Canyon, but she was killed instantly." The seeming grammatical blunder disappears when the sentence is read in context. The antecedent of the pronoun is found in the statement which preceded the quoted portion of the news item: "A woman (name withheld) was the driver of the vehicle which went out of control in last night's sleet storm."

When the rules of grammar are ignored and creedal dogma is read into a text, ignoring both the immediate context and all that is communicated in the Scriptures elsewhere, a "proof text" becomes but a pretext.

d. *Elements of faith.* We have defined faith as the belief of testimony. While such a definition arises naturally from such texts as Romans 10:17

207

and kindred Scriptures, faith involves more than simple belief, or acceptance of testimony. It includes also trust and reliance. This is illustrated
by the classic story of the stunt man who walked a tightrope strung
across Niagara Falls, pushing a loaded wheelbarrow. When the cheer-
ing of the crowds subsided enough that his voice could be heard, he
asked if anyone believed he could wheel a man back across to the
other side. Many expressed the belief that he could. But not one was
willing to trust himself to him, relying on his skill to do with one of
them what he did with a wheelbarrow load of bricks.

Faith also includes an element of affection, and desire. Many a
parent or mate or friend has stood by one accused of crime despite
extensive incriminating evidence of guilt. Their affection, their heart's
desire, moves them to believe the attestation of innocence on the part
of the accused. The renowned evangelist, R. A. Torrey, told of an
attorney who consented to attend church with his wife one Sunday
morning (on the day commonly called Easter). The preacher earnestly
proclaimed the resurrection Gospel. At the door the attorney remarked,
"You spoke as though you really believe that this Jesus whom you
worshipped was raised from the dead." The preacher replied, "I am
glad I came across that way for I really do." The attorney then introduced himself as to name and profession and added, "As an attorney,
I must have evidence for what I believe." The preacher proceeded to
explain that he too had received a degree from a reputable law school,
but had given up the legal profession for the higher law, the law of God,
and asked: "If I would prepare for you a brief on the resurrection such
as would be used to present a case in court, would you read it?" The
attorney agreed to do so, whereupon the preacher presented in legal
style the case for the resurrection, using Greenfield's ten principles
designed to test the credibility of witnesses.[1] When the attorney had

---

1. The ten principles alluded to are as follows:
    1) The number of witnesses (2 or more)
    2) Agreement of the testimony
    3) Integrity, honesty of the witnesses
    4) Those before whom the testimony was first given
    5) The place where the testimony was first given
    6) The time when the testimony was first given
    7) Was the testimony given under stress
    8) The motives of the witnesses
    9) The earnestness of the witnesses
    10) The immediate results of the testimony

completed his study of the document he stated that on the basis of the evidence presented, he was now convinced that Jesus was raised from the dead. "At least," said he, "the testimony would stand up in court, and apparently did in the time of the apostles." But he went on to state that he was not ready to become a Christian, explaining that previously he thought his problem was with his head (intellect) but now he recognized it was with his heart (his pride, and emotions). Well has it been written: "Take heed, lest haply there be in any one of you an evil heart of unbelief" (Heb. 3:12).

In addition to the foregoing elements, 1) belief, acceptance of testimony; 2) trust, reliance; 3) desire, affection; 4) expression, action is included in the makeup of faith. James summarizes two illustrations by stating succinctly:

> Ye see that by works a man is justified, and not only by faith . . . For as the body apart from the spirit is dead, even so faith apart from works is dead (James 2:24, 26).

The "Naughty" History of One Little Word—Not

Once Satan finds something that works for him he makes the most of it. Such is the "naughty" history of one little word—*not*. Consider:

1. Of the tree of knowledge of good and evil, God said: a) "Thou shalt *not* eat of it, for b) in the day you eat thereof you shall surely die," (Gen. 2:18). But Satan had a better idea, or so he convinced Eve. Satan said: a) Thou shalt *not* surely die! b) Actually you ought to eat of it, you will be as wise as God (Gen. 3:4, 5). Who told the truth?

2. Jesus said: "He that 1) believeth and 2) is baptized shall be saved" (Mark 16:16). Thus James wrote: "Ye see that a man is *not* justified by faith alone . . . for as the body apart from the spirit is dead, so faith apart from works is dead" (James 2:24, 26).

What are we being told today concerning this? Is this not the most popular preachment of our time: "He that is *not* baptized, who only believeth, shall be saved." "For you see, a man *is* justified by faith only."

e. *The object of Christian faith.* While faith comes by hearing and hearing by the Word of Christ and God, it needs to be kept in mind the purpose of the written word of God is to lead us to faith in the living Word of God—Christ. John stated the purpose of the Gospel he wrote, as follows:

> Many other signs did Jesus in the presence of his disciples which are not written in this book, but these are written *that* you may believe *that* Jesus

is the Christ, the Son of God, and *that* believing, you may have life in his name (John 20:30, 31).

Not What, But Whom

Not what, but whom I do believe
That in my hour of deepest need
Has help that no mortal man
Nor mortal creed can give.
Not what, but whom, for
Christ is more than all the creeds
And his pure life of noble deeds
Shall all the creeds outlive.

Not what I do believe, but whom—
Who walks beside me in the gloom
Who bears the burdens wearisome
Who all the dim ways doth illume
And bids me look beyond the tomb
The fuller life to live.
Not what, but whom.

— *John Oxenham*

"I know him whom I have believed, and I am persuaded that he is able to guard that which I have committed unto him against that day" (Paul in II Tim. 2:12).

PREVIEW—REVIEW QUESTIONS

1. Locate a text which specifically states the manner in which one arrives at the point of faith, particularly Christian faith.
2. Locate a text which indicates that principle was at work on the day of Pentecost, and at other crucial moments in the dissemination of the Christian faith.
3. State a synonym for hearing which underscores the sense in which hearing is linked to saving faith.
4. State the gist of one of the propositions with which Alexander Campbell challenged the Calvinist, N. L. Rice.
5. Do you know of anyone who arrived at faith in Christ without having first heard or read the Word of God?
6. State a practical definition of faith.
7. Distinguish between faith and knowledge.
8. Distinguish between faith and credulity.
9. Cite a text which commends a cautious hearing and acceptance of testimony.

10. State the twofold function of faith.
11. State the source from which Christian faith is derived.
12. State the Calvinist doctrine of how one comes to believe.
13. Note the context of I Corinthians 12:9 as it relates to the Calvinist dogma.
14. Note the sense in which Ephesians 2:8 is to be understood.
15. State and apply a basic rule of grammar that is essential to understanding Ephesians 2:8 once it is confused with creedal eisegesis.
16. Besides the primary element of faith, belief, list three others.
17. Identify a common three-letter English word that has been shifted about to serve the cause of Satan, the deceiver, from the beginning until now.
18. Identify the object of our faith, as Christians, and cite a significant text to that effect.

15

MAN'S RESPONSE INTENSIFIED: REPENTANCE, CONFESSION OF FAITH

Akin to the question as to which came first, the chicken or the egg, is the question as to whether faith precedes repentance or repentance precedes faith. The two texts which speak of both in the same phrase place repentance before faith. Mark 1:14 reports that after John was delivered up, Jesus came into Galilee preaching the Gospel of God, saying: "Repent ye, and believe in the gospel." In Acts 20:20, 21, Paul, in his farewell to the elders of the church at Ephesus, reminded them that he had taught them publicly and from house to house, "testifying to both Jews and Greeks, repentance toward God and faith toward our Lord Jesus Christ. (Cp. Heb. 6:1.)

The question as to which precedes the other, or the possibility that they are reciprocal, is primarily an academic question unless one has a doctrinal axe to grind. And some do. The two texts cited are particularly useful to those who are persuaded that one is saved "the moment one first believes," but who are not quite ready to reject repentance as well as baptism as essential "for the remission of sins" (see Acts 2:38). By positing repentance prior to faith the doctrine of instant and eternally secure salvation by faith alone is enhanced. As intimated, the doctrine of salvation by faith alone and the doctrine of eternal security are interdependent. If there is nothing that one needs to do, except believe, in order to be saved, there is nothing one needs to do to *stay* saved, else that would be something one needs to do besides believe.

Acts 2:36-41 (along with other case histories of the conversion process reported in Acts) poses a problem to those who insist on placing repentance before faith to accommodate the dogma of instant eternally-secure salvation the moment one first believes. It would be quite difficult to argue that the guilt-stricken crowd on Pentecost had not yet come to believe the Gospel preached by Peter, even though it is said: "Now when they heard this (the Gospel preached), they were pricked in their heart and said unto Peter and the rest of the apostles, men and brethren, what shall we do?" (Acts 2:37). Note Peter did not tell them to "repent and believe the gospel." He told them to repent and be baptized. If they had to repent before they could believe, did they have to repent and also be baptized before they could believe? Was the format instituted on Pentecost under the supervision of the Holy Spirit: 1) hear the Gospel, 2) repent, 3) believe, 4) receive the remission of sins, 5) be baptized as a witness to your salvation? Or was the format: 1) hear the Gospel, 2) believe it so deeply you are pricked in your heart, 3) repent and 4) be baptized for the remission of sins, and 5) receive the gift of the Holy Spirit?

Which precedes the other, faith or repentance? The two are inseparably linked together in the process of conversion. One is scarcely going to "repent towards God" if one does not even believe in God. The more fully one believes in the preachments of the Christian Gospel, particularly the first major premise thereof, that "Christ died for our sins," the more readily and the more fully one is likely to repent. And conversely, until one makes the "change of mind" of repentance, one can scarcely make a commitment of faith and loyalty to Jesus.

3. Repentance

a. *Repentance defined.* Our English words repent and repentance are carry-overs from the Latin Vulgate, via the KJV. It is unfortunate that such is the case. This is particularly so with the principal Greek word so translated. The Latin word from which our word repent is derived is *repoenitere*. It means "to repine," that is, "to grieve, to be sorry." The idea communicated is that of an emotional state in the context of sadness, regret.

214

As a translation of the Hebrew *nacham* it is not too bad a choice. *Nacham*, like the Latin word from which our words repent and repentance stem, refers to an emotional state. There is a Greek word used in our New Testament that means much the same thing, *metamelomai*. That word is derived from *meta* (change) and *melomai* (feeling). *Metamelomai* is used five times in the New Testament (Matt. 21:29, 32; 27:3; II Cor. 7:8; Heb. 7:21). It is not to be confused with *metanoeo* and *metanoia*. (The latter verb is used 34 times and the noun 24 times, and it is these 58 usages which are especially germaine to the subject under consideration.) *Metanoeo* is derived from *meta* (change) and *noeo* (mind) hence refers to a change of mind. (See Heb. 12:17 where it is actually, literally translated—ASV, NIV.)

The distinction between *metanoeo* and *metamelomai* (and the Hebrew counterpart of the latter, *nacham*) is helpful in understanding the Old Testament references in which God is said to repent. See Gen. 6:6, 7; Exod. 32:12-14; Judg. 2:18; I Sam. 15:11; II Sam. 24:16; Jonah 3:9, 10. Such passages are difficult to understand when equated with the Greek word *metanoeo*. Did God actually second-guess himself with regard to the creation of man? Did he also have a change of mind about several other things?

The Hebrew word *nacham* is to be equated with the Greek word *metamelomai*. *Nacham* speaks of God's sorrow over man's sin. Man's sin did not catch God by surprise, as though it were something he never anticipated. Parents are hardly taken by surprise when their children do not live up to their hopes for them, or even their rightful expectations. But the foreknowledge of what might happen, whether of sin, disease, or accident, does not ease the sorrow when such occurs.

Metanoeo is quite a different word. This has to do primarily with a mental state. It refers to a rational response to a bad situation whereas *metamelomai* relates to an emotional response.

It is unfortunate that translators of our common English versions of the New Testament have seen fit to translate *metanoeo* in plain English only once. In Hebrews 12:17 it is said of Esau that "he found no place for a change of mind in his father, though he sought it with bitter tears." The idea communicated is that Isaac's mind was made up, and he was not about to allow Esau's tears to change it. When Esau despised his birthright, exchanging it for a mess of pottage, Isaac determined that Esau would be obliged to live with his crass decision.

It is when we really make up our minds to do something that we do it. Our emotions may be involved, and often are. But our emotions fluctuate. What we do by way of an emotional response does not and should not chart our course. Such is the lesson to be learned from Esau.

Metanoeo is the word which confronts us in such texts as Matthew 3:2; 4:17; Mark 1:15; Luke 13:3, 5; Acts 2:28; 3:19; 8:22; 17:30; 26:20; Rev. 2:5, 16, 21, 22; 3:3, 19; 9:20, 21; 16:9, 11.

b. *Misconceptions of Repentance.* Because of the failure of translators to distinguish between *metanoeo* and *metamelomai,* translating both words, along with the Hebrew word *nacham,* by a derivative of the Latin word for repine, the first of several misconceptions of repentance has come to be established in the popular mind.

1) Many mistake sorrow for repentance. Were that all that is involved, everyone would at some time "come to repentance." Sooner or later, one's sins will either "find him out" (Num. 32:23) or cause others to "find him out," or otherwise bring one to grief or pain. But you cannot measure repentance by catching one's tears in a measuring cup. Many weep (repine) who never repent. And since they do not change their mind, they do not materially change their ways.

This is not to say that sorrow (*metamelomai,* repining) has no part in repentance. II Corinthians 7:8-10 has somewhat to say about this. Paul uses both *metamelomai* and *metanoeo* in this instructive passage. Writing with reference to the reaction of the Corinthians to his first (rebuking) letter he says:

> For though I made you sorry (Gr. *elupesa,* lit., "I grieved you") I do not *repent* (Gr. *metamelomai,* lit., "regret"), though I did *repent* (Gr. *metemelomen*), [Apparently Paul's first response to their emotional response to this letter was an emotional response to their reaction. He goes on to explain.] for I see that that epistle made you sorry (Gr. *elupesen,* "grieved" you) but for a time. I now rejoice, not that you were made sorry (Gr. *elupethete,* "grieved") but that you were made sorry (Gr. *elupethete* unto *repentance* (Gr. *metanoian,* "a change of mind"), for you were made sorry (Gr. *elupethete,* "grieved") after a godly sort. For godly sorrow (Gr. *lupe,* "grief") worketh repentance (Gr. *metanoian,* "change of mind") unto salvation, but the sorrow (Gr. *lupe* "grief") of the world worketh death.

From the foregoing passage which makes a play on the two words commonly translated repent, repentance, we are able to see the distinction between them. Sorrow, of itself, not even grief, is to be equated with repentance. Repentance calls for a change of mind which brings about a change of life.

2) Fear, especially fear of death, is often mistaken for repentance. This is the heart of the so-called "deathbed repentance" syndrome.

In one of my early ministries an old-fashioned doctor was a member of the congregation. When he reckoned patients might be dying, he frankly told them so (if they were old enough to handle it) on the premise there might be some things they would want to take care of if they knew they might not be long for this world. Many made a profession of repentance, especially "repentance toward God and faith toward our Lord Jesus Christ" (Acts 20:21). By the time I arrived on the scene one hundred cases of "deathbed repentance" had been witnessed by him, in which the patient (often to the doctor's surprise) rallied and "arose to walk in newness (?) of life." However, only three out of the one hundred kept their deathbed repentance (?) vows.

(3) There are many who would substitute penance for repentance. But this is not an innovation of the apostate church. The Pharisees did the same. But one cannot please God by afflicting the body for the sins of the soul. Were ashes on the forehead, or giving up watermelon for lent, or other vain acts of penance a true expression of a change of mind toward God, the Pharisees of Jesus' day along with the hapless heathen would outdo any of us. Of the Pharisees who disfigured their visage and stood on street corners in sackcloth looking sad Jesus had only words of scorn and ridicule. He called them hypocrites. John called them something worse. "You offspring of vipers," John said, "bring forth works worthy of repentance" (Matt. 3:7).

4) Reformation is often confused with repentance. The renowned evangelist, Sam Jones, defined repentance thusly in his famous sermon entitled "Quit Your Meanness." That should result from changing one's mind. That is the kind of evidence John the immerser was asking of the Pharisees, but of itself that is not repentance.

One of my professors related the case of a man with a compelling taste for strong drink who promised a young woman he would quit drinking if she would marry him. She wisely put him on probation, so to speak, to test his sincerity and the strength of his resolve. After two years of testing, she consented to be his bride, and "until death did them part" he kept his bargain, and without complaint. But following her death after nearly twenty years of marriage, he took to drinking again. Why did he quit in the first place? He did so to please her. He had not repented toward God.

The trouble with reformation is that it can never go far enough to bring us to that state of justification whereunto one may be saved. It is society or self-oriented. It is not unto God. Breaking the worst of our bad habits is like breaking a few bad limbs off of a diseased tree when the axe needs to be laid at the root of the tree (Matt. 3:10). A ship with seven holes in the hull will sink even if all but the least of them is plugged. It is not enough to turn over a new leaf. We need to turn up with a new life. Only by the transforming power of the Gospel appropriated through the obedience of faith can that be done.

Let us face the fact. Sin is against God. When Joseph was tempted by Potiphar's wife, his response was not: "How can I do this and sin against your husband who trusts me?" or "against my parents who raised me to know better?" or "against a vow of chastity I have taken?" He asked rather, "How can I do this great wickedness and sin against God?" There was one who would know even if they fooled all else— God.

5) There is still at least one other misconception that needs attention. Contrary to what we are told repeatedly, the word repent does not mean "to turn." Who has not heard the story of the scholarly preacher who was preaching on repentance and so clouding the issue with his much learning that an eccentric old man sitting in about the second row could stand no more. As the story goes, the old codger arose and headed for the door shouting "I'm going to hell!" Half way out the door he is said to have turned and come running back down the aisle shouting "I'm going to heaven! I'm going to heaven!" Upon reaching the front of the auditorium he is said to have then faced the audience and said, "That's repentance." The evangelist from whom I first heard the story added: "And that old man preached a better sermon on repentance than the scholarly preacher in his clerical robe had preached from the pulpit." I was so impressed I used the story several times. But that is before I indulged in that ofttimes reviled activity called research. Honestly, I thought the evangelist had checked it.

Perhaps the accompanying diagram may make the truth of the matter as plain as ABC. If a sinner is running away from God, and sinners certainly are (see point A of diagram), and if repent means to turn around and come running back to God (see point B of diagram), then what shall we make of Acts 3:19 where Peter commands: "*Repent* (turn around?) and *convert*" (Gr. epistrepho, "turn again")?

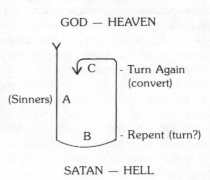

GOD — HEAVEN

(Sinners)

C - Turn Again (convert)

A

B - Repent (turn?)

SATAN — HELL

(See point C of diagram.) Cp. discussion concerning conversion, Lesson 12.

When one is traveling down the wrong road, he must first be convinced he is doing just that, and change his mind about the propriety of going on before he will *convert* (turn around) and head in the other direction. The old saying, "One good turn deserves another" is not always true. Two 180° turns are "too much of a good thing." To repent (if that is to turn) and convert (which certainly is to turn) is to "turn again" (Gr. *epistrophos*). Those who do so are like the dog and hog to which Peter likens those who "*turn* back (Gr. *hupostrepsai*) from the holy commandment given them," II Peter 2:21, 22.

c. *Who may, and who must repent?* According to II Peter 3:9 God is not willing that any should perish but that all should come to repentance. That hardly conforms to predestinarian doctrine which limits salvation to those whom God arbitrarily elected from the foundation of the world. Not only is God willing that all should come unto repentance, they are commanded to do so. The words of Jesus in Luke 13:3-5 are specific. Acts 2:38, 3:19 have already been cited. Paul's words on Mars Hill, addressed to a Gentile audience, are much to the point: God has now commanded all men everywhere to repent, and has appointed a day in which he will judge the world in righteousness by the the one he has ordained; Christ, whom he raised from the dead (Acts 17:30-31).

4. *The Confession of Faith*

The inclusion of a verbal confession of faith in Jesus as "the Christ, the son of the living God," in the process which brings one into a saving relationship with Christ is more supported by implication than by explicit command. Matthew 10:32, 33 is commonly cited as a supporting text. However, Jesus did not express those words in the context of an initial confession of faith as a prelude to baptism and enrollment in the church. Confessing Christ before men, as opposed to denying him, has a much wider range of application than responding to an evangelistic appeal at the close of a preaching service. There are many other ways in which one can confess Christ before men, or deny him, besides repeating the words of Peter's confession at Caesarea Philippi (in response to a hymn of invitation), or electing not to do so in that setting.

It also needs to be noted that the one recorded instance of one making such a confession of faith as an immediate prelude to baptism (see Acts 8:37, KJV) is omitted by many ancient MSS of the Greek New Testament. It is included, however, in the Western Text favored by some evangelical scholars.

Whether the text in question was lacking in the original text of Acts, or was inadvertently omitted by some later transcriber, the confession is comfortable to what the eunuch might very well have been expected to reply in response to Philip's response to the eunuch's request to be baptized. If Philip could find occasion in his exposition of Isaiah 53 to make the need for baptism so explicit, he certainly would not have found it difficult to so instruct his hearer concerning the person of Christ as to elicit from him a confession conformable to the one Peter made at Caesarea Philippi.

a. *Confession defined.* Our English words confess and confession are derived from the prefix *con* (with) and the Latin verb *fateri* (speak), particuarly by way of admission of guilt or acknowledgment of faith. Hence it means to "admit with," that is to speak in accord with one's accusers (or one's instructors).

In our New Testament the word confess is commonly used to translate the Greek word *homologeo,* derived from the prefix *homo* (same) and the verb *logeo* (to speak). Hence it means "to speak the same."

The basic idea that is common to all three languages, Latin, Greek, and our own, is that of voicing agreement; not just agreeing with someone but expressing that agreement vocally. In our common usage of the term confession we follow closely the idea enshrined in the Latin word from which our words confess and confession are coined. To confess is to admit to something, generally guilt or fault.

In our religious usage of the word we follow the lead of both the Latin and the Greek. 1) The admission of guilt or fault is called confession, and 2) the voicing of agreement with what we have been taught (the speaking forth of our faith in the same) is also called confession. In the confession of fault we agree with our accusers; in the confession of faith we agree with our instructors.

As concerns the first we are told in I John 1:9 that

> If we say we have no sin we make him (God, who says we do) a liar, and
> the truth is not in us. But if we confess our sins he is faithful and righteous
> to forgive us our sins and to cleanse us from all unrighteousness.

In Acts 19:18 it is said of those to whom Paul preached at Ephesus: "And not a few of them came, confessing and declaring their deeds."

As concerns the second, Paul states in Romans 10:9, 10

If thou shalt confess with thy mouth Jesus Christ as Lord and shalt believe in thy heart God raised him from the dead, thou shalt be saved, for with the heart man believeth unto righteousness and with the mouth confession is made unto salvation.

It is the latter usage of the word that is the focal point of our study at this time. This is not to minimize the need of confessing our sins. It is thereby we acknowledge our need of a Saviour, or acknowledge him openly.

The Scriptures witness to certain facts concerning the person of Christ. (See I Cor. 15:1-4 for a summary.) To that witness our hearts must give assent. If there is no agreeing state of mind or answering response arising from our hearts, what we may say with our lips will be to no avail. But if we believe in our hearts the witness of the Scriptures, we will make confession of the same (with the mouth) unto salvation; unless, of course, we have been programmed by modern mass evangelism techniques and faith only tracts to do differently.

To acknowledge anything less about ourselves and about the person and work of Christ than what the Scriptures teach is not confession in the Biblical sense of the term. We must speak the same thing! We are sinners. Christ is Lord and only Saviour.

In our courts criminals known to be guilty of gross crime are often allowed to confess to a lesser crime of which they are also guilty, to speed the trial process. In so doing they receive a much less severe sentence. The justice of God will not be so mocked. At the great white throne judgment, the record books shall be opened, and both the great and the small shall be judged according to their works, as recorded by the angels of him who knows even the thoughts and intents of our hearts (Rev. 20:12, 13; Heb. 4:12, 13). Only through the advocacy of Christ may we escape the wrath to come.

Likewise in the realm of faith, to confess that Jesus was a good man, a master teacher, a martyr to his high principles, is not the same thing as that to which the Scriptures bear witness. To say that he was "a son of God" or "the first and highest of God's creatures" or aught else short of the New Testament witness is not a confession of faith that is the same thing to which we are called to believe.

b. *The origin and authority for the confession of faith.* Matthew 16:13-18 is a crucial text in the light of what we have just noted. At the approach to the city of Caesarea Philippi Jesus inquired of his disciples concerning the prevailing estimate as to who he was. This was not done because he was not aware of public opinion, but rather to

221

elicit from his disciples their estimate of him. The prevailing estimate of the populace was readily stated. Of interest is the fact no one apparently regarded him as aught less than a reincarnation of one of the prophets of old, or the lately martyred John the baptizer. At the point of his question: "But who do you say that I am?" Peter answered: "Thou art the Christ, the Son of the Living God." Jesus' response to that was that what Peter stated was in voiced agreement with what God himself had revealed concerning him.

While it was Peter who made the confession that day, he did not make it up! God had revealed the same in many ways. 1) God did so at Christ's baptism (Matt. 3:17). 2) He did so through John the baptizer (John 1:29). 3) He did so at the transfiguration (Matt. 17:5, cp. Deut. 18:15-19). 4) He did so through the visitation upon him of the Holy Spirit through which he was empowered to perform credential-izing signs. (See Luke 4:14, 15; 7:18-22; John 5:30-47.)

c. *The content, substance of the confession of faith.* The confession of Peter (and Martha, John 11:27) embodied two essentials: Jesus' Divine sonship and messiahship. John in stating the purpose for which he wrote the fourth Gospel states:

> Many other signs did Jesus in the presence of his disciples which are not written in this book, but these are written that you may believe that Jesus is the Christ the son of God, and that believing you may have life in his name (John 20:30, 31).

Peter's Confession of Faith:
Its all inclusiveness — Its all exclusiveness

10. GOD — atheists, agnostics excluded
9. LIVING — pantheists, idolaters excluded
8. THE — polytheists, animists excluded
7. of (preposition, shows relationship)
6. SON — unitarians, liberals excluded
5. THE — JW's, Mormons, liberal theologians excluded
4. CHRIST — Moslems, pagans, unbelieving Jews excluded
3. THE — JW's, Mormons, liberal theologians excluded
2. ART — present active tense of the verb of being
1. THOU — the form of direct address

Who can make the above confession? Only those who can look to Christ and say what Peter said: "*You* (Christ) *are* (yesterday, today, yea and forever), *the* (one only), *Christ* (the Messiah, God's anointed

222

one), *the* (one and only begotten of the Father) *Son, of* (in a sense no other is, ever was or can be) *living* ("Who only hath immortality!"), *God* (creator, ruler, blessed potentate, who was before all things, in whom all things consist).

   d. *Nature (form) of the confession of faith.* Having noted the essential content of the confession of faith which Christ commended with a statement of benediction upon the confessor, note the form and nature of the confession. 1) It is a prescribed confession. Such is the inherent meaning of the very word so translated, *homologian.* We are to speak the same thing concerning Jesus that God declared to be true concerning him, as epitomized in the words Christ saw fit to especially commend. 2) It is an oral declaration. It is to be made with our mouths, expressing a faith that wells up in our hearts (Rom. 10:9, 10). Sneaking one's hand up while everyone's eyes are closed, save the manipulating evangelist who teaches men so, is hardly a confession of faith. 3) It is a public confession, "before men" (Matt. 10:32, 33). Paul admonished Timothy, saying, "Fight the good fight of the faith, lay hold on life eternal, whereunto thou wast called and didst confess the good confession in the sight of many witnesses" (I Tim. 6:12, 13). Were Timothy converted in a modern revival setting, Paul could not have said that. The great crowd of potential witnesses would have been instructed to close their eyes while Timothy slipped up his hand to ask the evangelist to pray for him. Thus committed, he may have been then asked to do several semi-public things, none of which are mentioned in the Scriptures but done rather in lieu of the things which are. If persuaded in a less feverish context, his confession may have consisted in signing a prepared statement in the back of a tract.

   As concerns "the other side of the street," I find myself becoming increasingly skeptical of the now nigh universal practice which prevails in the churches of Christ and Christian churches confession (?) ritual. Why should even mature, articulate, prior-taught men and women be restricted in their public testimony to the "little sir echo" exercise whereby they are permitted only to parrot a phrase at a time what the one who "takes their confession" says? Words are vehicles of thought. If a person in the midst of a highly supportive congregation cannot find the words or the courage to confess what he believes about Christ, what can we expect of such a one at work or school the next day?

   Here is an actual account, the tale of two persons. The first, a Bible college teacher of long experience, whose favorite course is the life of Christ. Having accepted the invitation of a struggling congregation to come and help them he steps forward as the invitation hymn is being sung and is asked to repeat, a phrase at a time, the words of Peter's confession. How ludicrous! Across town a child of about ten years of age steps forward during the invitation. An elder takes her by the hand, and looking intently into her eyes, and she into his; he said, "Tell me, who do you believe Jesus is?" Her quick answer was, "Jesus is the son of God!" The words were spoken in a tone that seemed to say, "Anybody ought to know that." That sure she was about who Jesus is. The elder then asked her, "What does Jesus mean to you personally? Why have you come here just now?" Her answer, "I want to be a Christian, and have him save me," and then with a voice that quivered a bit with emotion, she said, "He's the only one that can save anyone." I was that elder. I was satisfied. Her words were not precisely the same as the words of Peter. She did not say: "*su ei ho christos ho huios tou theou tou zontos*" (or however the same would have been spoken in Aramaic, which it probably was), but she "homolegoed" (if I may modify a word to fit our form of expression). She "spoke the same" truths concerning Jesus that Peter did. And best of all, she confessed with her mouth what she believed in her heart. May her kind increase.

e. *Finally, consider the subjects.* That is, consider those who are under solemn obligation to "confess the good confession in the sight of many witnesses." This may surprise some, but both the obligation and the performance extends to 1) all who would be saved (Rom. 10:9, 10), and 2) all who "would be lost" (Phil. 2:9-11; Rom. 14:11). Let us consider the latter first. Jesus once said to the hostile Jews, "You *will* not come to me that you may have life" (John 5:40). Looking down from the Mount of Olives, he lamented, "O Jerusalem, Jerusalem . . . how often *would I* have gathered thy children together, even as a hen gathereth her chickens under her wings, but *you would not*" (Matt. 23:37, 38). But there is coming a day when those who have denied him will be compelled to confess him as Lord to the glory of the Father before the whole assembled universe (Phil. 2:9-11 and Rom. 14:11 so state).

We commonly think of the confession of the lordship and sonship of Christ as a voluntary matter, something we may elect either to do or not to do. In this life that is so. But on the great day of God Almighty's great white throne judgment, it will be done on a non-elective basis, and it will be done to the glory of God, and the vindication of his own dear Son who might have been the saviour of all. But it will no longer be "unto salvation." It is a sobering thing to consider that those whom we neglect to evangelize, and those who reject all efforts directed toward their evangelization, will one day be brought face to face with the ultimate reality concerning who Jesus is, and with future life and judgment. Well it has been written:

> We are ambassadors therefore on behalf of Christ, as though God were entreating by us: we beseech you on behalf of Christ, be ye reconciled to God. Him who knew no sin he made to be sin on our behalf that we might become the righteousness of God in him. And working together with him we entreat also that you receive not the grace of God in vain: for he saith:
>
> > At an acceptable time I hearkened unto you,
> > And in a day of salvation did I succor
> > (come to the help of) you;
>
> Behold, now is the acceptable time; behold, now is the day of salvation (II Cor. 5:20—6:2).

PREVIEW—REVIEW QUESTIONS

Repentance

1. Which comes first, repentance or faith? Or are they reciprocal? Explain.
2. State the literal meaning of the primary Greek word that is commonly translated repent. Is it ever translated literally? If so, where?
3. Identify another Greek word translated repent(ance). Distinguish between the two words as to actual meaning.
4. How does the Hebrew word translated "repent" compare with the two Greek words so translated?
5. How does such knowledge help to explain Old Testament texts in which God is said to have "repented"?
6. List the four most common misconceptions of repentance.
7. Evaluate, negate any one of them.
8. Identify the text which underscores the fact that the Biblical word for repent does not mean to turn. Diagram it.
9. Who is privileged to repent? Cite a supporting text.
10. Who will repent? Cite a supporting text.

Confession

1. State the literal definition of the Greek word translated confess(ion).
2. What is the derivation of our English word confess? What do the two have in common?

3. State the two things we most commonly associate with confession.
4. How does the fundamental meaning of the term apply in each case?
5. When is a "confession" not really a confession? Apply to the context of this discussion.
6. Take note of the origin and authority for the confession that is basic to the Christian faith. Identify the text.
7. Document the fact that while Peter made the confession that Jesus commended, he did not make it up.
8. State the two basic truths affirmed in Peter's confession.
9. State some facts concerning the form a confession of faith should take, according to New Testament teaching.
10. Evaluate the routine practices which have become an almost unvarying ritual: a) in modern revivalism b) in churches professing to have restored New Testament practice.
11. Who will confess Jesus Christ as Lord? Cite some pertinent texts.
12. How should such knowledge affect us evangelistically?

16

MAN'S RESPONSE DRAMATIZED: CHRISTIAN BAPTISM

Few subjects related to the Christian faith are as steeped in controversy as the subject of baptism. Every facet of the subject draws disputation from some quarter; so much so that it has become a topic virtually taboo in preachment or practice in almost every kind of inter-church cooperative effort or fellowship.

Charles G. Finney, renowned nineteenth century evangelist, correctly noted more than a century ago that:

> In the days of the apostles . . . the Gospel was preached and those who were willing to be on the Lord's side were called upon to be baptized. It (baptism) held the precise place that the anxious seat (or mourner's bench) does now, as a public manifestation of their determination to be Christians (Finney, *Revivals of Religion*, p. 254).

Mr. Finney who, probably more than any other man of his time, popularized the substitution, went on to explain why he and others among his contemporaries were (quote) "obliged to adopt some substitute" (note the language). The reason cited was pragmatic, *viz*, "otherwise they could not get along in promoting a revival." Baptism had become that controversial. It still is, in fact more so, today. For in our time, those who have adopted the substitute have gone on the offensive and commonly disparage baptism, if performed with a view to salvation. And despite the feverish activity which often goes along with the substitute for baptism, they profess to believe that salvation is attained through faith alone.

Have you ever wondered how a vast sector of the Bible-thumping segment of Christendom could be persuaded to accept a substitute for something they well know that Christ personally commanded as a part of the Great Commission? The answer is simple. Charles G. Finney, in his Oberlin College lectures (preserved in the aforementioned book), stated it as simply as words can express anything. Conducting a successful revival was assigned priority. Obedience to Christ, fidelity to the apostolic practice—those considerations were reckoned as dispensable. In evangelism numbers is the "name of the game."

By the artful device of instituting a substitute, ostensibly as but a temporary expedient rather than an outright and permanent substitute for a Divine ordinance, the innovation was made to appear as but a practical delaying tactic. Thereby the various denominations can attend the Divinely appointed matter "each in his own way," (simple baptism, face-forward triune baptism of the upper torso, pouring, sprinkling), and each for whatever purpose they might assign to the rite of baptism.

The foregoing bit of history serves to point up the fact that Christian baptism is a highly controversial subject. We will do well to consider carefully what we say. We will do even better if we will consider carefully what the Scriptures say. Fortunately (or unfortunately, depending on whether one expects a quick and easy answer to questions over which Christendom has been long divided), the Scriptures have much to say on the subject. Over one hundred references, in fact 122 different texts, employ some form of the Greek word *bapto*, from which such words as baptize and baptism are derived.

In order to set forth in capsule form all the reference data essential to a comprehensive view of the subject, we have appended to this lesson a special study aid entitled: "Concerning Baptism(s), Baptizing: Textual Data." All 122 texts that use the root *bapto*, or a derivative thereof, are listed categorically; with a minimum of interpretative comment. If the reader will take the time (and it does take time) to read each text in its context, a comprehensive view of the whole subject of baptism as set forth in the New Testament may be obtained in the process. In view of the extensive controversy which surrounds this subject, anyone professing to be informed on the subject owes it to himself and to those he may attempt to instruct to examine each and every reference listed on the data sheet. Those who do so will be somewhat amazed that so much controversy surrounds a topic so extensively and clearly set forth in the Scriptures.

By way of summary of the textual data: 1) The simple verb root, *bapto*, is used 3 times in the New Testament: Luke 16:24; John 13:26; Rev. 19:13. Since the usage is non-ritualistic in each instance, the translators have not hesitated to translate the word "dip"; otherwise transliteration is resorted to in order to veil the meaning of the term. 2) *Baptizo* (the act of dipping) is used 75 times. It is merely transliterated (baptize) in each case. 3) *Baptisma,* a noun form, is used 22 times, and again transliteration has been resorted to in every case. 4) *Baptismos,* another noun form (used in the plural) appears 4 times in the Western Text, 3 times otherwise, and is translated washings. See Mark 7:4, (8, KJV); Col. 2:12 (some mss.); Heb. 6:2, 9:10. 5) *Baptistes,* the title given to John (the dipping one) to distinguish him from the many other "Johns," appears 14 times, and 6) *baptizon,* a variant, is used once (Mark 6:14). Finally, 7) *embapto* appears 3 times, and since it is used in each case in a non-ritualistic context, the translators have not hesitated to translate the word dip in each instance, as they did the simple verb root form, *bapto.* See Matthew 26:23; Mark 14:20; and John 13:26, and compare references listed under 1) above.

A. *Baptism Defined*

With the foregoing reference data in view, it is not difficult to arrive at a definition of baptism. Wherever any form of the word appears in the New Testament apart from a ritualistic setting, the term is uniformly translated dip, its closest English equivalent.

Etymologically, *bapto,* the Greek verb from which all the other forms of the word stem, is an onomatopoetic word. A word which derives its *name* (Gr. *onoma*) from the sound that is made when something is *done* (Gr. *poieo*), is so designated by grammarians. Examples thereof include such words as pop, snap, crackle, buzz, squish, rumble, fizz, roar, crack, ping, splat.

The sound made when a descending object breaks the surface tension of water came across to the Greeks as "bapt." To our English ancestors, it sounded like "dip." The suffix letters *ize* are a verb forming suffix which signifies to make, or do. Thus to glamorize is to make glamorous, to chastize is to make chaste, to scandalize is to make scandal, to pulverize to make powder. Baptize is to make the sound of an object breaking the surface tension of water, hence it is an onomatopoetic term for "the act of dipping."

When used as a metaphor in such expressions as the baptism of the Holy Spirit, baptism of fire, and baptism of suffering, the word means to overwhelm. When an object is submerged (hence immersed) it is immediately engulfed, overflown by the element in which it is dipped. For example, when Cornelius and his household were baptized in the Holy Spirit, in like manner as the apostles were "at the beginning" (of the church age, see Peter's explanation, Acts 11:15-18), they were not dipped into the Holy Spirit and forthwith drawn out. They were overwhelmed by the Holy Spirit, brought under the control of the Holy Spirit. (See the author's essay, "A Third Look at the Baptism of the Holy Spirit" in the Appendix.)

B. *Distinction between Christian Baptism and Other New Testament Baptisms*

It is very important that one be able to distinguish between Christian baptism (baptism administered by the authority of Christ, as set forth in the Scriptures) and substitutes which have been devised over the years. It is also important that one be able to distinguish between Christian baptism and various other baptisms which are mentioned in the New Testament. There are five such baptisms to be considered: 1) the baptism of John, 2) the baptism of the Holy Spirit (in its miraculous manifestation), 3) the baptism of fire, 4) the baptism of suffering, and 5) the baptism for the dead. Such a listing of itself poses a problem in the light of Ephesians 4:5 wherein Paul affirms "there is one baptism." Was he, of all the New Testament writers, unaware of such an array of variant "baptisms"? He was at least aware of the last one listed, for he is the only one who even so much as mentioned "baptism for the dead."

The key to the problem noted is to be found in the context in which Paul stated there is "one baptism." In v. 3 Paul has exhorted his readers to "keep the unity of the Spirit in the bond of peace." That sets the stage for what follows, the enunciation of the seven pillars of unity. Paul speaks of those facets of Christian experience, doctrine, and practice which make us one. Thus when he says there is one baptism, he is speaking of that one which is the common experience of all

Christians. There is indeed such a baptism. At least it was so then. Which one might that be? To arrive at the answer to that question, we need to engage in a perceptive process of elimination.

1. *The Baptism of John.* The baptism of John had much in common with the baptism instituted by Christ in the Great Commission. But there are some important differences also. The similarities will be noted first.

a. John's baptism was also *of Divine origin.* Recall the "hot potato" Jesus dumped into the laps of the carping Pharisees when they agreed to engage in a question exchange (Matt. 21:23-27). "The baptism of John, whence was it? from heaven or from men?" That called for a huddle. They quickly concluded they were trapped either way they might answer. So they lied, "we know not" (v. 27). Jesus' humor comes to light as he proceeded to play their game by the rules they were making up as they went along: "Neither will I *tell* you by what authority I do these things" (v. 27).

The question of Jesus with regard to John's baptism is particularly pertinent today in the light of the history we have reviewed via the startling confession of Charles G. Finney. The baptism of Christ, whence is it? From heaven or from men? Is the baptism Christ commanded of such lesser authority and significance that it can be set aside, and an expedient concocted by men can be put "in the precise place baptism occupied in the days of the apostles"? So it would seem to be. But "what saith the oracles of God?" (Rom. 11:4).

b. John's baptism was also a *baptism of repentance unto the remission of sins.* Mark 1:4 plainly so states: "John came, who baptized in the wilderness and preached the baptism of repentance for (Gr. *eis,* into) the remission of sins." (Cp. Acts 2:38.)

The repentance facet of John's baptism is underscored by his rebuke to the Pharisees: "You offspring of vipers . . . bring forth fruits worthy of repentance" (Matt. 3:7, 8). That his baptism was unto the remission of sins is commonly overlooked, as is a text found in Luke's Gospel, saying:

> And all the people when they heard, and the publicans, justified God, being baptized with the baptism of John. But the Pharisees and the lawyers rejected for themselves the counsel of God, being not baptized of him.

That kind of rejection is still going on, only now it is done by the order which call themselves fundamentalists/evangelicals, and consists of the repudiation of the efficacy and need of the baptism commanded by Christ.

c. The baptism administered by John was also, as the name of the action described connotes, *the act of dipping.* Rarely is this denied in the instance of John's baptism. The place chosen, the Jordan River, at Aenon, "because there was much water there" (John 3:23), and the description of the baptism of Jesus (Matt. 3:16) leave little room for argument: "And Jesus, when he was baptized, went up straightway from the water" (Gr. *anebe,* "went up," *apo,* "from" *tou hudatos,* "the water"). The description of the baptism of the Ethiopian eunuch (Acts 8:38, 39) uses the same language, plus an additional descriptive phrase, to describe baptism of one yielding himself to the authority of Christ. It is said of both Philip and the eunuch that they "went down" (Gr. *katebesan,* "descended") "into" (Gr. *eis*) the water, and that they "came up" (Gr. *anebesan,* "ascended") "from" (Gr. *ek,* "out of") the water.

In view of the close parallel between the two baptisms, the question arises: why did Paul rebaptize the twelve baptist disciples at Ephesus? (See Acts 19:1-5.) Should someone have witnessed both baptisms, but out of earshot, the second likely would have appeared as an encore. The answer is bound up in a crucial distinction—a difference in dispensation. The preceding paragraph in Acts (18:24-28) notes that Apollos preceded Paul at Ephesus. Though he was eloquent, fervent in spirit, mighty in the Scriptures, and persuasive, like many others of whom the same could be said, his knowledge of the subject of baptism was faulty. He preached and practiced what he knew, but he "knew only the baptism of John" (18:25) prior to his encounter with Priscilla and Aquila who "instructed him in the way of the Lord more accurately" (18:26). It would appear that the twelve men Paul encountered had been discipled by Apollos for they had been baptized with John's baptism.

Note that in his lifetime even Jesus baptized with John's baptism, or, to be more precise, he had his disciples do so for him (John 4:1, 2). And, as is well known, he himself, though sinless, was baptized with John's baptism. Why so? "To fulfill all righteousness" (Matt. 3:15). Surprise! If Jesus had not been baptized with John's baptism, he would have needed to be for the reason others did. He would have been a sinner, setting himself above an ordinance enacted by his Father. Recall the question he put to the Pharisees? "The baptism of John, whence is it? of men or of heaven?" (Matt. 21:25). Does this disclosure have anything to say to us today?

John's baptism was not into (*eis*) the name of the Father, the Son, and the Holy Spirit, nor was it accompanied by the promise of the gift of the Holy Spirit (Acts 2:38, 39, cp. 19:2-6). Neither was it administered "in (Gr. *en*, by) the name of Jesus Christ," that is, by the authority of Christ. John's authority terminated with his death whereas the authority of Christ came into full covenantal force with his death. (See Heb. 9:16, 17.)

A Mormon tract left in my hands argues that the reason Paul rebaptized the twelve men is that their baptizer was not a qualified "priest" (as the Mormon church professes their baptizers to be). That explanation fails on two crucial points. 1) The administrator does not validate baptism, else no one could actually know this side of eternity whether his or her baptism were really valid, and 2) even if only a "priest" were authorized to baptize, the Scriptures teach that the whole church constitutes a "royal priesthood" (I Peter 2:9, cp. Rev. 1:6, 5:10), of which priesthood Christ is the only high priest.

Unfortunately the insidious error openly espoused in the Mormon tract neither originated with the cult, nor is it limited in its practice to the cult. The "clergy" (by whatever name the order is called) of virtually every segment of Christendom practices the error even if they do not openly acknowledge or espouse it.

2. *The Baptism for the Dead.* This is an even more insidious error that it is promoted and practiced by the so-called Church of Jesus Christ *of the Latter Day Saints.* Of "the latter day saints"? How latterly? I never fail to press that question upon the youthful "elders" of the cult who come to my door. What other kind of saints are there in view of the fact the ranks of the "former day saints" closed when the former days gave way to the inauguration of the latter days, the days the church began over 1900 years ago (Acts 2:16, 17ff.; Heb. 1:1, etc.).

The Mormon cult is the prime contender for proxy baptism, "baptism for the dead." The practice has but one proof text to support it, an enigmatic verse found in I Corinthians 15:29, versus several plain pronouncements of Scripture to controvert it.

It is a dictum of Divine revelation, to which we have alluded (and documented) several times previously, that "by the word of two or three witnesses a thing shall be established." See Numbers 35:30; Deuteronomy 17:6; Matthew 18:16; II Corinthians 13:1. In addition to failing that crucial test, the teaching and practice is controverted by such plain passages as Romans 14:12; Matthew 12:36, 37; 16:27; Revelation 20:12, 13, and 22:11, 12. Moreover, there is not one Biblical example, nor even so much as a suggestion elsewhere that any such thing was being practiced. Moreover, in the parable of the rich man and Lazarus, it is stated that the gulf which separated the righteous dead from the wicked is fixed (Gr. *esteriktai*, "firmly fixed"). No one crosses that gulf in either direction (Luke 16:26).

It is a sound hermeneutical principle that unless a passage is couched in obviously figurative language, it is to be taken at face value for what it seems to say, unless: 1) what it seems to say is unsupported by any other Scripture and 2) plainly contradicts what is elsewhere taught and supported by two or more Scriptures. I Corinthians 15:29 is such a text. Whatever the passage means, it cannot mean what it appears at first glance to be saying; else God is "a god of confusion." In the preceding chapter, Paul said God is not (I Cor. 14:33).

According to the *International Standard Bible Encyclopedia,* Vol. I, approximately two score "more or less strained" interpretations have been offered. At one end of the spectrum is the view that the text alludes to such a practice as the text seems to suggest—proxy baptism for the dead. Historians are cited who report that the gnostic heretic, Marcion, actually initiated such a practice at Corinth. If so, the question arises: which came first, the text of I Corinthians 15:29 which the gnostics then seized as a basis for the practice (as the Mormons have done), or was Paul alluding to a practice already begun? If the latter, why then did he not repudiate the practice as out of harmony with the Biblical doctrine of personal accountability? My judgment is the text of I Corinthians 15:29 came first.

What then could Paul have possibly meant by the saying? An interpretation, admittedly "somewhat strained" (eisegetical in fact, not exegetical *except in the larger context* of the Scriptures) translates the text to read: "What shall they do who are baptized *on account of* the dead?" That is to say, in view of the fact baptized believers die and thus join the ranks of the dead. If there is no resurrection of the dead, why be baptized? Baptism is without meaning except in the light of the historic facts of the Gospel, which Paul defined at the outset of the chapter as focusing on the death, burial, resurrection, and appearances of Christ (I Cor. 15:1-4).

Whatever may be the true import of the text, the one thing that is clear is that "baptism of the dead," proxy baptism, if such an interpretation of the text is valid, is not, *definitely not,* the one baptism that is the common experience of all believers. It is not therefore one of the pillars of unity of which Paul writes in Ephesians 4:1-6.

3. *The Baptism of Suffering.* The phrase "baptism of suffering" is not found in the Scriptures, but neither is the phrase "baptism of (in) the Holy Spirit" or "baptism of (in) fire." But when baptizing is done, regardless of the place or the element in which the baptizing is done, it is common and proper to refer to the same as baptism(s).

Matthew 20:20-23, Mark 10:35-40, and Luke 12:50 provide a Biblical basis for the coining of such a phrase as the baptism of suffering. In these three texts, addressed by Jesus to his disciples, he asked: "Can you be baptized with the baptism wherewith I am baptized and drink of the cup whereof I drink?" Obviously, he was not asking them if they could submit to John's baptism as he had done, or drink out of the same drinking vessel he used. He is using the terms in a metaphorical sense as we do when we speak, for example, of soldiers encountering for the first time actual field conditions in a pitched battle, submerged as it were with battle fire. Such soldiers are said to receive the baptism of fire.

So too in the passage cited above. The form of reference is similar to such expressions as plunged into sorrow, despair, or immersed in care, overwhelmed with anguish. The analogy is suggested by a number of Old Testament passages such as Isaiah 43:2; 51:17, 22; Jeremiah 47:2; Lamentations 3:54; Psalms 69:2; 75:8; 125:4, 5.

Not every generation of Christians, and not every Christian, even in times of fierce persecution drinks the cup of suffering to its lowest dregs. The "baptism of suffering" is not the universal unifying experience which unites us as one body in Christ.

4. *The Baptism in Fire.* How thankful we should be that the baptism *in* fire is not the one baptism which unites believers in Christ. However, more than once I have heard misguided zealots pray for the baptism *of* fire as an adjunct to their prayer for the baptism of the Holy Spirit. The latter, they were led to believe, is a second-stage experience posterior to water baptism and/or salvation.

The expression "baptize . . . in fire" appears only twice in the Scriptures. Each of the four Gospels record the prediction of John to the effect his successor (the Christ) would baptize in the Holy Spirit (Matt. 3:11; Mark 1:8; Luke 3:16; and John 1:33). Peter, in Acts 11:16, recalled the promise in connection with his report to the church at Jerusalem concerning the Cornelius episode. But only two of the texts make mention of Christ's fiery judgment of the wicked. Incidentally, there was no fire on the day of Pentecost, nor wind, when the baptism of the Holy Spirit was visited upon the apostles to equip and credentialize

235

them for the work to which they had been commissioned. There was "a *sound like as of* a mighty wind," and there was a visual aspect of the miracle of Pentecost that was "*like as of* fire" (Acts 2:2, 3).

Matthew and Luke, in recalling the prediction of John, make mention of the baptism *in* fire, as well as *in* the Holy Spirit. And they do so by including his prediction of Jesus' fiery judgment of the wicked. Note the same as recorded in Matthew (3:9-12). The words are particularly addressed to the Pharisees:

> Think not to say unto yourselves, we have Abraham to our father: for I say unto you, that God is able of these stones to raise up children unto Abraham. And even now the axe lieth at the root of the trees: *every tree therefore that bringeth not forth good fruit is hewn down, and cast into the fire.* I indeed baptize you in water unto repentance: but he that cometh after me is mightier than I, whose shoes I am not worthy to bear: he shall baptize you in the Holy Spirit *and in fire:* whose fan is in his hand, and he will thoroughly cleanse his threshing floor: and he will gather his wheat into the garner, *but the chaff he will burn with unquenchable fire.*

Note that an engulfing fire is mentioned three times, once in connection with the burning of the corrupt trees, once in connection with the destruction of the chaff, and between the two, in connection with the imagery of the engulfment which ensues when one is "baptized." Is it reasonable to suppose that the fire spoken of in the middle of the threefold illustration is different in purpose and scope from the other two? The two baptisms spoken of engulf universal humanity. If we are not baptized in the Holy Spirit, we will be baptized with fire. Whatever your understanding of the baptism of the Holy Spirit may be, it should be obvious that at least the baptism in fire is not the one baptism of Ephesians 4:5.

5. *The "One Baptism" of Ephesians 4:5.* The one baptism of Ephesians 4:5 is a baptism which is both outward and inward, visible and invisible, physical and spiritual. It is both an event and a state of being, a baptism in water administered by a fellow man (viewed from the earthly perspective) and a baptism in the Holy Spirit (viewed from the heavenly perspective.

To my readers who may be at first somewhat taken aback at what has just been said, attention is again called to the author's prior published essay: "A Third Look at the Baptism of the Holy Spirit." See the Appendix sector of this publication.

The problem which has long vexed the church, dividing believers into hostile camps which tend to polarize into a deeper and deeper rift, is that we fail to recognize that baptism in the Holy Spirit is, or to be more precise *was*, manifested initially in two phases: 1) a somewhat restricted manifestation accompanied by signs serving to credentialize the apostles and certain other chosen vessels at critical points in the expansion of the church, 2) an unrestricted manifestation which was (and is) moral rather than miraculous in expression. The miraculous manifestation was necessarily *bestowed*. The moral manifestation (the fruit of the Spirit) is just as necessarily "growed" (grown).

One vociferous segment of the church, the self-styled evangelical or "fundamentalists" (the majority voice today), follows somewhat the lead of the Darby-Scofield dispensational model in which the most that may be admitted is that baptism in water "for the remission of sins" may have been prevalent in the Jewish phase of the emerging church as a carry-over from John's ministry. But when the emphasis shifted to the evangelizing of the Gentiles, that was shortly phased out, and "the distinctive (?) New Testament doctrine of salvation by faith only (?) became the Divine model." Thereafter baptism was administered subsequent to salvation as "an outward sign of an inward grace." Those of such persuasion read "water baptism" out and Holy Spirit baptism into those Scriptures which speak of baptism as related to salvation (Rom. 6:3-5; Gal. 3:27; Col. 2:12; I Peter 3:21, etc.).

Cracks in the Stony Wall of Resistance

The stony wall of resistance to the Biblical doctrine of baptism for remission of sins is beginning to crack. For example, the renowned evangelical scholar, F. F. Bruce, in the publication, *Questions and Answers,* fielded a number of loaded questions concerning baptism in which he acquitted himself as accepting the Scriptures at face value when they speak of baptism as being "for the remission of sins." He cited Acts 2:38 and 22:16 as speaking specifically to that point, and proceeded to derail the tactic which attempts to solve the issue by erecting a *post*-Pentecost dispensational change in the redemptive format.

When a questioner pitted W. Graham Scroggie against him, noting that Scroggie takes the position that such texts, plus Mark 16:16, Galatians 3:27, Romans 6:3-5, and Colossians 2:12, refer to baptism of the Spirit as opposed to water baptism, Bruce rose to the challenge. He noted Holy Spirit baptism is contrasted with water baptism *only* when John's baptism is the frame of reference. The New Testament never separates Christian baptism (in water) and "baptism in one Spirit into the body of Christ" (I Cor. 12:13). They are the outward and inward facets of the one baptism.

What was but a crack here and there in the stony wall of resistance to the Biblical doctrine of baptism has been turned into a gaping hole by the eminent international Baptist scholar, Dr. George R. Beasley-Murray. His landmark treatise, *Baptism in the New Testament*, was addressed primarily to his own brethren, the Southern Baptists. They quickly got the message, but they were not about to receive it. In fact they succeeded in coercing the publisher to recall the publication and take the edition off the market. Fortunately it has since gained a publisher (Eerdmans) and is now available in a 422 page paperback.

In a shorter interim publication, *Baptism Today and Tomorrow,* Dr. Beasley-Murray quotes a typical "Baptist leader" in the act of denying that baptism has any efficacy as a means for the transmission of God's saving grace, and adds:

> It is my impression that most Baptists in the USA and in the countries of the Commonwealth would still subscribe to that statement, but that a majority of their theologians would repudiate it. The theologians, however, appear to exercise little influence on the preaching and administration of baptism in the (Baptist) churches (p. 14).

He ought to know whereof he speaks. He has recently served on the faculty of the Southern Baptist Theological Seminary, Louisville, Kentucky.

Summary: Christian Baptism Redefined

By way of concluding this extended process of elimination, we have undertaken to determine which baptism Paul was speaking of when he affirmed there is "one baptism." I offer my personal definition of Christian baptism. The baptism which fulfills the terms of the Great Commission must be recognized as both a Divinely given mandate and the repentant believer's devout response. Thus I define Christian baptism as:

> 1. An ordinance of Christ enjoined upon (1) all who, in "the obedience of faith," yield their wills to his will for the remission of sins and enrollment in his church, and (2) upon all who teach and preach his redemptive message; to be performed in behalf of those who would obey the Gospel to the saving of their souls. It consists of the immersion (submergence) and emergence (in and from the water) of a penitent believer in the name of (authority of) Christ.

2. Christian baptism is the obedience from the heart to that form of doctrine which was delivered us, whereby a penitent believer in Christ yields his will to the will of Christ, and consequently his body unto God as an instrument of righteousness. (See Rom. 6:2-5, 13, 16-18.) Outwardly, Christian baptism consists of the surrender of the body to the overwhelming waters in an act symbolic of the death, burial, and resurrection of Christ. Inwardly, it consists of the surrender of the human spirit (will, self) to the overwhelming of the Holy Spirit in an act that symbolizes the death of the carnal mind and renewing of our minds by the Holy Spirit (See I Cor. 12:13, Titus 3:5, Rom. 12:1, 2.) A baptism that does not engulf both the body and the soul, that fails to recognize Jesus as both Lord and Christ; an obedience that is not from the heart or which does not conform to that form of doctrine which was delivered us, is not Christian baptism. (See Rom. 16:17.)

PREVIEW—REVIEW QUESTIONS

1. Note the relevance of the innovation of the "altar call" ("mourner's bench syndrome") to the current practice of downplaying the role of baptism.
2. Why was the mourner's bench substituted, at least as a temporary expedient?
3. Identify the Greek verb root for such words as baptize, baptism, baptist. Where does the simple root form appear in the Greek New Testament, and how is it uniformly translated (KJV, NIV, et al)?
4. What is meant by an onomatopoetic word? Identify some which we use in our common speech. Relate to baptism.
5. How does the metaphoric usage of baptize, baptism, differ from its literal use? Cite an example.
6. List the different kinds of baptisms mentioned in the New Testament.
7. In view of the fact the New Testament speaks of so many, how could, why would, Paul say there is *one* baptism?
8. How can one determine which one Paul was speaking of? Illustrate.
9. Note some similarities between John's baptism and the baptism Christ ordained in the Great Commission.
10. In view of the fact John's baptism was a baptism of repentance for the remission of sins, why was Jesus baptized therewith?
11. Note two differences between John's baptism and Christian baptism.
12. Why did Paul rebaptize the twelve baptist disciples he encountered at Ephesus?

13. Did Jesus baptize anyone during his ministry? Explain John 4:1, 2.

14. What serious problem arises when it is taught or assumed it requires a valid (priestly) administrator to make baptism valid? (a la Mormonism, Catholicism, and Protestantism, generally).

15. Evaluate and respond to the Mormon practice of proxy baptism. Among other things, how does it relate to the Biblical dictum for the validation of the witness to a thing?

16. How do the Greek nouns *baptisma* and *baptismos*(ois) differ? How is the latter generally translated? See appendix which follows.

17. Explain the phrase, "baptism of suffering." Have you received that baptism?

18. Identify the baptism of fire. Did anyone receive that baptism on Pentecost? Explain why some so believe.

19. How does the author identify the "one baptism" of Ephesians 4:5? What two facets of baptism does he believe to be so interrelated they constitute one baptism?

20. Explain the dispensationalist attempt to confine water baptism for remission of sins to the first two or three decades of the church.

21. As cracks, and even gaps, begin to appear in the stony wall of resistance to a view which links water baptism to remission of sins, in what direction is the dissident group moving?

22. Can those among us who have inclined to take a position in the opposite direction learn anything from this? If so, what?

23. Is the author's identification and definition of the "one baptism" (Christian baptism) threatened or supported? How so?

CONCERNING BAPTISM(S), BAPTIZING: TEXTUAL DATA

ROOT: Βάπτω (bapto) "to dip"

Actually, the word stems from a phonetic syllable, "bapt," the "sound" (as the Greeks thought they heard it) made whenever anything was dipped or plunged into the water. *Bapto* appears in this simple form 3 times in the New Testament: Luke 16:24, John 13:26, Rev. 19:13.

DERIVATIVES:

Βαπτίζω (*baptizo*) "to baptize"

Literally, *to make* "bapt" or *the act of dipping*. Forms of the verb used 75 times.

1. References to baptizings administered by John and/or his disciples: Matt. 3:6, 11, 13, 14, 16; Mark 1:4, 5, 8, 9; Luke 3:7, 12, 16, 21; 7:29; John 1:25, 26, 28, 31, 33; 3:22, 23 (twice), 26; 4:1, 2 (Jesus—actually his disciples) 10:40; Acts 1:5; 11:16; 19:4.
2. References to baptizings administered by Christian evangelists: Matt. 28:19; Mark 16:16; Acts 2:38, 41; 8:12, 13, 16, 36, 38; 9:8; 10:47, 48; 11:16; 16:15, 33; 19:3, 5; 22:16; Rom. 6:3 (twice); I Cor. 1:13, 14, 15, 16 (twice), 17; Gal. 3:27.
3. References to baptizings in the Holy Spirit, and *in fire (a metaphor): *Matt. 3:11; Mark 1:8; *Luke 3:16; John 1:33; Acts 1:5; I Cor. 12:13.
4. References to baptizings in (or by) affliction—"the baptism of suffering": Matt. 20:22 (twice), 23; Mark 10:38 (twice), 39; Luke 12:50.
5. References to symbolic baptism: I Cor. 10:2 "Our fathers were all baptized unto Moses . . ." I Cor. 15:29 ". . . baptized for the dead" (verb used twice).

NOTE: WHEN USED AS A METAPHOR, BAPTIZE, BAPTISM, TAKE THEIR MEANING FROM THE *RESULT* OF THE ACT RATHER THAN THE ACTUAL ACT, HENCE—"TO OVERWHELM."

Βάπτισμα (baptisma) a noun referring to the process of immersion, submergence, and emergence. This form is found only in the New Testament and later literature contingent upon the New Testament. It differs from baptismos (see below) in that it is a "once and for all," non-repetitive act. It is used in the New Testament 22 times to refer to:

1. "John's Baptism" (the baptism of repentance and preparation initiated by John) Matt. 3:7; 21:25; Mark 1:4; 11:30; Luke 3:3; 7:29; 20:4; Acts 1:22;10:37; 13:24; 18:25; 19:3, 4.
2. Christian Baptism (the baptism commissioned by Christ) Rom. 6:4; Eph. 4:5; Col. 2:13; I Peter 3:21.
3. As a metaphor (see note above) to denote the overwhelming effect of trials: Matt. 20:22, 23; Mark 10:38, 39; Luke 12:50.

Βαπτισμός (baptismos) a noun, with the same general meaning as baptisma except that it refers to the repetitive ceremonial "cleansings" which were common to the Mosaic system, and certain of the contemporary religions. It is widely used in Jewish literature (Greek translations thereof) and pagan literature. It appears four times in the New Testament and is often mistaken for Christian baptism by the "anti-baptism, faith-only cultists."

1. It is translated (?) "washing," 3 times: Mark 7:4, 8 (KJV); Heb. 9:10.
2. It is translated "baptism" in Col. 2:12 (some mss.) and "baptisms" in Heb. 6:2.

Βαπτιστής (baptistes), "the dipper" (14 times)
Matt. 3:1, 11, 12; 14:2, 8; 16:14; 17:33; Mark 6:24, 25; 8:28; Luke 7:20, 28, 33; 9:19.

Βαπτίζων (baptizon), "the dipping one": Mark 6:14.

Ἐμβάπτω (embapto) non-ritualistic usage (3 times): Matt. 26:33; Mark 14:20; John 13:26. Cp. Bapto (see first paragraph).

17

CHRISTIAN BAPTISM, CONTINUED: SALIENT FACTS

In the preceding lesson, we took pains to distinguish the "one baptism" which conforms to the mandate of Christ, as set forth in the Great Commission: the baptism which is enjoined upon all who preach the Gospel, to be performed in behalf of those who are thereby called to obey the Gospel unto the remission of their sins and unto salvation. In order that those evangelized and taught may obey Christ in baptism according to the Scriptures, we need to note: 1) the *action* of Christian baptism, "that form of the doctrine which was delivered us" (Rom. 6:17), 2) the *elements* (pl.) in which we are baptized, 3) the *proper subjects*, 4) *those authorized to administer* Christian baptism, and 5) "the formula," that is, the words (if there be such) that must be spoken for the act to be valid.

Since that which Christian baptism is divinely designed to accomplish is God's responsibility to effectuate, we will reserve the discussion of the *resultants* of Christian baptism (the purpose and design) for another lesson. We may be assured of this: that the Father, Son, and Holy Spirit will fulfill the promises which attend the "obedience of faith," and will do so much more discerningly and perfectly than we who are

243

called upon to teach on the subject and obey in all things according to the Scriptures. Our attention in this lesson will therefore be focused on those facets of Christian baptism through which we are called upon to render unto God "the obedience of faith among the nations" (Rom. 1:5, 6:17, 16:26).

A. *The Action of Christian Baptism*

The action described by the word baptize may be deduced in several ways. An article in the *Encyclopedia Americana* contains this succinct comment: "If this word were not associated with a disputed church ordinance, there would never have arisen a question as to its meaning."

1. *The etymology of the word.* In the preceding lesson attention was called to the fact that baptize is an onomatopoetic word; a word that was formed to imitate the sound that was heard when the action occurred. That sound was the sound that was heard when something was dipped (Gr. *bapt*) into the water. The act of baptizing indeed makes such a sound, provided, of course, that which is done conforms to the New Testament model, "coming to the water, *going down into* the water, coming up out of the water" (Matt. 3:13-16, Acts 8:36-39, cp. Rom. 6:3-5, Col. 2:12, 13).

2. *The testimony of Dictionaries and Lexicons.* Dictionary definitions will differ from Greek lexicons in that the latter will define the word according to its ancient (etymological) usage, whereas dictionaries will report modern usage also. But almost any quality dictionary will note first of all (generally in italics) a) the root from which a word stems and the original meaning thereof, and b) the history of the word leading up to its introduction into our language. Such terms as OL (old Latin), ME (middle English), etc., will advise as to how that came about. After that a dictionary will list meanings which accrue to words as they are stretched to fit different contexts. No dictionary, however, assigns any other definition to baptize but *dip* as the primary and etymological (real, root) meaning thereof.

3. *A comparison of the Greek Septuagint (LXX) text of the Old Testament with the Hebrew text in those passages where the word dip (dipped) appears in our Bible.* The Hebrew word so translated, *tabal*, appears in the Hebrew text fifteen times: Gen. 37:31; Exod. 12:22; Lev. 4:6, 17; 9:9; 14:6, 16, 51; Num. 19:18; Deut. 33:24; Josh. 4:15; Ruth 2:14; I Sam. 14:27; II Kings 5:14 and 8:15. In all but the first instance the LXX replaces *tabal* with *baptizo*. In Genesis 37:31

the verb for dye, stain (*moluno*) is used, to emphasize the result, the purpose for which Joseph's brothers dipped in blood the coat they had stripped from him before selling him as a slave.

Leviticus 14:15, 16 is of special importance to this inquiry. The text describes one of the priestly rituals of the Mosaic Law and reads as follows (with the Hebrew and the Greek LXX verbs inserted parenthetically at the points in which they appear in the text):

> And the priest shall take of the log (cruse) of oil, and *pour* (*yatsaq, echeo*) it into the palm of his own left hand; and the priest shall *dip* (*tabal, baptizo*) his finger *in* the oil that is in his left hand, and shall *sprinkle* (*nazah, rantizo*) of the oil with this finger seven times before Jehovah.

Note that three entirely different actions were commanded to be performed in the ritual. And it required three entirely different words in all three languages (and indeed in any language) to accurately describe the action. In no language are such words as pour and sprinkle derived from the same root as the word for dip. Neither the Latin Vulgate translators, nor the King James translators, nor any other have rendered *tabal* or *baptizo* by such entirely different action words as sprinkle or pour.

4. *Associated Biblical data.* The incidental details recorded in connection with baptismal narratives are non-supportive of aught else but "the act of dipping," baptism. For example, it is reported that John chose the site of his baptismal ministry (Aenon, near Salem) "because there was much water there" (John 3:23). Jesus and the Ethiopian Eunuch came to the water where they were baptized. In the case of the latter it would be incongruous to assume that a man of his political position (equivalent to Secretary of the Treasury of Egypt) would not even have a jar of drinking water in the chariot as he undertook the long journey down the Gaza Road. If his baptism could be accomplished on a token basis, he should have said to Philip, "There is water here in my jug, what hinders me from being baptized as I go my way?" Instead they came to a certain water, and both the evangelist and his convert went down into (Gr. *katebesan eis*) the water, and came up out of (Gr. *anabesan ek*) the water (Acts 8:38, 39). Of the baptism of Jesus the descriptive language is equally precise. Whenever the act of baptism is described in the Scriptures, it is described as a dipping.

5. *The metaphors used with reference to baptism.* a) Baptism is spoken of as a birth (of water and of the Spirit). Nicodemus' question is very much to the point, whether mistakenly arising out of a crassly

literal interpretation of Jesus' words, or otherwise. He certainly could not enter again into (Gr. *eis*) his mother's womb and be born again, much less could he enter a few drops or a handful or "dipper" of water, and be born of something so much smaller than himself. b) Baptism is also pictured as a death, burial, and resurrection (Rom. 6:3-5, Col. 2:12), and as "the bath of the beginning again" (Titus 3:5). The term "bath" (*loutron*) is a noun, not a participle. c) Romans 6:5 speaks of the baptized as being planted together, engrafted with Christ (Gr. *sumphutoi*). Whatever the metaphor used, none corresponds in imagery to standing still, while a bit of water is sprinkled or poured upon one's head.

6. *A technicality to be noted.* Ocassionally one comes across the argument that unless one is cremated and the residual ashes be sprinkled, or that the body should be put through a meat grinder, it is impossible for a person to be sprinkled. That is a weak argument. Technically it is true, but the fact is, even the Scriptures speak of sprinkling in a non-technical sense with persons (among other things) said to be sprinkled. Hebrews 9:13 speaks of the blood of a heifer "sprinkling them that are unclean." V. 19 speaks of Moses "sprinkling the book (of the law) and *all the people*," and v. 21 states, "Moreover, he sprinkled with blood both the tabernacle and all the vessels of the ministry."

On the other hand, to use these texts in support of "sprinkling for baptism" is also a weak argument, for an entirely different Greek word (*rantizo*), a word of an entirely different .neaning from *baptizo*, is used in each case.

There is a sense in which sprinkling, pouring, and dipping are all essential to salvation. But care needs to be given to the element involved in each action, and the particular facet of a believer's being that receives the action. It is the "heart" that is said to be "sprinkled by the blood" (Heb. 10:22b). The expression is obviously metaphoric. The Holy Spirit is said to be "poured out upon us richly" (Titus 3:5) as we undergo "the bath of the beginning again" (commonly translated the washing of regeneration), and "the body washed with pure water" (Heb. 10:22c). These observations become a striking commentary on I John 5:8: "For there are three who bear witness, the Spirit, and the water, and the blood: and the three agree in one." In Christian baptism, administered according to the Scriptures, they most certainly do agree in one solemn sanctifying and saving act. Before the baptismal controversy became superheated by the faith-only reactionaries, virtually every commentator of note saw in I John 5:8 a baptismal text, relating baptism to redemption. Even Luther and Calvin did so, openly.

It is a basic principle of reasoning that things equal to the same thing are equal to each other. Regardless of preference or practice in Christendom, all agree that every figure of speech used in the New Testament to speak of Christian baptism and every New Testament description of the action involved can be readily equated with the submergence and emergence of a pentitent believer (into and from the water) as an expression of the obedience of faith called baptism. When sprinkling or pouring (or even triune immersion) are substituted, the equation becomes forced, strained, if indeed it can be maintained at all. Thus no one who has ever undergone "that form of doctrine delivered us" (Rom. 6:17) elects later in life, upon gaining further knowledge about baptism, to be "sprinkled," rejecting the former for the latter. But every year thousands are lost to the effusionist denominations, as members of long standing find their "baptism" does not provide for them "the answer of a good conscience towards God" (I Peter 3:21).

B. *The Elements of Baptism*

In the previous lesson it was noted that Christian baptism has two facets, one inward, the other outward. Christ administers the one in accordance with Divine promise (Matt. 3:11; Acts 11:16, 17; I Cor. 12:13; Titus 3:5; I John 5:8). Those who bring their fellows to the point of obedience are commanded to administer the other. Since one cannot obey a promise, but can and should obey a Divine command, the promise is received when the required obedience is given. (See the author's treatise: "A Third Look at the Baptism of the Holy Spirit," Appendix.)

On the day of Pentecost, Peter voiced both the command to be obeyed and the promise(s) to be received, saying: "Repent ye and be baptized, every one of you, in the name of Jesus Christ, for the remission of your sins, and you shall receive the gift of the Holy Spirit" (Acts 2:38). At Caesarea, in the pilot case of the extension of the Gospel to the Gentiles, God took the initiative, for obvious reasons. Peter got the message and challenged the six Jewish brethren who accompanied him to the house of Cornelius: "Can any man forbid the water that these should not be baptized who have received the Holy Spirit as well as we?" (Acts 10:47). In view of what they had both seen and heard, none could or did. Whereupon Peter commanded them to be baptized. At Damascus, Ananias said to the pentitent Saul of Tarsus: "The Lord, even Jesus, who appeared unto you in the way

247

which you came, has sent me that you may receive your sight and be filled with the Holy Spirit." Then he commanded: "Arise and be baptized, and wash away your sins, calling on the name of the Lord" (Acts 9:17; 22:16).

In each case, water baptism served as a visible, viable vehicle of demonstration of the convert's willingness to die to the former manner of life, and to be raised to walk in newness of life. Peter, in his first epistle, calls to our attention the fact that Noah and his family were saved *by* water (note the preposition used, not just *from* water, but *by* water), being thereby translated out of the world that was into a world in which they were privileged to begin life anew (I Peter 3:21).

In view of the analogy drawn between Christian baptism and the Noachian flood, a pertinent question arises. If water is so important an element in salvation, *how much* is required? John 3:23 bears on this question. John, whose baptizing involved multitudes of penitents, chose a site where there was enough water to accommodate mass baptisms. (In the light of John 4:1, 2, it may be conjectured John did not singlehandedly baptize the multitudes who responded to his preaching. He chose a site therefore extensive enough to facilitate mass baptizing.)

Abraham Lincoln is said to have been asked by someone, "How long ought a man's legs to be?" His quick answer was, "Long enough to reach the ground." How much water is needed for baptism? Enough to cover the subject; or subjects, when many are being baptized into Christ at the same time.

C. *The Proper Subjects for Baptism*

Who is a proper subject for baptism? The Biblical answer to this question leaves no room for doubt. In the Great Commission Christ was very specific. The commission specifies we are to baptize those who have been taught (Matt. 28:19). Mark's account states it a bit differently, but in a sense is even more specific. Mark also reports Jesus as commanding that the Gospel be proclaimed to all mankind, and notes: "He that believes and is baptized shall be saved" (Mark 16:16). It is obvious that the apostles understood that only those who had been so taught that they had come to believe the Gospel proclamation should be baptized. A resume of the book commonly called Acts of Apostles makes this clear. It also makes clear the fact that not only was baptism reserved for all who had been brought to a state of repentance and faith, all such were forthwith baptized. Baptism was viewed as the essential accompaniment of faith.

The following texts underscore the pattern prescribed by Christ in his final words to the apostles. Note two things are common throughout: 1) that which preceded baptism, 2) that which proceeded from faith. See: a) Acts 2:37, 38, 41, b) 8:12, 13, c) 8:36-38, cp. 22:16, d) 9:1-6, 18, *e) 10:33, 44, 47, 48, *f) 16:13-15, *g) 16:30-33, *h) 18:8, i) 19:4, 5.

The asterisked texts record "household" baptisms. Such are seized upon by those practicing infant baptism (?), commonly called pedo-baptists. Aside from the fact that the pedobaptists beg the question by assuming the households included infants, they fail to note what the Scriptures declare to be true of those who made up the households. 1) Lydia was a traveling saleswoman from a city of Asia Minor, and her household consisted of the "women" who were of her company. To assume infants were in such a party would be ludicrous. (See Acts 16:13, 14.) 2) Cornelius greeted Peter with the announcement: "We are all here present in the sight of God to hear all the things commanded you of the Lord" (Acts 10:33). 3) Acts 16:32 reports concerning the conversion of the jailer and his household that Paul and Silas "spake the word of the Lord unto him, with all that were in his house." And following the baptisms that ensued, we are told that they returned to the jailer's house where he set food before them and "rejoiced greatly with all his house, having believed in God" (v. 34). Rather precocious infants, were they not? Amazing that they could not only hear and believe, but understand well enough what their baptism signified that they greatly rejoiced. 4) Less is known of Crispus, ruler of the synagogue at Corinth, but those who made up his household are specifically reported as having "believed" the message Paul proclaimed.

Pedobaptism is a reversal of an essential change which distinguishes the new covenant of Christ from the old covenant which was given through Moses. That difference is clearly set forth in Jeremiah 31:31-34 and repeated in Hebrews 8:8-11. Under the old covenant those of fleshly Israel were born into covenant relationship with God. When they were old enough to understand, they were taught concerning the relationship into which they were born. Thereafter they were obligated to keep the commandments written on stone. But under the new covenant, those who make up spiritual Israel (see Rom. 2:28, 29, Gal. 3:6, 7; 6:14-16) are first taught (Matt. 28:19) and then born anew of the water and the Spirit to enter into the kingdom of God" (John 3:3-5).

Old Covenant	New Covenant
1. Born	1. Taught
2. Taught to know Jehovah, whose they were	2. Born (baptized of the water and the Spirit)

Recall that Moses was born of the seed of Abraham, but if Miriam had not persuaded Pharaoh's daughter to get a nurse for him from among the Hebrew women, and hence brought Moses' own mother to him, he would have known nothing about Jehovah, much less the fact he was "a prince of God." Similarly, every child born into the nation of Israel had to be taught. But under the new covenant, we do not have to teach a child of God to know the Lord, for they all know him, "from the least to the greatest of them," being taught and then "born" into the kingdom of the Son of God's love.

George R. Beasley-Murray calls attention to the debacle that exists throughout the greater part of the pedobaptist world, which includes Anglican England and the British Commonwealth of nations, Catholic and/or Calvinistic-Lutheran Europe, and Latin (Catholic) America. Virtually every one is a "baptized" (?) member of the church. But few attend except for festival days, and few have any semblence of a personal relationship with Christ. Pedobaptism is somewhat like a vaccination, it generally innoculates the one receiving it from the real thing.

How did such a contradiction ever occur? It has its roots in the dogma of total hereditary depravity. Once mothers were persuaded their offspring were born under the curse of Adamic guilt, living in a day when no one was as yet taught to deny the fact that baptism is for the remission of sins, and therefore leads to salvation, the logical thing to do was to have the child baptized at the earliest time possible. Infant mortality was too prevalent to await a time of instruction and personal accountability. Never mind the fact the New Testament plainly taught the baptism of believers. What had they to lose? The child could certainly be no worse off "baptized" with no inkling of what was happening, or why, with no knowledge of either God nor Christ. That could come later, if the child lived. Thus Lin B. Fishback, one of my early professors, defined infant baptism as "an unscriptural method of performing an unscriptural ordinance to save the unscriptural candidate from an unscriptural sin." To that he added, wryly, "Apart from that there isn't much wrong with it, or left of it."

For an expose of the dogma of original sin, and tragedy of errors that have stemmed from that noxious plant that found root in the post-apostolic church, see my treatise on "The Big Lie" in the Appendix of *What the Bible Says About the End Time* (Boatman).

D. *The Administrator of Baptism*

One of the many carry-overs from the papal system is the notion that only duly ordained clergymen are properly qualified to administer baptism. The notion prevails throughout the greater part of the Protestant sector of Christendom. It is the dogma of such cults as Mormonism, and is of moot acceptance among most of the congregations professing to be heirs of the American Restoration Movement which set out nearly two hundred years ago to restore the doctrine and practice of the priesthood of believers. Few are the preachers who would openly teach that those who are led to Christ by members of congregations should wait till Sunday to be baptized before the church; by the preacher, no less. But the practice is so common that congregations take it for granted, and even the elders acquiesce thereto. And it is currently in vogue for the "senior minister" to underscore the pecking order by exercising the prerogative to administer baptism regardless of who discipled the candidate.

Such preachment and/or practice presupposes two fundamental errors: 1) It presupposes a priesthood exists in the church that is above and superior to the priesthood of believers (I Peter 2:9). This runs contrary to a second important distinction between the old covenant and the new. We have noted one in connection with the practice of pedobaptism. Note now another. Under the Mosaic covenant there were four levels: 1) Deity (Jehovah), 2) the High Priest, who alone could enter the Holy of Holies and appear before Jehovah, 3) the priesthood, and 4) the congregation. But under the New Covenant, Deity and the High Priest are are merged in the person of Christ, and the priesthood and the congregation are merged in the persons of the church. In Christ we are a kingdom of priests (Rev. 1:6, 5:10; I Peter 2:9).

Old Covenant	New Covenant
DEITY	
	} Christ
High Priest	
Priesthood	
	} Church
Congregation	

251

The administrator of baptism may be compared to a person who assists in the delivery of a baby. Many a taxi driver has found himself in that role. In doing so he in no way affects the hereditary factors, the chromosomes and genes which determine the sex, race, and other characteristics of the child. A midwife might have performed a bit more expertly, and an obstetrician even more so. But none of them affects in any sense the parentage of the child. Since baptism is by no means as complicated a task as assisting in the birth of a child, there is no reason that a parent should not baptize his own believing children. And there is no reason a Christian who has led a neighbor, friend, or relative to Christ should have to put the convert on layaway, so to speak. Nowhere does the Scriptures teach that "baptism is an outward sign of an inward grace" and such outward witness must therefore be made before the greatest number of people; hence the convert should be put on hold till Sunday morning, step forward at the close of the sermon, and be baptized by the preacher. The "behold our custom is" syndrome, unfortunately, continues to be an affliction with which we shall likely be obliged to contend for years yet to come.

2) The second error enshrined in the notion under scrutiny is that it presupposes some form of apostolic succession. Do you *know* that the one who administered baptism to you was duly ordained, and was baptized by someone who was duly ordained, and that person also, and so on and on, all the way back to the apostles? If the administrator's qualifications validated the act, no one could be really sure their baptism is valid.

An interesting inconsistency is exhibited by those who insist baptism has nothing to do with salvation (else that would put a man between a believer and the Saviour). They reverse their field when it comes down to the bottom line. They would not think of being baptized by someone other than a clergyman of their persuasion. In fact the late J. Frank Norris (of Forth Worth, Texas, fame) has stated in an article in my files:

> John, the Baptist, baptized Jesus. That made Jesus a Baptist. Jesus established the church. That made the church a Baptist church. Since only a Baptist baptizer can make of the one baptized a Baptist, then only a Baptist can baptize one into the Baptist church.

When that bit of audacious bigotry was shared with the late Isaiah Moore, black evangelist and long-time Dean of The College of the Scriptures (Louisville, Kentucky), Moore replied with a characteristic twinkle in his eye:

Quite the contrary. Even after John baptized Jesus, along with multitudes of others from Jerusalem, Judea, Galilee, and from beyond the Jordan, John was still called *the* baptist. And the baptist (the only one) said of Jesus: "I must decrease that he may increase." Now when you take one from one, you hardly have enough left to start a church.

Moore went on to note that the closest thing to the starting of a "Baptist" church this side of Pentecost was at Ephesus, but Paul rebaptized into the name of Jesus *every one of them.* He further noted it was not the fact that Apollos was the baptizer that caused Paul to do so. It was because they had been baptized with John's baptism out of dispensation.

E. *The Formula of Baptism*

What must one say when administering baptism to validate the act? Does one actually have to say anything as the body of a duly qualified candidate is baptized? Is there something that happens or fails to happen insofar as the candidate is concerned, depending on whether the properly formulated words are spoken?

This issue is being raised in different quarters, and for different reasons. There are "baptizers" who are careful to say nothing that would remind anyone of such baptismal texts as Mark 16:16; Acts 2:38; 22:16; Rom. 6:3-5; Col. 2:12, etc.; lest someone hearing what was said might get the idea that baptism is essential to salvation, leading to the remission of sin, uniting one with Christ, etc.

In overreaction to that, there are others who refuse to accept the validity of the baptism someone has received, if at the time of the baptism due attention was not called to what Peter said on Pentecost in response to the question: "Brethren, what shall we do?" (Acts 2:37). But there is not so much as a hint that an echo of those words was pronounced upon a one of the three thousand who gladly received the word and were baptized. If the candidate does not know why he is baptized before he is dipped, he was probably duped into what he was doing and is not thereby rendering the obedience of faith.

Others have expanded the overreaction and insist on including key phrases of other baptismal texts in the forumla. The reading of key baptismal texts definitely is a timely and legitimate teaching device employed upon behalf of spectators who otherwise might not know what is going on, but such a recital does not add to the validity of a candidate's baptism.

Still another controversy has arisen in connection with the Sabellian dogma, developed in the course of the one hundred-year controversy which consummated in the Nicean Council and Creed (325 A.D.). The long-drawn and bitter conflict was sparked by the Arians who taught a view of the person of Christ strikingly similar to the Jehovah's Witnesses, and the followers of Athanasius who reacted along the lines that were made the official doctrine of the church nearly a century later. Sabellius offered what he thought to be a mediating position. He taught that the three personalities revealed in the Scriptures were not coexistent (contemporary) but successive manifestations of the one true God. In the Oneness Holiness reconstruction of the doctrine, the name of Jesus is said to be the name of the Father, the Son, and the Holy Spirit, thus they "baptize in the name of Jesus only."

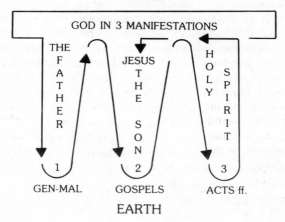

The "proof texts" of this strange construction are found in the fact (?) that while Jesus commanded the disciples to "baptize in the name of the Father, Son, and Holy Spirit" (Matt. 28:19), they actually baptized "in the name of Jesus" (only), Acts 2:38. And when Paul rebaptized the twelve disciples at Ephesus, he baptized them "in the name of Jesus" (only), Acts 19:5. They reason therefore that the name of Jesus is the name of the Father, the Son, and the Holy Spirit.

The Oneness Holiness construction is full of holes. If there is but one person in the Godhead, to whom did Jesus pray? Or was he schizophrenic? Who spoke out of the heavens at his baptism, and his transfiguration? Or was he a super ventriloquist who bounced his voice off a cloud? Such a construction sounds strangely like the gnostic heresy, under a different guise, which John denounced as of the antichrist:

> Who is the liar but he that denieth that Jesus is the Christ? That is the antichrist, even he that denieth the Father and the Son (I John 2:22).

In the gnostic construction, Jesus was regarded as a creature of the Father—the first and highest of his creation, but nonetheless a creature. The Oneness doctrine is unitarian in a form which demeans God, the Father. See I Corinthians 15:27, 28.

But what about the proof texts advanced by Onenessites? They have neglected a simple bit of homework. They have failed to check the prepositions. Prepositions denote the direction in which action is flowing, or relationship. In Matthew 28:19 the preposition is "into" (Gr. *eis*). In Acts 2:38 the preposition which relates to the name of Christ is "in" (Gr. *en*). That preposition could well have been translated "by," in the sense of "by the authority of." *Eis* is a forward looking preposition. *En* is backward looking. By the authority of Christ (in his name) one is baptized into the name of the Father, Son, and Holy Spirit. Christopher Columbus was financed by Queen Isabella when he set forth on the exploration trip which brought him to the western hemisphere. In return, wherever he discovered land, he planted the flag of Castile, and took possession "in the name of Queen Isabella." Christian baptism is administered (*en*) in the name of Jesus Christ, (*eis*) into the name of the Father and of the Son and of the Holy Spirit, unto/for (*eis*) the remission of sins.

Matthew 28:18-20 affirms 1) the authority which lies behind the ordinance of baptism and 2) the relationship into which one enters when a penitent believer bows to the authority of Christ.

PREVIEW—REVIEW QUESTIONS

1. State a basic fact relative to the etymology of the word baptize which bears on its root meaning.
2. State one respect in which dictionary definitions sometimes vary from that of lexicons and encyclopedias.
3. State the manner in which the Greek Septuagint (LXX) translates the Hebrew word (*tabal*) translated "dip" in English.

4. Identify a text which includes all three words—dip, pour, and sprinkle—in a context which clearly shows the meaning of each.

5. List some incidental details associated with baptism in New Testament accounts of baptisms, or references to baptism.

6. List some metaphors associated with baptism which suggest dipping rather than affusion (sprinkling, pouring).

7. Note the technicality relative to a secondary usage of the word sprinkle. Does that open the door to sprinkling as a substitute form of baptism? Explain.

8. Since sprinkling and pouring are in a sense related to salvation, state how so.

9. Apply to the issue over the mode of baptism the principle of reasoning; "Things equal to the same thing are equal to each other."

10. In what respect are there two elements, not just one, involved in Christian baptism?

11. Cite a text which indicates all who are in Christ are baptized in the Spirit as well as water.

12. How does the fact that Holy Spirit baptism is a promise of Christ, water baptism an ordinance of Christ, relate to the baptism controversy?

13. How much water is necessary to make a baptism valid?

14. According to the Great Commission, state two prerequisites for baptism.

15. Take note of several New Testament conversions and check the recorded data. Does it jibe with what Jesus commanded?

16. Take note of some "household" baptisms. What evidence mitigates against the notion infants were included?

17. Note the manner in which pedobaptism is a reversion to the circumstances of the Old Covenant.

18. Finish the Fishback quote: "Infant baptism is . . ."

19. State and refute the two common errors to the effect it takes a valid administrator to validate baptism.

20. Note a distinction twixt the two covenants which is violated when the priesthood of believers is not recognized.

21. Does the New Testament provide a guide as to what one must say when baptizing to validate the act? Explain.

22. Evaluate the Oneness doctrine as it relates to the so-called baptismal formula.

23. Explain the difference between the preposition in Matt. 28:19 and Acts 2:38 as they relate to baptism.

18

CHRISTIAN BAPTISM, CONCLUDED: PURPOSE SERVED

A. Pertinent Background Information

Persons reading the New Testament without benefit (correction, blight!) of creedal blinders are mystified by the controversy over the purpose and benefits of baptism. From the first mention of baptism in the New Testament (Matt. 3:5-17) to the last (I Peter 3:18-21) and consistently throughout all the references in between (of which there are more than a score), baptism is set in the context of remission of sins, salvation, unity with Christ, participation in the death, burial, and resurrection of Christ, regeneration, receiving the Holy Spirit, etc. Nowhere is the doctrine or practice of baptism disparaged in the New Testament or presented as an option. Those who begin reading the New Testament on their own invariably and readily note such things. They are surprised and unsettled when professedly mature and knowledgeable Bible students represent the facts to be otherwise.

Paul's statement in I Corinthians 1:17, to the effect he had not been sent to baptize and that he was thankful he had personally baptized only a few of the Corinthians (if taken out of context), might provide the lone exception to the positive thrust of the New Testament doctrine of baptism. But the very context of the passage communicates the fact that every one of the Corinthian Christians had been baptized, regardless of who evangelized them. The problem Paul is addressing was the sectarian spirit that was developing among them, evidenced by the fact each was taking special pride in the fact that their favorite evangelist had baptized them. In that context Paul was thankful he had followed the example of Jesus (see John 4:1, 2) who wisely had his disciples administer baptism lest some would think their baptism made them a cut above their fellows, in that they had been baptized by the hands of Christ (cp. I Cor. 1:15).

One indeed has to put on creedal blinders to read into I Corinthians 1:14-17 anything that would support the jaundiced view of baptism that is characteristic of those caught up in the faith-only syndrome. Is it not amazing that the faith-only precept is heavily indebted to Martin Luther, yet the Lutherans continue to practice infant baptism (?) lest the infant die before arriving at the point of faith and go to hell. In that respect Lutherans actually practice baptism-only salvation. By a curious form of reasoning they would deny that, insisting it is the parents' faith operating on behalf of the infant that is the saving factor. A question remains unanswered. Why cannot the parents' faith save the child without baptism, if one is saved by faith alone?

Were that not problem enough, the Baptists, the most vocal champions of the dogma of salvation by faith alone, actively proselyte Lutherans to their own sect; but when successful, they refuse to accept those proselyted into the membership of their sect unless the defectors submit to a public baptism administered by a Baptist preacher. Consistency of reasoning or practice has never been a hallmark of creedal reconstruction of the Scriptures.

Such observations should suffice to underscore the scope of the problem now before us, and its source. It is not that the Scriptures have not spoken, or that what has been spoken is not plain in statement as to the specified benefits and even essential resultants of the obedience of faith. The problem is that what the Scriptures teach concerning the purpose of baptism, and what results therefrom, does not square with the dogma of salvation by faith alone. What then should be sacrificed?

Martin Luther who coined the phrase, "salvation by faith alone," was soon thereafter confronted with the problem of which we have just spoken. History records that Luther was "working" his way up the cathredral steps, in conformity to established ritual, when some words of the Scripture flashed into his mind: "the righteous shall live by faith." Arising, he returned to his room and found the place where that is written (Rom. 1:17b). In conformity to the pendulum principle, Luther took his pen and wrote (obliquely) into the text the word "sola," making it to read: "the righteous shall live by faith sola" (solely, only, alone). Luther thus moved from one extreme to another.

What a shock it was to him, as he began to bury himself in the reading of the Bible, to come to James 2:24 and find the Scripture there stating exactly the opposite of what he had amended Romans 1:17 to read. James concluded an argument in which he had used Abraham as an illustration, by affirming one "is *not* justified by faith alone." Now what was Luther to do? It should be obvious what he ought to have done. But being still in the throes of reaction to dead works of the papal system, instead of deleting the word he had added to Romans 1:17, he chose to delete the entire book of James from the Bible. He labeled (libeled) it "an epistle of straw."

The spiritual heirs of Luther have learned to live with the book of James by doing with James 2:17-24 what they do with such texts as Mark 16:16; Acts 2:38, 22:16; Romans 6:3-18; Galatians 3:27; Colossians 2:12; I Peter 3:21. They assume what the Scriptures mean to say in those places cannot be what they plainly, unequivocally communicate, else the dogma of justification by faith "sola" would be violated. Thus like Luther, the author and prototype of their theological format and fellowship, they abandon exegetical principles and resort to eisegesis to read into the passages whatever is required to fit their creed. Thereby every baptismal passage which does not specifically mention water is interpreted as referring to Holy Spirit baptism, *only*.

B. *Some Pertinent Questions*

The question rises: why then baptize anyone in water, in any fashion, for any cause? Why do Lutheran clergymen (among others of pedo-baptist tradition) continue to ceremoniously sprinkle water on the foreheads of infants, incanting the phrase, "I baptize thee *in* the name of the Father, and the Son, and the Holy Spirit"? And why do Baptist ministers publicly and ceremoniously dip those old enough to make a personal profession of faith, incanting the same phrase (including the substitute of the preposition "in" for "into," Gr. *eis*)? If baptism "for the remission of sins" is to vainly "add to the finished work of

259

Calvary" (a popular phrase in the liturgy of Faith-Onlydom), then why does not water baptism administered for any cause vainly add to the regenerative work of the Holy Spirit? The answer given is that baptism is "an outward sign of an inward grace," or more succinctly "a witness." Scripture? There is none that says any such thing.

The rationale is that one is not adding to the "finished work of Calvary," nor the "regenerating work of the Holy Spirit," if baptism is administered only as a symbol, stripped of an sacramental or efficacious benefit. Thus the command of Christ can be carried out, and his personal example followed, and their creedal reconstruction of the Scriptures can still be maintained.

But we repeat what was said at the outset. No one reading the Scriptures without creedal blinders would ever come to any such conclusion. Well may we ask: 1) To whom did the Ethiopian eunuch feel constrained to witness when he asked to receive water baptism? Where did he even get the idea he should be baptized? Philip "preached unto him Jesus." Did preaching Jesus originally include preaching what Jesus said in the Great Commission? Why did Philip go along with it? Why did he not suggest that the eunuch should wait till he got home and give his "baptismal witness" in a more public situation? 2) To whom did Cornelius and his household witness by being baptized in water? Had not Peter and those who came with him seen enough already? Was not their baptism in the Holy Spirit so manifest that even the six Jews who came with Peter were obliged to acknowledge that even though Cornelius and his household were Gentiles, they had definitely been baptized in the Holy Spirit? What else needed to be proved? They certainly were not baptized into a local Baptist church. 3) Why was the Philippian jailer baptized in the middle of the night? To whom did he and his household bear witness? Why did not Paul and Silas suggest they wait till morning and have Lydia and her company come and "witness" the baptism, and vote them into the church? 4) The fundamental question remains. Where does the New Testament teach any such thing? And if it does not, for what reason or reasons is baptism to be administered? Why was it attended to so quickly upon one's acceptance of Christ? Why the urgency? Why the consistency of the pattern, without regard to race, time, sex, or place? Let creeds be set aside. "What saith the oracles (Gr. *chrematismos*—Divine response) of God" (Rom. 11:4).

260

C. *The Purpose, the Resultants of Baptism*

This should not be difficult to ascertain if one will simply take the time to note, one by one, the Scripture texts which speak of Christian baptism. There are no subtleties to decipher, no hidden meanings, in fact, no surprises; unless one has been led to expect not to find what the Scriptures so simply express.

Nowhere in the New Testament is the subject of baptism presented in the context of controversy, as though someone had a proverbial axe to grind, or as though a deviant practice or doctrine of baptism needed correction. For the most part, references to baptism are of the incidental, "in passing" sort. What we find is generally simple reporting. Even the one discourse on baptism which has been preserved for us was not written to answer a single one of the questions being raised today. Romans 6:3-17 was written neither to settle questions concerning the "mode of baptism" nor to inform us of the purpose of baptism.

Sprinkling and pouring are practices so far removed from Romans 6:3-17 in point of time, and from the intrinsic meaning of the word *baptizo*, Paul was in no way responding thereto. Such practices awaited generations of drifting from the apostolic order before they were even to be introduced provisionally. And as for the purpose of baptism, that was not as yet gainsayed by any sect or schism threatening the unity of the church in either doctrine or practice. Paul's baptismal discourse in Romans six was written to apply what was universally understood about baptism to a reactionary development growing out of his doctrine of justification by faith vs. the works of the Mosaic Law.

Our contemporary faith-only hyper-reactionaries go beyond the original reaction. The Jews were not saying, "If God's grace is as great as Paul declares it to be, why be baptized?" They were saying only, "Let us sin the more that grace may abound" (v. 1). Paul answers by noting were they to do that, they would be acting in violation of everything their baptism was designed both to do and teach. Romans 6:3-17 serves as a kind of pictorial summary of the implications which are intrinsic in the design and *modus operandi* of baptism. His expression of abhorrence: "Let it not be!" (Gr. *me genoito*) is followed by a graphic reminder of what baptism is supposed to have signalized, the state into which they were thereby supposed to have come.

Any delineation of the purpose and the resultants of baptism will best begin by noting the Divine Author and the authorization of Christian

261

baptism. With this our verse-by-verse listing of the textual data will now begin.

1) *Matthew 28:18-20* should remind us of the question Jesus put to the Pharisees: "The baptism of John, whence was it? from heaven or from men?" (Matt. 21:25). Cp. Luke 7:29, 30 for a startling announcement concerning failure to submit to John's baptism. Does one need to ask whence came the baptism Christ has enjoined upon us, even unto the end of the world, in his Great Commission? What happens when one who has been discipled by the Gospel of Christ submits to Christ's authority in the baptism he has commanded? Answer: Obedience itself is one thing that happens. And as a result of that obedience, one is baptized into (Gr. *eis*) the name of the Father, and of the Son, and of the Holy Spirit.

Is this not worth pondering? Only once in all history, as of the Biblical record, have the Father, Son, and Holy Spirit been manifested simultaneously. At Jesus' baptism, the Father sent the Holy Spirit in a visible form to abide upon him (John 1:33), and at the same time God audibly declared Jesus to be his only begotten son, in whom he was well pleased. The trinitarian concept of the Godhead has no reference data more cogent. It is then exceedingly significant that in the whole of the Scriptures only one act of faith and/or obedience is said to place one "into the name of the Father, and of the Son, and of the Holy Spirit."

2) *Mark 16:16* specifies another important result which ensues when one believes the Gospel and is baptized: "He that believeth and is baptized shall be saved." To that promise is added a warning note: "He that believeth not shall be condemned."

Those who have a creedal dogma that must be defended at all costs hasten to point out that Jesus did not also say: "He that is not baptized shall be condemned." How ridiculous can one get? What is the use of discussing baptism with one who will not believe? What good would it do to baptize someone who does not believe? Baptism is an act of faith. It is at the core of the "obedience of faith" (Rom. 1:5; 16:26; cp. 6:17, 18). Except as an expression of faith, even though one were baptized until he was waterlogged, it would profit nothing. Hebrews 11:6 plainly warns: "Without faith it is impossible to be well pleasing unto God, for he that cometh to God must believe that he is, and that he is the rewarder of them that diligently seek after him."

Suppose a weary traveler, afoot in a burning desert, faint and athirst, should draw near to a wayside inn astride an oasis. Suppose the traveler, almost at the point of delirium from the oppressive heat should be noticeably hesitant to come in. Whereupon the observant innkeeper opened the door and said, "Come in, and stay awhile, and my servants will bring you a cool drink, and set food before you to refresh you. But suppose the traveler, whether too near heat exhaustion to think clearly, or by reason of stubbornness or stupidity, should continue to hesitate. Would not the concerned innkeeper attempt to reason with the man, saying: "You must heed my invitation. If you do not come in, you will suffer a heat stroke and die 'neath the burning sun"? Would he also have to say, "If you won't stay awhile, you will die out there 'neath the blazing sun"? The first act, an act of the mind and the will, would be a necessary predicate of the more passive act, staying awhile within. Thus our Lord has promised earth's pilgrims: "He that believeth (an act of the mind, and of the will) and is baptized (a passive, compliant act, contingent upon believing) shall be saved."

The foregoing texts, drawn from Christ's final instructions to the apostles whom he had chosen, plainly state 1) the Divine authority that underscores the command both to be baptized and to baptize, and 2) the all-encompassing purpose for baptism—that those discipled and believing "shall be saved." The texts which follow, drawn from the book of Acts and the apostolic epistles plainly show how the apostles understood the commission given them. We shall continue the numerical sequence as they are noted one by one.

3) *Acts 2:38*. Here Peter is answering the question of a vast multitude stricken with guilt upon hearing proclaimed the Gospel of the death, burial, and resurrection of Christ. We shall resist the temptation to state what Peter would have had to say if Pentecost were the prototype of typical evangelistic campaigns today. That it was not! Few indeed are the mass evangelists, and even mini-evangelists who would dare to answer the question put to Peter in the manner that he did. The creeds of evangelicalism and the constitution and bylaws of most of the churches would have to be revised if they did.

The answer Peter gives, "Repent ye, and be baptized every one of you *in the name of* (by the authority of) Jesus Christ, for the remission of your sins, and ye shall receive the gift of the Holy Spirit" agrees perfectly with what Christ commissioned them to say, as recorded in Matthew 28:18-20, Mark 16:16, and Luke 24:47.

Modern interpreters have taken off in two directions to avoid the difficulty of reconciling their preachments and practice with what Peter said. The most common diversion (perversion, to be more precise) is to say that the preposition for/unto can sometimes be interpreted to mean "because of," hence is to be understood in this text as looking back upon what has already been realized, not what is about to result. Toward the close of this lesson, we shall review that bit of deceit in depth.

The ultra-dispensationalists have come up with another escape hatch, or so they think. As one of them undertook to explain it to me: "My Baptist brethren are being flagrantly dishonest when they try to make Acts 2:38 read, 'be baptized *because* of remission of sins.' But," he continued, "you are in error when you teach that baptism is for remission of sins today." He then undertook to explain that baptism for remission of sins was only a carry-over of John's baptism till the close of the Jewish phase of the church. After that, salvation by grace alone through faith became the way of salvation. When we opened our Bibles and read Matthew 28:18-20, noting the *duration* of the Commission as Jesus enunciated it, and Acts 2:38 and the *distribution* of the command to be baptized as Peter enunciated it, he was quite unable to come up with a Scripture that could be warped to sustain his thesis and stand up under scrutiny. The thesis there are two Gospels discernible in the Scriptures, a provisional Gospel for the Jews which ended (or rather, was suspended) at the fall of Jerusalem, and another for the Gentiles that became a Gospel of grace alone through faith, on or about Acts 18:6, is little short of heresy. It makes a mockery of the doctrine of the unity of believers in Christ, as pled for in his intercessory prayer (John 17:20-23) and as articulated in Ephesians, chapters 2 through 4, and elsewhere.

4) *Acts 22:16* is a striking commentary on Acts 2:38. Saul of Tarsus, stricken blind on the Damascus Road, asked of Jesus, "What shall I do, Lord?" (Acts 22:10). The answer received was: "Arise, and go into Damascus and there it shall be told you all the things which are appointed for you to do." In the initial account (ch. 9), the answer is stated more tersely, "Arise and go into the city and it shall be told you what you must (Gr. *dei*) do" (v. 6). The verb, *dei*, is used in the New Testament 105 times: 65 times it is translated "must" (KJV) and even "must needs be"; otherwise it is rendered "ought" and "should." Paul therefore was not just receiving some advice. He was placed under Divine command.

Upon arriving in Damascus no one awaited him there to tell him anything. So he did all he knew to do or could do under the circumstances. He fasted and prayed. It would seem that if anyone could simply "pray through," Saul ought to have done so. But when the Lord sent Ananias to instruct him, Ananias said, "And now, why tarriest thou, arise and be baptized and wash away thy sins, calling on the name of the Lord." Then Paul was not saved when he "only believed," or "saw the light," or fasted and prayed, else he was saved while still in his sins. It was not even when the Holy Spirit came upon him (see 9:17). Not even *Holy Spirit* baptism is a substitute for water baptism. That belongs to the Divine side of the redemptive process. Witness the case of Cornelius (Acts 10:47, 48). To submit to water baptism in acknowledgment of the authority of Christ, for the remission (washing away) of sins is something we must do.

A. T. Robertson notes the verb (baptisai) is the *"first aorist middle* (causative), not passive, and should read 'Get thyself baptized'" (Robertson, *Grammar,* p. 808), "and get washed (apolousai) of thy sins." But having said that, he throws to the winds his expertise in Greek grammar, for which he is renowned, and lets his theology take over. Candidly admitting: "It is possible, as in 2:38, to take these words as teaching baptismal remission, or salvation by means of baptism." He adds: "But to do so is *in my opinion* (note the basis on which he now moves: opinion supersedes grammar) a complete subversion of Paul's vivid and picturesque language." He then cites Romans 6:4-6 (Robertson, *Word Pictures in the New Testament,* p. 391). Is it really? Unless one is creedal bound and "opinion" blinded that is a complete subversion of what Paul wrote in Romans 6:4-6, *and elsewhere.*

5) *Acts 2:41.* In this Scripture baptism is said to result in being added to the *ekklesia* (the called) of Christ (cp. v. 47; see also I Cor. 12:13). It was the *body* of Christ (his flesh) that was raised "on the third day" (as promised). And it is the body of Christ (his "called out" ones) who shall be raised, as promised, "in the last day" (John 6:39, 40).

6) *Romans 6:3-6.* This text, amplified and applied as the chapter unfolds, plainly teaches that we enter into the redemptive death of Christ when we are "buried with him through baptism," and that we are raised to walk in newness of life even as he was raised to "give life also to our mortal bodies" through his Spirit that dwelleth within in us (Rom. 8:11, 5:11; I Cor. 15:17, 18).

7) *Colossians 2:12.* This text is an echo of Romans 6. Included is a phrase often overlooked by those on both sides of the efficacy of baptism

controversy. Again baptism is said to bring us into union with Christ, both with respect to his death and to his resurrection. But note that in baptism our faith is not in the act itself but in the "working (energizing, Gr. *energeias*) of God who raised him (Christ) from the dead." Few, if any, who acknowledge baptism as a solemn command effectuating our redemption can rightly be charged with believing it is the water that washes away sins. We readily agree with Peter. Baptism is "not the putting away of the filth of the flesh, but the answer of a good conscience toward God" (I Peter 3:21). But what is wrong with having a good conscience borne out of taking Christ at his word, doing what he commanded, and for the reasons he gave us such a commandment?

8) *Romans 6:16-18.* This text will be dealt with more fully in a later lesson as the Divine commemorative institutions are discussed under that title. For the purpose of this present study we shall simply take note of the fact that baptism is said to make us "free from sin" (as Acts 2:38; 22:16 also state), but we also thereby "become servants of righteousness." That expression is an echo of Jesus' words to John when he presented himself to John for baptism, despite the fact John was baptizing "for the remission of sins" (Mark 1:4). The populace could think what they pleased. Jesus was more concerned about the will of his father who immediately endorsed his course of action by audibly declaring himself to be "well pleased" with his beloved son (Mark 1:11).

9) *Galatians 3:27* is but a variant expression of what is affirmed in Romans 6:3-5 and Colossians 2:12. It adds, however, a significant phrase. We are said thereby to "put on Christ" (Gr. *enedusasthe*, lit., "enclothe," from *enduo*). This is the same verb used in I Corinthians 15:53, 54 where we are told that in the resurrection we mortal, corruptible beings shall put on immortality and incorruption. If one is minded to bypass being raised up by Christ in baptism, will such a one be equally content to bypass being raised up by Christ in the consummation of the ages? Raised up by Christ we shall be: some unto the resurrection of life, all others to the resurrection of damnation; and all at the same hour! (See John 5:28, 29.) Thank God, those who have part with him in the first resurrection will have no part in the second death. (See Rev. 20:6, cp. v. 14.)

10) *I Peter 3:20-22.* In this text baptism is again specifically linked to salvation, and to a good conscience toward God as well. Some years ago a lady attending evening services where I was preaching asked to talk with me privately about some doctrinal differences which

concerned her. Since she carried a Scofield (Commentary) Reference Bible and her expression from time to time betrayed what she was thinking, I was sure that baptism was likely one point of issue. It was. In fact it was the chief point of issue. I elected to keep the discussion on a textual, exegetical basis, rather than argue creedal or theological positions. Thus I started going through the New Testament, calling baptism references to her attention, and asking her to write down each time what the Scriptures state or implied baptism was for. Obviously this was something she had never done before, and she was a bit shaken at the number of references to baptism, and the number of rather crucial things that are linked with baptism. But she stood her ground, insisting there had to be some other interpretation, for her "pastor" who was a much older man than I had clearly shown her that salvation is through faith alone. At length I was down to the last text to be set before her.

At this point I paused and asked, "What would the Scripture have to say before you would believe that baptism now saves us? As far as I am concerned, Mark 16:16 says that very thing, but you refuse to believe it." Again she explained that dispensationally that was no longer true. When Paul turned to the Gentiles baptism was no longer administered for the remission of sins. So I rephrased my question: "What would a text of Scripture written after Paul turned to the Gentiles have to say before you would believe that baptism saved *us, now*?" I handed her a pen and told her to write that down, and I would see if I could find a Scripture somewhere that said something like that. She did it. Admittedly, I felt a bit guilty for having taken advantage of her ignorance by feigning a bit of ignorance on my own part. Taking her own Bible I turned to I Peter 3:20-22 and asked her to read it out loud. She got down to the very phrase she had written, read it haltingly, with a touch of anger showing in her voice, and answered testily, "I still won't believe baptism saves us." I said to her, "At last the truth is out. You probably admitted more than you intended to say. I noted you did not say, 'I don't believe it,' or 'I cannot believe it.' You said you *won't* believe it." Jesus closed one of his encounters with the unbelieving Jews by saying, "You *will not* come to me that you may have life" (John 5:40).

I Peter 3:20-22, the final baptismal text of the Bible, links baptism to salvation and a good conscience toward God. The text also calls attention to the typology of the flood by way of illustration. Note what is said: The Noahites were not just saved from water, though that they were in one sense. But the point of typology to which Peter calls attention is that they were saved by/through (Gr. *dia*) water. The ark saved them (physically) *from* the water. But the water saved them spiritually by washing away that sinful generation that had so encroached upon the righteous there were but eight such souls left. "Even so," Peter says, "after a *true likeness* (Gr. *antitupon*/antitype) baptism doth now save us." It is more than the putting away of the filth of the flesh. It is the answer of a good conscience toward God.

BAPTISM *Essential* or
an *Elective?*

If God says what he means, means what he says, what is God trying to say to us?	An ESSENTIAL: The text, taken at face value so says.	U N C L E A R	An ELECTIVE: Any suggestion of essentiality is lacking.
1. Matt. 28:18-20	_____	_____	_____
2. Mark 16:15, 16	_____	_____	_____
3. Acts 2:38, 39	_____	_____	_____
4. Acts 22:16	_____	_____	_____
5. Acts 2:41, 42	_____	_____	_____
6. Rom. 6:3-5	_____	_____	_____
7. Col. 2:12	_____	_____	_____
8. Rom. 6:16-18	_____	_____	_____
9. Gal. 3:27	_____	_____	_____
10. I Peter 3:20-22	_____	_____	_____

In the light of the closing warning of the sacred Scriptures, Revelation 22:18, 19, and the foregoing Scripture references:

(   ) Those who teach that baptism is essential to salvation have "added" to the Word of God and are in danger of the wrath to come.

(   ) Those who teach that baptism is not essential to salvation have "taken away" from God's Word and are in danger of the wrath to come.

(   ) The Scriptures are unclear on this subject.

268

D. *Assaying Some Paste "Jewels"*

In popular theology, indeed "consistency is a jewel." It is that rare. But cheap imitations that fool the unwary are to be found on every hand. The following are a few samples of paste baptismal "jewelry" being peddled as Biblical theology.

1. Dr. A. T. Robertson's *"eis"* theology is a classic example. The Greek preposition, *eis*, pronounced "ice," as in the slang for diamond, is handled by Dr. Robertson with masterful inconsistency. In Volume 1 of his popular seven-volume publication, *Word Pictures in the New Testament,* the renowned scholar provides an interesting commentary on Matthew 26:28. Jesus, in the institution of the Lord's Supper, took a cup and said: "This is the new covenant in my blood, which is poured out for many, *unto the remission of sins."* The underlined phrase draws this comment:

> Unto remission of sins (*eis aphesin hamartion*). This clause is in Matthew's account alone, but it is not to be restricted for that reason. It is the truth. This passage answers all the modern sentimentalism that finds in the teaching of Jesus only pious ethical remarks or eschatological dreamings. He had the definite conception of his death of the cross as the basis of forgiveness of sin. The purpose of the shedding of his blood of the New Covenant was precisely to remove (forgive) sins (p. 210).

Now that the author has explained to us *precisely* what the phrase *eis aphesin hamartion* means (vs. what "modern sentimentalism" would have us believe), let us turn to Volume 3, *The Acts of the Apostles,* and see how he handles Acts 2:38 where the phrase is repeated, except that Peter in his use of the phrase is even more precise and personal in his application. Peter's answer to the question, "What must we do?" reads: "Repent and be baptized every one of you *for the remission of your sins (eis aphesin harmartion)."* Now what will he say the phrase means? Here it is, verbatim:

> This phrase is the subject of endless controversy as men look at it from the standpoint of sacramental or evangelical theology. In themselves the words can express aim or purpose, for that use of *eis* does exist.

Note: At this point, out of 1,783 references in which eis is used in the New Testament, he cites I Corinthians 2:7, just about the most inocuous reference that could be found. Why did he not cite the aforementioned Matthew 26:28? Ah, that would draw attention to what he has already affirmed to be the "precise" meaning of the phrase. So in Acts 2:38 he reverses his field and says:

> But then another usage exists which is just as good Greek as the use of
> *eis* for aim or purpose (p. 35).

At this point he cites two texts: Matthew 10:41, 12:41. Apparently those are the two best proof texts he can come up with. Indeed they may be the only two he could call to mind. They are not all that convincing. But again, having diverted his reader's attention to texts quite oblique to the issue at hand, he concludes:

> One will decide the use here (Acts 2:38) *according as he believes that baptism is essential to the remission of sins or not. My view is* decidedly against the idea that Peter, Paul, or anyone in the New Testament taught baptism as essential to the remission of sins, or the means of securing such remission. So *I understand* Peter to be urging baptism on each of them who had already [sic] turned, repented, and for it to be done in the name of Jesus Christ on the basis of the forgiveness of sins *which they had already received* (p. 35, italics my own).

Consistency, thou art a jewel! Theology, thou art something else! A study was made by Wm. E. Paul, who surveyed 72 available translations of the New Testament to see how they saw fit to translate Acts 2:38. The 72 include several translations done by individuals. Only one was bold enough to revise the verse to teach what Robertson espouses. No committee, no matter what their makeup, has yet seen fit to expunge from the text what Robertson disparages as "sacramental" theology. Kenneth Wuest, working alone, stands alone in that. He awkwardly renders the phrase: "in relation to the fact that your sins have been put away." To obscure the obvious, he uses twelve words to do the work of five.

Question: Did the Greek language lack the facility to express the concept "because of"? Did Luke have to take the word *eis*, reverse its meaning, and hope no one would take literally what he reported Peter as having said in Acts 2:38? Actually, it abounds with words he could have used. Fourteen are so translated. One, *hoti*, is translated *because (of)* 183 times. *Eis*, used 1,783 times in the New Testament *never* is. Only in commentaries, sermons, etc., of those blinded by creeds is Acts 2:38 ever represented as teaching that baptism is to be administered "because of" instead of "*for* the remission of sins."

2. Another classic example of creedal inconsistency "paste jewelry" is found in a vehement "letter to the editor" signed by one who called himself Reverend (no less) . . . (name withheld to protect the not so innocent) of Mt. Airy, N.C. A Christian brother, Edward Werner, had

published *An In-depth Study of the Greek Word Eis* which aroused the ire of the self-styled Reverend (see Ps. 111:9). His reply was as follows:

> If *baptism* is essential for salvation or remission of sins, then *the baptizer* is just as essential in God's plan of salvation as Jesus Christ. Since persons can't *baptize* themselves, having to depend on another to do it for them, the one *baptizing* is coequal with Jesus Christ, MEANING THAT THE BIBLE IS NOT TRUE, and the Scriptures should read: Rom. 5:9, "justified by his blood AND WATER BAPTISM," and Eph. 1:7, "redemption through his blood AND WATER BAPTISM," and Col. 1:14, "redemption through his blood AND WATER BAPTISM," and Eph. 2:14, "We are made nigh by the blood of Christ AND WATER BAPTISM," and Heb. 9:22, "Without the shedding of blood AND WATER BAPTISM there is no remission of sins," and I Pet. 1:19, "We have been redeemed with the precious blood of Christ AND WATER BAPTISM," and Rev. 7:14, "and have washed their robes and made them white in the blood of the Lamb AND WATER BAPTISM," and Rev. 12:11, "They overcame by the blood of the Lamb AND WATER BAPTISM."
>
> (Hogwash!)
>
> What you need is to get saved by grace through faith, and that not of yourself, it is the gift of God, not of works (baptism). I'll stand on God's Word.
>
> Signed: Rev. _____

Suppose we test the consistency of the Junior Reverend by deleting the words baptism, baptizer, and water baptism, and supplying one of the words he (correctly) links with salvation (faith, grace) in his final paragraph, or the resurrection of Christ, or repentance, or the preaching of the Gospel. (The first and the last two mentioned are things we do ourselves.) Reprint his letter, leaving blanks where he assails baptism, and insert any one of the terms suggested, and see how his logic (?) works out.

As an example of how such an exercise exposes the utter absurdity of his tirade, a few lines hereby follow so treated:

Exhibit A. If (faith) is essential for our salvation or remission of sins, then (the one who leads us to believe) is just as essential in God's plan of salvation as Jesus Christ. Since persons cannot (lead) themselves (to believe), having to depend on someone else to do it for them (Rom. 10:14-17), then the one who (leads them to faith) is coequal with Jesus Christ, MEANING THAT THE BIBLE IS NOT TRUE, and the Scriptures should read: Romans 5:9, "justified by his blood (AND FAITH)," and Ephesians 1:7, "redemption through his blood (AND FAITH),", etc., etc., etc. (Hogwash? Hogwash!)

Exhibit B. If (the Gospel is the power of God unto salvation unto everyone that believeth, Rom. 1:16), hence is essential for salvation or the remission of sins, then (the preacher/teacher who brings the Gospel) is just as essential in God's plan of salvation as Jesus Christ. Since persons can't (evangelize) themselves, having to depend on another to do it for them (Rom. 10:14-17), the one (bringing the Gospel to them) is coequal with Jesus Christ, MEANING THAT THE BIBLE IS NOT TRUE, and the Scriptures should read . . . . (Hogwash? Hogwash!)

Exhibit C. If (the resurrection of Christ) is essential for salvation (see Rom. 5:10) or remission of sins, then (Jesus' resurrection) is just as essential in God's plan of salvation as Jesus Christ (himself, or his death, perhaps? cp. I Cor. 15:17). Since persons can't (raise Christ from the dead) themselves, having to depend on (the Spirit that raised up Christ, see Rom. 8:11) is coequal with Jesus Christ, MEANING THAT THE BIBLE IS NOT TRUE, and the Scriptures should read . . . . (Hogwash? Hogwash!)

Consistency, thou art a jewel! The self-styled Reverend is a paragon of inconsistency. His pearls of wisdom are paste artifacts. He would do well to reconsider the swill he is feeding to his congregation and apologize to Bro. Edward Werner.

The inimitable evangelist, Archie Word, once quipped that creeds can so narrow one's sight and mind that "a mosquito could land on the bridge of the nose and kick both eyes out without shaking its hips." How urgently, how desperately, is this creed-bound world needing to hear "the whole counsel of God" with regard to the destiny-laden question: "What must one do to be saved?"

3. Another inconsistency arising out of creedal blindness is to be seen in the aforementioned "Reverend's" use of Ephesians 2:8. The faith-only syllogisms are about 90% silly, and only about 10% logic. For the unitiated, syllogisms are a rhetorical (and presumably logical) device used to sort out and test what things belong to, or may be included in, a certain class or category. They consist of a major premise (the class or category), a minor premise (a specific to be tested, or sorted out), and a conclusion. For example:

> Virtue is worthy to be praised.
> Honesty is a virtue.
> Therefore, honesty is to be praised.

Does that not make sense? It should. The major premise is true. The minor premise is true. Thus the logical conclusion that is drawn is also true. But unfortunately, just as the old saying goes, "Figures do not lie, but liars figure," even so logical syllogisms lead to logical conclusions, but a lot of silliness passes for syllogistic reasoning. Sometimes this is done innocently, based on lack of information, or proper definition. For example:

Bicycles are prohibited from use on interstates. Motorcycles are bicycles (two-wheeled vehicles). Therefore motorcycles may not be used on freeways.

Right? Wrong. They are used on freeways, and legally so. What then is the problem with the syllogism? The problem is one of definition. Motorcycles are not, by definition of public law, bicycles. They are licensed as motor vehicles, capable of maintaining highway speed in excess of the minimum speed limit, 40 MPH. But are they not "two-wheeled" vehicles? Yes, but so is an ox-cart. But I do not know of a boy wanting an ox-cart for his birthday. Not all two-wheelers are "bicycles."

Now let us apply this to the topic at hand, from two perspectives, a) creedal, and b) Biblical.

a) Creedal-oriented syllogism

Major Premise: We are not saved by works (Titus 3:5)
Minor Premise: Baptism is a work (Scripture?).
Conclusion: Therefore baptism in no sense saves us.

But I Peter 3:21 says it does, and Mark 16:16 implies as much, along with a lot of other texts such as Acts 2:38, 22:16; Galatians 3:27; etc. What is the problem? Unless God is a god of confusion, and it takes a faith-only indoctrinated theologian to straighten things out, baptism must not be a work, according to Biblical definition. Only by the definition of such persons as the two we took time to refute is baptism a "work."

b) Biblical-oriented syllogism

Major Premise: We are not saved by works of righteousness which we do ourselves (Titus 3:5, cp. Eph. 2:8).
Minor Premise: Baptism now saves us (I Peter 3:21).
Conclusion: Baptism is not therefore a work of righteousness which we do ourselves.

What then is it? It is "the obedience of faith" (Rom. 6:17). It is faith in action. Faith had better be in action, for if it is not, it is dead (James 2:24-27). Hearkening back to the problem dealt with in the North Carolina preacher's hangup, we repeat what was noted when we reviewed the role of synecdoches in Biblical revelation: Only a denominational bias (creedal blindness) would lead one to reject one (any one) factor in God's redemptive system because he has, in some other text, spoken of some other factor as being a means of his redeeming grace.

PREVIEW—REVIEW QUESTIONS

1. When baptism is mentioned in the Scriptures, is it by way of reproof? Warning? Commendation? Commandment? Or is it treated with indifference?
2. Is there any exception to the rule? Is any text in which baptism is specifically mentioned ever cited as such? Locate, if so.
3. Explain, contextually, texts some cite by way of disparaging baptism.
4. How does the prevailing practice of infant baptism belie the Lutheran doctrine of salvation by faith alone?
5. How does the baptizing of proselyted confirmed Lutherans do much the same thing?
6. What word did Luther add to Romans 1:17 in conformity to the "pendulum principle"? Explain the circumstances.
7. State the problem that confronted him later when he came to the book of James. How did he attempt to solve it?
8. How do his spiritual heirs handle the problem today?
9. State the inconsistency which exists when the dogma of total hereditary depravity leads to infant baptism in a sect of Christendom teaching salvation is by faith alone.
10. Respond to the saying that baptism for the remission of sins is a denial of the finished work of Calvary.
11. Relate the circumstances of baptisms recorded in Acts (beyond the day of Pentecost) to the teaching that "baptism is our witness to the fact we have been saved."
12. Where does the Bible say anything to the effect that baptism is our witness, or is the outward sign of an inward grace?
13. State the problem which Paul was dealing with in his baptismal discourse in Romans 6. How does he bring the doctrine of baptism to bear on that problem?
14. Was Romans 6 written to refute or correct the practice of sprinkling? Does it do so? Relate the two questions.

15. State two resultants of baptism which may be deduced from Matthew 28:18, 19.
16. Take note of the only recorded instance of the simultaneous manifestation of the three persons of the Godhead. Relate to what is said about baptism in Matthew 28:18, 19.
17. State a specific result of being baptized according to Mark 16:16. Without the preposition *eis* to hassle over, how do the faith-only adherents try to get around this verse?
18. State the results which are said to follow baptism according to Acts 2:38.
19. Note the distinction between being baptized "*in* the name of Jesus Christ" and "*into* the name of the Father, Son, and Holy Spirit."
20. Note two ways faith-only adherents attempt to reason around Acts 2:38.
21. In view of the fact Acts 22:16 does not use the disputed preposition (*eis*), how does the text bear on the issue as to when sins are remitted?
22. What results when one is baptized, according to Acts 2:41? Where else is baptism said to result in the same estate?
23. State the benefits which result from baptism according to Romans 6:3-5.
24. Wherein ought our faith to be placed when we are being baptized, according to Colossians 2:12?
25. Relate Romans 6:16-18 to the theme of the book of Romans as stated in the prologue and epilogue. According to Romans 6:16-18, what results when one is Scripturally baptized?
26. Take note of the variation of imagery used in Galatians 3:27 as compared to Romans 6;3-5, Colossians 2:12. Are they contradictory?
27. Note the consequence of being baptized, according to I Peter 3:21. Relate baptism to the typology of the flood.
28. Fill in the blanks of the chart, *Baptism: Essential or an Elective.*
29. Note the inconsistency of Dr. A. T. Robertson when he moves from Matthew 26:28 to Acts 2:38.
30. Does the Greek text not have a way to express the concept, "because of"? If so; identify, explain.
31. Do translators of the New Testament, loners and/or committees, ever translate *eis* "because of," or anything else to that effect?
32. Is *eis* used so rarely in the New Testament it is difficult to ascertain its precise meaning? How often is the term used?

33. Document the fact the "precise" meaning of eis is recognized and insisted upon when creedal dogma is not at stake.
34. Note the hole the faith-only "Reverend" dug for himself in his tirade against baptism for remission of sins.
35. Define and illustrate the term "syllogism."
36. Note how the proper use of the device can lead one to the truth, when Scriptures are not taken out of context.

SECTION SIX:
ORGANIZATIONAL STRUCTURE OF THE CHURCH

19

THE VALIDITY OF ORGANIZATIONAL STRUCTURE

Surprise! Organization is not a dirty word. While it is true that the term itself does not appear in an English translation of the Scriptures, the idea communicated thereby is by no means lacking. Our English words organize and organization are derived from the Greek root *ergon*. The term, in its simplest form, appears 177 times in the Greek text of the New Testament. It is translated "work" 152 times, "deed" 22 times; "doing," "labour," and "trade" account for the other three usages. *Ergates,* a derivative of ergon, translated "worker," "workman," "labourer," appears 15 times. Other derivatives such as *ergazomai* (used 41 times) and *ergasai* (used 7 times) provided additional reference data. The first is translated work, wrought, minister, and labor; and the other is rendered craft, business, gain, works, and deeds.

In English usage the word *organ* refers to something that works. Anatomically, we use the term to refer to those parts of the body which work spontaneously, automatically, and for the most part, continuously. Our arms and legs, our hands, and our speech apparatus work only as directed. Fortunately, we do not have to instruct our heart to beat, our lungs to bellow, and our gastronomic apparatus to proceed with the function for which it has been designed. When we lie down for a night of sleep we do not have to instruct our ears to monitor the noises which may ensue and alert us to wakefulness if the phone rings, or some other sound needs our wakeful attention. Neither do we have to instruct our skin, our basic thermostatic apparatus, to monitor the temperature and induce our subconscious minds to pull up the covers, or shed some, to maintain our comfort through the night. We call such members of the body (of which there are many) *organs*, because they *work*. Fortunately, they work together in harmony, according to Divine design, and thus a living creature is called an *organism*.

Time and time again, speakers whose avowed intent has been to enlighten their auditors as to the true nature of the church have used as an opener the familiar cliche: "The church is not an organization; it is an organism." That is a bit of sophistry that needs to be rethought. It is but a half-truth at the best. Cite one example of an organism that is not intricately organized. Break up the organizational structure and organic functioning of even the simplest organism and note how quickly it sickens, dies, and thereupon ceases to be an organism. An inert mass of dead cells, soon to disintegrate, is all that will remain of what was once a living, functioning organism.

Paul repeatedly spoke of the church as "the body of Christ" (I Cor. 12:13-27; Eph. 1:22, 23, 4:16; Col. 1:18). Would anyone care to argue Christ's fleshly body was unorganized? Was not each individual part of his physical organism fitly framed together, each member having a specific function? Do not I Corinthians 12:12-27, Romans 12:3-8, and Ephesians 4:4-16 teach that Christ's spiritual body likewise is intricately organized and able to fulfill its Divine mission by reason thereof?

What the speakers we have alluded to undoubtedly mean to say is that the church is not just an organization. Mere organizations can survive the loss of a "head." Various members of the organization can be shifted about and can take on a new function quite unlike any they have performed before. A filing system is organized; so is a phone directory, and scores of other things. However, it takes an organism, operating at least at the level of human intelligence, to design or employ any one of them.

Organization is not incompatible with Divine design. Even heaven has organizational structure. The presence of archangels (ruling angels) implies lesser angels; ruled no less. I Corinthians 15:27, 28 affirms there is even stratification within the Godhead. And from such a passage as Matthew 19:28 (cp. Luke 22:30), we may anticipate some stratification of the redeemed in glory. All society is organized to some degree. There can be no social structure without it.

The church, according to Divine design, exhibited organizational structure from its inception. That it is to continue to do so, and that the form the organization is to take is subject to Divine direction, are underscored by a plethora of Scriptures.

Our word organization is comprised of the root *ergon* and two important suffixes. The suffix letters *ize* are a verb-forming device, signifying to make, or to do. The context normally suggests which of the two meanings applies. It should go without saying that the church is not organized to make work for someone, but to do the work it has been commissioned to do. The suffix letters *tion* are a noun-forming suffix, signifying the "state of." Thus the word organization literally denotes "the state of doing work." It would be hard to improve upon that state of being, provided the work the church is doing is the work it has been Divinely commissioned to do. Not until both facets of the Great Commission, the evangelization of the world and the edification of the saints, have been fully consummated, need the church to restructure itself, or reassign itself, as though it were needing to find something to do.

When Isaiah received his exalted vision of God and heard the voice of the Lord saying: "Whom shall I send? and who will go for us" (Isa. 6:8), Isaiah was caught up in the rapture of the occasion. Like a youth hearing a stirring challenge at a Christian service camp, Isaiah said: "Here am I, Lord, send me." Immediately the answer came back: "Go, tell this people . . . " Isaiah's response: "How long, Lord? How long?" reflects a bit of second-guessing perhaps. God's answer was: "Until cities be waste, without inhabitant, and houses without man, and the land be utterly waste" (v. 11). In short, as long as there remained so much as one person to hear God's message, Isaiah's commission was still in effect. Is it not even so with Christ's commission to the church?

The only justification for the organizing of the church is to facilitate the carrying out of the Great Commission. While there is a sense in which it is every Christian's duty to be about that task, Christ knew full well how true it is that "everybody's business is nobody's business." Thus it is written of Christ that when he ascended on high he gave gifts to men. Included in those gifts were gifts of service, gifts of leadership, and gifts of specialized ministries. Paul states it on this wise:

He gave some (to be) apostles; and some prophets; and some evangelists; and some pastors and teachers; for the perfecting of the saints unto the work of ministering, unto the building up of the body of Christ: till we all attain unto the unity of the faith, and of the knowledge of the son of God, unto a fullgrown man, unto the measure of the stature of the fullness of Christ . . . from whom all the body fitly framed and knit together through that which every joint supplieth, according to the working together of each several part, maketh the increase of the body unto the building up of itself in love (Eph. 4:11-13, 16).

Implications of the Head/Body Analogy

Several important implications are to be seen in the foregoing analogy. 1) As to *government*, there are three. a) In matters of faith, that is, in areas where God's word has been given us (cp. Rom. 10:17), the church is a theocratic society—a Divine monarchy. It has been said that a monarchy is the best form of government, provided we have the right kind of monarch. In Christ we have the perfect monarch. He has the power of God and the wisdom of God (I Cor. 1:24), and is the love of God personified (I John 4:9, 10).

b) In matters of opinion, in those decisions in which we have no "thus saith the Lord" or approved precedent, the church is free to operate as a democracy—congregationally. Time-honored custom may have much to commend it, but must never be equated with Divine commandment. On the other hand, we should not be caught up in the Athenian syndrome. It was said of even the strangers sojourning there that they too "spent their time in nothing else, but to tell or hear some new thing" (Acts 17:21).

c) In matters of inter-congregational relationships, the church is autonomous. But while there is a sense in which each congregation is a law unto itself (within the bounds of Biblical directives), no congregation should seek to live unto itself. Such texts as Acts 11:27-30; I Cor. 16:1, 2; II Cor. 8:1-5; and the Jerusalem conference (Acts 15) set a precedent for inter-congregational cooperation.

2. The head/body analogy also has implications as to behavior. In our manner of life, individually and collectively, every thought and deed should reflect the mind of Christ. As persons we are certainly assessed and held accountable for the actions of the various members of our bodies. Philippians 2:1-18 has some pertinent things to say concerning this.

The fact that Chirst, as head of the church (Col. 1:18, Eph. 1:20-23), has "all authority, both in heaven and on earth" is underscored by the Great Commission (Matt. 28:18-20). Any binding or loosing done on earth must be subject to him that sits at the right hand of God, and so shall it be unto the end of the world (the age) (Matt. 28:18-20). After that "he shall deliver up his kingdom to God, the Father . . . that God may be all in all" (I Cor. 15:27, 28).

Concerning the Functioning of the Body

The head/body analogy was a favorite illustrative device of the apostle Paul. In I Corinthians 12 and Ephesians 4, he elaborates upon the imagery, providing some special insights. From what he has written we may conclude that the "organs" of the body (the functionaries, the working parts) may be classified under three heads: 1) vestigial, 2) indigenous, 3) supplemental.

The term vestigial means, literally, "pertaining to a trace." It is used anatomically to refer to those organs (or functions) of the body which cease to function when the body reaches a more advanced state. Our navel is an example. The navel is a vestige, but a trace, of what was once the most important organ we had—the umbilical cord. The umbilical cord was our lifeline. Every bone and cartilage, every bit of tissue, every nerve fiber, and every drop of blood in our veins were developed and nourished via the umbilical cord. Yet the time came when, by the wise design of our creator, that cord was cut. Think of it. Our lifeline was severed. But we did not die. Instead we moved on to a fuller, higher life without it. For all the while the umbilical cord was doing the job for which it was designed, part of its work was to develop within the body a replacement for itself—the alimentary canal and the pulmonary apparatus and the circulatory system.

At the moment of our birth a number of functions essential to the development of the body to that point cease, never to resume. And other functions which were previously latent now take over. And as the newborn infant matures, it develops the capacity to make use of tools, implements, and other aids to extend indigenous and acquired abilities. So too has it been (and is) with the body of Christ.

There are those who have laid claim to having restored the apostolic church, the church that was brought forth on the day of Pentecost. That simply is not so. It has not been done. It cannot be done. It is not supposed to be done.

Let us reconcile what we profess with what we express. (See accompanying diagram, with explanatory notes: *The Functioning Church— Then, and Now.*) The apostolic church included a number of specially endowed functionaries not with us in the flesh, not the least of which are the apostles themselves. The qualifications for the apostleship (see Acts 1:21, 22) are scarcely duplicable today, and likewise the powers they demonstrated. The term itself simply denotes an envoy. It is derived from the preposition *apo* (from) and the verb meaning "to send." It is not of itself a word with special religious significance. Any emissary, or to use a more familiar form of expression, any missionary, is an apostle. In Acts 14:14 the term is so used. There we read of Barnabas and Saul who were sent forth from the church at Antioch on a mission to be directed by the Holy Spirit. Saul was an apostle in a twofold sense, having been 1) called and qualified by the appearance unto him of Christ himself, and thus made an apostle of Christ, and 2) having been called to go forth from the church at Antioch in the role of a missionary sent from that congregation. Our word missionary comes from a Latin root (*missio*) from whence comes such words as missal, missile, and even message and messenger. It is the Latin equivalent of the Greek word *apostolos*.

In that the word apostle has come to be equated in the popular mind with that select company who made up the apostolate whom Christ personally called, empowered, and commissioned; we do well to use the less innocuous term, missionary, to designate those "sent forth" today to carry the message of Christ to those beyond our reach.

The same is true of the word prophet. Actually, it simply denotes a spokesman—one who "speaks for" another. (See Exod. 7:1, 2 for a simple illustration.) An evangelist, in the larger context, could be called a prophet, but to do so in our day would be misleading. A prophet is popularly thought to be a *fore*-teller instead of a *forth*-teller. Timothy, whom Paul charged to "preach the word," "do the work of an evangelist," and "fulfill (his) ministry" (II Tim. 4:2, 5) was earlier exhorted (see I Tim. 4:14) to "stir up the gift of prophecy" which had been given him through the laying on of hands. But it was Paul who foretold to Timothy the things which were to come to pass.

Every "title" used in the New Testament (job description would be a more suitable term) is used in its generic sense, with a diversity of applications, and also in a specialized sense. Those who object to such terms as "life-work recruit," or "full-time Christian service" as applied to those who respond to the call to prepare for and give themselves to paid vocational Christian service, for the sake of consistency ought not refer to anyone as an evangelist, or even a deacon, for are we not all supposed to "tell the good news" and "serve" him in every way we can? But it will ever be true that what everyone ought to do would soon be nigh unto vanishing away, unless someone takes the lead and makes the doing of that thing his or her life's vocation. Or to state it simply: "Everybody's business usually turns out to be nobody's business." Thus Christ saw fit to provide an organizational format for the church consisting of specially endowed functionaries to provide those services necessary to the bringing forth and early nurture of the infant church, and a core of functionaries drawn from the mature members of the church to continue the oversight of congregations at the congregational level. He provided also for the ministry of those who would eschew the gain of the secular world to devote themselves wholly to the ministry of the Word, and for the appointment of willing and worthy men or women to various services of mercy and administration.

The Primary Function of the Church

The primary function of every living thing is to reproduce itself. For whatever purpose the various life forms have been created, the primary function of each of them is to reproduce their kind, lest their kind should perish from the face of the earth. Since the life chain is interdependent, one form of life feeding upon another, or others; it is doubly important for each life form to reproduce itself in profusion, not just one for one.

God's order to Adam and Eve was that they should "be fruitful, and multiply, and have dominion over the earth, and over every (other) living thing" (Gen. 1:28, 29). Note that man is not instructed to have dominion over man. That is God's prerogative, and rightly so, as creator and all-wise ruler of the universe.

The lesser creatures likewise were so constituted as to reproduce their kinds. Even inanimate life forms were so endowed, and were endowed to do so profusely. God sometimes seems to be prodigal in the lavishness with which he has endowed certain of his creation with the power of reproduction, but the food chain of the total organic world is interrelated, and the amazing abundance of fossil fuels in the bowels of the earth, so essential to our present industrial civilization and distribution, witnesses to the prescience of God.

The first business of the church is to reproduce itself, and the second is to nurture and care for its own. Let no one despise the office of the evangelist. The man called to be an evangelist may sometimes be despicable. Judas was. But the office itself is the highest under heaven.

283

The Functioning Church — *Then, and Now

The *APOSTOLIC Church

Vestigial Offices

"God hath set in the church . . ."
(I Cor. 12:28, 29)

1. APOSTLES - "ones sent," envoys. (Cp. Acts 14:14 - *church* sent "missionaries")

2. PROPHETS - "ones who *speak for* . . ." (cp. Exod. 7:1, 2)

3. TEACHERS (Context suggests they *were* especially endowed for the task)

4. MIRACLES (Gr. "powers")

5. GIFTS (pl.) of HEALINGS (pl.) Gr. "charismata"

6. HELPS (support)

7. GOVERNMENTS (guidance)

8. TONGUES (and INTERPRETERS, cp. vs. 10, 30, 14:28)

Note:
These offices/gifts are not given on demand (see v. 11) nor did all have one.

The "CHRISTIAN" Church

Indigenous Offices

(Christ) "gave some apostles, prophets, and some . . ."
(Eph. 4:11)

1. EVANGELISTS, the "good news bearers" cp. preachers, see II Tim. 4:2, cp. v. 5

2. PASTORS (shepherds) & TEACHERS
Also called:
   a. Bishops (overseers), Titus 1:5, 7
   b. Stewards (house managers) Titus 1:7
   c. Elders (older "mature" men) Acts 20:17, cp. 28

Plus

Appointed "Servants" (see Acts 6:2-4)
   a. DEACONS (male servants), I Tim. 3:8-10, 12, 13
   b. DEACONESSES (female servants) Rom. 16:1, 2, 6; Phil. 4:3, I Tim. 3:11 - Gr. "women" [not "their (deacons') wives"]

Supplemental Offices

We elect, appoint, choose, use, etc., some to be . . .

1. Trustees
2. Janitors
3. Song leaders
4. Choir directors
5. Secretaries
6. Treasurers
7. Clerks
8. Ushers
9. Youth Sponsors
10. Bible School Officers
11. Committee men Committee women galore!

Note:
In doing so we are extending the principle exercised by the apostles, Acts 6:1-4. When a need arises, search out and find qualified persons to meet the need that those called to the ministry of the word and prayer may continue therein.

The apostolic churches were served, at least in its initial stages, by all those listed in columns 1 and 2. Our congregations are served by those listed in columns 2 and 3. We have not restored the apostolic church. We are not supposed to do so. What we are supposed to restore is the church the New Testament revelation makes provision for. It provided for the cessation of vestigial offices, the perpetuity of the indigenous offices, and for the appointment of servants to supplement as needed.

284

It is therefore ordained by the Lord that "they who preach the Gospel should live of the Gospel" (I Cor. 9:14). Those called to preach may occasionally become so involved in work that is not their own, the work of church administration for example, that the ministry of the Word is slighted. Such is the pattern of our time, and church growth statistics underscore the fact. The average congregation this past year added barely over two new members per month (including transfers!). Think of it. If the average congregation (the whole congregation, mind you, including its "evangelist") wins only one soul per month, then in view of the few that are winning souls week after week, how many are winning none? What a travesty! What a tragedy!

There are some "paid ministers" who are able to involve others in "one-on-one" witnessing, while they themselves attend the chores of the church and fill the pulpit on Sunday morning; but not many. Christ gave some to be evangelists. Let those so called (and that can be taken two ways) not miss the lesson the apostles early on taught the church at Jerusalem. "It is not fitting that we should forsake the word of God and serve tables" (Acts 6:2b).

Note they did not say the serving of tables was not a fitting thing to be done. The fact that seven men of excellent credentials were chosen testifies to the fitness of the task to which they were assigned. The fact a plurality of men was assigned to the task witnesses to the fact it requires a plurality of persons to do most of the things which need to be done. Especially is this so when unpaid volunteers forego their leisure time to be "ministers" of Christ.

Many in the church can do most things the paid ministers do, and could receive a blessing in doing so. Meeting a felt need is service and satisfaction at its best. Let the evangelist "continue in the ministry of the word and in prayer" (Acts 6:4).

Perhaps this is as good a time as any to step in where angels might fear to tread. Some comment is due the one-man, paid-pastor system which is now burgeoning into the one-man, paid-pastor, paid-assistants system. The point at issue is not over the principle of a paid ministry, or a multiple ministry. Not only did "the Lord ordain that they who preach the Gospel shall live of the Gospel," the principle is extended on behalf of others also. The words of Jesus, "the labourer (Gr. *ergastes*) is worthy of his hire" (Luke 10:17) apparently included elders in New Testament times. (See I Tim. 5:17, 18, and I Peter 5:1, 2.)

Any time a congregation makes a significant demand upon the time, energy, and abilities of a person, male or female, that person deserves to be recompensed. The sheer magnitude of modern "church plants" and crowded "church calendars" has given rise to paid custodians and paid secretaries. The apostolic church apparently put a premium on the care of the flock, a work which the New Testament uniformly assigns to the elders, not the evangelist. (See Acts 20:17-32 and I Peter 5:1-7.)

Three of Paul's epistles (I, II Timothy and Titus) are commonly called "the pastoral epistles." That is a misnomer, born out of a perversion of New Testament church polity. The Greek word, *poimenos* (pastor/shepherd), and the verb, *poimaino* (feed/tend), are strangely and altogether absent. Correction: they are indeed absent, but not strangely so. Timothy and Titus were evangelists, preachers of the Word, not pastors.

Our Baptist neighbors attempt to justify the takeover of the title "pastor" by the preachers via the artful device of assuming Acts 14:23 refers to the appointment of preachers for the several churches. They affirm likewise that when Paul asked the elders from Ephesus to meet him at Miletus, it was really the preachers of several congregations in the city who were so spoken of. And when Titus was left in Crete to "set the churches in order and ordain elders in every city," he was to appoint pastor-preachers for each congregation. This is sheer eisegesis. Is it not interesting that the qualifications for elders which Paul so painstakingly detailed to Titus and Timothy are passed over lightly? It is also worthy of note that wherever the Baptist model is adopted, the role of the elders is greatly diminished.

Those who adopt, or adapt, the Baptist system justify doing so on the ground that it works. That it does. And the papacy which epitomizes the clergy system in full flower has for centuries enjoyed phenomenal success, as men reckon success. But let one read carefully the words of Peter in I Peter 5:1-7 and the full text of Paul's farewell address to the elders at Ephesus in Acts 20:17ff. Compare the apostolic mind with the current mind set. Paul who could have exploited his apostolic prerogatives shrank from any semblance of so doing. And Peter who could have exploited his position as chief among the apostles chose rather to count himself a "fellow elder" (Gr. *sunpresbuteros*) and set forth Christ as the "chief shepherd/pastor" (Gr. *archipoimenos*). The term, "the pastor," and even more, "the head pastor" and/or "senior minister" have a Romish ring.

Some forty plus years ago this writer was extended a call to serve as resident minister-evangelist of a congregation which had nearly twice as many members as the community I was then serving had people. My immediate response was that I was ill-prepared for such a task. My only experience to that time was limited to weekend ministries to small rural churches as a "student preacher." I had had no administrative experience. The elders explained to me they were not looking for an administrator. There were enough of them, a score or more, with approximately twice that many deacons appointed to assist them, to handle that. They were looking for an able pulpit man with an evangelistic temperament who could teach publicly and from house to house, and were convinced I could fulfill that role. On that basis the challenge was accepted. The elders made good on their promise, and I seemed to fulfill their expectations to their satisfaction. I served in that capacity until called to the presidency of Minnesota Bible College. While believers were not added to the Lord daily, they were certainly added weekly. New members were added to the fellowship at a rate of at least one every other day throughout the course of the four-year ministry.

While wrestling with the decision to step into a job which I feared was well beyond my abilities, I happened to come upon the following quotation from the pen of the late Carl Patton. The quotation influenced that decision, and the decision to become a recruiter and teacher of preachers. Patton's words were:

> I can well understand and appreciate all those activities by which a preacher makes himself useful and beloved. But I here declare they are all secondary to his high calling. They are so now, always have been, and will always so be. Blessed indeed is the preacher who knows that however well he does any or all of those things they can never of themselves make a preacher.
>
> The church lived eighteen hundred and fifty years without a boy scout troop. Henry Ward Beecher was not an expert in pitching pup tents and tying knots. Robert Chalmers probably never met a Friendly Indian. Dr. Gladden paid no attention to the finances of the church. That could be taken care of by men appointed to that business. No record has come down to us of what filing system Spurgeon used, or what Talmadge did with his annual reports.
>
> The leaders of the church who made history, who deeply affected the life and thought of their times, the men who made the church a real power in their community, and in the lives of those who were associated with them the most closely, never did so by any secondary or accessory means. They did it by their preaching.

Is it not written, "It was God's good pleasure through the foolishness of preaching to save them that believe" (I Cor. 1:21)? Notice who is

287

to be pleased, and how he is said to be pleased, and how men are said to be saved. To this end, Christ "gave some to be evangelists."

PREVIEW—REVIEW QUESTIONS

1. Identify and note the basic meaning of the Greek root from whence stem our words organize and organization.
2. State the general meaning of our English word "organ." Note its anatomical use.
3. Is the church an organization or an organism? Explain.
4. Does the New Testament represent the church as an unorganized, free-floating society? Explain.
5. Does the New Testament represent the heavenly society thusly? Explain.
6. State and explain the significance of the suffixes "ize" and "tion."
7. State the lesson to be drawn from the commission to Isaiah, as it relates to the Great Commission of the church.
8. Note the implications of Paul's head/body analogy as related to the organizational structure of the church.
9. Note the implications as related to the behavior of the church.
10. List the threefold classification of functioning body parts, according to the author's analogy.
11. Explain and apply the term vestigial.
12. State the root meaning of the terms "apostle" and "prophet."
13. In what respect do our churches fail to express what we profess? How ought the restortation ideal be better phrased?
14. Note the generic and specialized sense in which various "job-description" titles are used in the New Testament.
15. State the primary and essential function of every living thing.
16. State the case for a "paid" ministry. Does the New Testament provision apply to the preaching function only?
17. Take note of the attempt to equate the role of elders in the apostolic church with the one-man, paid-preacher (pastor).
18. Respond to the pragmatic rejoinder, "It works."
19. Compare the apostolic mind (Paul and Peter, for example) with the mind set of many front-ranking clergymen today.
20. According to I Corinthians 1:21, who is to be pleased through preaching, and how is he most pleased thereby?

20

THE ROLE OF THE ELDERS

In the previous lesson the validity of organizational structure was noted. Attention was given to those whose role (function) is no longer directly involved in the ongoing ministry of the church. These were likened to such physical functions as are provided by the umbilical cord and kindred prenatal systems which cease to be directly involved in the development of the body when the function they were designed to fulfill is completed, or "perfected" (Gr. *teleios*; see I Cor. 13:10).

It is readily acknowledged that this analogy does not provide a perfect parallel. None ever does. Even the analogies Jesus used could not be pressed too far. He knew that. Thus, he used a number of different analogies in an effort to instruct his disciples concerning the nature of the kingdom. Some of his parabolic analogies contained only one or two points of comparison. If pressed further, they could be made to teach that which is contrary to the nature of Christ's kingdom. For example, is God "an unrighteous judge" who will only grant our fervent requests to "get us off his back," so to speak?

Paul, in I Corinthians 13:8-10, used the analogy of a child outgrowing certain habits and needs in an attempt to get the Corinthian

Christians to see that 1) they were behaving childishly in their use of certain spiritual gifts (tongues particularly), and that 2) some of the gifts which were necessary for a time would cease to be needed, and would cease to be given.

Some attention was also given to the role of the evangelist, an ongoing office (function). Today, this ministry has been crossbred with prevailing custom and culture to produce a kind of hybrid employee of the local church. The same is variously called (sometimes erroneously) preacher, pastor, minister, senior minister, minister-evangelist, and even reverend.

In this and the following lesson our attention will be focused on those persons chosen out of the congregation, commonly called (but not Biblically so) the official board, or the church board. Before doing so, some attention needs to be given to the propriety or impropriety of the use of such terms as office, officer, and official.

Paul wisely counsels that no man should be selected to serve as an elder who is a novice (I Tim. 3:6), and even one considered for the diaconate should "first be proved" (I Tim. 3:10). These service roles should be viewed as a public trust in recognition of one's practice (way of life), not an office in the popular sense of that term. The NIV wisely underscores this fact by translating Romans 12:4 to read: "Just as each of us has one body with many members, and these members do not all have the same *function*, so in Christ we who are many form one body." The head of that body is Christ. He is the only "officer" the church has. All authority is resident in him. As the various members of our bodies are functional, but not official, being subject to the will that is resident in the head, so, by Divine design, is the body of Christ.

What we have just noted is somewhat obscured by the traditional translations of several key Scriptures. For example, the KJV translation of I Timothy 3:1 reads: "If any one desires the *office* of an elder . . ." But the word "office" is supplied by the mindset of the translators; it is not in the text. Vs. 10 and 13 of the same chapter have likewise been clouded with verbage conveying ecclesiastical overtones. I Timothy 3:10 simply says of those aspiring to be deacons (servants), "Let these also first be proved, then let them serve, if they be blameless." The KJV reconstructs this to read: "Let them *use the office* of deacon . . ." So too with v. 13. The text simply says: "The one having ministered (served) well acquires a good standing." The KJV revised this to read: "They that have *used the office* of a deacon well purchase to themselves a good degree."

Out of such revision of the Biblical text, against the backdrop of the ecclesiastical structure of the Anglican church (but a step removed from the model of the Roman church from which the Anglican church had lately seceded), came the concept of an official board directed by the resident clergyman. King James, as "head of the Anglican church" apparently found the revisions of the text acceptable in his sight. *The New King James Version,* 350 years removed from the original, has followed the lead of the NIV, deleting the word "office" where arbitrarily superimposed upon the text, and replacing "office" with "function" in translating the word *praxis* (cp. Rom. 12:4). A step backwards is well taken when it is a step back towards the original connotation of the sacred text.

The Church Board

Traditionally the church board, or official board, has been comprised of a board of elders and a board of deacons, generally convening jointly to conduct the "business affairs" of the church. Paid employees whose work is considered to be a "ministry" are generally regarded as ex-officio members. Custodians, secretaries, etc., who perform the "chores" of the church are normally excluded. A growing practice among the rising success-oriented genre of ministers is for "*the* Pastor" (sometimes called Senior Minister) to be the chairman of the board, president of the congregation, superintendent of the Bible school, advisor (at the least) of all committees, and captain of the athletics teams. The latter was added somewhat in jest, but not altogether. Many of this rising order censor all information, communications, and appeals addressed to the' congregation or any committee thereof; police the bulletin board and publications; and decide which Christian service camps and Bible colleges the youth may attend.

Such a role, and it has not been overstated insofar as its full development is concerned, is indeed a hybrid role. It has been crossbred with organizational concepts which are foreign to the New Testament doctrine of church polity and practice, and is an open violation of the New Testament doctrine of the priesthood of all believers.

That the system works is not to be gainsaid. Usually it does. Rome provides a dual example. Power ploys of strong natural leaders generally achieve their intended goals whether in government, industry, or church administration. Nationally, dictators can (and do) seize opportunities for decisive action while democratic processes are tied up in

291

congressional debate. But God did not so ordain. What he has ordained deserves to be given all due consideration, particularly as it relates to the church.

Facts About the Eldership

To appreciate to the full the Biblical ideal and role of the work of the eldership (Gr. *presbuteroi*), one needs to be made aware of the extensive Biblical data which relates thereto. Not the least is the fact that the title elders is only one of several significant terms used in the New Testament to designate this important service role.

A. *Titles, Form of Reference*

At least five titles are used in the New Testament for this function. Job descriptions might be a better term to use.

1. *Elder.* This is the only term used which borders on being an honorific title. It is used to translate the Greek word *presbuteros.* The term refers to a mature man, not necessarily an aged one. *Presbutes* more commonly designates an aged man.

When a Jewish man became thirty years of age he was considered to be old enough to hold any office. He could even be elected to the Sanhedrin. Witness the case of the "young man," Saul of Tarsus (Acts 7:58, cp. 26:10). Jesus wisely delayed entrance upon his Divine mission until he had become thirty years of age (Luke 3:23). He knew full well his ministry would provoke enough controversy without the charge of being a young upstart used against him (cp. I Tim. 4:12). As a title the term elder compares with the Latin word from which is derived the term senator. Maturity, not advanced age, is communicated by the term.

It is my observation that in congregations which reserve the office of elder for men approaching the senior citizen status (a common occurrence among rural churches), a tension often develops between the elders and the deacons. The latter often includes young to middle-aged farmers, businessmen, school administrators, etc., whose maturity of judgment and business acumen have gained for them the respect of their community but not of the elders. They are reckoned too young to hold that high office. Soon their desire to see the church become more adventurous places them in an adversary role with the elders. In time they are moved to take advantage of the fact that as deacons they outnumber the elders. In the one-man, one-vote pattern that prevails in the typical church board setting this often occurs. One safeguard is to return to the Biblical pattern which places the congregation under the rule of the elders. But when senior citizen status is made a prerequisite of the eldership the potential for rebellion is ever present.

We repeat what has already been said. The term *presbuteros* emphasizes a mature state of mind, not of the body. As one grows older, one tends to want to freeze history, hold the line, and maintain the status quo. A "board of elders" consisting of men in their declining years will produce a declining church. The decline and death of many a congregation reflects the aging and death rate of those who control the church.

It is of interest that in business and industry young, vigorous, resourceful persons are recruited for salesmanship and management, but the board of directors consist of business-wise and experienced, older men. But these are also persons who want to see the corporation grow and keep in step with the times. They recognize their own limitations and therefore seek out resourceful, young executives and salesmen whose energy and drive and innovative ideas will complement the areas in which they themselves are no longer aggressive and strong.

Note the New Testament precedent. Elders are first mentioned in connection with the church in Acts 11:30. The benevolent offering sent to the saints at Jerusalem by the church at Antioch was sent to the elders, not the deacons. It is the elders who filled the role of stewards (Gr. *oikonomos,* "house/estate managers") and bishops (Gr. *episcopos,* "overseers, supervisors"). Acts 14:23 speaks of elders being "ordained/appointed" in every city. "Set forth publicly" (as men duly selected) would be an accurate rendering of the text. In Acts 15:2, 4, 6, 22, 23 and 16:4 elders are associated with the apostles at the Jerusalem conference. This is highly significant and in contrast to modern times. Today it is the preachers who convene to consider general church polity. In Acts 20:17 it is the elders of the church at Ephesus who were called to meet with Paul at Miletus. In Acts 21:8 Paul is reported to have conferred with James (generally believed to be that James who was a half brother to Christ), but it is stated: "and all the elders were present."

Timothy was counseled by Paul to "not rebuke an elder," but rather to "exhort him as a father" (I Tim. 5:1). In v. 17 elders who "rule well" are said to be "worthy of double honor, especially those who labor in the word and in teaching." From this we may conclude that some among them ministered on a full-time basis and thereby shared with the preachers in the right to receive their livelihood from those for whom they labored. In v. 19 Timothy is admonished to protect elders against gossip. An accusation against an elder is not to be received except upon the testimony of two or three witnesses.

Titus, whom Paul had left in Crete to set in order the things that were lacking, was given specific instructions concerning the selection of elders (Titus 1:5-11). The verb translated ordain/appoint is *kathistao*. It is illustrated by the context of Acts 6:3 where it has been previously used. Titus, as an evangelist of the Word, was to state the qualifications for the office, and, no doubt, the attending responsibilities; and the churches from place to place were to make the selections. They would have to "live with their choices." Titus would likely be moving on soon. Preachers have an advantage here. They can *leave* their mistakes. The congregation has to *live* with them.

Peter, in his first epistle, adroitly used some wise psychology in counseling elders. Rather than putting the weight of his apostolic office behind his words, he speaks of himself as a fellow-elder (Gr. *sunpresbuteros*, I Peter 5:1) and exhorts them to exercise their over-lordship (Gr. *katakurieuontes*) and pastorate (Gr. *poimanate*) in humility. They would thus rule by example and not the weight of office. It may reasonably be suggested they needed that counsel. To their discredit elders often do. Notwithstanding, younger Christians are exhorted to submit to the elders (see v. 5).

The last mention of elders (as the epistles have been arranged in our New Testament) is in James 5:14 where the sick are instructed to call for the elders (pl.) of the church to anoint them with oil, and pray over them, with the assurance that healing would be forthcoming. Actually, the epistle of James is one of the earliest books of the New Testament, and the passage alluded to is in keeping with the principle enunciated in the author's "Excursus on Mark 16:17, 18" (included at the end of Lesson Six).

2. *Bishop.* Elders are also spoken of in the New Testament as bishops. (See Acts 20:17, cp. v. 28, and Titus 1:5, cp. v. 7.) Our word bishop is an anglicized form of the Greek word *episkopos* with both ends cropped. It is derived from *epi* (over) and *skopeo* (to see); hence to oversee. Our word supervisor, derived from the Latin *supervidere*, is a precise equivalent.

The Greek word *episkopeo* carries the idea of a visit of mercy and compassion. It commonly implies looking in upon someone with a view to helping. In classical Greek literature it describes a mother keeping a vigil throughout a long night over a sick child, or a nurse looking in upon a patient with a view to help in any way possible.

In the New Testament the word is used by Jesus in Matthew 25:36, 47. Note the context. "I was sick, and in prison, and ye *visited* me" (or visited me not). It is the word used in James 1:27 where pure religion is defined as *visiting* the widows and the orphans in their affliction. It is used of the visitation of God upon his people, bringing them redemption (Luke 1:68, 78). (See also Luke 7:16; Acts 7:23; 15:14, 36; and Heb. 2:16). The oversight to be administered by bishops is the oversight of benevolent, caring love. The role of bishops in current ecclesiastical power structures almost invariably obscures the New Testament ideal.

3. *Steward.* In Titus 1:7 elders/bishops (cp. vs. 5 and 7a) are called stewards. The term is used to translate the Greek word *oikonomos* (literally house-ruler, or estate manager). Two parables of Jesus, Luke 12:35-48 and 16:1-13, and such texts as I Corinthians 4:1, 2; I Peter 4:10, 11 provide a commentary on this role. A number of Jesus' parables are based on the steward's role in society without directly using the term. From the whole of them we learn that not every steward bore equal responsibility to his Lord except in one particular—each was to serve to the best of his ability. The steward entrusted with five talents who gained five others in the exercise of his stewardship and the one entrusted with two who likewise doubled his master's investment in him were each given responsibility in keeping with their ability. Thus, though one produced two and a half times as much as the other, the latter was as fully commended. This principle is often overlooked in modern practice.

4. *Pastors/Shepherds.* The translation of the Greek word *poimen* is somewhat arbitrary. When used with reference to Christ, translators go with the word shepherd. When used of men appointed to "tend," "feed," "lead" (Gr. *poimaino*) "the flock (Gr. *poimnion*) they opt for the word pastor, derived from the Latin word *pasture* from which our word of like spelling is derived. The word shepherd emphasizes the leading of the flock and pastor the feeding of the flock. These are basic needs. Sheep are not independent travelers. They have no homing instincts. They cannot sniff out watering holes or grassland. They have neither weapons of offense or defense. The fact is, if the theory of evolution were true, it is hard to figure out how sheep survived for eons before man supposedly evolved to care for them.

In the Scriptures the work of shepherding and pastoring the flock of God is uniformly assigned to the elders. (See Acts 20:17, 28-31; I Peter 5:1-4; Eph. 4:11.) Three of Paul's epistles, addressed to young evangelists who were proteges of the apostle Paul are commonly called the Pastoral Epistles. But the fact is the words noted in the preceding paragraph appear nowhere in any one of them.

Timothy is called upon to "be a good *minister* (*diakonos*) of Christ Jesus" (I Tim. 4:6), to "neglect not the gift of prophecy" which had been given him through the laying on of the hands of the elders" (I Tim. 4:14), to "preach the word" (II Tim. 4:2), and to "do the work of an evangelist" (II Tim. 4:5). But nowhere is he called upon to pastor the church, to do the work of the elders, nor is he called a pastor or shepherd.

Titus was left at Crete to set the churches on that isle in order and to direct them in the choosing of elders, but Timothy was not so instructed. The difference is that Timothy was residing in Ephesus where the church had long enjoyed the benefit of a strong eldership whereas Titus was serving in an area where the churches were yet to arrive at that state of development. Timothy was to relate to an established eldership. Titus was to lead in the appointment of elders. Obviously, Timothy, as a preacher, prophet, minister, and evangelist, would have enough to do without usurping the role of the elders. Titus would do well to bring the churches at Crete to a state of order whereby he would have the benefit of a functioning eldership.

5. *Teachers.* Elders are also called teachers (Eph. 4:11). The Greek construction in this text indicates that the phrase "pastors and teachers" relates to the same persons. In I Corinthians 1:28, 29 teachers are designated as a third instructional office. In Acts 13:1 teachers are specifically associated with the prophets at Antioch and shared with them in the ordination of Barnabas and Saul to the work to which the Holy Spirit was calling them. As previously noted, elders participated in the ceremony of the laying on of hands in the ordination and equipping of Timothy for the ministry to which he was called.

In view of what has been noted, it should be obvious why the role of the elders is pluralized within the organizational structure of a congregation. There are two good reasons. 1) For one thing it provides protection for the congregation against the tyranny of one-man rule. Considering the implications of the several terms applied to the role, such protection is prudent and providential. 2) In view of the multiple responsibilities suggested by the job descriptions, the pluralizing of the role provides protection for the elders. Considering the fact that elders are generally what is commonly called laymen, men who give their time after business and working hours and taking time from their families, the responsibilities are mercifully shared by a plurality of men appointed to the role.

B. *Duties of the Elders*

The duties of the elders can be readily deduced from the titles (job descriptions) and the list of qualifications.

1) Elders have a duty to themselves (Acts 20:28a). Self-mastery is a must. They are to rule by example and demonstration. Jesus, in his farewell prayer, prayed first for himself, then for those through whom we have come to believe on him, and then for us. This was not selfish on his part, nor a reflection upon his low regard for us. His first obligation was to steel himself for the ordeal he was to undergo. If he had failed in being all that he needed to be, and in doing all he needed to do, we would be lost. I am reminded of the girl whose first public prayer implored: "God, please take care of yourself. If something would happen to you, we would all be sunk." After I and the rest of the campers in our prayer circle had recovered our composure, one of the young men apologized for our first reaction, noting that on reflection it occurred to him that her prayer may have been the most sensible and sincere prayer that was offered. An elder's first duty is to take heed to himself.

2) Elders have a duty to their own households. See I Timothy 3:4 and Titus 1:6. An unruly, ill-managed, and unbelieving household renders a man incapable of commanding respect or exhibiting the qualities and abilities needed to be an example and a leader. It is possible for a man who was never privileged to have a family or one whose children grew to adulthood before he became a Christian to relate well to children and to gain the confidence of the congregation and community. There are men who have devoted their lives to working with children, who for one reason or another were denied the privilege of having sons or daughters or raising to adulthood a child taken by death. Such men are not to be automatically and arbitrarily excluded from consideration. The home offers the most common and relevant proving ground, but is not the only proving ground. The Biblical injunctions are logical but not letter-of-the-law legalities. Years ago I took note of the fact that in Jesus' encounters with the carping Pharisees, the Pharisees generally had the letter of the law on their

side. The apostle Paul, whose stated principles such as the one under consideration are often quoted by legalists, noted: "The letter killeth, but the spirit giveth life," (II Cor. 3:6). In that he was perceptive. In that he had "the mind of Christ."

3) Elders have a duty to the flock of God, the church. (See Acts 20:28-31; I Peter 5:2, 3; Titus 1:9-11; I Tim. 3:5.) a) Elders should feed/lead/tend the flock. (The Gr. word *poimaino* includes all three facets.) They are therefore called teachers. b) Elders are to protect/ guard the flock lest "wolves" from without devour them, and men arise among them to lead them astray. They are therefore called pastors/ shepherds. c) Elders must by example and by the Word of God "rule" the flock. (See I Tim. 5:17; Heb. 13:7, 17; I Peter 5:2, 3.) They are therefore called bishops (overseers). Two Greek words are used to express this. *Proistemi* means literally to stand before, hence to lead by example. *Hegeomai* means to guide. The idea of rule by force is nowhere associated with the elders' role. Nowhere in Scripture does the Lord give elders "authority" which gives them the "right" to dominate fellow Christians. Notwithstanding, elders must on occasion rise to the challenge and "convict the gainsayers, and stop the mouths of those who would overthrow whole households" (Titus 1:10). Such responsibility calls for an admixture of courage and discretion. d) Elders must serve as "house (estate) managers" of the house of God. They are therefore called stewards (Titus 1:7). This stewardship most certainly includes the management of the financial affairs of the church. Popular opinion assigns this role to the deacons, but Acts 11:27-30 should dispel this notion. While deacons were appointed to care for the widows, the relief offerings that were sent to Jerusalem from afar were sent to the elders, not the deacons. It needs to be noted that the Greek word *diakonian*, translated "relief" in Acts 11:29 (KJV, ASV), is the same word translated "ministration" in Acts 6:1.

The budget of any institution or association—family, fraternal, government, etc.—is the expression of their value judgments and activities translated into dollars and cents. Whoever controls the finances of any group of people controls their goals and actions. Tell me how a person or institution secures and then handles its money, and I can readily discern whether they are spiritual or carnal. If the elders are indeed charged with the oversight of the spiritual affairs of the church, but the finances of the church are entrusted to the deacons (presumably yet too immature spiritually to be elders), how can the elders fulfill their role as God's stewards? And how can the program of the church, prescribed and facilitated by the budget, be spiritual?

e) Elders also have a community responsibility. If nothing else, they are to so conduct themselves as "to have a good testimony among them without" (that is, outside the congregation), I Timothy 3:7.

Qualifications for Elders

The qualifications for the eldership may be listed under four categories: 1) commitment, 2) character, 3) circumstances, and 4) capabilities. Extended lists of qualifications are found in two texts: I Timothy 3:1-13 and Titus 1:5-9. In all cases the overriding qualification is whether one sufficiently desires the work (not the office) to qualify himself for the task. Paul's words in I Timothy 3:1 are adroitly chosen. "Faithful is the saying, If a man desires (or aspires) the episcopate he desires (longs for) a good work." The KJV translators allowed their Anglican church structure to revise the saying to read: "If any man desires *the office of a bishop.* . . ." There are two words for desire used in the text. The first is *oregatai.* The word is taken from the arena, and describes the dedication and commitment of contestants who subject themselves to a rigorous regimen controlling every facet of their lives including diet, entertainment, and other forms of self-discipline in order to qualifiy for the Olympic games. The kind of dedication to a goal and self-discipline which makes champions is enjoined upon those who would aspire to be elders. The second word Paul used is the one Jesus used with reference to himself when he expressed to his disciples his longing to eat the Passover with them before his crucifixion. The word is *epithumia* (cp. Luke 22:15). Paul used the same word when he expressed to the Philippians his desire to be with Christ (Phil. 1:23). Men who possess this kind of desire to serve are at least worthy of consideration as candidates for the oversight of the church. They may fall short in certain circumstantial considerations. A man may be widowed, or his wife may be barren. They may have had triplets, but only one survived leaving them with only one child, not children. He may have some character traits which are not yet perfected, but he is pressing on toward the mark of the prize of the high calling of God in Christ Jesus. Like Paul, there may be aspects of his past that he is trying to forget; and others should allow to be forgotten.

When a composite list is made of the qualifications as stated in the two texts cited above, a bit of comparison brings some interesting facts to light. Altogether, twenty-six (26) reference points are noted. But of the twenty-six, only seventeen appear in Paul's instruction to

299

Timothy, and but fifteen in his instruction to Titus. Only five are *common to both lists*. The letter to Timothy contains twelve that are not included in the letter to Titus. And there are ten in the letter to Titus that are not included in Paul's instruction to Timothy.

The foregoing observations raise some interesting questions. 1) Which of the congregations which were the beneficiaries of Paul's letters to his two proteges were thereafter blessed with "Scripturally-qualified" elders? 2) Or are we to assume neither of the two men did anything until each had checked with the other, and perhaps with still other possible recipients of letters from Paul; and only after a composite list of qualifications was thereby gained, did they set about expediting the task enjoined upon them?

Some forty years ago the writer delivered an address on the subject, "The Musts of a Scripturally-Qualified Eldership," taking my cue from I Timothy 3:2 and Titus 1:7. The full text of the address was printed in the *Christian Standard*. A number of persons took the liberty to mimeograph the same for use in clinics, seminars, etc., on church leadership. Included in the address and made available to the audience was a sample ballot. The composite list of "qualifications" appeared under the heading: "A Scripturally-Qualified Elder Is:" Along the right-hand side of the page several parallel columns were printed. At the top of each of the columns space was provided to write in the names of nominees and/or men who otherwise might be under consideration. The first of the columns noted that a "Scripturally-qualified elder" *is* one who merited a check (✓) vs. an (x) at every point, thus setting the standard.

Following the address I was besieged to deliver the same message to various congregations represented by the conclave of brethren who had come together. My first appointment was with a congregation that was scheduled to vote on a slate of candidates the same morning I was scheduled to speak.

At the close of my address the chairman of the elders, one of the most devout and able elders I have ever known, arose to his feet and tearfully asked that he be allowed to resign, stating he had never before realized how unworthy he was to hold such an exacting office. The other elders likewise, both those whose terms had not expired and those up for reelection, and every one of the candidates anticipating serving for the first time, asked to step down from their office, or from consideration for the office. Not one of them expressed any resentment towards me, or the things I said. They had simply looked down the list of absolutes I had compiled (the "musts" of a Scripturally- qualified eldership) and failed to see themselves mirrored by that imposing list. Among them were fathers of sons who had entered the work of the preaching ministry, and of daughters who had married preachers and missionaries, and of sons and daughters in Bible college preparing for specialized Christian service.

That was the day my eyes were opened to how legalistic and un- realistic I had allowed myself to become. We spent many an hour before that Lord's day was done searching our hearts and searching the Scriptures. I have never delivered that address again. I had mistaken an ideal, a goal, for a legal decree. I had forgotten the warning that "the letter killeth, but the spirit giveth life" (II Cor. 3:6).

Paradoxically, the very men who counted themselves the most unworthy were the men who were the most qualified to serve. Near the summit of an alpine range is a monument to a man who set about to carve a trail over a formidable barrier of ice and rock to facilitate concourse with villagers on the other side of the mountain. He almost did what his fellow villagers had agreed could not be done. But near the crest he slipped and fell to his death. The villagers took it upon themselves to finish the work he had started, and did. At the point the trailblazer slipped, they raised a monument bearing his name and the simple legend: "He Died Climbing." Tribute to whom tribute is due! He made a miscue that cost him his life, but he died climbing. He died with his face set toward the summit. He died while pursuing a lofty goal.

Thank God, we serve one who sees that toward which we strive, not just where we have arrived. In this regard we too need the mind of Christ. The only one who never makes a mistake is the man who attempts nothing. But that is a mistake within itself. It is better to fail trying to do something beyond our ability than to be successful in doing nothing.

Correlation of I Timothy 3:1-13, Titus 1:5-9

Qualifications, listed by categories:	Timothy	Titus
1. COMMITMENT:Desire (Gr. oregetai and epithumia— fervent and compelling)	v. 2	
2. CHARACTER: Personality traits, life-style, demeanor		
a. Blameless, irreproachable (Gr. anepilempton) "without handles": anegkletos, "invulnerable")	2	6, 7
b. Vigilant (nephalion- alert, awake)	2	

Correlation of I Timothy 3:1-13, Titus 1:5-9 (continued)

Qualifications, listed by categories:	Timothy	Titus
c. Soberminded (*sophron* - of a wise, prudent mind)	2	
d. Orderly (*kosmion* - cp. cosmos, God's creation)	2	
e. Temperate (not a *paroinon* - one alongside of, associated with wine)	3	7
f. Gentle (*epeike* - patient)	3	
g. Given to hospitality (*philoxenon*)	2	8
h. Not contentious (*amachon* - free from strife)	3	
i. Not a striker (*aplekton* - not quarrelsome)	3	7
j. Not a lover of money (*aphilarguron* - not eager for base gain, not "after a fast buck")	3	
k. Not greedy for filthy lucre (*aischrokerde* - not coveteous)		7
l. Not a novice (*neophytos* - new convert) (Note reason stated.)	6	
m. Not self-willed (*authade* - arrogant, selfish)		7
n. Not soon angry (*orgilon* - emotional excess)		7
o. Just (*dikaion* - fair, impartial)		8
p. Holy (*hosion* - undefiled, pure)		8
q. Lover of good (*philagathon* - lover of good things)		8
r. Self-controlled (*egkrate* - temperate, self-mastered)		8
s. Holding to the faithful word (*antechomenon* - cleaving, steadfast)		9
t. Having a good standing with them without	7	

3. *CIRCUMSTANCES* Note: The following relate to social (primarily family) situations which provide a testing area for one's interpersonal relationships.

	Timothy	Titus
a. Husband of one wife (*mias gunaikos andra* - lit., one-woman man vs. a polygamist, adulterer)	2	6
b. Ruling well his own house (*proistamenon* - presiding over, in charge of, his household)	4	
c. Having children in subjection with dignity	4	6
d. Having children that believe, not accused of riot or unruly		6

4. *CAPABILITIES*

	Timothy	Titus
a. Apt to teach (*didaktikon* - skillful in teaching)	2	
b. Able by sound doctrine to exhort and convict gainsayers		9

The foregoing list is imposing. If flawlessness in every detail at all times, including past history, is demanded of candidates, no one could qualify. Fortunately, preachers are not screened by such a checklist, rigidly interpreted and enforced, else the ranks of the ministry would be thinned exceedingly. These qualities ought certainly to be represented by the elders in the aggregate, and to be striven after by each one individually. A flagrant variance from the ideal should not be countenanced. Paul instructed Timothy "against an elder receive not an accusation, except at the mouth of two or three witnesses. Them that sin reprove in the sight of all, that the rest may be in fear" (I Tim. 5:19, 20). This Scripture recognizes the fact that elders too may have lapses in proper conduct. Because of their public role in the church, their sin is to be dealt with in a manner that should serve as a warning to others. It is unclear whether the word "all" in the foregoing quotation refers to all the elders or all the church. In the opening verse of the chapter, Timothy is cautioned to "rebuke not an elder, but exhort him as a father." Circumstances and common sense should determine the extent of publicity that should be given to a sinning elder's misconduct, and the manner in which he is to be reproved. Paul does not say, at the first offense, on any count, an elder should be dismissed. By the same token, a past offense should not disqualify a man from candidacy.

In summary, the thrust of the foregoing Scriptures is that the best men available, the most reputable and willing men of the congregation, the men who have proved by their steadfastness and concern for the church their commitment to Christ: such men though imperfect will "grow in the grace and knowledge of the Lord Jesus Christ," to borrow a phrase from Peter (II Peter 3:18). He did.

Questions as to the method of selection, duration of the appointment, and other such matters will be reserved for the next lesson, and included with a survey of the role of the diaconate. Further comment concerning marital and parental standards will also be included, since they are again mentioned in Paul's instruction concerning deacons.

PREVIEW—REVIEW QUESTIONS

1. Where, if ever, does the New Testament speak of the church board, or describe its function?
2. Obviously the original KJV translators allowed the milieu in which they lived to influence their translation of the Scriptures. Have we proved immune to such temptation? Cite specifics.
3. Distinguish between the Greek words *presbutes* and *presbuteros*. Which designates the role of elders?

4. Note some problems which arise out of the notion that elders must be chosen from among the old men of the congregation.
5. Note the literal meaning of the Greek word transliterated bishop, and note the sense in which the verb form of the word is used in the New Testament.
6. What is the literal meaning of the Greek word translated steward, and how does that relate to the role of elders?
7. What is the difference, if any, between a pastor and a shepherd? How do translators incline to choose between the two?
8. Are preachers ever referred to as the pastors of the church? List the titles which are applied to them in the New Testament.
9. State two reasons the eldership is pluralized, there being no record of one man being alone appointed as an elder.
10. List, categorically, duties of the elders.
11. Note the manner in which the several titles applied to them indicate their responsibilities in the church.
12. State the four categories in which qualifications for elders may be distributed.
13. Evaluate the practice of combining Paul's instructions to Timothy and Titus concerning elders and rigidly enforcing the same in the selection of elders.
14. Discuss the mindset which demands perfection of elders, individually, though the strength of one may compensate for the weakness of another, but allows preachers to serve with less stringent qualifications demanded of them.
15. Are there other circumstances besides the family setting in which a man's ability to fulfill the role of an elder may be tested?

21

THE ROLE OF THE DIACONATE

Who is the greatest in the kingdom of God? What are the criteria? Is it whom you know? What you know? Is it determined by seniority? By rank? Who is the greatest in the local church? Is it the one whose name appears at the top in the typical pyramid chart of the power-structure chain of command?

Consider this startling affirmation: "Whosoever is the greatest among you shall be your servant" (Gr. *diakonos*), Mark 10:43. Jesus said that. And by way of illustration he added: "Even as the Son of Man came not to be served (Gr. *diakonethenai*) but to serve (Gr. *diakonesai*) and to give his life a ransom for many."

Obviously Jesus did not have (quote) "the office of deacon" in mind when he said that. But what he said most certainly needs to be kept in mind by those called deacons, and by elders and preachers, evangelists, missionaries, Bible college personnel, editors and publishers, and the untitled of the pews.

The role of the diaconate, both deacons (male and servants) and deaconesses (the female of the species) needs to be restudied and over-hauled in the light of New Testament teaching and early church practice.

Today, the "office of deacon" is commonly regarded as the junior branch of what is commonly called the church board. The "office of elder" is viewed as the senior branch, with the preacher representing an adaptation of the United States presidency, thus completing the adaptation of what is regarded as a Christian form of government (politically) to the organizational structure of the Christian church.

It is inevitable that some adaptation of the prevailing culture will reflect itself in the church in every age and place. The Roman Catholic church found the model for its organizational structure in the political milieu in which it arose and flourished. Fortunately, the founders of our republic were seeking to establish a form of government based upon Christian principles. They therefore, provided for us a better model— but not the best. That is found in the church revealed in the Scriptures. The New Testament teaching concerning the diaconate, and its relationship to the presbytery (eldership), is not set in concrete (to borrow a popular phrase) nor spelled out in detail in every respect; but guideline principles are discernible.

Diaconate Defined

In this study we are using the term diaconate as a collective noun, much in the sense in which we speak of the elders as the eldership. Some balk at the use of both terms, charging that both are unbiblical. If to be "biblical," a term has to be found in traditional translations of the Bible, we are attempting to freeze history at some arbitrary date this side of the penning of the sacred Scriptures.

When followers interrelate, they have fellowship. When people become partners in an enterprise, they form a partnership. When members of the body of Christ form a local congregation, they constitute the membership of that congregation. It would be quite impossible for a congregation to exist as a visible, viable entity, having members, but without a membership. All this is simply to say that it is proper to refer to the deacons as the diaconate (or even the deaconship).

The term deacon has become encrusted with male exclusiveness. And the situation persists, despite the fact the only person directly named in the New Testament whose role in the church is immediately and specifically designated as a *diakonon* of a congregation is a woman (Phoebe), not a man (see Rom. 16:1).

The seven men named in Acts 6:5 are readily conceded to be the first church deacons, but they are not directly so called in the context, nor elsewhere in the New Testament. But Phoebe is specifically designated as deaconess (Gr. *diakonon*) of the church at Cenchreae (Rom.

306

16:1, cp. v. 2). Moreover, several women are named in the context of the chapter and are salutarily honored for their service. One of them (Mary) is said to have "bestowed much labor on the church" (v. 6).

In view of the fact that women served the apostolic church, formally and with distinction, and their service is included in the New Testament usage of the title under discussion, diaconate is used in this study as an innocuous generic term embracing all who so served and their modern counterparts.

Origin of the Diaconate

As stated above, the seven men in Acts 6:5 are generally conceded to be the first persons to be formally appointed to the diaconate. The reason cited for their appointment is important to this study. They were appointed to fill a specific need.

A complaint had arisen in the congregation. The Grecians (a term designating Jews who had been dispersed amid the Grecian culture) were complaining that their widows were being neglected in the daily ministration (Gr. *diakonia*, translated *relief* in Acts 11:29). The apostles wisely suggested that a committee of seven should be appointed to administer the service, stating that it would be inappropriate for themselves to forsake the word of God, which they had been appointed to administer, to serve (*diakonein*) tables. They were hardly suggesting it was beneath their dignity to do so, but it would not be in the highest and best interests of the church should they do so.

Moses' father-in-law, Jethro, observed Moses becoming wearied and worn by duties others could very well handle. He suggested that Moses would do well to expand the organization of the expedition by appointing rulers over thousands, over hundreds, over fifties, and even down to groups of ten (Exod. 18:13-26). Moses did so, and Jehovah did not rebuke him for taking counsel other than that which he had given. Common sense is ever in order.

The apostles applied the principle cited by Jethro to their own circumstances, though on a smaller scale commensurate with the need to be met. Out of that circumstance came the appointment of the first deacons.

Jethro also wisely counseled Moses with regard to the qualifications or standards that should be required of the subordinates he was encouraged to appoint, saying: "Thou shalt provide out of the people able men, such as fear God, men of truth, hating unjust gain" (v. 21).

Those same qualifications could well have been used in the selection of the first deacons. The situation needing attention was fraught with emotional overtones. Race, money, and women were intermingling factors.

In either case the men chosen were appointed to a specific need. They were not appointed to an office, or enlisted in an officers' corps, in the event something might arise that would need their attention. They were appointed to a specific service. In the case of the seven deacons, they were in effect a committee of seven to see to it that the widows of the Grecians were treated fairly in the daily administration of needed benevolence.

It would be ill advised to conclude that the only Biblical role open to deacons is that of serving as a benevolent committee. That was simply the need that was pressing at the time. Note the apostles assured the multitude of the brethren, "We will appoint them over this business" (Gr. *chreias*—need, want, lack). If it could be assumed that no other want or lack has ever arisen in the life of the church it could then be assumed that the sole duty that can be Scripturally assigned to deacons is that of serving as a benevolent committee.

As an example of the penchant for patternism that persists among us is the fact that the statement of the apostles, "It is not fit that we should forsake the word of God and *serve tables,*" has been picked up and used as the basis for the practice of having "deacons" serve at the communion table somewhat in the role of waiters. Thus the physical elements of the Lord's supper are "served." They are catered to the congregation and passed by the deacons from row to row. The fact is in many congregations the only discernible difference between the elders and deacons is that the elders stand beside the communion table and the deacons line up in front of it. But in "board meetings" the business is not conducted around the communion table. In board meetings often about the only difference between the elders and deacons is that there are more of the latter. They can therefore outvote the elders and thus control the business of the church with regard to every item on the agenda, and sometimes do.

It is for this reason that congregations are chary about accepting the idea that the diaconate may (and in New Testament times did) include women. We have troubles enough at the present. Why add further to the imbalance of voting power? The answer to that is, where in the New Testament is it suggested the deacons (male or female, or both) ever met with the elders and voted on anything? The elders are

308

called the overseers, senators (Gr. *presbuteros*—presbyters/elders), stewards, pastor/shepherds, and exercise the leadership (I Tim. 5:17, cp. 3:4, 5; Heb. 13:7, 17; I Peter 5:2, 3).

No one minds women working, performing various chores for the church. The fear is that were they appointed as deaconesses, they might follow the lead of the deacons and vote as a power block, and thus eventually run the church. The Biblical solution to that potential problem is not to disavow that the New Testament provides for deaconesses, but to return the deacons to the place the New Testament places them—as servants under assignment.

Duties of the Diaconate

The duties of deacons and deaconesses are not detailed in the New Testament, and wisely so. This provides the latitude congregations need to appoint members to the work needing done, as such varies from time to time and from place to place, as well as to the routine tasks which prevail generally.

Elders, as has been noted, are referred to by a variety of job-description titles. But the diaconate is simply designated by the ubiquitous Greek word that has been merely transliterated to form our words deacon and deaconess. When the term is used in a different context, it is translated minister and servant. Both these terms are of Latin derivation. The latter normally relates to a more servile role, including the role of a slave.

The duties of the first deacons were such as were necessary to provide an equitable distribution of the relief funds of the church, particularly as they were needed to meet the needs of the widows. Later, as a famine reduced considerably more persons to such straits, churches from afar sent relief offerings to the church at Jerusalem. But as we noted in the previous lesson, the funds were sent to the elders, not to the deacons. (See Acts 11:27-30.) That fits into the fundamental difference between the two offices. Elders are designated as overseers (bishops), estate managers (*oikonomos*—stewards). Deacons are servants under assignment.

Nowhere do the Scriptures teach that deacons are in charge of material matters, particularly the finances of the church. Were that so, they could readily control the work of the church. The budget of a church is simply the program of the church translated into dollars and cents.

An Enigmatic Situation

An enigmatic situation prevails today in many congregations seeking to be Biblical in their practice. They refuse to recognize the role of a deaconess, but many women of the congregation are appointed, sans the title, to the *work* of deaconesses. The enigma is that they fill the role of deaconess much more Biblically than those openly called deacons fill the Biblical role of deacons.

To be specific, women are assigned to specific tasks. They prepare the table for the serving of the Lord's supper, and clear the table afterwards. They wash and store the utensils. They spread and care for the linens. Some may be in charge of the consumables, seeing to it that the supplies are on hand. Some bake the bread. A few make and/or store the fruit of the vine. Women are placed in care of the baptismal supplies, and are assigned, of course, to the women's robing room. They promote and expedite fellowship meals, both preparing the food and cleaning up afterwards. They visit the sick and look after the indigent. And they generally serve as pianists and organists; often serving as song leaders and/or choir directors. All this, and more, women servants of the church do without demanding the right to attend the board meeting with full voting rights. But deacons(?) who often do little more than take their turn passing the offering and communion trays have equal vote, man for man, with the elders.

Women do not usurp the servant roles they occupy. They are chosen, and assigned. The piano stool is not occupied by the woman with the fastest car, or who is fleetest of foot, or lives closest to the church, or otherwise arrives the earliest. She is chosen on the basis of her ability and availability, and hopefully for her character, dependability, and good taste in the choice of selections left to her discretion.

Why is the title deaconess so grudgingly and often fearfully withheld from those to whom it is so becoming? Must the rising pressure of the women's liberation movement, supporters of the Equal Rights Amendment, and governmental pressures force upon us changes which long since ought to have been made?

The New Testament provides for the appointment of persons to meet whatsoever need arises in the discharge of the responsibilities which confront us as Christians. The persons best suited to do what needs to be done should be the persons appointed to do it. When such persons are women, let the women who are best qualified and willing do it.

As for what they ought to be called, it would likely be best that the title deaconess be held in abeyance, as being already sullied in its true import by their male counterparts who are called deacons. We have long since done this in the case of the elders with regards to the title bishop. We have likewise found the terms apostle and prophet so restricted in their application, insofar as the average person is concerned, that we substitute the title missionary (Latin-based equivalent of the Greek *apostolos*) for "the ones sent" forth by the church today (cp. Acts 14:14). And we do not even employ a viable synonym for the general sense and meaning of the term prophet. We would do well to drop the term deacon, and call male servants of the church by such titles as usher, greeter, maintenance committeeman, etc., etc.

The cliche, "everybody's business is nobody's business" is actually a truism. We might get far more work out of our "deacons," more of them would likely come nearer to fulfilling the "office," if they were assigned to specific tasks and given job-description titles, identifying their assignments.

Qualifications for the Diaconate

Again we see fit to use the generic term for the generalized service-role personnel of the church. The same is in keeping with the writer's studied conviction that both men and women filled such roles in the apostolic church. To those who ask: if that be true, why then did not the apostle Paul provide a list of qualifications for deaconesses as he did for elders and deacons in I Timothy 3:8-13? My rejoinder is that he did. Support for such an affirmation is not lacking though admittedly it is not clearly discernible. But part of the problem is that a key text has been obscured in its import by the unwarranted eisegetical liberties which the translators of the KJV took with I Timothy 3:11.

In the context of Paul's categorical listing of standards of conduct and personal relationships for those appointed to service roles in the church, the KJV translators added a pronoun. They thereby changed the thrust of what Paul might otherwise be understood as saying. The text of I Timothy 3:11 was altered to read "their wives" instead of simply reading "women." The pronoun was inserted without any textual basis. The fact is subtly acknowledged to a degree by the NKJ in which the added word is italicized, but the rendering of *gunaikas* as "wives" continues the distortion of the text. *Gunaikas* (a plural form of *gune*) is the ordinary mode of addressing or designating women, married or otherwise. Jesus, for example, addressed his mother thusly from the cross, saying: "*Woman*, behold your son (the disciple John). (See John 19:26).

311

Does it not seem strange that Paul would take occasion to inform Timothy what behavior patterns a deacon's wife should display, yet said nothing about the standards to be set for the wives of elders? If he had closed the entire discussion with what is said in I Timothy 3:11, the instruction might be construed as relating to both service roles, elders as well as deacons. But v. 11 is set instead in the midst of his instruction concerning the diaconate. The NIV follows the lead of the KJV, rendering *gunaikas* (women) as "wives," without even benefit of italics. But in "a moment of truth," they appended a footnote reading "deaconesses." For the uninformed, footnotes generally betray the fact that the popular rendering of a text is not always the one truest to the sense thereof; or at the least, it is not the only viable translation.

Contextually, vs. 8-10 contain five specifications for male servants. Four of the five are slightly rephrased in v. 11 and applied to the women of whom he saw fit to make mention. The verse is parenthetical. Vs. 12 and 13 focus on the male role as it relates to family relationships. This has already been spelled out for elders in vs. 2 and 5.

The four specifications which apply to the diaconate without regard to sex distinctions are these: 1) Grave. The Greek word (*semnos*) has two applications. It denotes dignity and gravity. That is, it relates to persons and things to be regarded with due respect and to a seriousness of purpose, hence a mindset not given to frivolity and vanity.

2) Tongue control. Men servants are not to be double-tongued (Gr. *dilogos*, literally two-worded). The slang expression for it is "speaking out of both sides of the mouth"; that is, saying one thing to one person and quite the opposite to another, saying what suits the occasion instead of what fits the facts. Women servants are not to be slanderers (Gr. *diabolos*, literally, she-devils). The root means an accuser. Satan is called the devil because he is an accuser of the worst sort. In his first encounter with mankind, of record, he accused God of lying to Adam and Eve, implying they would not really die, as God said they would if they disobeyed him. He suggested instead that God was resorting to a bit of Divine chauvinism, trying to hold them back from becoming as he is. In the text before us, it is unclear why the difference of application was made. It might be conjectured that gossip or slander was more of a temptation of women, and proneness to falsehood generally was more characteristic of men.

3) Wine drinking. What is said here is difficult to understand amid our culture. Elders, deacons, and deaconesses, were not forbidden to drink wine. That would have been quite unrealistic. But they were to be

temperate, not given to wine. In I Timothy 3:3 the word used is *paroinon*, literally, alongside of wine. The translation, "not given to wine" is metaphoric. In marriage, men marry, women are given in marriage. Women are thus to submit themselves to their husbands who thereupon have rule over them. But elders are not to be given to wine. They are not to lie alongside of wine. They are not to be given to wine, with the wine becoming their husband, so to speak, their lord and master. The phrase in I Timothy 3:8 is *me oino pollo prosechontas*, literally, "being not addicted to much wine." This is only a variant of the former expression. As our translations read, it is sometimes suggested that deacons can drink a little wine, but elders are to be total abstainers. The latter is not what is communicated in I Timothy 3:3. The word translated temperate in I Timothy 3:11 (and sometimes rendered sober) is *nephalious*. It means to be free from the influence of intoxicants.

All three expressions bespeak the same thing, but in different words. They do not refer to different degrees of intoxication or addiction, but neither do they demand total abstinence. They demand sobriety, and freedom from excess, hence temperance.

I write the foregoing observations as a militant, outspoken foe of the beverage alcohol industry, at all levels. I am a life-time, evangelistic, total abstainer. I do not even drink coffee. When invited to do so, I attempt to decline with a note of humor, saying: "I do not even drink beer, unless it has the 'root' in it." And I only buy the decaffeinated product. These things are not said to proclaim my own righteousness, or to put down coffee drinkers, but to underscore the fact I have not "gone soft on drinking." My persuasion is that were Paul writing to those in our culture, he would encourage, if not demand, total abstinence. But the fact, is, the language of I Timothy 3:3, 8, and 11 does not of itself so charge.

Grape cultivation and wine processing receive frequent mention in both testaments without censure. The vintage fermented quickly. Considering the processing conditions, equipment, climate, and storage facilities, this was inevitable. Pasteurization, pressure cookers, canning, and refrigeration were centuries removed. But wine, though commonly consumed with daily meals, was ordinarily diluted by three to four parts of water. The supply was thereby extended, hopefully, from one year to the next. The vintage was deintoxicated, and the wine "cauterized" the water. The latter is reflected in Paul's admonition to Timothy, "Stop drinking only water, and use a little wine because of your stomach and your frequent illnesses" (I Tim. 5:23, NIV).

Today, we have the benefit of more sophisticated medicines, a wider range of tasteful (many of them healthful) beverages which may be consumed without risk of addiction or of countenancing and supporting the beverage alcohol industry. In view of the pressure advertising and the carnage wrought on our highways by accidents in which alcohol is involved in over half of all fatalities, I am persuaded Paul would not have given the same counsel were he writing today.

4) Deacons and deaconesses alike were expected to be persons of exemplary faith (I Tim. 3:9, 11). In addition, deacons were to be men not marked by greed and to be exemplary in their family relationships. Concerning the latter, as promised in the previous lesson, we will shortly have more to say. But first, v. 13 of the chapter deserves comment. "They that serve well as servants (deacons) gain to themselves a good standing and great boldness in the faith that is in Christ Jesus." Stephen did. Philip did. Undoubtedly, others did.

Good deacons do not remain deacons long. They become evangelists, elders. They become a resource pool for leadership roles. Elders are logically selected from those who have apprenticed and served well as deacons. In turn, those appointed to the diaconate should "first be proved" (I Tim. 3:10). How so? There are occasional "one-time" situations particularly suited to the interests and abilities of persons not already involved in leadership or service roles. They can be included in the planning and promotion of spot programs and activities. If they show resourcefulness, initiative, the ability to work with others, to yield and to adapt, to bear criticism, and to eschew bossiness and a desire for the credit and the limelight; they have "first been proved." It is then time to heed the rest of Paul's counsel. "Then let them serve as deacons (or deaconesses, as the case may be), if they be found blameless."

Must all these be married, having children?

Included in the qualification consideration for both elders and deacons is the phrase, "the husband of one wife," (Gr. *mias gunaikos andra*), I Timothy 3:2, 12; Titus 1:6. In addition, we find such phrases as, "one that rules well his own house, having (his) children in subjection with all gravity" (I Tim. 3:4), and "having children that believe, who are not accused of riot or unruly" (Titus 1:6). Of the deacons it is written: "Let deacons be husbands of one wife, ruling (their) children and their own houses well" (I Tim. 3:12). By inference, if the role of deaconess be acknowledged, or if wives automatically become "deaconesses" when their husbands become deacons (but without "voting rights" and "church board" status), as some interpret I Timothy 3:11, then deaconesses must be the wives and mothers.

How can all these things be reconciled? If to qualify as an elder, a man must be an older man, but not too old, that is, he must have children (pl.) old enough to believe, yet young enough they are in subjection to him, being ruled as a part of his household; the tenure of an elder is circumscribed "coming on and going out." They must enter younger than commonly supposed and vacate the office when their children leave home. A rigid and literal interpretation of what is said would so decree.

As for the marriage and divorce factors, as these considerations relate to both elders and deacons, are we dealing with absolutes, or with principles? Many would say the word "must" settles that. It means the same in this context that it does in John 3:7 ("ye must be born again"). It is hard to argue with that brand of logic. But Jesus did so repeatedly in his conflict with the Pharisees who took the hard line, the-letter-of-the-law stance, on every issue.

I recall the case of two brothers, but a year apart in age. They were commonly thought to be twins. We will call them Jim and John. Jim was a very serious person. While he socialized with girls his age, seemingly enjoying their company and they his, he rarely dated formally. He graduated from college with honors, still single, and became gainfully employed, rising rapidly in the firm. He was a dedicated Christian, faithful in attendance. Occasionally he was called upon to usher or pass the collection and communion trays, but was deemed unqualified to be elected to the board.

With his younger brother it was quite different in most respects. Dating consumed most of his evenings. He married shortly upon graduating from high school. His first child was born "prematurely" by several weeks, even months. His church attendance was spotty, though his wife attended regularly and took her turn in the nursery to which she contributed a new enrollee at frequent intervals. At this point, someone suggested that if John were given a "job" (office) in the church, he might become more interested. Largely through the faithfulness of his wife in bringing her growing brood of children to Sunday school and assisting in the nursery, John garnered enough votes to be elected. He was flattered somewhat and responded favorably, serving for the most part as well as most of his peers. Eventually, he was elected to the eldership.

315

Meanwhile Jim enrolled in the extension classes of the area Bible college. He became the teacher of a growing singles class and did some supply preaching in the area. On occasion he filled the pulpit in his home church. Many said he belonged in the pulpit. But though he was deemed qualified for that important leadership role, he was rejected as a candidate for the board of deacons. He did not have a wife and children. However, he served on various committees, chairing many of them, and participated effectively in evangelistic calling.

In his late thirties, he was moved by compassion to marry a young widow whose husband was killed in a car wreck, leaving her burn-scarred, crippled, and with two children. At last, he was deemed qualified to be a deacon. However, one stickler for details insisted they were not really "his" children, since they were not his biologically. Question: When did Jim become qualified to be a deacon, if ever?

Is the marital and parental relationship the only arena in which a man can prove himself? Granted that it provides a natural setting for certain aspects of the work of an elder, but are there no facets of church work where business experience and common sense might prove of value? Were Jesus among us today as a thirty-year-old bachelor, he would not be counted qualified to stand at the door and pass out bulletins in some congregations. He could not qualify as a deacon, much less an elder.

Does the phrase *mias gunaikos andra* disqualify not only bachelors, but widowers as well, remarried or otherwise? And does it rule out the divorced and those persons married to such persons, regardless of time and circumstances? A sin that is held against a person is a sin that is not forgiven. Paul was once a murderer and a blasphemer (I Tim. 1:13), yet he became an apostle. Fortunately, he was not divorced. Are there two unpardonable sins? Or is divorce, even before one comes to Christ, that sin? These are hard questions. The letter of the law would seem to demand one answer, the spirit of Christ another. Granted that a prior marriage which ended in divorce calls for a second look — or does it? Does such a person not deserve a second look? What God has cleansed, must we count otherwise regardless of the change that Christ has wrought?

Paul wrote to the church at Corinth, saying: "Neither fornicators, nor adulterers, nor effeminate (male prostitutes, NIV), nor abusers of themselves with men (homosexuals), nor thieves, nor covetous, nor drunkards, nor revilers, nor extortioners shall inherit the kingdom of God," but added: "And such were some of you: but ye were washed, ye were sanctified, ye were justified in the name of our Lord Jesus Christ and in the Spirit of our God" (I Cor. 6:9-11). Which of them, if any, having first been proved, could be appointed to service and leadership roles in the church, and which cannot? Would it not be fair to inform candidates for baptism in which class they fall, and in which caste they shall remain, if the latter is their lot? Or would it be better that the latter learn of their irrevocable estate only when spiritual growth prompts them to seek service and leadership roles in the church? These are indeed hard questions. Tension between the letter of the law and the spirit of Christ calls for a blend of courage and charity, grit and grace.

Methods of Selection

The method of selecting church leaders is not spelled out in large letters, nor does it follow a rigid pattern. 1) Matthias was chosen by lot to fill the vacancy created by Judas' defection and suicide. He was one of two candidates produced by an unspecified screening process in which some basic guidelines were first laid down (Acts 1:16-26).

2) In the selection of the seven deacons(?) of Acts 6, the apostles declared the need, the number of men to be chosen to meet it, and the qualifications. Incidentally, the qualifications specified are quite dissimilar from those set forth by Paul in I Timothy 3:8-13. Nothing is said to the effect they should be married, or have children, or rule their houses well. The brethren were instructed to look out (Gr. *episkepsasthe*—oversee/visit) among themselves to find men of good report, full of the Holy Spirit and wisdom (v. 3), whom the apostles would then appoint (Gr. *kathistao*—literally, put into position) over the business to be attended. In doing so, the apostles prayed and laid their hands upon them (v. 6).

Barnabas and Saul were named by the Holy Spirit for the mission to which they were sent. There were five such men in the congregation said to be "prophets and teachers." How the Holy Spirit made known to the congregation his choice from among them is not stated. The congregation responded by fasting, prayer, and laying their hands upon them (Acts 13:1-3).

Near the close of their first missionary journey, Barnabas and Saul (the latter now called Paul) retraced their steps and appointed elders in every city (Acts 14:23). The word for appoint (KJV ordain) used here is *cheirotoneo* (literally, to vote by outstretched hands). Prayer, fasting, and the laying on of hands completed the ordination process.

317

In Titus 1:5 the evangelist Titus whom Paul had left on the Isle of Crete was instructed to appoint (Gr. *kathistemi*) elders in every city. A list of qualifications follows. No details of the process of selection are given.

From the foregoing we learn that the Holy Spirit, the apostles, the evangelist, and the congregation were all involved in the selection of qualified personnel. No precise unalterable pattern is discernible. Congregations, however, were not left to decide for themselves the qualifications to be sought, only the persons who met the qualifications. When the inspired apostles or the Holy Spirit were directing the choice, the precise number to be selected was named. In the instance of replacing Judas, there was, of course, only one opening to be filled. The apostles specified seven to be appointed to the care of the widows in the church at Jerusalem. Two men were specified by the Holy Spirit for the missionary outreach stemming from the church at Antioch. Aside from the choosing of Matthias, there is no hint of one man being pitted against another in a popularity contest. He was chosen by lot, not by popular vote. The two-party, popular vote contest, with twice as many nominees as positions to be filled, has more in common with our political system than with Biblical precepts, and is generally more political than spiritual in operation.

Duration of the Appointment

The duration or time span embraced by an appointment is nowhere stated. Whether appointees were subject to review, replacement, or reelection from time to time can only be conjectured. No rule would likely fit all circumstances. Experience teaches that "life-time" tenure is fraught with perils. There is absolutely no hint that an elder appointed by one congregation may expect to assume the same role in another, should he happen to move. The position is one of trust and respect gained amid and under the observation of those who chose him to have oversight of them. It is government by the consent of the governed.

We choose our doctors and express our confidence in them by following their instructions, distasteful though such may sometimes be. This is government by the consent of the governed. We choose our lawyers and submit to their counsel. This too is government by the consent of the governed.

A woman, considering a marriage proposal, should ask herself, "Would my best interest be served were I to submit myself to this man, becoming subject to him in everything?" (Eph. 5:22, 24). This is government by the consent of the governed. So should it be, even to a greater degree, in our relationship with Christ. We choose him as Lord. Why call him, "Lord, Lord," if we do not the things which he commands us?

The church in its organizational structure is not a democracy. From the human side, it is a republic in which we choose those who represent us and assume responsibility for our spiritual welfare and associated needs. From the Divine side, it is a monarchy whose affairs are administered by those who recognize they are also stewards of the manifold grace of God, and who will give an account of their stewardship when he returns for a reckoning and to receive that which is his own.

PREVIEW—REVIEW QUESTIONS

1. According to Jesus, who is the greatest among us?
2. By his word choice, was Jesus actually meaning to say the deacon's office ranks above all others? Explain.
3. In what respects does the organizational structure of the average congregation exhibit a "Made in America" label?
4. Why is the term diaconate preferred by the author to the term deaconship? Do you agree to any degree?
5. Note the origin of the diaconate. Relate a circumstance in the life of Moses called to mind thereby.
6. In what way did the appointment of the first deacons set a pattern? What principle(s) can be cited?
7. What duty did they perform which is taken out of context and made the routine (sometimes only) duty for deacons today?
8. What change in the role of deacons tends to make congregations chary about calling women who fill service roles deaconesses?
9. Were the first deacons actually placed in charge of the care of the needy, with free access to the church funds? Explain.
10. In what respect do women appointed to definite service roles often more readily fit the New Testament pattern of the diaconate than the deacons?
11. Why would it likely be expeditious to discontinue the terms deacons and deaconesses? Have we set any precedent for this?
12. Relate the cliche, "Everybody's business is nobody's business" to the principle which relates to the diaconate.
13. Comment concerning the KJV reconstruction of the language of I Timothy 3:11.

14. Note four guidelines for men and women servants that are closely parallel.
15. Discuss the issue of temperance vs. total abstinence.
16. Does our culture differ sufficiently to tip the balance from one towards the other? Explain.
17. How can a person first be proved as to his fitness to serve as a deacon without being elected to a trial term?
18. What is the literal meaning of the phrase commonly translated, "husband of one wife"?
19. Was such a qualification exacted of the first deacons? What about having children?
20. How does a letter-of-the-law interpretation of the marital and parental stipulations relate to the limitation of the tenure of elders?
21. Could Jesus qualify for a position on the church board were he to return to again dwell among us? If not, why not?
22. What is there about the ministry of the Word that makes it possible for a bachelor to fulfill that role single-handedly, but not one elder or deacon can be included on the board if unmarried or without children in subjection?
23. Is divorce the unpardonable sin? Why should this be asked?
24. Discuss the tension between the letter of the law and the spirit of the law.
25. Was Jesus ever placed under this tension? How did he respond? What does that say of "the mind of Christ"?
26. In what way does our method of selecting "board members" reflect a "Made in America" label?
27. Apply the principle expressed in the phrase, "government by the consent of the governed."

SECTION SEVEN: THE DIVINELY GIVEN NAMES AND COMMEMORATIVE INSTITUTIONS

22

THE DIVINELY GIVEN NAMES

In the comic strip, *Peanuts*, one of the woebegone characters around whom Charles Schultz's humor often revolves is seated at her desk in the schoolroom. She is depicted pondering a true-false test, her insecurity showing. At length, she calls out to the teacher: "Ma'am, what if it is only half true?" That is a good question. It is pertinent to the subject at hand.

There is a half-truth that has been around so long most people believe it. At least they would have us think they do. You have heard the old saw: "What's in a name? A rose by any other name would be just as sweet." That is a half-truth. As with most half-truths, it is worse than an outright lie. There is just enough truth in it to subtly obscure the lie which is its inner core.

Some time ago my wife and I were visitors in the morning service of a flourishing young congregation. The preacher, effusing charisma, announced as his sermon topic: "Suffering as a Christian." His opening remark was, "You know, of course, that the name Christian was given in derision. Being a suitable nickname, it has stuck." I glanced about to see how others responded to that bit of effrontery, and it appeared they agreed. I was minded to take a cue from Aquila and Priscilla, and take him aside and expound to him the Word of God more perfectly (see Acts 18:26). But the church reputedly had a strong eldership, so I left the matter up to them.

Some weeks later we again had occasion to visit the congregation, and were invited by an elder to attend an adult class he was teaching. In introducing us, he explained that it was an open class, and if at any time I wanted to say something to feel free to do so. That was somewhat like saying, "sic 'em" to a dog.

The class had hardly gotten under way when one of the men cited a happening at work, and added, "He calls himself an Evangelical, or something like that." The teacher (an elder, no less) replied: "I couldn't care less how someone worships, or what they call themselves, as long as they worship the same God I do. After all, what's in a name?" Since the class sat in a circle to engender the camaraderie that was sought, it was not difficult to see that most of the class agreed with him. I waited for a moment for someone to challenge him. When no one did, I asked, "May I take you up on the invitation you extended me to speak out, if I were minded to do so?" He nodded approval. I said more than I had intended at first, kindling as I spoke.

Christianity Today carries a one-panel cartoon series entitled, "What if . . . ," lampooning various facets of current religiosity. Calling attention to the same, I spoke to this effect:

1) What if the angel who clued Joseph in on the full story of Mary's pregnancy should have said: "When he is born, thou shalt call his name, uh, let's see now. Oh you will think of something. It doesn't really make any difference, regardless of what the prophet Isaiah predicted. After all, what's in a name?"

2) Or what if what's-his-name (uh, you know who I mean, Joseph's stepson) should have said in his commission to the apostles: "Go make disciples of all the nations, baptizing them into the name of every Tom, Dick, and Harry; or John the baptist maybe, or Jeremiah, or one of the prophets. I am not a stickler for details."

3) Or what if Peter on the day of Pentecost should have answered the question of the inquiring multitude, "Repent ye and be baptized in the name of the coming kingdom. Hey, how about calling them the Kingdom Kids? That sounds catchy, doesn't it?"

4) Or what if Peter should have said to the cripple at the gate of the temple, "In the name of common sense, you panhandling beggar, get up and walk. Yeah, you heard me, it's that simple. One name is as good as another. It's what you feel in your heart that counts."

5) Or when arrested by the temple officers who demanded of him: "By what authority (power) or in what name have you done this?" what if Peter should have answered them: "Name, schmame, ask me again, and I will tell you the same. Where do you get that stuff, 'by what authority, or power, or in what name have we done this?' What's in a name?"

What's in a Name?

What's in a name? Authority is in a name. The incident detailed in Acts 3:6—4:12 plainly affirms this to be so. In fact, Peter closed his defense by saying, "There is no other name under heaven that is given among men whereby we must be saved" (Acts 4:12).

Personally, I believe that if Peter had commanded the cripple to rise up and walk in the name of Evangelicalism (or whatever might have been currently popular), he would have died a cripple. Paul rebuked the church at Corinth for the very thing we shrug off as of no consequence. He charged that they were dividing the body of Christ. And he pleaded with them "in the name of the Lord Jesus Christ" to be of one mind in him. We need to take up again what was once a part of our plea for unity in Christ or quit calling ourselves the Christian Church.

What is in a name? Would a rose by any other name indeed be just as sweet? Chemically, yes. It is not its name which gives to a rose its sweetness, nor does its sweetness give to a rose its name. Irrespective of aroma, any flower having the same petal formation is a rose. Aesthetically, emotionally, romantically, a rose would not be just as sweet if called by another name. The name has so long been associated primarily with flowers of such exquisite beauty and sweet fragrance that the senses are heightened at the sight, or even mention, of a rose. Suppose a young swain should dump a dozen long-stemmed American Beauty roses in the lap of his fiancee, saying, "Here are some skunk cabbages for your birthday," she would scarcely respond, "What's in a name? A rose by any other name, even skunk cabbage, is just as sweet."

What is in a name? Does anyone really believe that it makes no difference what something, or someone, is called? Call a member of some ethnic minority by a name that is traditionally used as an ethnic slur and see the response. Call a member of any sect, or denomination of Christendom by the distinctive name of some other, or call a Christian a Buddhist or a Buddhist a Moslem. Correction. Do no such thing;

neither in jest, nor as a test. It will not be funny, and it will not be appreciated. One can call a member of any sect of Christendom a Christian, and the beneficiary of that grace will be flattered. Yet, most any one of them will defend a divisive sectarian name by parroting the old saw we have taken the pains to unmask.

One can sugarcoat a poison pellet, and it will go down as smoothly as an M & M chocolate drop, but its inner core of poison will do its deadly work when the veneer has been dissolved. We repeat, "a half-truth is worse than an outright lie." And such is the subterfuge we have taken time to lay bare.

But What Saith the Oracles of God?

Again we have occasion to consider the question of Romans 11:4. It is especially pertinent to our present inquiry, for it focuses on the word that is the key to the interpretation of the key passage which relates to the subject—*chrematismos*. Dr. Alfred Marshall translates it, "Divine Response" (*The Interlinear Greek-English New Testament*).

Does God count names important? He most certainly does. One can scarcely read the first ten verses of the Bible without having that called to our attention. God promptly named everything he made. He called the light Day, the darkness Night (Gen. 1:5). He called the firmament Heaven (v. 8), the dry land Earth, and the waters Seas (v. 10).

When God made man he named him, and likewise his wife. "He called their name Adam" (from the ground) 5:2, and apparently approved when Adam gave to Eve a distinguishing name, Woman, "because she was taken out of man" (2:23).

He named the garden he planted for man's first home (2:8), and gave distinguishing names for each of the four branches of the river of Eden (2:11-14). He brought the animals and birds before man "to see what he would call them" (2:19), if anything. Adam was apparently observant, imitative, and perceptive. He gave names to all of them, and God seems to have been pleased with his performance, for "whatever man called every living creature, that was the name thereof" (v. 19).

The third commandment of the decalogue underscores the fact that God does not regard it lightly when man regards his name lightly (Exod. 20:7). He gave his chosen people a name, Israel, "Prince(s) of God," and showed himself especially solicitous of those whom he called "My people, who are called by My Name" (II Chron. 7:14). The name of his son was foretold, categorically (Isa. 7:14) and the name of the spiritual Israel that he (Jesus) would call out from all the nations was foretold, categorically, also (Isa. 62:2-5). The specific name to be given his son, and the specific name to be called upon his new elect race were adroitly held in abeyance until the proper time for their disclosure.

There can be no doubt about it. God counts names important. It should not be difficult to understand why. They serve several important functions.

The Function of Names

Names serve several important functions. Communication would be difficult, and identifications especially so, if there were no fitting and distinguishing names for persons, places, and things. Nouns, the generic term for such manner of speaking, are among the first words a child learns to say.

1. *Names are descriptive.* They describe features, feelings, and functions. Our English words, noun and name, are derived via Latin, from the Greek word *onoma*. To nominate is to put someone's name forth for consideration of some kind. To be anonymous is to have no name, or at least no disclosed name.

The more descriptive a name is, the more readily communication is facilitated. In our language, vehicles which were designed to carry things were originally called carriages, and what they carried was called cargo. Very appropriate, is it not? Our word car is "shorthand" for carriage. When self-propelling vehicles were first developed, they were called horseless carriages. They were also goatless, oxenless, elephantless, and even "manless" in that context. So a more descriptive and distinctive name was sought. Since they were mobile (able to be moved), and were even "self-moving" vehicles, they came to be called automobiles.

Vessels which ply beneath the surface of the sea are aptly called submarines. The first flying machines were called precisely that, or airships. They are now called airplanes, because their wings plane the air. Our spacemen are called astronauts (star-sailors). That is more suited to our high aspirations than to actual accomplishment.

When one has come into a saving relationship with God, in and through Christ, how ought that relationship be described? How ought the grace, the love, the sacrifice, the love, the power, and the person that made it possible be expressed? Should we call ourselves Gospelites, or Baptists, or Born-Againers, or Calvarians? Or ought the centrality of Christ take precedence? Would not the name Christian more properly describe the new relationship we have gained, and give to Christ the honor that is due him? In view of Acts 4:11, 12, "what think ye of the Christ?" Is he worthy to be exalted above ordinances, forms of church government, renowned reformers; indeed above all others and all things?

2. *Names are used to distinguish one person or thing from another.* If Adam had given the same name to every animal they might as well not have been named at all. Imagine Adam and Eve trudging along outside the protective domain of Eden. Let us assume they had seen enough of the raw life of the wilds that they are now keenly aware of what a hungry carnivore can do to his prey. Suppose Adam should see what we call a lion crouching in a thicket, getting ready to spring upon them. But when he was asked to name each of them, he had said, "What's in a name? What you call them won't change them in any way. I will just call them all, *oneofthem*." But now Eve needs to be alerted to their danger. "Pssst," Adam whispers, "I see *oneofthem*." Eve turns in the direction Adam is pointing and sees what we call a squirrel scampering up a tree. Can you not hear her say, "Adam, are you nuts? *Oneofthem* can't hurt us."

Names are used to distinguish persons and things, each from another. You meet a man named Jones. The name tag on his work jacket tells you that. But you are aware there are a lot of folk in the area with that name. So you say to him, "Sir, what is your first name?" "John," he replies. "Oh yes, you are the fellow that has that tremendous oak tree in his front yard." "No," he says, "that's a different John Jones. We are no relation. I am John Jacob Jones." You answer that by saying, "I thought John Jacob Jones was the mayor of the town. Didn't he pass away last week?" That, you learn, was the man's father. You have been talking to John Jacob Jones, Junior. But since the death of his father, he can now drop the name Junior.

Every time you add a name, you make another distinction. There are denominations that would have you know on what side their forbears fought during the Civil War. There are others who would have you know they broke away from the corrupt power structure of their heritage and they are free. Others would have you know they do not mess around with sprinkling infants; they baptize folk old enough to choose for themselves whether they want to be baptized and be affiliated with the church. Others would have you know they are the missionary

326

or the free will, or the fundamentalist, or the primitive branch of that denomination. And so it goes. Organizational structure, the day they opt to worship, their ethnic heritage, etc., etc., they proudly proclaim on their bulletin boards, their publications, their ads in the newspaper and in the phone directory, and in what they call themselves personally. But they will not admit they are dividing the church thereby. Not even I Corinthians 1:10-13 can convince them of that. But the fact is, names are distinctive, they are divisive. They distinguish and separate one from another.

Is there a name that does not distinguish one from another those who are in Christ? Is there a name that does the important thing, however, distinguishing those in Christ from those who do not choose to be identified thusly? There is one—only one. I will not insult the reader's intelligence by stating what that one is.

3. *Names are commemorative in character.* We often name our children in commemoration of someone dear to us, someone we admire. Our first son bears, besides the family name, the given names of his two grandfathers. Many name children in honor of persons who have made history, or to honor friends. Conversely, some names are avoided as having become dishonored by someone so named. Jezebel means "uncohabitated." It is the Hebrew equivalent of the name Virginia. But Jezebel tarnished her name as Judas did the name given him.

Jacob called a certain place Bethel, "House of God." Aforetime it was called Luz, "Almond." Israel paused at a certain place to assess their state and concluded, "hitherto the Lord has helped us." So they set a stone up as a memorial pillar, and called the memorial Ebenezer, "stone of help" (I Sam. 7:12). Have your raised your Ebenezer lately? Did you know what you were saying when you went along with the crowd and sang that you were doing so? Do we have Someone whose name would be an honor to wear? Is there One who stands out above all others, and all things?

4. *Names are progressive.* An old saying declares that "New occasions teach new duties." New relationships call for new names. Recall how it is in courtship that flowers into marriage. Boy meets girl. Her name is Dorothy, but soon she is being called Dotty. Soon, it is Honey, and/or Sweetheart. In time she may even be called Mrs. Josef Zoankahlovitchsky, or she may become just another Mrs. John Smith. But the progression may very well not stop there. She may become Mama, and then Grandma.

New relationships call for a progression in nomenclature. Have we entered a new relationship that might well dictate a new name, a name which according to Divine promise "the mouth of the Lord has named" (Isa. 62:2)? Have we now advanced beyond that high estate so that our Christian growth is best articulated by reminding folk by the name which we wear spiritually how indebted we are to someone or something else? Is that really progression?

Facts Concerning the Name Christian

1. There are prophecies concerning a new name for God's chosen in a new age and a new relationship. Isaiah (Isa. 56:3-5) predicts a time when the foreigners and the emasculated who would fain join themselves to Jehovah would no longer be minded to say, "Jehovah will separate me from his people" (v. 3). For it is written: "Thus saith Jehovah . . . Unto them will I give in my house and within my walls a memorial and a name better than of sons and daughters; I will give them an everlasting name, that shall not be cut off." Israel is not that name. Nor are the party names of a divided Christendom such a name. Isaiah 62:2-5 is even more to the point:

> For Zion's sake I will not hold my peace, and for Jerusalem's sake I will not rest until her righteousness go forth as brightness, and her salvation as a lamp that burneth. And the nations (Gentiles) shall see thy righteousness, and all kings thy glory, and *thou shalt be called by a new name which the mouth of the Lord shall name* (vs. 1, 2).

As the promise continues, the imagery of marriage is employed to dramatize the joyous relationship which ensues. The words "Hephzibah," meaning "my delight is in her," and "Beulah," meaning "married," are used metaphorically, not nominally, to describe the estate. The passage is akin to Isaiah 7:14 where the relationship of the Messiah is stated categorically, not nominally. Matthew quotes the passage affirming the Messiah would be called Emanuel (God with us), and sees no contradiction in that and the words of the angel to Joseph, declaring, "And thou shalt call his name Jesus (Saviour), for it is he that shall save his people from their sins" (Matt. 1:21-25).

In all the New Testament, despite the plethora of terms used to describe those who are in Christ, there is only one name that is 1) *new*, and 2) said to be *Divinely given*.

This brings us again into direct confrontation with the meaning of the verb used in Acts 11:26 to describe the introduction of the name

Christian. But first, let us note the conditions surrounding that auspicious moment.

Antioch is not the first place that Gentiles were baptized into Christ. A step was taken in that direction when the Samaritans were evangelized by Philip. A further step was taken when Peter finally got the message of the thrice-given vision with which he wrestled and, with the help of even further demonstration of God's will, not only preached to the Gentile household of Cornelius, but baptized them as well. But aside from the evangelistic contact, no fellowship or co-mingling of either the halfbreeds or the Gentiles is reported.

The founding of the church at Antioch became therefore a milestone event. Philip had gone half a mile, so to speak. Peter had gone the whole first mile, but at Antioch, the evangelists went the second mile. Luke, who took time out between Acts 8:4 and 11:19 to detail through an extended hiatus the chain of events which led the way to the happening of Acts 11:26, returns to the point he had made in Acts 8:4. With the intervening events in mind, read Acts 8:4 and immediately move to Acts 11:19. The first text reads: "They that were scattered abroad went everywhere preaching the word." Now hear this:

> They therefore that were scattered abroad upon the tribulation that arose about Stephen travelled as far as Phoenicia, and Cyprus, and Antioch, *speaking the word to none save only to Jews. But there were some of them* (men of Cyprus and Cyrene) *who when they were come to Antioch spake unto the Greeks also,* preaching the Lord Jesus (vs. 19, 20).

As the story unfolds, we are told "the hand of the Lord was with them, and a great multitude that believed turned unto the Lord." The news of this got back to Jerusalem, and Barnabas was dispatched, presumably to look into the matter. Being full of the Holy Spirit and faith (v. 24), he was delighted. Soon he took time out to go to Tarsus to seek for Saul, and upon finding him, he brought him to Antioch. They worked together there for a whole year. Sometime in the course of that chain of events, God did something that he had not done before, neither in Jerusalem where a Jewish church flourished, nor in Samaria where a halfbreed church was to be found, nor even at Caesarea where with a signal demonstration of the Holy Spirit he had demonstrated that he made no longer any distinction between Jew and Gentile. "The disciples were Divinely called (*chrematisai*) Christians first in Antioch" (v. 26).

That is precisely what the text says. That is not what our English translators say. That is not what most commentaries say. That is certainly not what theologians and preachers ordinarily say. How then can we speak with such certitude? It is simple. Simply note the various texts of the New Testament where the same verb appears, but can be translated without embarrassment to sectarian practice.

2. Some questions are highly in order. There are several texts of Scripture in which translators have inserted into our English text some words which indicate there was a degree of Divine interaction in the events reported. The texts have one thing in common. They all include the Greek word that is now under consideration.

a) How did it happen that the Wise-men learned of Herod's dire design concerning Jesus? The text says they learned of it in a dream. But might that not have been just a nightmare? Our translators would have us know they were "being warned *of God* in a dream." The text does not include the phrase *tou Theou*. The translators have inserted the words into the translation of the text. Why? Because Matthew used a word which according to Greek lexicons, based on its usage in the Greek Septuagint and in secular Greek literature, means "to appoint or nominate by Divine direction." The form of the word used in Matthew 2:12 is *chrematisthentes*.

b) How did Joseph learn when it was safe for his family to return from Egypt? He had a dream. But the same Greek word appears (Matt. 2:22). So the translators again add the words "of God" to their rendering of the text.

c) Luke 2:26 leaves no room for questioning the source of the revelation given Simeon. The text reads that "it was revealed unto him by the Holy Spirit that he should not see death until he had seen the Lord's Christ." Luke used the same verb Matthew used (2:12 and 22), even though it was a bit redundant for him to have done so in this instance.

d) Luke uses the same verb again in Acts 10:22, just one chapter prior to what he reports concerning the origin of the name Christian in Acts 11:26. How did it happen that the Gentile Cornelius was moved to send for Peter? How did he know him by name, and where to find him, and what Peter could do for him? The messenger he sent informed Peter it was "of God." At least that is the way the translators have made it to read. That should not be surprising. The verb is again the same.

e) We will bypass Acts 11:26 for the present and take note of Paul's usage of the same verb. He uses it twice. In the first instance, Romans 7:3, the translators handle the word as they have done with Luke 2:26. In contrasting God's law with man's reasoning, Paul states that a woman joined to another while her husband liveth "shall be called an adultress." For that to be stated, Paul was obliged to employ a verb which speaks of "the action of God in making known his will." Such a verb was readily at hand in the form of *chrematisai*.

g) Hebrews 8:5 is instructive. How did Moses know he was to exactly follow God's blueprint for the tabernacle? The Hebrew writer tells us he "was warned *of God*" (*kechrematistai*).

h) A parallel situation is found in the case of Noah, cited in Hebrews 11:7. No man could have contemplated such a flood, or how to cope with it. Fortunately, he "was warned *of God*" (*chrematistheis*).

i) This leaves Acts 11:26 to be interpreted in the light of the usage of the same word in eight other texts. What happened here that the word *chrematisai* would appear to have lost its distinctive meaning, leaving open the possibility that "an enemy has done this," to take a text (Matt. 13:26) out of context to express the popular opinion?

Etymology of the Name Christian

The name Christian is derived from the three principle languages of the Mediterranean world. Literally, it means "belonging to, or of the anointed one." The Hebrew word Messiah was rendered *Christos* when carried over into the Greek LXX. The Greek word was of the same meaning in its literal connotation, but among the Hebrews it had overtones of hope and Divine promise beyond what its counterpart communicated in Greek. To form the word Christian, the Messianic concept, universalized through its Greek counterpart, was given a Latin suffix (ian) denoting relationship—belonging to, or a follower. The Greek suffix (os) denoting number and gender was now affixed forming a new word, *Christianos*. When translating into English, the gender designation is dropped, resulting in our word Christian.

To those who prefer not to believe that Christian is the Divinely revealed name for those who are redeemed to Him through Christ, I beg to ask: "When is the prophecy of Isaiah concerning a new name to be given by the mouth to the Lord to be fulfilled? If the name Christian is not that new name, and if the circumstances chronicled in Acts 11:19ff. do not fit the circumstances of the prophecy, what might provide a suitable occasion for God to give us a new name—better than sons and daughters, an everlasting name that shall not be cut off? Many of the sectarian names of our religious neighbors are admittedly novel, but they are hardly suitable as a vehicle for glorifying Christ (I Peter 4:16).

331

Miscellaneous Informal Names

A number of common nouns are used in the New Testament to describe or designate various aspects of the Christian way of life. But none of them can be construed as a name, a proper noun. Believers, brethren, children, disciples, friends, household, etc., could be as readily applied to secular social orders. They most certainly are not the new name of Divine promise.

Miscellaneous Congregational Names

Christians are commonly assumed by the speakers and writers of the New Testament as constituting identifiable local assemblies (churches) and as members of "the general assembly (Gr. *panegurei*) and church (Gr. *ekklesia*) of the first born (ones) who are enrolled in heaven" (Heb. 12:23).

The most common form of reference in this regard is simply, *the church*. Such reference is often to a local congregation as in Acts 2:47; 5:11; 11:26. At other times, the whole of the called-out ones, the church at large, the church in every place believers were known to be, are included in the form of reference, as in Ephesians 1:22; 3:22; 5:24; Col. 1:18.

The second most common form of reference is *the church of God*. See Acts 20:28; I Corinthians 1:2; 15:9; II Corinthians 1:1; Galatians 1:13; I Thessalonians 2:14; I Timothy 3:5. There is no hint that the "churches of God" differed in any respect, or were not included in "all the churches of Christ" which Paul affirmed joined him in saluting the saints at Rome, and vice versa. "God was in Christ reconciling the world unto himself" (II Cor. 5:19). Christ did not act as a free agent, carving out a kingdom for himself (I Cor. 15:22-28).

The church is sometimes spoken of in terms of its geographical distribution. Thus we read of the churches of Asia (I Cor. 16:19), the church of the Thessalonians (I Thess. 1:1; II Thess. 1:1), the churches of Galatia (Gal. 1:2). In one instance a group of congregations were spoken of ethnically as "the churches of the Gentiles" (I Cor. 16:4), but not in a sectarian setting is this so.

The repeated use of the term, the church, qualified only by the designation of the location, can mean only one thing. In the beginning, churches differed only in location, not in doctrine, practice, and sectarian spirit. The latter might be charged against the church at Jerusalem at the outset, but not for long.

The congregations were also called *churches of Christ*. In the light of Matthew 16:18, it would be quite inconceivable that the churches would never be so called. Paul used the term to embrace the whole of Christendom in Romans 16:16. Acts 20:28 in some early manuscripts reads "the church of our Lord" (meaning Christ), and the text continues on to read, "which he (Christ) purchased with his own blood." This should have some bearing on the sense in which the phrase, the church of God, as used elsewhere should be understood.

The phrase, churches of Christ, could also be rendered, Christ's churches, or Christian churches, when the phrase is brought over into our tongue. In English we have three ways of expressing the possessive case. We can do so by a prepositional phrase, the most common form of reference in Greek. We can use the apostrophe with an "s," or we can employ the Latin suffix, ian, as was done in forming the name Christian for introduction at Antioch. The Philippian jailer, Philippi's jailer, and the jailer of Philippi could hardly be construed as being three different persons. The American flag, America's flag, and the flag of America all look the same and are the same. It is a travesty that men pleading for the unity of believers should actually sever themselves from believers with whom they hold the most in common by making distinctions where there is no essential difference.

When individual Christians congregate, assemble, for Christian worship, they constitute a Christian assembly. No one seems to have trouble with accepting that truism. But when the word church is substituted for assembly, as a substitute for *ekklesia*, common sense ceases to prevail. Legalists would do better to translate the phrase, *ekklesiai tou Christou,* "assemblies of Christ." Or more precisely still, "the called-out ones of the anointed one." That should be literal enough to suit those who champion the letter of the law above the spirit. But somehow they have failed to research the word church, and its introduction into the text of the Scriptures as a substitute for *ekklesia*.

The church is what it is, and whose it is, regardless of what we call it. But we do well to call Biblical things by the name the Bible (rightly translated) uses, or warrants.

A plea is in order for a return to the one name that is above every name. Sinners are asked to believe in the name of the Lord Jesus Christ, to repent in the name of Jesus Christ, to confess the name of Jesus Christ, to be baptized *into* the name of the Father, and Son, and Holy Spirit, *in* the name (by the authority) of Christ. Is it not then strange that followers of Christ, those who profess to be in Christ, to

333

belong to Christ, should then elect to spend the rest of their lives, living and serving him(?) in other names than his own? Colossians 3:17 remains strong and wise counsel:

> Whatsoever ye do, in word or deed, do all in the name of the Lord Jesus, giving thanks to God and the Father through him.

PREVIEW—REVIEW QUESTIONS

1. Define a half-truth. Why are such more dangerous than outright lies?
2. Evaluate the saying, "What's in a name? A rose by any other name would be just as sweet." What is true about it, if anything?
3. Does anyone really believe that, enough to practice it consistently?
4. Cite evidence God considers names important.
5. State and illustrate, Biblically and in common usage, the four functions served by names.
6. Locate two prophecies concerning a name to be given God's people in the Gentile age.
7. How does the more explicit of the two texts indicate the new name will be made known?
8. State the circumstances that will prevail, distinct from the Mosaic dispensation, when the new name is to be given.
9. Identify the time when such circumstances became the most openly visible.
10. What is said in Acts 11:26, fully translated, which links the text with prophecy?
11. What reason have we to believe that the translators of our Scriptures obscured the true import of it (Acts 11:26)?
12. List some information names used in the New Testament to refer to Christians. What function do such terms provide?
13. Is any one of them new in the sense it has no counterpart in the Old Testament? Cite example.
14. Concerning congregational names, which form of expression is most often used in the New Testament?
15. Complete the quotation: "The repeated use of the term 'the church,' qualified only by the designation of location . . ."
16. State the second most common form of reference to the church. How may that be reconciled with Matthew 16:18?
17. Note two other forms of expression in which Romans 16:16 might be acceptably translated into English.

18. What would be the most literal translation of the key phrase of Romans 16:16?
19. At what point in the redemptive process is the name of Jesus commonly set aside in favor of party labels?
20. Cite a text which precisely charges us to do otherwise.

23

THE LORD'S SUPPER

The word remember rings out in the Scriptures like a trumpet blast. More than two hundred times God's word calls our attention to things we do well to remember; things "written for our admonition upon whom the ends of the ages are come" (I Cor. 10:11). Fifteen times, Moses, in his farewell addresses to Israel, challenged them to remember certain things that ought never to be forgotten. One of the ten commandments required them to "remember the sabbath day and keep it holy" (Exod. 29:3). In Deuteronomy 5:15 he tells them why.

When the noun remembrance is included in the textual data, another fifty plus references command our attention. Obviously God expects us to use the gift with which he has endowed us to remember spiritual things as well as things mundane. Life as we know it would be nigh impossible were it not for the facility we call memory.

Historical Perspective

In every dispensation God has made use of memorials to commemorate certain events which signalize both his judgment and his grace. 1) In the patriarchial age he used the rainbow to serve as a reminder of his judgment upon the antediluvian age, and his promise that never again would he use a flood to destroy all flesh (Gen. 9:8-17). 2) In the Mosaic dispensation God appointed a number of commemorative institutions, the chief of which was the feast of the passover, detailed in Exodus, chapter 12.

3) In the Christian dispensation there are four commemorative institutions, appointed with reference to the four historical facts which Paul cited as the substance of the Gospel (I Cor. 15:1-4). a) The Lord's supper is a commemoration of the death of Christ. b) Christian baptism depicts his death, burial, and resurrection, with a focus on the burial. In the symbolic reenactment of the Gospel, it is the burial in baptism which is the most immediately discernible facet. In the long-range view, which only time can afford, it will be discerned whether the one baptized really died to sin and was raised to walk in newness of life. c) The Lord's day commemorates the resurrection, supplanting the sabbath being restricted to fleshly Israel. (See Deut. 5:2, 3, cp. 12-15; note particularly v. 3, 15b.) d) The Christian life commemorates the manifestation (appearances of Christ, very much alive, after his resurrection. Note there are four facts of the Gospel, not just three, as commonly affirmed. (See I Cor. 15:5-8; cp. Acts 1:3.)

Definition of Terms

Our word memorial may be defined as "pertaining to memory." The Greek counterpart, *mnemosunon* (see Matt. 26:13; Mark 14:9; Acts 10:4), is derived from the Gr. *mnemon*, "mindful." Vine defines *mnemon* as "that which keeps alive the memory of someone, or something that has happened." Our words, remember and remembrance, stem from the same Greek root.

Almost everyone makes excuse for forgetting things by blaming their memory. I once heard the president of a large corporation, a man who memorized a minimum of ten verses of Scripture daily, say that he would not knowingly keep on his payroll, except at the most menial level, an employee whose excuse for failing to do something he was supposed to do was, "I forgot." His challenge was, "If you forget, you don't care! A young man who really cares for a young lady does not forget a date."

We are endowed with remarkable memories. Daily we read with understanding newspapers, magazines, books, letters, etc. To do so

338

requires the retention of thousands of idea symbols. We remember where hundreds of things are located. We have stored in our minds thousands of facts, faces, and configurations which can be called to mind, many of them at the slightest suggestion. We shall give an account of the deeds of the body on the day of judgment. The rich man in the parable of Lazarus and "Dives" was told, "Son, remember . . ." (Luke 16:25).

Now concerning the Lord's supper. The appointment of memorial institutions, as we have noted, is a practice common to both God and man. The observance of the Lord's supper is the one thing Jesus has commanded us to do "in remembrance" of him.

1. Scripture References

One does not have to have a vast array of Biblical knowledge to be informed concerning the Lord's supper. Jesus obviously wanted this to be comprehensible even by babes in Christ. One only has to read approximately 33 verses of Scripture (the equivalent of approximately one chapter) to bring to mind all that the Scriptures have to say on this important subject. Each of the synoptic Gospels records the essential details in simple terms: Matthew 26:20-30, Mark 14:22-27, Luke 22:14-20. Acts 2:42 and 20:7 record the simple fact the commandment of Christ was observed on a "continual" basis. Paul, in I Corinthians 10:16, 17, alludes to the Lord's supper, and, in 11:20-30, provides a commentary on the subject in the light of certain mispractices on the part of the Corinthian Christians.

2. Terminology Used in the Scriptures

Three terms are used with reference to the Lord's supper, each focusing on a different aspect of the institution.

a) *Kuriakon deipnon*, "the Lord's (own) supper," I Corinthians 11:20. The intrinsic meaning of the adjective was discussed in some detail in Lesson Two. The term means "of, or pertaining to, the Lord." That which Jesus on the night he was betrayed commanded to be done in remembrance of him is in truth, in a sense no other meal can be, the Lord's own supper.

The Biblical usage of the word supper requires some explanation. The term has little, if any, reference to the time of day. The mode of partaking a meal in Biblical days would be regarded as quite uncouth in our society. The meal itself was relatively simple. Beans, peas, or other cereal grains were boiled into a thick soup which was then placed in the middle of the table. Those who partook of it did so by breaking off portions of coarse, dry (often stale) bread which were "baptized" (Gr. *bapto*, see John 13:26; Matt. 26:23; Mark 14:20) into the soup. The bread sopped up the soup and was thus called the sop (John 13:26). They then supped the sop saturated with the soup, and called it supper. Eventually the term came to be applied to a meal that was eaten, even when the mechanics of doing so were somewhat altered. In the institution of the Lord's supper, Jesus broke bread and gave it to them, with instruction to eat it; and then instructed them to drink of the fruit of the vine, with no hint of their dipping the one in the other. Quite the contrary.

b) *Te klasei tou artou*, Acts 2:42, "the breaking of the bread." This form of reference is synecdochical, a manner of speaking in which "a part stands for the whole," often (as in this case) the more forward part of a process or thing giving its name to the whole. As noted in the preceding paragraph the breaking of the bread was the initial act which facilitated the eating process.

Today we have removed ourselves so far from the ancient custom that even in the partaking of the Lord's supper the term "the breaking of the bread" has become meaningless. My speaking schedule has for years taken me into approximately forty different congregations annually. Rarely have I been privileged to break bread with anyone. In this day of convenience, "instant" everything, I am obliged to "pop pellets" when my arthritic fingers finally manage to pick up one of the anemic looking miniscule loaves far too small to share with anyone.

c) *Koinonia*, "communion," I Corinthians 10:16, 17. The word used in this place signifies a sharing, or participation. It is frequently translated fellowship. But inasmuch as "the breaking of the bread" receives direct mention in that text, *koinonia* is obviously used in Acts 2:42 in the more general connotation of the term. The term may, however, be rightly applied to the Lord's supper, or any meal shared in common. The very manner in which meals were shared in ancient times accounts for that. This accounts for the differences of opinion as to what is being referred to in v. 46. (Cp. 20:7 and 11.)

3. *Terms in Common Use, but not so Used in Scripture*

a) The term *Holy Communion* is commonly used in liturgical churches. It is used as a sacramental term, suggesting that certain mystical powers accrue to the communicant by virtue of the transubstantiation or con-substantiation miracle which occurs when the ritual words are spoken as the duly ordained "priest" incants the Divine blessing upon the bread and wine.

1) Transubstantiation is a Roman Catholic dogma which teaches that the elements are "changed in substance" into the actual body and blood of Christ, retaining however their physical appearance (including, we may well add, the taste, smell, texture, weight, calories, and in the case of wine, alcoholic effect of the original substance.

2) Consubstantiation is a Lutheran modification of the dogma. In this reconstruction the teaching is that the body and blood of Christ are *with* (*con*) the elements of the supper, as fire is *with* a poker that has been embedded in fiery coals. Of course, the hypothesized presence is not quite that obvious.

Does anyone really believe that happens? Does anyone really believe that when Jesus took bread and said, "This is my body," that bread suddenly became his body, and the hands of his physical body which a split second earlier held the bread, suddenly disappeared leaving the bread suspended in midair? Or did his words of blessing merely cause the elements to take on the properties of his real presence, even to the constituent elements of his flesh and blood, but not so that anyone could have noticed that, or known it, if they had not been told? What do you think? And when he said, This is my blood of the new covenant which is poured out for you," did his face turn ashen as his blood was suddenly transferred to the cup he had in his hands, in concentrated form, displacing the fruit of the vine, or united with it (as per the Lutheran modification) without any increase in the amount therein?

The disciples would have laughed at all such surmisings. When Jesus said, "I am the door of the sheep" (John 10:9), he did not suddenly disappear and show up somewhere stretched out across the entrance into a sheepfold. When Joseph interpreted Pharaoh's twin dreams, he said: "The seven fat cattle and the seven fat ears (of grain) are seven *years* of plenty, and the seven lean cattle and lean ears are seven *years* of famine which shall follow" (Gen. 41:25-27). The Scriptures abound with such manner of speaking.

b) *The Eucharist* is another term that is currently in vogue, especially in "scholarly" circles. The term is derived from the Greek word for thanksgiving (*eucharisteo*). It is a synecdochical expression, such as the breaking of the bread. Before Jesus did the latter, he did the former. But if we are wanting to really point up the first thing he did, why not call it the *lambon arton?* Before he gave thanks for anything, he "took bread."

4. *Other Pertinent Terms*

a) *Bread.* In both Testaments the term is used as 1) a general term for food of any kind (cp. the first use of the term, Gen. 3:19), and 2) for the specific article of food that comes to mind when we hear the word used today. As regards the latter usage, the New Testament has two words for bread: A) unleavened bread, without fermentation (Gr. *azumos,* Heb. *matstach*). From the latter comes our word matzos, a popular form of "communion bread." Surprisingly (at least it was to me, even this late in life), *azumos* is never used in the New Testament with reference to the Lord's supper. b) *artos,* a loaf, the more commonly used Greek word for bread, appears 70 times in the New Testament. It is a generic word for bread, and may include unleavened bread as one of its meanings, but rarely is so used in the New Testament. Only by inference can it be said that it is so used anywhere. That inference is, of course, very strong when the word appears in the three synoptic accounts of the institution of the Lord's supper. From Exodus 12:15 we learn that all leaven had to be removed from the house for the duration of the seven-day feast of unleavened bread. The passover was observed as one facet of that feast.

All three synoptic writers make specific mention of the fact that it was on the first day of "unleavened bread" (*azumos*) that the preparation got underway for Jesus to keep the passover with his disciples. But all three of them likewise switch from the word *azumos* to *artos*— the word that is used in Acts 2:42, (46); 20:7, (11); I Corinthians 10:16, 17; and 11:23, 26, 27, 28. I repeat, surprisingly, *azumos* (unleavened bread) is *never* used with reference to the Lord's supper. It is not used of the "bread" Jesus "took" the night the Lord's supper was instituted (even though that was likely, even most certainly, the kind of bread he used). And it is not used in any of the texts which afterwards record the observance of the Lord's supper, or instructions concerning its proper observation. Inasmuch as the earliest of the synoptic Gospels was written some two decades after the crucifixion and after the extension of the Gospel to the Gentiles, and I Corinthians and Acts were written later still, what we have just observed has some interesting spinoffs.

b) *The cup* (Gr. *poterion,* a diminutive of *poter,* "a drinking vessel." The term provides no basis for cultural hangups. The phrase of which it is a part provides no basis for the "one-cupper" sectarian patternists. If it were "the cup" itself Jesus blessed, we had better try to find *that* one. This is another synecdochical expression, wherein "a part stands for the whole," the container actually referring to what was in it.

c) *The fruit of the vine.* (Gr. *genematos tes ampelou*), "generation (fruit) of the vine." The Greek word *oinos* (wine) is never used with reference to the Lord's supper. Considering the culture and circumstances of the time, it would be folly to argue that the ultimate product of "the fruit of the vine," fermented grape juice, was never used. But one may reasonably argue it should not be preferred. The generic term used by all three evangelists (the fruit of the vine, Matt. 26:29; Mark 14:25; Luke 22:18) compares with the generic term for bread (*artos*). The brief accounts of the institution of the Lord's supper, and the later references to the observance, appear to be couched in language deliberately chosen to avoid the sectarian schisms which hard-core patternists have visited upon the church.

d) *The table of the Lord.* (Gr. *trapezes kuriou*), I Corinthians 10:21. This is another synecdochical expression. Termites might literally eat the piece of furniture that is oft so called; but we eat (and drink) that which is placed upon a table, or whatever may serve the purpose.

The Significance of the Lord's Supper

1. Primarily, the Lord's supper is a memorial service. It is designed to commemorate Christ's atoning death. It is not a funeral service. There is no *corpus delicti,* dark ages dogma and reformation theology notwithstanding. Several facets of the commemorative character are worthy of special attention.

a) It is a costly memorial; costly to Christ, not us. The budget outlay for the communion service is negligible. Deep down in a New England coal mine two young men who had made their way there by following the route of the tram cars stepped onto an elevator platform and were quickly hoisted to the surface. At that, one said blithely to the other, "That was an easy way to get up and out." The venerable operator, whose son had lost his life in the building of the shaft, replied: "Yes, indeed, it was easy; easy for you. But have you any idea how much it cost to sink that shaft?"

Salvation is easy. In one sense it is even free. But it cost Calvary, it cost the life of God's dear son, for God to sink the shaft! Well has the poet said:

> Oh the love that drew salvation's plan.
> Oh the grace that brought it down to man.
> Oh the mighty gulf that God did span,
> At Calvary!
>
> (Wm. R. Newell)

Another, Elizabeth Claphane, has written:

> But none of the ransomed ever knew
> How deep were the waters crossed
> Or how dark the night our Lord passed through
> Ere he found his sheep that were lost.

b) It is also an enduring memorial. Many of the world's historic monuments are in sad state of disrepair. The pyramids of the pharaohs have been ransacked for their treasures. Many shrines have been ravaged by time. The Statue of Liberty is currently undergoing extensive repairs. But the memorial to the death of Christ is renewed year by year, and shall endure till time is no more.

c) It is also a universal memorial. As a lad it seemed to me that Peter's suggestion on the mount of transfiguration was a good one, and I wondered why it was not commended and carried out. In the light of what we have just noted I came to understand. Had that been carried out, it would likely long since have been reduced to ruins by the wars which have continuously ravaged the land. And even though it were spared that fate, there is yet another reason that Christ's death has been memorialized instead in the Lord's supper. Only a few are ever privileged to visit the places where Jesus once walked. But there is something much better than "walking today where Jesus walked." The important thing is to walk today *as* Jesus walked. We can do that in our own city and countryside. The purchase price of our redemption, as it has been ingeniously memorialized and universalized in the Lord's supper, is a constant incentive to every ransomed soul to do that very thing.

2. The Lord's supper is a proclamation. a) It is the longest sermon on record. It began the night our Lord was betrayed, and is to continue until he comes again to claim his own. b) It is a sermon on the greatest of themes. When the greatest triumvirate ever to come together on this earth held a summit conference on the mount of transfiguration, "they spake of his death *he was about to accomplish* at Jersualem" (Luke 9:21). The underscored phrase is worthy of contemplation. Jesus was no martyr to a lost cause. His death was an accomplishment. To that end came he into the world.

c) This is also the most universal of sermons, viewed in the light of who it is that is commanded to proclaim it. In I Corinthians 11:26, Paul writes, "As often as you eat of the bread, and drink of the cup, *you* proclaim the Lord's death till he come." Herein is your ordination certificate. The Lord's supper makes preachers of the cross of every faithful Christian who honors Christ's dying wish and most solemn command.

Our religious neighbors, whose creedal heritage and denominational superiors bind them with practices not bound in heaven and loose them from practices which are solemnly sealed by the blood of Christ, are persuaded to believe that to "continue steadfastly" in the breaking of bread, along with the other matters mentioned in Acts 2:42, would be to make the communion "too common" (an interesting phrase, is it not?). Is it not strange that in "evangelical" churches it is not considered "too often" for a preacher to preach Christ crucified Lord's day after Lord's day, and in between? But the Lord's supper is limited to once a month, or once a quarter, and in a few circles but once a year. And one sect has abandoned the observance altogether, a bit of effrontery which brings to mind that Jesus said, "You are my *friends* if you do the things that I say" (John 15:14).

3. The Lord's supper is a participation in Christ's death. It serves as a continuing renewal of our covenant relationship with Christ which began with our baptism. I Corinthians 10:16, 17 speaks of it as a *koinonia* (communion) in the blood and body of Christ. As we have already noted, this is the language of symbolism, but symbols often point to realities which need to be dramatically and frequently brought to mind. The two elements of the Lord's supper were carefully chosen, and are Divinely designed to accomplish that purpose.

a) The loaf, in its constituency, is suggestive of his body. As we break it, we are reminded of how his flesh was torn by the scourge, the nails, and the spear. This is an analogy that is not to be pressed too far. His body was not dismembered, as the bread which we break is torn into pieces, and like the passover lamb which typified his death, not a bone of his body was broken (John 19:36). There are many who believe that the use of unleavened bread would enhance the symbolism by reminding us that his flesh did not see corruption. We have shown already that we may not insist upon that as a necessary demand, but it is certainly a viable option.

b) The fruit of the vine is suggestive of his blood. In the instance of certain varieties the color enhances the imagery conveyed. It is my preference that we make the most of modern technology and use unfermented juice as a more fitting symbol of his sinlessness. Again, as we have noted, the language of the Scriptures carefully guards against pressing this facet also too far. A military expedient, pouring the juice upon the bread, "tincturing" the bread thereby, is used on the battlefield. It is reported that the "tincture method" is infiltrating civilian communion services. Christ's blood left his body when it was "poured out." My judgment is that serving the elements separately, and having the two recombined within us, is more in keeping with the design of the Lord's supper as a symbol of his death, but imparting life to those who partake (cp. I Cor. 11:30).

4. The Lord's supper is designed to feed the mind, the heart, our inner man, promoting spiritual life, giving health to the soul (I Cor. 11:29, 30). Abuse or neglect can lead to spiritual sickness and death.

5. It is a bond of unity, according to I Corinthians 10:17. There were twelve tribes of Israel, and the table of showbread in the tabernacle had therefore twelve loaves. The pelletizing of the communion bread may effectively dramatize that today the body (?) of Christ is divided into hundreds of denominations. But that, of course, is not the intent of the pelletizing innovation.

6. Last, but not least, it is a formal, dying, covenantal request of our Lord and Saviour. Ordinarily such requests are carefully observed by those who profess to love and care. There come to mind some lines penned by the late Evangelist James Earl Ladd, which I have likely rephrased a bit here and there.

I've Got a Date

I've got a date with the Lord.
He set the time for me
When I am to remember his sacrifice
He made on Calvary.

Remember the night in the upper room
When he blessed the cup and the bread.
This is my blood for the remission of sins
To remember me when I am dead.

But the Lord isn't dead anymore.
He's risen and reigns above.
And he left this feast for me to keep
As a token of my enduring love.

And when I think of the sins I commit
Then I think of his words to me:
Remember me when they break the bread
And the blood which was shed for thee.

And so I want to tell you, friends,
That whenever I am able,
I am going to keep my date with him
At his communion table.

Questions and Observations

1. Concerning transubstantiation and consubstantiation: How can one be sure Jesus was not speaking literally when he said, "This is my body, this is my blood"? If the Word could be made flesh (and blood) and at the same time the eternal Word could be hidden in the form of the infant that was born from Mary's womb, could not he in turn become bread and wine and his flesh and blood be hidden therein? The answer to that is: With God all things, of course, are possible, but not probable. The issue is not over what God can do, but what he has done.

If the bread to be eaten at the Lord's supper either is, or contains, the actual body of Christ, we are commanded to participate in an act of cannibalism. If the juice either is, or contains, Christ's blood, then he commanded his disciples (and us) to participate in an act which was strictly and repeatedly condemned in the very law under which he and they were living. See Leviticus 3:17; 7:26; 17:10, 14; 19:26; Deuteronomy 12:16, 23; 15:23; cp. Gen. 9:4. To guard against doing such a thing, the throats of the sacrificial animals were slit, their carcasses disemboweled, and drained of blood. How do we know Jesus was not speaking literally? We are to use both common sense and the Scriptures. Either would suffice. Together, all doubts are removed.

Both Ezekiel (Ezek. 2:9—3:4) and John (Rev. 10:9, 10) were given books and told to eat them. Had they done so literally, what a waste of sacred literature that would have been. They would have learned that the books were a poor substitute for a bowl of their favorite cereal, but what would they have learned from the revelation contained within? Jesus countered Satan's suggestion as to how to break his fast by reminding him that it is written, "Man shall not live by bread alone but by every word that proceedeth out of the mouth of God" (Deut. 8:3; Matt. 4:4). The invitation of God extended through Isaiah is still open. "Come, let us reason together," saith Jehovah (Isa. 1:18).

2. Is the drinking of the fruit of the vine under church auspices for the remission of sins? This argument is used on occasion to whip delinquent church members into line. It works for a time, but like the concept itself, it is short-lived. But it has recuperative powers and can

be used effectively again, for a time. Simply stated, the idea communicated by the doctrine is that in the communion service we come under the Divine "blood blanket" which stretches from one Sunday morning service to the next. Or does it stretch from one Sunday morning back to the previous Sunday? It would about have to (would it not?), if that is how Christians stay under the blood of Christ; unless it is a kind of indulgence which guarantees that you will "go home free" (of sin) even if you die in a drunken orgy on Saturday night; provided, of course, you had communion the previous Sunday. Shades of Romanism!

Admittedly, the proponents of the theory do not present it quite that crassly, but neither do they care to be questioned too penetratingly as to how the system works.

But did not Jesus say, "This cup is the new covenant in my blood which was poured out for many unto the remission of sins"? Precisely. And did not Peter use similar language when he said one should "be baptized for remission of sins"? Precisely. Then baptism cleanses one of the sins committed prior to becoming a Christian, and the Lord's supper takes care of the same on a weekly installment basis thereafter. Taking communion is something like getting a booster shot of the blood of Christ on a weekly basis. Such is the substance, if not the actual phrasing, of this innovative doctrine.

We admitted what Jesus said. Now let us note what he did not say. He has nowhere said "*drinking* of the cup is for the remission of sins." It was the outpouring of his blood which was to make provision for that. We are commanded to be baptized "for the remission of sins." We drink of the cup in commemoration of the provision he made for our sins to be forgiven.

In his first epistle, John reaffirms the fact that Christians sin, and need cleansing therefrom. He who denies that is a liar, and makes God out to be one (I John 1:8, 10). What then are we to do? Stay close to the water's edge? No! Christian baptism (*baptisma*) is a "once and for all" act. In this it differs sharply from the "divers washings" (*baptismoi*, Heb. 9:10) of the old covenant. Likewise the blood of Christ was poured out once for all in ratification of the new covenant (Heb. 9:12, 24-28).

How then are we cleansed of our sins after baptism? Peter told Simon Magus to "repent and pray" (Acts 8:22). John is speaking in the same vein when he writes: "If we confess our sins, he is faithful and righteous to forgive our sins and cleanse us from all unrighteousness" (I John 1:9). Neither Peter, John, Paul, nor any other New Testament writer ever instructed any erring saint to do differently. Does partaking of the Lord's supper have then nothing to do with the forgiveness of our sins? That would be to overstate the matter in the opposite direction. It is a time of introspection (I Cor. 11:28). A proper observance of the Lord's supper should move us to repentance, prayer, confession, and hence to forgiveness of sins. But the Lord's supper is not the magical blood blanket that serves as a booster shot for our baptism. John says that the blood of Jesus Christ "*is cleansing*" (Gr. *katharizei*, third person, singular, indicative, active voice) us of all our sins." We are not in and out of grace, batted back and forth like a tennis ball in and out of first one court and then the other. But neither do "we have it made," God being stuck with us in his court, because of a good blow Christ got in for us long ago. Truth is rarely found at the extremes in any area of inquiry.

3. A third question relates to the issue of how often is "too often." Who is to decide that? Did Jesus so legislate? Should we observe the Lord's supper only at the passover season in keeping with the setting in which he instituted it? What limitations as to frequency, if any, was he legislating when he said, "As often as you do this, do it in remembrance of me"?

Does Acts 2:42 specify a Sunday only observance of the Lord's supper? If so, how so? Why, if so, is only one of the four activities mentioned limited to Sunday morning? And how do we know it refers to a morning service, or for that matter, a Sunday service? And when does Sunday begin? Are we to follow the Jewish reckoning of time, as the narrative of Acts does? Then perhaps what is called Saturday night by western calculation (cp. Acts 20:7-12) would be the more advisable time to "meet together to break bread."

It has been affirmed that one can distinguish between an ordinary meal and the Lord's supper by the fact the latter is *always* spoken of as "the breaking of *the bread*," and the other simply as the "breaking of bread." Here is how the four relevant phrases in Acts read in the Greek text:

    2:42 *te klasei tou artou* - the breaking (of) the bread
    2.46 *klontes . . . arton* - breaking (from house to house) bread
    20:7 *Klasai arton* - to break bread
    20:11 *Klasas ton arton* - breaking the bread.

If Acts 2:42 refers to the Lord's supper, but v. 46 to a common meal, then it would appear from the wording of Acts 20:7, 11 the church at Troas met for an evening fellowship supper, and the Lord's supper took place the next morning.

How often is too often? Apparently any more often than those who would set the rules allow for themselves. I strongly dissent. Let those who are sated with but a little not seek to play God and legislate restrictively those who long for more. I partake with the shut-ins when I take the Lord's supper to them. Let others assume the role of priests; I prefer to share with the shut-ins. Is not that why it is also called "communion"? How many "come together in Christ's name" does it require to constitute a church? Or is the problem the fact I have already eaten? No "second helpings" from the Lord's table!

Is it not odd? There is always someone to our right, and to our left. Our religious neighbors decry our excessive frequency, while many among us insist it must never be any more frequent than what they have concluded to constitute both limits, the maximum and the minimum. "But ye did not so learn Christ!" (Eph. 4:20).

4. A fourth question is with regard to how far we can go in altering the original setting and incidental details of the Lord's supper without violating the spirit, or the letter, or both, of Christ's command. This is a moot question. I often find myself caught in the middle. Two subquestions are:

a) How much of the original setting and details can be deleted, and
b) how many innovations can be introduced without violating either the letter, or the spirit, or both? With regard to such inquiry the question arises: What are we attempting to do? Reduplicate as much as possible the scene in the upper room? Or make the service as brief, antiseptic, or entertaining as possible?

If we are to discern the body of Christ, broken and bleeding; if we are seeking to bring to mind Christ's agony; pray tell me, what is the purpose of an instrumental concert in which the expertise of the musicians, their improvisations of a familiar hymn (cross-centered or otherwise), is forced upon all who partake? Why "dinner music" when we are supposed to be surveying with "the eyes of the heart" (Eph. 1:18) the cross on which the Prince of Glory died?

As one whose family tree has deep roots in the non (even anti) instrumental Churches of Christ, I have tried to keep the lines of communications open. Granted that many among them remind me of Paul's sorrowful estimate of his brethren whose zeal for God he commended (Rom. 10:2) but whose legalism he was obliged to condemn, like their ancient counterparts they are often technically right. That is to say, if the letter of the law is the most important facet of the topic of discussion, they often have the better of the argument. Jesus was confronted with that on more than one occasion. But it is ever true that "the letter killeth, but the spirit giveth life" (II Cor. 3:6).

All this is said to lead to this observation: My judgment is that it is not instrumental accompaniment to singing that is more than their "righteous" souls can bear. It is rather having to endure musical accompaniment not only to prayers but even the communion of the Lord's supper. That is *much* too much!

If we are looking for some common ground on which to seek re-approchement, we have it in the Lord's supper. Nowhere are we even commanded to sing in a service of Christian worship, much less be entertained or lulled with music. In fact, aside from an inference drawn from I Corinthians 14:26, it cannot be demonstrated that any congregation in apostolic times ever sang a congregational hymn. The lone reference to which we have alluded refers to a solo. But we are commanded to observe the Lord's supper, and Acts 2:42 and 20:7 bear record that the apostolic church did so regularly. Is it asking too much for a congregation to silence their musical instruments during the communion service as a gesture of respect for the conscience of those who might be led thereby to lower the walls which separate us?

2) Now to address a word to the die-hard patternists. It needs to be remembered that the Lord's supper was instituted on a weekday evening; evening, mind you, not Sunday morning. And the only recorded communion service was likewise an evening affair; likely Saturday evening (Acts 20:7), "the first day of the week," according to Jewish time, not ours. It most certainly was not just before noon on Sunday morning. If v. 11 refers to the Lord's supper instead of breakfast, we might have a pre-dawn Sunday morning communion service, not by design and intent however, but because of the long-windedness of Paul, the preacher. Moreover, to those hung up on rigid patternism, it needs to be noted that the first communion service was a stag affair. There were no women present, nor youth, nor any aged. All present were of one race, even of one locale. They were all Galileans (Acts 2:7). Moreover, the service was preceded by a meal and a foot-washing ceremony. As to the latter, Jesus strongly intimated his example in washing his disciples' feet should be emulated. "Ye also ought to wash one another's feet," he said (John 13:14). He then spoke to them at some length, and prayed an intercessory prayer. In concluding, they sang a hymn and departed for the Garden of Gethsemane where they slept while he prayed. But of all the things that happened that night, only two things are enjoined upon us in

351

Paul's discourse on the Lord's supper (I Cor. 1:20-30). In v. 26 Paul simply says: "As often as you a) eat the bread and b) drink the cup, you proclaim the Lord's death till he come."

We must conclude therefore the time of day, or even the day, the recipe for the bread, the specific state of the fruit of the vine, the number of prayers and their wording, the mode of distribution, the things preceding, the things following, the constituency of those assembled; all such are incidentals of varying degrees of importance and indifference. Few, if any, are crucial to the keeping of the command. I therefore take what is set before me, strive (often vainly) to shut out the dinner music, ignore the impropriety of many of the prayers, and a) eat of the bread (such as it is) and b) drink of the cup (such as it is) in remembrance of him whose death, I am remembering, was not under ideal circumstances either. That does not mean I do not undertake, when occasion is afforded, to make suggestions and even recommendations; but I refuse to allow circumstances to deter me from doing the two things I can do which are crucial, the two things whereby Paul affirms we proclaim Christ's death. The one thing I refuse to do is to attend a Lord's day worship service with those whose practice and power structure deny me the privilege of doing either of those two things, contrary to our Lord's most solemn command.

In conclusion, be it remembered that we appreciate being remembered, especially by those we have loved and served, and for things we have done which have been costly, inconvenient perhaps, and gracious. Marvel not that Christ has asked us to remember his death, until he comes again.

PREVIEW—REVIEW QUESTIONS

1. Define commemorative, memorial.
2. List the four basic facts of the Gospel, and identify the commemorative institutions which relate to each of them.
3. How extensive are the New Testament references to the Lord's supper? Locate two references in each of these: Gospels, Acts, Epistles.
4. Identify and define literally the phrase translated, "the Lord's supper."
5. What ancient custom lies behind our word "supper"?
6. Explain the background of the phrase, "breaking of bread."
7. Do we actually break bread in our communion service?

8. What is the significance of the Greek word for "communion"?
9. State the overtones in the term "Holy Communion."
10. Define and distinguish transubstantiation and consubstantiation.
11. State the two violations of custom and Scripture of which one would be guilty, if the substantiation dogmas were true.
12. What does eucharist mean? How did it happen to become a synonym for the Lord's supper?
13. Identify and distinguish between the two Greek words for bread. Which is used exclusively with regard to the Lord's supper?
14. What, if any, special significance is to be attached to the phrase, "the cup"?
15. Comment perceptively concerning the phrase, "the fruit of the vine."
16. State three facets of the memorial aspect of the Lord's supper.
17. Of what is the Lord's supper a proclamation?
18. How does the bread serve to suggest Christ's body?
19. How does the cup's contents suggest his shed blood?
20. How does the time frame of the institution of the Lord's supper increase our obligation to observe it, as commanded?
21. In what sense do we "eat and drink Christ's flesh and blood"?
22. Explain and evaluate the "blood blanket" theory.
23. State the two questions which must be solved in determining how far we must go in reduplicating the original "Lord's supper."
24. What Divine commandment would we need to delete from our communion services to accommodate the conscience of the non-instrumental brethren? Is it too steep a price for unity?
25. List several facets of the setting of the original supper seldom duplicated in our observance, if duplicable at all.
26. Can we draw a lesson from such observations which ought to help us to be more forbearing with those whose customs differ? Explain.

EXCURSUS ON THE
BOOSTER SHOT COMMUNION DOCTRINE

What is the Biblical role of the Lord's supper in Christian worship? Is it commemorative in design, intended to call to mind the price of our redemption? Or is it sacramental in its effect, a sort of "booster shot" to our baptism, essential to the maintenance of our initial immunization from the wages of sin? This issue is being raised by the current spate in the sporadic outbreak of a doctrine that contends for the latter position.

The teaching in question has never really taken hold. To my knowledge no sect or cult of Christendom has adopted the position and elevated it to the level of dogma. But from time to time individuals arise who do so and by their zeal gain for a time a small following. The teaching has some affinity to the Catholic dogma of transubstantiation and its weaker counterpart in Reformation theology, consubstantiation. The degree of affinity can not be readily assessed in that the doctrine is 1) sporadic in appearance, normally short-lived, 2) contenders are generally individualists, representing no major segment of any religious party, and 3) a want of literary sources documenting what the protagonists precisely believe and how they might respond to probing questions.

Since the Biblical doctrine of baptism "for the remission of sins" is almost totally rejected by evangelicalism (except for the anomaly of "infant baptism"*) despite the fact the same is clearly so stated in the Scriptures and augmented moreover by a plethora of supportive and illustrative metaphors, it follows therefore that no segment of current evangelism would be open to the "booster shot" communion model. If one need not do anything, even once (be baptized, for example) for remission of sins, certainly no one would need to participate in a recurring act of obedience to maintain a state ostensibly achieved by faith alone. Contenders for "booster shot" communion as essential to the weekly renewal of remission of sins are virtually (if not exclusively) limited to the most legalistic interpreters of the role of baptism. Any success they may gain in this regard can only alienate the more the evangelical community. It is not to be rejected, however, for its want of popular appeal, else baptism for the remission of sins would have to be rejected. It is to be rejected because it is devoid of a Biblical basis.

Proof-text Cited for the Doctrine

The proof-text cited for the doctrine in question is lifted from Matthew 26:28. Jesus, in instituting the Lord's supper, passed a cup among the disciples, saying: "This is my blood of the covenant which is poured

---

* Somehow those caught up in the faith only syndrome find only believer's baptism for remission of sins incompatible. The "baptism" of infants to save them from the guilt of Adam's transgression is too deeply rooted in denominational tradition for the inconsistency thereof to be noted. And besides, the appeal of evangelistic crusades is to adult audiences, or at least to those of the age of accountability. What they may do when they get home (or have homes and children) is not the focal point of evangelistic crusades.

out for many unto the remission of sins." In requesting they drink it he commanded that they do so in remembrance of him. But some would have us believe that the real reason for having them (and us) to do so is for the maintenance of remission of sins. To support this contention the theorists moved to Acts 2:38 where "identical language is used concerning Christian baptism." That is but a half-truth.

There is considerable difference between saying, "My blood is poured out for remission of sins" and saying "*Do* this for remission of sins." Nowhere in the whole of the New Testament is anyone commanded to drink of the communion cup "for remission of sins," nor is it recorded that any one ever did so.

In His great commission Jesus authorized believer's baptism in response to the preaching of the Gospel as a channel of salvation. Thus Peter, on Pentecost, told the guilt-stricken multitudes: "Repent and be baptized for the remission of your sins." But nowhere did he nor any apostle or prophet say anything to the effect a weekly booster shot, via the communion service, is required to maintain that state.

Throughout the book of Acts it is recorded of virtually every person, or group of persons, whose conversion is chronicled that they responded to the Gospel by being baptized. Even Saul of Tarsus who not only was personally singled out for salvation and service by Jesus but who subsequently prayed for three days awaiting further instruction, was commanded to "be baptized, and wash away thy sins." But nowhere was it suggested to him, nor through him, nor through any one else that any one must drink of the communion cup on a routine basis lest the statute of limitations should run out on the remission of sins.

Why is so much attention given to baptism as a divine imperative, but such slight mention made of the Lord's supper if the state gained by baptism must be maintained by the Lord's supper?

When Simon Magus sinned grievously following his baptism why did Peter command him to "repent and pray" for forgiveness if the communion service is the vehicle of grace which sustains our redemption? And if it be so, what do we do between Sundays?

The "Blood-Blanket" Hypothesis Examined

Crassly speaking, and I quote verbatim an acquaintance of many years, once a vigorous contender for the teaching in question: "As alien sinners receive remission of their sins through baptism, Christians receive remission of their sins through the Lord's supper. If one wilfully misses

355

the Lord's supper he moves outside the blood blanket. Such a one is no longer covered by the blood of the lamb."

That made "better preaching" than dialogue. Outside of the pulpit, which facility often provides a protective pillbox for its occupants, he was unable to deal with certain pointed and pertinent questions. For example, if the communion blood blanket only stretches from one Lord's day to another (echoes of Isa. 28:20), precisely how does it fit our needs? Is the forgiveness attained thereby retroactive? That is, does taking communion on a given Sunday atone for the sins of the *past* week? If so, what happens to those who sin, *and die*, between Sundays? To "cover" that problem he agreed that for the system to work the "blood blanket" would have to stretch from one communion service to the next (give or take a few hours to accommodate discrepancies arising from time zone and daylight savings time adjustments, and differences in schedules followed by various congregations). But this smacks heavily of the Roman Catholic system of indulgences. At length he modified his preachment to affirm that a proper observance of the Lord's supper provides an ideal setting for a Christian's supplication for the remission of sins. That position is defensible.

What Saith the Oracles of God?

Since the doctrine in question is not directly taught in the Scriptures, being but inferential at best, as even its strongest contenders are obliged to admit, it should not be surprising that the refutation of the doctrine will likewise not be directly communicated in the Scriptures. A relatively strong inference may be deduced from the typological data set forth in the epistle to the Hebrews, chapters 9, 10.

The 8th chapter of Hebrews closes (8:9-13) with a quotation taken from Jeremiah 31:31-34 contrasting the two covenants, the old (Mosaic) and the new (Christian). The two chapters which follow provide an amplification of the quotation from Jeremiah. Underscored by the two chapters is the fact that under the old covenant the priests were obliged to offer "continually" (9:6) ritualistic sacrifices for sin which "could never take away sin" (10:2, 4, 11). Week after week (in fact even daily), through the course of nearly fifteen centuries, the weary rituals were carried on. But Christ in one fell swoop made end of sacrifice by the sacrifice of himself (9:25, 26; 10:12, 18).

The notion that participation in a weekly communion ritual is essential to the remission of sins has far more in common with the abrogated law of Moses than it does with the new covenant of Christ. Christian baptism (Gr. *baptisma,* a once and for all cleansing, stands in contrast to the *baptismoi* (Heb. 6:2; 9:10; Mark 7:4), repetitive washings prescribed by the law of Moses (cp. I Cor. 6:11).

One can press this too far, as do those who teach the dogma of eternal security, no matter what. But that provides no excuse for going to the opposite extreme, teaching a state of such precarious salvation that the benefits of the death of Christ have to have a booster shot every Sunday in order to be maintained. Truth is seldom found at either of the extremes to which any doctrine can be carried.

Near the close of the apostolic age John stated the case on this wise: "If we confess our sins he is faithful and righteous to forgive us our sins and to cleanse us from all unrighteousness" (I John 1:9). That is in harmony with the advice of Peter to Simon Magus near the beginning of the Christian era (Acts 8:22).

We are neither teetering precariously on the brink of perdition from one communion service to another nor are our sins, "no matter what," covered by a blood blanket "one week wide" following our participation in the Lord's supper. But it bears repeating, a proper observance of the Lord's supper provides an ideal setting for a Christian's supplication for the remission of sins.

Pertinent Reflections

Against a backdrop of fifty years in the Christian ministry, the last forty of which have been spent in the formal training of Christian ministers, certain pertinent reflections come to mind.

1) Prior to World War II congregations were not as quick to divide when differences arose among them, and preachers were not so prone to encourage divisions. Preachers generally elected to move to a new field of service when confronted with intransigent opposition. Seldom did they force a split either by a power play or by taking the "loyal" members across the street or across town to start a "loyal" church. In turn, church members were not so prone to quit the church when they opposed the preacher but found themselves in a minority role in that respect. The more common practice was to register their dislike for the preacher by assuming their usual pew through the communion service, then walking out just before the sermon. Many a preacher countered that form of opposition by moving the Lord's supper after the sermon. I sincerely doubt that the Lord's supper provided a proper

357

setting for either the preacher or the offended members to supplicate the Lord's forgiveness for their sins. But it does underscore the fact that historically our brethren have considered the observance of the Lord's supper a solemn obligation, if not a privilege.

In the past few years many ministers have maneuvered their congregations into moving the communion service to the close of the service for a different reason. The practice permits them to maximize their role as the spokesman for the congregation and the person in charge of the service. Almost invariably this results in minimizing the role of the Lord's supper. Not only is the time slot reduced in length but the celebration of the Lord's supper comes to have a tacked on appearance. Seldom does it attain a climactic role, as promised by the promoters of the change in the order of the worship service.

2. A second observation is that the sacramental concept which places souls in jeopardy who miss a week is often a subconscious ploy to increase attendance according to the precept that "where love does not lead the law must rule." Whether the Lord is pleased to have members attend out of a sense of guilt and fear is questionable. But this is beyond question: Those who worship Him in spirit and in truth, drawn to Him and to one another by love and in appreciation for the atoning work of Christ whose death they lovingly come together to commemorate in the observance of the Lord's supper, of these it may be said: "for such doth the Lord seek to be His worshippers" John 4:23b.

THAT FORM OF DOCTRINE

Excursus on the Commemorative Significance of Christian Baptism

Christian baptism has been discussed extensively in previous lessons. But one aspect of the subject, rarely noted, was touched upon only briefly—the twofold typology of Christian baptism. The Divinely appointed commemorative institutions: 1) the Lord's supper, commemorating the death of Christ, and 2) the Lord's day, commemorating his resurrection, form by Divine design a continuum in the assembly and worship of the redeemed. But baptism is a one-time, once and for all, commitment experience.

In contrast to *baptismos*, the Greek word used in reference to the repetitive washings of the Mosaic system (see Mark 7:4 (8, KJV); Heb.

6:2; 9:10), *baptisma* is a non-repetitive, one-time act. *Baptisma* is a word unique to the New Covenant Scriptures and subsequent literature contingent upon the New Tesatment.

Typology of Christian Baptism

Twice in the New Testament Christian baptism is spoken of as having typological significance. In Romans 6:17 Paul used the Greek word *tupon* to express the relationship of Christian baptism to what he speaks of definitively as "the Gospel"—the death, burial, resurrection, and manifestation (post-resurrection appearances) of Christ (see I Cor. 15:1-4). In I Peter 3:21 Peter uses the term with the prefix *anti* in comparing the salvation of the household of Noah "by (Gr. *dia*) water" and "baptism which also (says he) after a *true likeness* (KJV, like figure, Gr. *antitupon*) now saves us."

The Greek word from which our English words type, typology, typical, etc., are derived denotes primarily a mark or impression left by a blow. Typewriters are so called because the writing accomplished thereby consists of impressions (figures, letters, symbols) left on the paper by the blows struck thereon as selected keys are activated. The typewriter ribbon serves to accentuate the impressions.

New Testament Usage of Tupon

The Greek word under consideration appears in the Greek New Testament seventeen times. In our English versions it appears variously translated, but the core concept embodied in the word generally persists. In John 20:25 mention is twice made of the "*print* of the nails" in the hands of Christ. Acts 7:43 speaks of the *figures* which the apostate Israelites "made to worship." In the verse which follows Stephen reminded his hearers of God's command to Moses to "make all things according to the *pattern*" which God had shown him on Mount Sinai (see also Heb. 8:5). In I Corinthians 10:1-11 Paul reminds his readers of God's wrathful judgments upon the Israelites whom he had redeemed out of Egypt but whom he afterward destroyed in the wilderness. Twice in the course of the analogy which he details Paul wrote: "Now these things happened unto them by way of *example* and are written for our admonition" (vs. 6, 11). To translate the texts more literally, Paul is saying the dire judgment God visited upon them is *typical* of what we too may receive if we commit the same folly. But despite the added

359

warning of v. 12, "Wherefore, let him that thinketh he standeth take heed lest he fall," many persist in teaching the dogma of once saved always saved. Is nothing to be learned from typology? Not even when it is expressly spelled out and illustrated as it is in I Corinthians 10:1-11? See also Hebrews 2:1-4, 3:7—4:13.

The word *tupon* is used with a positive thrust in such texts as Philippians 3:17; I Thessalonians 1:7; II Thessalonians 3:9; I Timothy 4:12; and Titus 2:7. See also Acts 23:25 and Romans 5:14.

Romans 6:17 is unique in that it is an exception to the dictum that "a type *always* prefigures something future." (See *The International Standard Bible Encyclopedia*, Vol. V, p. 3029.) Paul does not hestitate to speak of baptism as looking backward, "post-figuring," so to speak, something past. Specifically, he speaks of baptism, viewed in its larger context, as being a *form* of the doctrine of the death, burial, resurrection, and appearances (alive again, manifestly so) of Christ. Those four happenings are defined by Paul as the essence of the Gospel which he proclaimed, and by which we are saved. In Romans 6:16-18 Paul summarizes his treatise on the intrinsic significance of baptism by saying:

> Know ye not that to whom ye yield yourselves servants to obey, his servants ye are whom ye obey; whether of sin unto death, or of obedience unto righteousness? But God be thanked that (whereas) ye were the servants of sin *ye obeyed from the heart that form of doctrine* which was delivered you. Being then made free from sin ye became servants of righteousness. (KJV)

To fully appreciate what Paul has just said one needs to read the entire chapter. Paul compares two deaths, two burials, two resurrections, and two manifestations of a new life. The actuality of the one constitutes the four cornerstones of the Gospel. The fidelity of the other constitutes that "obedience of faith" which is the theme of the book of Romans (see 1:5, 16:16, cp. 6:16-18). Baptism is the Divinely conceived and commanded "obedience from the heart to that form (*tupon*) of doctrine that was delivered us." In that dramatic act of self-surrender and faith we become heirs of eternal life, the "free gift" (Gr. *charismata*) of God which is in Christ Jesus (Rom. 6:23).

Note we are not said to obey the *doctrine* that was delivered us but rather the *form* (type) of the doctrine. Or to be more specific, we are to obey *that* form of the doctrine that was delivered us. In view of the context in which the saying occurs, it ought not to be difficult to identify the commandment delivered us which is manifestly a form, likeness (type) of the death, burial, and resurrection (and manifestation—alive again!) of Christ our Lord.

It would be a startling revelation to many to reread Paul's baptismal discourse, Romans six, underscoring every sentence in which the word *like, likeness* (and other comparative expressions) appear, and noting what ordinance of Christ is precisely identified as being *that form* of doctrine through which we are made free from our sins.

The typology of Christian baptism illustrates both the function and the form of baptism. The *dead* are buried, not the living. It is those who are *made alive again* that shall be raised up in the last day. Note how carefully Paul chose his words.

> Are you ignorant that all we who were baptized into Christ were baptized into his death? We were baptized therefore with him through baptism into death, that like as Christ was raised from the dead through the glory of the Father, so we also might walk in newness of life. For if we have become united with him in the likeness of his death, so shall we be also in the likeness of his resurrection, etc. (Rom. 6:3-5).

What "mode" of baptism is a likeness of death, burial, resurrection, and appearance (alive anew!)? What function (purpose) of baptism is said to be accomplished through *our obedience from the heart to that form of doctrine delivered us?*

Other relevant questions are also touched upon. What validates baptism? The office or ordination of the administrator? The words which are incanted over the subject? The fullness of one's knowledge and understanding? No! If the *heart* of the one being baptized is right (that is, if the obedience rendered is "from the heart") and the *form* of baptism is right (that is, it is *that form* of the doctrine that was Divinely conceived and commanded of us), then it is *all right.* Baptisms (?) performed for other reasons than those set forth in the oracles of God, or by some other mode (if there be any rightly so called) are not "that form of doctrine" Paul has taken pains to explain in Romans, chapter six.

An old-fashioned country doctor in a congregation I served as an undergraduate student dramatically illustrated the point we are making. The church baptistry was beneath the platform floor. To use it the pulpit furniture had to be removed and a section of the floor which actually was a trap door had to be raised and leaned against the back wall. The underside, thus exposed to view, was unsightly to say the least. The women of the church remedied the situation somewhat by draping the upturned floor/door with a bed sheet. The doctor had a better idea. He procured a sign cloth on which he drew six rectangles and sketched in five scenes. Across the top he printed the words: IF YOU WOULD BE "BURIED" (Like This:) In the upper left-hand panel he sketched a casket sitting on top of the ground, with a preacher sprinkling a handful of dust on the casket. In the middle panel he scketched a similar scene, except in this instance a bowl of dirt was being poured upon the coffin lid. In the right-hand panel a full burial was depicted. Below the three panels a line read: YOU SHOULD BE "BAPTIZED" (Like This:). The first two panels depicted kneeling figures with a few drops of water being sprinkled/poured upon their heads. In the right-hand panel the words LIKE THIS appeared in large letters with an arrow pointing to the baptistry below. This panel also included the Scripture reference, Romans 6:3-18.

Every baptism performed in view of the doctor's relatively crude art work spoke more eloquently concerning "that form of doctrine that was delivered us" than any sermon ever could. A series of baptisms generally ensued.

To those whose theology and practice persuade them to differ, I solemnly ask: If one does not "obey from the heart that form of doctrine delivered us" in the ordinance of Christian baptism, then pray tell me when *does* a believer "yield himself as a servant unto disobedience" in an act that typifies the death, burial, and resurrection unto newness of life?

Christian Baptism as an Antitype

No discussion of the typology of Christian baptism would be complete without some attention given to I Peter 3:18-22. In v. 21 Peter relates baptism to typology in the more common frame of reference. Peter speaks of the salvation of the eight Noahites "through/by (Gr. *dia*) water" (that is, the waters of the flood) as having its antitype in *baptism,* "which also after a true likeness/like figure (ASV/KJV, Gr. *antitupon*) doth now save us."

This is a troublesome verse to those whose theology has lately driven them to come up with the pontification that texts (of which there are a dozen or so) which plainly relate baptism to salvation refer to Holy Spirit baptism, not water baptism. That does not "wash" with I Peter 3:21. It is impossible to "wring the water out" of the text before us without destroying the typology that is plainly affirmed.

The key to the typology of the passage is in the phrase, "through/by water" (Gr. *dia*), not *from* (Gr. *apo, ek*) water. *Dia* appears 627 times

362

in the Greek New Testament (if I have counted correctly, including the text before us). Establishing the meaning of the preposition is thereby made easy. Note what the text affirms. The Noahites were saved by/through water. The ark saved them physically, but physical death was only delayed by that "salvation." Peter speaks of a salvation more transcendent and enduring. The flood waters *saved* them from a fate worse than drowning. Sin had so encroached upon the messianic line in the days of Noah that he and his family alone were spared from the wrath of God. By/through the flood waters God washed their world clean of that wicked generation, and bore Noah and his own above the flood to replenish the earth.

Therein is the typology of baptism. Hear it from Peter, I Peter 3:21 (NIV), "and this water symbolizes baptism that now saves you also." Lest we miss the point of the typology, Peter hastens to explain that the cleansing we receive in baptism is not physical (although some measure of physical cleansing is inevitable when baptism is baptism indeed, rather than a mere token—sprinkling. Baptism is not a bizarre bath. In yielding ourselves unto God as servants, through obedience to that form of doctrine that was delivered us, it is our hearts that are cleansed. It is the answer of/for a good conscience toward God. (The Greek word, *eperotema* is a legal term denoting an appeal.)

Twice in the New Testament baptism is related to a good conscience. Hebrews 10:22 informs us that when we draw nigh unto God with a true heart, in the fullness of faith, our *hearts* are *sprinkled* from an evil conscience as our *bodies* are *washed with pure water*. This brings us back to Romans 6:17. Paul and Peter are agreed as to the role of baptism. Both stress the importance of our obedience being from the heart. Both find the efficacy of baptism rooting in significant events in the drama of redemption. Both relate baptism to salvation.

It has well been noted that the Gospel in its larger context consists of 1) facts to be believed, 2) commands to be obeyed, and 3) promises to be enjoyed. Romans, chapter six, underscores the fact that obedience is often the missing link. In rebuking the Jews who, like their modern evangelical counterparts, jumped upon the doctrine of grace as though salvation were by grace through faith alone, Paul penned his treatise on baptism. Twice he resorts to an expression of abhorrence, *me genoito*, "let it not be!" Neither faith alone nor baptism alone saves anyone. We must die to sin as he died for our sins, be baptized with him into his death, and rise to walk in newness of life.

363

THE GOSPEL

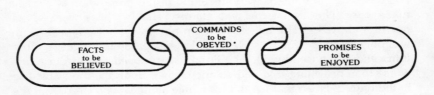

* OBEDIENCE — "The Missing Link"

John 3:36; II Thessalonians 1:7, 8; Hebrews 5:9; Romans 6:17

BAPTISM: THAT FORM OF DOCTRINE

O tell the good news that we preached to you,
You too can preach if you will.
There's something our Saviour would have you do,
His commission to fulfill.
He died for our sins, the Scriptures so teach,
Was buried and raised from the dead.
This is the gospel your life will preach
When your baptism is spirit led.

Our dear Saviour's passion is dramatized
In keeping his blessed command:
Repent each one of you and be baptized
And enter my bloodwashed band.
When we through faith do obey from the heart
That form of doctrine given
Both our sins and our guilt from us depart
Tis his promise sent us from heaven.

When buried beneath the baptismal wave
We're into his death baptized;
And enter thereby our Saviour's grave:
Thus buried with him who died.
With Christ we die that made free from our sin
With Christ we may then arise:
New life and new hope and new joys to win
And a new home beyond the skies.

Chorus:
    He that believes and is baptized is saved.
    For on the cross his cleansing blood he gave.
    My sins are all forgiven
    And I'm on my way to heaven.
    He that believes and is baptized is saved.

Russell E. Boatman
(Tune: Heaven Came Down and Glory Filled My Soul)

24

THE LORD'S DAY

Strange as it may seem, at least upon first notice, nowhere in the Scriptures are we commanded: "Remember the Lord's day (the first day of the week, the resurrection day) and keep it holy." Moreover, nowhere in the Scriptures is Sunday (the first day of the week, the day on which Christ was raised from the dead) specifically identified as "the Lord's day." That form of expression, found only in Revelation 1:10, was, however, uniformly so identified by the early church "fathers."

Ignatius (c. 101), for example, writing but six or so years removed from the commonly accepted date for the book of Revelation, wrote: "Let us no more sabbatize; but let us keep the Lord's day, the highest of all days." Theodoret, speaking of the Ebionites, a judaizing sect zealous for the law, had this to say: "They keep the Sabbath according to Jewish law, but sanctify the Lord's day as we do." Justin Martyr (martyred c. 145), writing concerning times and customs of his day, noted:

> On the day called Sunday there is a meeting in one place of all Christians that live in town or country. [Note the unity implied, and the identifying

name.] The memoirs of the apostles (the Gospels) or the writings of the prophets (Old Testament literature) are read, and the president (one presiding) or bishop (overseer) exhorts to the imitation of those notable examples, after which we arise and begin to pray.

An account then follows concerning the observance of the Lord's supper, and closes by citing several reasons for meeting on the first day of the week, the chief being in commemoration of our Lord's resurrection.

To understand how, without specific command (at least of record) the first day of the week so quickly superseded the Sabbath day observance, one needs to take precise note of the nature and function of time.

Time Defined

Categorically speaking, time is the reckoning of duration. Webster defines time as "an interval in which a process occurs." Such a definition obviously alludes to a segment of time bounding the beginning and ending of an occurrence. The pattern for the measurement of time in this manner was divinely revealed when God said of the luminaries he ordained to shine on us: "Let there be lights in the firmament of heaven to divide the day from the night: and let them be for signs, and for seasons, and for days and years" (Gen. 1:14).

Were the earth designed to rotate at a different speed or to orbit the sun at a greater or lesser distance, or at a faster or slower pace, our days and nights and months and years would differ measurably from such as we know.

If time is indeed an interval in which a process occurs, then that which invests any specific segment of time with significance for any one of us is the process or happening that occurs which in some way affects our present life and/or our destiny.

The month of August in which these words are being written is, generally speaking, an interval of mediocrity. There is no national holiday in the month of August. Yet for the writer it is extra special. Four days are celebrated by our family in August. The 6th marks the anniversary of the birth of our firstborn child, a son. The 13th is the anniversary of my ordination to the Christian ministry. The 19th is the anniversary of my own birth, and the 25th marks the anniversary of a marriage which is soon to enter its 50th year.

What constitutes a calendar day? And what distinguishes one above another? Of itself a calendar day is just one more in an ongoing series of axial rotations of the planet Earth. It bears repeating: the thing that invests a given rotation (day) with significance for any one of us is a happening that may occur which significantly affects either our present life or our destiny.

The foregoing observation underscores the reason the first day of the week came so quickly to be invested with special significance for the church. No explicit command needed be given; or if given, recorded. A time-honored custom hallowed by examples of divine approbation, and on occasion, decree, set the precedent for the Lord's day institution.

When Jehovah, who dealt with Israel as with children, delivered them from the bondage of Egypt he instituted the weekly recurrence of the day of their deliverance as a day of rest, saying: "Remember the Sabbath (rest) day, to keep it holy . . . thou shalt not do any work, thou, nor thy son, daughter, man/maid servant, cattle, nor the stranger that is within thy gates" (Exod. 20:8-10). As a wise father he cited his own example. He labored six creative days; and on the seventh day having finished his creation, though the Lord God is omnipotent, he rested from all his creation which he created and made.

Moses, in his farewell address, repeated the decalogue and explained the fourth commandment even more explicitly: "Thou shalt remember that thou wast a servant in the land of Egypt and Jehovah thy God brought thee out thence by a mighty hand and an outstretched arm: Therefore Jehovah thy God commanded thee to keep the Sabbath day" (Deut. 5:15, cp. v. 3).

Why then do we not observe the Sabbath? For us to do so would violate the very principles which occasioned the Sabbath law for fleshly Israel. Since neither we nor our forefathers were in bondage in Egypt the day cannot be invested with the significance for us that it bore for the emancipated Israelites. Other nations do not celebrate the fourth of July, nor do we celebrate the patriotic commemorations of other nations.

Why do we observe the first day of the week? We too have a day of deliverance to remember. We too were once in bondage. But we are privileged to recall a day of greater deliverance than that commemorated by the Sabbath. Whether Jew or Gentile, bondman or free, male or female, we were once in bondage unto sin and death. Romans, chapter six (see *excursus* appended to the preceding lesson), and Ephesians, chapter two, underscore that fact. Our great emancipator accomplished our deliverance when he arose from the dead, the victor over the world, the flesh, death, and the devil. That he did when he arose from the dead on the first day of the week, having in his hands "the keys to death and the grave" (Rev. 1:18). We do well to heed the admonition of Paul: "Remember Jesus Christ, risen from the dead" (II Tim. 2:8).

History of the Observance of the First Day of the Week

1. Under the law. As is true of many facets of the New Covenant, there is that in the Mosaic Covenant which foreshadows (typifies) the epochal events which signalize the emergence of the first day of the week as a day of Christian worship and celebration. The fifty-day harvest festival initiated by the offering of the sheaf of the first-fruits and climaxed by the feast of weeks (Pentecost) is detailed in Leviticus 23:15-21. (See also Deut. 16:9-12.)

Note that the celebration began and ended on the first day of the week. It began with the wave-offering of the first sheaf of standing grain that was harvested. This ritual, by divine decree, took place on the first day of the week. The precise instructions read:

> And he shall count unto you, from the morrow after the sabbath, from the day ye brought the sheaf of the wave-offering (first-fruits), seven sabbaths shall there be complete: even unto the morrow after the seventh sabbath shall ye number fifty days, and ye shall offer a new meal-offering unto Jehovah (Lev. 23:15, 16).

Note from the foregoing that the festival also climaxed on the first day of the week—the 50th day of the harvest festival, hence the name Pentecost by which it is known in the New Testament. Pentecost is a Greek term for the 50th day after the Passover Sabbath.

We are indebted to the Apostle Paul for the clue to the typology of the foregoing passage. As the first sheaf of grain that was harvested was offered to Jehovah in token of the entire harvest which in due season was to be gathered in, so Christ is the first-fruits of them that sleep. Paul writes:

> But now hath Christ been raised from the dead, the first-fruits of them that sleep. For since by man came death, by man came also the resurrection from the dead . . . but each in his own order: Christ the first-fruits; then they that are Christ's, at his coming (I Cor. 15:20, 21, 23).

As has already been noted, the festive season also climaxed on the first day of the week. It is worthy of note that the New Covenant which could not be inaugurated (be "in force") prior to the death of Christ the testator (Heb. 9:16, 17) was duly and dramatically inaugurated by the coming of the Holy Spirit, and the proclamation of the Gospel on the day of Pentecost, the first day of the week.

The implications of the foregoing observations are significant. Not one of the epochal events which Paul sets forth as constituting the four cornerstones of the Gospel (I Cor. 15:1-4) occurred on the Sabbath. Jesus died and was buried before the Sabbath. He was raised from the dead and initiated his post-resurrection appearances after the Sabbath. The Gospel which Paul declares to be the Gospel of our salvation does not root in any event which happened on the Sabbath. The confirming event by which Christ is said to be "declared the Son of God with power, according to the spirit of holiness," is the *resurrection* of Christ from the dead (Rom. 1:4). (Jesus so prophesied in veiled language, John 2:19, and elsewhere.) But when he was raised from the dead his disciples remembered what he had spoken, "and they believed the Scriptures, and the word which Jesus had said" (John 2:22). The resurrection is that crucial to the Gospel. Every first day of the week, not just at a spring festival, we do well to come together, proclaim and duly "*remember* Jesus Christ risen from the dead" (II Tim. 2:8). Such is the thrust of the typology of the first day of the week, as it is prefigured under the law.

2. In the Gospel age. As the Old Covenant drew to a close and the inauguration of the New Covenant drew near, the first day of the week began to figure prominently in the demonstration of the messiahship of our Lord. Admittedly Jesus kept the Sabbath. He was born under the law (Gal. 4:4). He lived and died under the law (Heb. 9:16, 17). But for his triumphal entry into Jerusalem, in fulfillment of an important messianic prophecy, and in bold demonstration of his kingship, openly accepting the plaudits of the people, Jesus chose the first day of the week for that signal and crucial demonstration (Zech. 9:9, 10; cp. John 12:12-19).

The first day of the week was also divinely chosen for the day of his resurrection, and for a number of his most important post-resurrection appearances. The fact is that of his ten recorded appearances every one that has been clearly chronicled as to the day it occurred was a first-day-of-the-week appearance.

3. In the Apostolic age. It is significant that the church was founded on Pentecost, the first day of the week, and is said to have continued steadfastly in the apostles' teaching, fellowship, breaking of bread, and prayer (Acts 2:42). Did it begin on Sunday and six days later revert to Sabbath keeping? Acts 20:7 and I Corinthians 16:1, 2 most certainly

indicate otherwise. It is true Paul visited Jewish synagogues and spoke to those gathered there on the Sabbath. As a point of contact with the Jews he also observed certain of the feasts which were abrogated when Christ became "the end of the law" (Rom. 10:4), "taking it out of the way, nailing it to the cross" (Col. 2:14). But Paul cared enough for his countrymen, and knew well enough where he might find the most devout among them, that he attempted to keep the lines of communication open. On the other hand, he bristled when any one of them undertook to bind any part of the law upon him.

4. In the sub-apostolic age. The literature of the sub-apostolic age is replete with quotations which demonstrate clearly that it was normative for Christians to observe the first day as a commemoration of the resurrection of Christ. Several were cited previously, dating back to well within the first decade following John's use of the expression: "I was in the spirit on the Lord's day" (Rev. 1:10). Others may be cited.

Barnabas, c. 120, affirmed: "We keep the first day as a joyful day on which Jesus rose from the dead." Clement of Alexandria, c. 192, wrote: "A Christian, according to the command of the Gospel, observes the Lord's day, thereby glorifying the resurrection of Christ." (Note: The expression, "according to the *command* of the Gospel," is a stronger statement than the Gospel records and the apostolic writings in general warrant, but is in keeping with the implications of the New Testament literature.) Tertullian (c. 200) bluntly stated: "The Lord's day is the holy day of the church. We have nothing to do with the Sabbath."

Such quotations stand in marked contrast to one of the subtle arguments of the Sabbatarians. The Seventh Day Adventists, for example, have found it to their advantage to widely publish a quotation taken from *The Convert's Catechism of Catholic Doctrine*. On page 50 of said catechism it is written:

Question: Why do we observe Sunday instead of Saturday?

Answer: We observe Sunday instead of Saturday because the Catholic church, in the council of Laodicea (336 A.D.) transferred the solemnity from Saturday to Sunday.

Two things are wrong with that: 1) The Catholic church as such did not even exist in 336 A.D., although it was definitely on the way. 2) How could the Catholic church, or any church, change the day of worship from Saturday to Sunday in 336 A.D. when the church had already been worshipping on Sunday for 300 years!

What actually happened was as follows: Among Jewish converts to the Christian faith the transition from Saturday *and* Sunday to Sunday only was gradual. The first converts were Jews, many of whom were intensely "patriotic." Nostalgia for the temple and/or a desire to keep the lines of communication open is reflected by such passages as Acts 2:46, 47; chapters 3, 4; 5:20, 21, 42; and chapter 21. The apostles made certain concessions to the judaizers, as witnessed by the Jerusalem conference. Recall also Paul's circumcision of Timothy, his keeping of the Passover, his shaving of his head in Cenchreae, and his submission to the purification ritual prior to his ill-fated attempt to worship in the temple (see Acts 21:17ff.).

Such concessions were but a delaying tactic at best. For example, the circumcision issue finally had to be met head on, lest the terms of salvation be judaized. Eventually the Sabbath issue had to be faced also. This was slower in coming. Such passages as Colossians 3:16, 17 and Romans 14:4-6 helped hold judaizers in line. The Laodicean conference of 336 A.D. attempted to do with the Sabbath issue what the Jerusalem conference (Acts 15) attempted to do with the circumcision issue.

Why Do We Honor the Lord's Day?

Why do we regard the first day of the week as the Lord's day, and solemnize it as an appropriate time for Christian assembly and worship? The reasons are manifold:

1. Because that was the day Christ arose from the dead.

2. Because of the emphasis placed upon it by his post-resurrection appearances on the first day of the week.

3. Because that was the day he fulfilled his promise to send forth the Holy Spirit to guide the apostles in all the truth.

4. Because that was the day the apostles, under the direction of the Holy Spirit, founded the church.

5. Because the full Gospel, now fully credentialized, was first proclaimed on that day.

6. Because the first-fruits, the first ingathering of the Gospel proclamation, was on that day.

7. Because it is recorded (Acts 20:7) the church came together to observe the Lord's supper on that day, bearing out a reasonable inference drawn from Acts 2:42.

8. Because of the reasonable inference that may be drawn from I Corinthians 16:1, 2.

371

9. Because the sub-apostolic fathers consistently identified the first day of the week with "the Lord's day."

10. Because it is a divine principle, clearly demonstrated in the Scriptures, that it is injudicious to put new wine in old wineskins that have long since served their purpose. The Sabbath is an old wineskin. The first day of the week is a new wineskin, suited to a new occasion, a new celebration, communicating a new event, the crowning event of the Gospel.

Why Do We Not Keep the Sabbath Day

1. For one thing it would be quite impossible to keep it as originally given. The restrictions imposed by the Sabbath law were fitted to the people, the place, and the purpose for which the Sabbath law was given.

2. There is not the slightest hint in the Scriptures that any Gentile convert to the Gospel ever kept the Sabbath, or was expected to do so. They had something better to remember.

3. A crucial distinction needs to be noted between the Sabbath commandment and the rest of the decalogue. All the rest are based on moral principles. Moral principles are right for all people at all times— day and night, day by day, year in and year out—always! When are we to honor our fathers and mothers? When are we to refrain from stealing, killing, adultery, taking God's name in vain, etc.? The Sabbath commandment is based upon an episode in the history of the Israelite nation. It was to be observed only on the recurring day of the week, and was to be observed by dramatizing the change of state that was wrought by the event they were commanded to commemorate in their ancestral heritage.

4. In keeping with the timeless character of moral principles, the other nine commandments have been carried over into the New Covenant and invested with deeper significance. Under the Old Covenant only overt acts were condemned and punishable. Jesus, in the Sermon on the Mount, altered that drastically. See Matthew 5:17-48. The man who has not committed murder only because he is a poor shot, or who has not become an adulterer for want of opportunity, is reckoned as being of the same mind, the same heart and soul as those who have committed such wanton acts.

5. In furtherance of the same principle, breaking of the other moral commandments of the decalogue is specifically prohibited in the New Testament. But not so, the Sabbath law.

a. The primacy of God is repeatedly enjoined upon us in the New Testament. For example, see Matthew 6:33; Mark 12:30.

b. Idolatry is condemned at least a dozen times. See Acts 15:20; II Cor. 6:16; I John 5:21, etc.

c. Profanity is condemned in all of its forms, including the minced profanity (by-words) by which Christians express the same feelings, and say almost the same thing, but not quite. See Matthew 5:33-37; James 5:12. God who knows our hearts will not be fooled by our "gee-whizzes, jeepers creepers, by crackies, goldarnits, doggone yas, what the heck," etc.

d. Remember the Sabbath day? Strange! No apostle, no Biblical writer (or record speaker), either in sermon or letter, gave instruction on Sabbath keeping. I have a list of over 150 different thoughts and acts (to say nothing of omissions of right doing) that are specifically named in the apostolic literature in the context of condemnation, but nowhere is Sabbath breaking chronicled or condemned. Did no one ever break the Sabbath in the apostolic age?

e. As for the rest, the commandment to honor parents receives attention at least six times (Eph. 6:1-3; Col. 3:20, etc.). Murder is condemned at least six times (see Matt. 5:21, 22; Rom. 1:29, etc.). Adultery is condemned repeatedly (Matt. 5:27-32; Gal. 5:19, etc.). Theft is likewise condemned (Eph. 4:28; I Cor. 6:10). Lying is condemned in all forms (Rev. 22:15; Rom. 1:25). Covetousness is condemned at least nine times (I Cor. 5:10, 11; Eph. 5:3, etc.).

Why such silence in the apostolic literature concerning Sabbath breaking, or keeping? Is God trying thereby to tell us something? He most certainly is, and has, and in a very positive way. See Romans 14:5, 6 and Colossians 2:16, 17. Within the context of the citation from Colossians we are informed that Christ has "blotted out the bond written in ordinances that was against us and contrary to us; and he has taken it out of the way, nailing it to the cross" (v. 14, 15).

The Sabbatarians would counter this by stating it was the ceremonial law that was annulled on Calvary, whereas the decalogue is God's eternal law, and the Sabbath commandment is specifically designated as binding "for a perpetual covenant . . . for ever" (Exod. 31:16, 17). Such an assumption is wreathed with problems.

1) The covenant that was fulfilled, and taken out of the way at Calvary, cannot be disassociated from the ten commandments. For example, it is written:

373

> And Jehovah said unto Moses, Write thou these words; for after the tenor of these words I have made a covenant with thee *and with Israel* . . . And he wrote upon the tables the words of the covenant, the ten commandments (Exod. 34:27, 28b).

And again, Moses in retrospect stated in his farewell address:

> And he (Jehovah) declared unto you *his covenant* which he commanded you to perform, *even the ten commandments;* and he wrote them upon two tables of stone (Deut. 4:13).

And in the following chapter it is written:

> Jehovah our God made a covenant with us in Horeb. Jehovah made not his covenant with our fathers, but with us, even us, who are all of us here alive this day (Deut. 5:2, 3).

Having so spoken, Moses then proceeded to recite the ten commandments, by reason of which the book of Deuteronomy, "Second Law" (actually second *giving* of the law), received its name.

2) To affirm on the basis of the language of Exodus 31:16, 17, the Sabbath is still binding and shall continue to be so even into the heavenly state when (according to Sabbatarian theology) we shall celebrate the Sabbath with God and the hosts of heaven—this is to void the distinction the Sabbatarians themselves have attempted to draw twixt the decalogue and "the ceremonial law." Virtually every facet of the Mosaic ritual was likewise appointed "for ever," "for an everlasting covenant," "a perpetual statute." For example:

a) The Passover: a day of memorial to be kept "throughout your generations . . . an ordinance for ever," Exodus 12:14.

b) The seven-day feast of unleavened bread: to be observed "throughout your generations . . . an ordinance for ever," Exodus 12:17.

c) The wave-offering (sheaf of the first-fruits): "a statute for ever throughout your generations," Leviticus 23:14.

d) The table of shewbread: Aaron and his sons to eat of "an everlasting covenant" and "a perpetual statute," Leviticus 24:8, 9.

e) The ritual of the day of atonement: "a statute for ever," "an everlasting statute," Leviticus 16:31, 34. How brash it was of Jesus to institute the Lord's supper instead! Or was he really behaving audaciously? Did he fulfill the law and institute a memorial feast commensurate with his role as the author of the New Covenant? Or are the rituals of the Old Covenant still binding despite what transpired on Calvary?

f) The Aaronic Priesthood: appointed "an everlasting priesthood

374

throughout their generations" (Exod. 40:15). Did the author of the epistle to the Hebrews (of all people) not know that? See Hebrews 7:11-17, 26:28.

g) Even circumcision was appointed as "an everlasting covenant" even before the giving of the Law of Moses, and incorporated into the law as binding even upon foreigners and sojourners before they could be admitted to the feast of the Passover (Gen. 17:13; Exod. 12:43, 44, 48). Yet the Jerusalem council determined that circumcision not be made binding upon the Gentiles (Acts 15:28, 29), and Paul wrote in the New Covenant Scriptures that circumcision availeth nothing (Gal. 6:15). Was that the beginning of "the great falling away," or was it not rather a recognition that a new *age* had been initiated and the former *age* had *passed away?*

The key to the understanding of the foregoing Scriptures is to be found in the fact that the Hebrew word olam and its New Testament counterpart aion no more mean for ever than an evergreen is "ever green." Olam and *aion* (from the latter we get our word *eon*) commonly designate an *age,* or something *age-lasting.* If for ever means for evermore, what would "for ever *and ever"* mean?

The Biblical expression "for ever and ever" commonly translated the Hebrew phrase, *le olam wa-ed* (unto the age and onward), *min ha-olam wad ha-olam* (from age to age) and the New Testament phrase, *eis tous aionous ton aionon* (unto the ages of the ages). Such expressions in the Scriptures are used to speak of the infinitude of God, and the future life and blessedness of the redeemed. The Sabbath enactment is nowhere spoken of in such language. As an ordinance directed toward man it lasted for the age for which it was enacted, and passed with the passing of that age.

6. At the heart of the Sabbatarian dogma is the postulate that assumes: 1) the seven days of Genesis 1:1—2:3 were literal twenty-four hour days, the first *week* of at least our solar system and the earth of which it is a part; and 2) when God "rested" from his creation on the seventh day he ordained that man whom he had just made should rest with him, despite the fact that man had done nothing of the sort from which he could "rest"; and 3) the whole created order of heavenly beings (angels, seraphim, etc.) were likewise obliged to rest with him.

The foregoing construction reads much more into the Scriptures than the textual data warrants. The account records only that God rested from "creating and making," Genesis 2:3. Since God is the energizer of the universe, and its cohesive force as well, utter chaos would ensue were God to "rest" from *all* his work at any time. But in the Sabbath command directed to Israel, they were to do "no work," nor were their servants, their stock, nor any strangers within their gates (Exod. 20:10).

The conjecture that God sets aside twenty-four hours at the close of each week to receive the worship of the angelic hosts and men on earth below is an unwarranted assumption. In the apocalypse (chapters 4-7) John was given a vision of the throne of God. The worship there said to be accorded him was not a twenty-four hour at-the-end-of-the-week affair.

7. The assumption God initiated the Sabbath commandment at the dawn of human history a) to be perpetuated throughout all the ages and b) to be extended throughout all the earth is contrary to both reason and revelation, science, and Scripture. If indeed at the close of every week there is a sacred twenty-four hour time slot in which God is to be worshipped, how do we go about determining when and where *that* day begins and ends?

The problem is that every solar day is upon the earth not merely twenty-four hours but forty-eight. Which twenty-four out of the forty-eight hour total are to be identified as God's holy Sabbath? To the ancient Israelites, confined to the land of Canaan, a narrow strip of territory nowhere as much as one hundred miles wide, hence less than one-tenth the breadth of an average time zone, the sun set on virtually every inhabitant at the same time. They could concertedly begin to "remember the Sabbath day and keep it holy" by recessing from any activity that could be classified as work. But to mankind dwelling upon the earth from sea to sea and almost from pole to pole, Sabbath keeping presents a number of problems. Not the least of those problems is determining when and where it is Saturday.

As civilization spread around the world, and travel increased in terms of both time and distance, men became aware of the fact the earth is not flat, but round; and when it is day time in one hemisphere it is night time in the other. Moreover the intermittent darkness and daylight "creeps" its way around the earth. Unless timing devices were reset as men traveled about, particularly when they traveled great distances in the pathway of the sun, their clocks communicated confusion. They found the sun rising and setting at strange hours.

Map makers drew imaginary lines on the globe that depicted the land masses and seas that appear on the surface of the earth. Those that circle the earth laterally were called parallels or latitudes and those

376

that depict the globe sectioned like a peeled orange were called longi-
tudes or meridians. The 360° of the earth's circumference (at the
equator) were sectioned into twenty-four 15° segments, each 1,000
miles wide at the equator. The result was twenty-four time zones. But
what time is it here and there? Where does a day begin? Where does
a merry-go-round start turning?

By international agreement the 180th longitude (meridian) was
agreed upon as constituting the *point* at which a day begins and mid-
night as the *time* when a day begins. (I am curious as to how the Jews
voted on that.) Thus when the 180th meridian reached that point in its
circuit when it would now start moving towards the sun, a new day
would thereafter officially begin upon the earth. An hour later the 165th
meridian of the western hemisphere arrives at the same point in relation
to the sun and the same day begins for that time zone. By the time
the last meridian has ushered in the day for the people dwelling in
that time zone, the day which began at the 180th meridian is over; but
for those in the last time zone the day has just begun. Thus every day
is on the earth forty-eight hours. Which of the forty-eight are to be
identified as the twenty-four hour, seventh day Sabbath God supposedly
instituted in the dawn of history and made obligatory on all mankind
for all time to come?

Other problems also arise with that theory. Examine a globe. Note
that in the south Pacific the date line has been shifted eastward in
the region of Samoa, from whence it moves to the south for thousands
of miles before it is repositioned westward in the region of New Zealand.
This was done to accommodate islanders dwelling in the bulge thus
created who occupied territory controlled by western powers. They
thereby moved one full day ahead of their next-door neighbors. If
there be any Sabbath keepers among them, which of them keep the
sacred twenty-four Sabbatarian Sabbath?

Now look at Alaska. There the date line has been shifted westward
to place Alaska in the same time zone as the United States, contingent
upon our purchase of the territory from Russia. Alaska thereby lost
a full day in its calendar. On what day of the week should a Sabbatarian
in Alaska attempt to keep the hypothesized sacred twenty-four hour time
slot ordained from creation to be the day of worship?

Such questions, and the facts which give rise to them, are troubling
to the Sabbatarians with whom I have shared them. In accord with
the adage, "misery loves company," when other arguments have
failed, their usual response is: "Don't those who keep Sunday instead

of Saturday have the same problem?" No. Perhaps some legalists among them do. But there is nothing sacred about a block of time per se. It is the events which take place in a time segment which invests time with significance. When the focus is kept upon the event, the event can be celebrated with due honor irrespective of a precise correlation with chronometers and calendars.

My wife and I were joined in marriage in a ceremony which took place, beginning at 4:00 p.m. one Sunday afternoon in August, nearly two thousand miles removed from our present home. When the 25th of August comes around each year, only one year out of seven does the day fall on Sunday; and due to distance and the innovation of daylight savings time, it is 7:00 p.m. in St. Louis, Missouri, at the time that would correspond to 4:00 p.m. in Los Angeles nearly fifty years ago. But to recapture the ecstasy of that bygone day and hour, we do not have to wait seven years between anniversary celebrations, return to Los Angeles, and turn our clocks back to standard time.

One fateful evening in the midst of what is commonly called the passion week, our Lord instituted the Lord's supper to be observed thereafter in commemoration of the death he would undergo the day following. But the apostles to whom he entrusted the matter guided the church in observing the Lord's supper on Sunday, the day of his resurrection. Sunday was a propitious time to meet, in view of his resurrection and the events of the day of Pentecost which followed. But to assume, or much more to insist, that it would be inappropriate or even unscriptural for Christians to meet on a different day, or at a different hour, to observe the Lord's supper or do aught else in his memory or service would be contrary to what is written in Romans 14:5, 6.

We therefore close as we began. Strange as it may seem, at least upon first notice, nowhere in the Scriptures are we commanded: "Remember the Lord's day (the first day of the week, the resurrection day) and keep it holy." But a Spirit-led church, from its inception on Pentecost, the first Lord's day of the church age, under the tutelage of the inspired apostles, had its beginning and thereafter continued steadfastly in the apostles' teaching and fellowship, in the breaking of bread, and the prayers. Love requires no further incentive. The letter killeth, but the spirit giveth life.

PREVIEW—REVIEW QUESTIONS

1. Aside from the day of the week involved, and the event commemorated by each, state a seldom noted distinction between the Sabbath law and the Lord's day observance.
2. How did the early church fathers, early on, interpret the phrase "the Lord's day"?
3. Define time, categorically and functionally.
4. Note the divine origin of the prevailing pattern for the basic segmentation and measuring of time.
5. State the principle by which a specific time segment is invested with significance for an individual, a group or a nation.
6. What event in the history of Israel invested the Sabbath day with a significance unique to that nation?
7. Of the two possible reasons for observing the Sabbath day, which did Moses capitalize upon in his farewell address to Israel?
8. Identify an act of divine deliverance of greater significance than Israel's deliverance from Egyptian bondage.
9. Note at least two respects in which said event is greater.
10. Note two somewhat related rituals of the Mosaic Covenant which foreshadowed important first-day-of-the-week events of the New Covenant era.
11. Note the language which specifically identifies the events as first-day-of-the-week happenings.
12. Note the Old Covenant name of the event referred to as Pentecost throughout the New Testament. What does each of the names signify?
13. Note at least two significant events in the life of Christ which invest the first day of the week with special significance.
14. Identify the event which even more specifically suggests the first day of the week was divinely selected to supersede the Sabbath in the church age.
15. Identify two texts which in an offhand manner of reporting suggest the observance of the first day of the week was of common practice.
16. Note two fundamental errors in the claim that the Catholic church changed the day of worship from Saturday to Sunday in 336 A.D.
17. List several reasons, short of a positive command, for observing the first day of the week as Christians.
18. List several reasons for not keeping the Sabbath.
19. Explain the difference between commandments based on moral principles and such a command as the Sabbath law.

20. Is there any sense in which, aside from the Sabbath command-ment, the others are incorporated in the New Covenant? Explain.
21. Respond to the Sabbatarian claim that it was the ceremonial law (not the decalogue which contains the Sabbath law) that was ful-filled and hence annulled by the death of Christ.
22. Respond to the Sabbatarian doctrine which affirms that inasmuch as the Sabbath is said to have been appointed "for ever," it is therefore ever binding.
23. State the manner of speaking in which the Scriptures communicate the concept of endlessness.
24. Explain the fact that every calendar day is actually on the earth forty-eight hours.
25. What bearing does the fact have upon the Sabbatarian dogma to the effect there is a sacred twenty-four hour time slot which con-stitutes God's holy Sabbath.
26. Would the problems just noted present any difficulty for the nation of Israel in the land of Canaan? Explain.
27. Do those who observe the first day of the week find themselves confronted with the same problem? Explain.

25

THE DIVINE DESIGN
FOR CHRISTIAN UNITY

Suppose you knew that tomorrow you would be executed—publicly, as a spectacle; that before this night were over you would be seized by an armed band, subjected to a farce of a trial, and condemned to die in one of the most agonizing, brutal, degrading, excruciating forms of execution ever contrived. How, if free to choose, would you spend this evening? Would you be up to sharing in a festal celebration with a circle of friends? Jesus did. He even initiated the arrangements.

What might you talk about? Would you avoid the subject of your eminent crucible? Or would you dwell on it in morbid apprehension? You would probably do some praying. Jesus did. But the burden of his prayer was for others. That prayer has come to be known as his intercessory prayer. It might very well be called his death wish, (John 17:1-26).

At the heart of that prayer is a fervent plea which he made for us, and with a view to the predicament in which we find ourselves. Having prayed for the twelve men whom he had called to be his apostles, he then turned his attention to such as ourselves, saying: "Neither for these only do I pray, but for them also that believe on me through their word . . ." (That includes us. How else do we, or anyone, come to believe on him except through the apostolic writings?) And what did he pray on our behalf? "*That we might all be one*. . . ." How much one? "even as thou, Father art in me, and I in thee, that they may also be in us: . . ." (v. 21a). And he cited three reasons for so praying: 1) That the world might *believe* that God sent him, (v. 21b). 2) That the world might at least *know* that God sent him, (v. 23a). And 3) that the world might know that God *loves* them, even as he loves his Son, (v. 23b). Surely, those should provide sufficient reason for us to eschew our bent for division and pursue the cause of unity.

I. *THE PARADOX OF CHRISTIAN UNITY*

The New Testament teaching concerning the unity of believers is somewhat paradoxical. On one hand, the unity of the church is affirmed as though it were both axiomatic and actual. On the other hand, the fact of schism is candidly and consistently recognized. At least the possibility of division is anxiously articulated in Christ's intercessory prayer. He prayed that we might all be one lest "the world" be left in ignorance and unbelief. In that he was prescient. That is precisely the result which accrues wherever the church is caught up in inter-tribal warfare.

That the church is one is affirmed by such texts as Romans 12:4, 5, I Corinthians 10:17, I Corinthians 12 (particularly vs. 12-14, 20, 24, 27), II Corinthians 11:2, Galatians 3:28, Ephesians 2:11-22, 4:4-16, Colossians 1:18. On the other hand, the fact that schism within the ranks of those who believe is not only possible but already existing is also affirmed in the Scriptures. See Romans 14:3-15, *16:17, 18, I Corinthians 1:10-13, Chs. 12-14, Galatians 5:16-21, *II Thessalonians 3:14, 15, *Titus 3:10, I John 2:18-20, 4:1-6, *II John 9-11. Moreover, in the texts which have been asterisked believers are asked to take action calculated to affix the blame for dissensions and divisions which arise. To such texts, II Corinthians 6:14-17 is commonly added and used as a proof text supporting the practice of "the moral and spiritual minority" breaking away to preserve the "new and true church." A self-published study by W. Carl Ketcherside, *The Twisted Scriptures*, provides some valuable insights on such verses. They are indeed oft-times "twisted" Scriptures.

The Key to the Paradox

The key to the paradox which confronts us is to be found in the fact that unity has two facets. There is 1) a unity of the spirit and the mind,

THE DIVINE DESIGN FOR CHRISTIAN UNITY

and 2) a unity of preachments and practice. The one is dispositional and idealistic. The other is propositional and substantive. The one has to do with our affections and our attitudes, the other with our affirmations and actions.

Spiritual unity is the kind of unity that emerges in times of mutual peril and distress. Animals fleeing before a raging fire or rising flood have been seen running side by side, predators and their normal prey temporarily stripped of their predatory disposition on the one hand and of mortal fear of their predators on the other hand. Wars and rumors of war often lead to strange alliances. Have you paused lately to consider who our allies were in World War II, and who our foes were? I vividly recall our commander in chief, the late Franklin D. Roosevelt, speak of Russia as "our gallant ally," and adding: "I like old Joe." Apparently he did—to the point of trusting him far beyond his deserving. The end of the war soon brought to light the fact we were not really one, certainly not substantively. There has been no significant shift in the political goals of either the USA or the USSR from that which existed when America and Russia were "allies" militarily.

In the context of the Christian faith unity also has two facts. There is a unity of the spirit, of mind-set, of disposition; even of pre-disposition. There is also a unity that is substantive, propositional. Paul speaks of both facets in Ephesians 4:1-16. In vs. 1-3 he writes:

I, therefore, the prisoner of the Lord, beseech you to walk worthily of the calling wherewith you were called, with all lowliness and meekness, with longsuffering, forbearing one another in love; giving diligence to keep the unity of the Spirit in the bond of peace.

That is one facet of Christian unity—a very important facet. Two congregations practicing and teaching the same things may exist in the same community, ostensibly united in faith and practice but actually devoid of the unity of the Spirit, in no way manifesting a bond of peace. The core membership of the two congregations may at one time have been part of the same congregation. But they failed to keep the unity of the Spirit in the bond of peace.

Congregations rarely divide over the issues which are publicized. When brethren love one another, and love Christ, differences of Scripture interpretation and procedure differences can generally be resolved. The works of the flesh are the motivating causes of division. But these are artfully camouflaged by the issues that are pressed to the point of congregational dispute. Few are so blatantly bold as to openly admit that they hate their brethren. But if they can convince

383

themselves and a following that those whom they speak against are a threat to the doctrinal stance of the church, or its fidelity to New Testament practice, they come across as crusaders for Christ, fighting the good fight of the faith.

It is important therefore that we heed the admonition of Paul to keep the unity of the Spirit in the bond of peace. Note that unity of the Spirit is to be kept, not contrived. Is it not written even of the strife-torn church at Corinth: "In one Spirit were we all baptized into one body," (I Cor. 12:13).

The second aspect of the unity of believers, fidelity and commitment to the New Testament Scriptures, provided the impetus for the Protestant Reformation. But both collectively as well as individually the reformers fell short of their goal. Their efforts were but piecemeal at best. The sparks flew as each of them set about "grinding his own axe." But few showed a disposition to cooperate in areas of reform being championed by others. Thus the fragmenting of the reformation into warring denominations.

Our generation has witnessed, via the Ecumenical Movement, a renewal of the appeal to keep the Spirit of unity in the bond of peace. But substantive unity is far removed from the so-called ecumenical mind. There is scarcely a substantive doctrine of the Holy Scriptures that has not been treated as expendable. The inspiration and authority of the Holy Scriptures, the deity of Jesus, his atoning work on the cross, his bodily resurrection—all have been toned down and made secondary to political expediency in the creation of an ecumenical church.

The unity for which Christ prayed can scarcely be effectuated by the abandonment of those truths which are the core of the New Covenant scriptures. A school boy once defined a net as "a lot of nothing tied together by a piece of string." If the abandonment of New Testament faith and practice in the interest of political expedience is a viable option, we might just as well sue for peace with Rome, forthwith and directly, rather than belatedly and indirectly in the effectuation of the second phase of the master plan contrived by the hierarchy of the Ecumenical Movement.

But grant the ecumenicists credit where due. The movement has served to focus attention upon the sin of division and its corollary— the attrition and emaciation of the body of Christ via the bloodletting that ever accompanies a divided church.

II. *INTERLUDE: DEFINITIONS AND DISTINCTIONS*

Before proceeding to a formal discussion of the second facet of unity we need to note some basic definitions and distinctions.

1. *Unity versus union.* Unity, rightly defined, is the "state of being one." Union is simply the result of two or more persons or things being joined together. As the old adage puts it: One may tie two cats together by their tails and throw them over a clothesline, but unity will not be achieved thereby, only a union. Even if the cats were of the same species, size, age, color and gender unity could never be forced upon them by such a union. A metal plate may be affixed to a block of wood, but both will remain the same in substance. Neither will assimilate the constituent elements of the other.

2. *Unity versus uniformity.* Two peas in a pod exhibit uniformity. Various mass-produced commodities do likewise. They are uniform in size, shape, texture, and substance. Each is complete in itself, and like so many marbles each unit exists completely outside of and apart from the others. In the animate world uniformity, no matter to how high a degree, is not enough to fulfill their needs. They need to interact and interrelate with their own kind; for the propagation of their species, if nothing else. But they need to do so for other reasons also. The higher the life form, the greater the need for interaction and inter-relating.

As we move toward the second facet of unity as it relates to the Christian faith, other terms need to be defined.

1) Denomination(al), un/non/inter-denominational. To denominate is to "name from," that is, to give to one person, place, or thing a name designed to distinguish that one from others. Adam's God-given assignment with regard to naming the animals that shared his domain illustrates how important denominating is to communication. The proliferation of life forms has made the naming of specimens (even in groups) an ongoing task. In the instance of persons, each needs to be denominated individually. With our population exploding, this is becoming quite impossible despite the creativity of the human mind.

In the context of the Christian faith, denominational names are devised to form a name which will aptly set forth the basic distinction of one body of believers from others. As these in turn split, further distinctions are called for—north, south, free, latter day, charismatic, etc., etc.

Such prefixes as un, non, inter (denominational) are generally subterfuges calculated to communicate the notion that the congregations thusly designated are embracive of the whole church, or at least all but the "way out" cults.

2) Ecumenical is a term coined from the Greek *oikoumene* (whole habitation). Cp. Matthew 24:14; Luke 2:1, 4:5, 21:26; Acts 11:28,

17:6, 31, 19:27, 24:5; Romans 10:18; Revelation 19:9, 16:14. The term is the Greek equivalent of the Latin *catholikus*, "universal."

3) Protestant is a term that has come to have a reverse meaning from its original import. Etymologically, it means to "testify for, on behalf of," not against. But when truth has been long replaced by error, any attempt to restore the truth will be interpreted by those entrenched in error as a frontal assault. It is not strange therefore that today any challenge of the status quo is called a "protest" movement.

4) Reformation and Restoration are often used interchangeably. The churches of Christ and Christian churches commonly speak of themselves as The Restoration Movement. But at the outset, the movement of which such churches are the heirs was originally known as The American Reformation. A technical difference can be drawn between restoration and reformation. Restoration primarily denotes a reinstatement to a former position, rank, or state. It may denote also restitution for loss or damage, or the renewal of a former normal or unimpaired state of being. It is in the latter sense that churches of Christ and Christian Churches use the term. To reform may be used in the latter sense, or merely to form anew. In the context of church history, it has taken on some of the overtones of its usage in the context of civil law. A reformatory is a place where those convicted of criminal offenses are incarcerated for punishment and, hopefully, rehabilitation. It is worthy of note that it was not until the papal church became grossly criminal that the reformation gained sufficient popular support to become indeed a movement.

III. *THE SIN OF DIVISION*

This brings us to grips with the seven deadly sins of division. That division is in itself sinful, apart from its effects, is plainly set forth in the Scriptures. In Galatians 5:19-21 both the seeds of division and the alienations which stem from it are catalogued with the works of the flesh. Every form and expression of the divisive spirit—envying, strife, jealousy, wraths, parties, factions—one and all, they are placed in the same category as fornication, uncleanness, lasciviousness, adultery, idolatry, drunkenness and revelling. And we are duly warned that "they who practice such things shall not inherit the kingdom of God," (v. 21b). Why is division cited as so monstrous an evil? For at least seven reasons it is so.

1. Division is sinful if for no other reason than the fact it makes void the prayer of Christ. If the church is indeed the body of Christ then

what Christ, the head, fervently prayed for the members of his body ought to work to attain. Is not that what a body is for? What a travesty, to have a body that works against the will of the head. That comes close to demon possession, could we not say?

2. Division is sinful because it hinders the work of evangelism. Christ readily foresaw that the world will be slow to believe the witness of a gainsaying and divided church. Moreover, much of the world will be deprived of even hearing the word of truth. A church that spends much of its energy and resources building corrals to separate and segregate its several flocks will have little time and money left for world evangelism.

3. Division is sinful because it mutilates the visible church. Division does to the church what even Christ's most inveterate enemies did not even attempt to do to his fleshly body. Division dismembers, and in a sense decapitates, the body of Christ.

4. Division jeopardizes the very existence of the church. Jesus once said: "A house divided against itself can not stand," (Matt. 12:25). Many a congregation torn by strife has ceased to exist. Others have survived, but crippled beyond any ability to function effectively. There are exceptions of course but that does not disprove what Christ said in Matthew 12:25. It only underscores what he said in Matthew 16:18. Were the church not a divine institution it would have long since perished from the earth. Few indeed are the movements which have long survived repeated self-mutilation.

5. Division is sinful because it is manifestly a work of the flesh. It is as carnal as fornication, adultery, lasciviousness, covetousness and drunkenness. It is of the world, the flesh and the devil.

6. Division is sinful because it exalts man. The Corinthian syndrome, wherein believers boasted: "I am of Cephas," "I am of Paul," "I am of Apollos," and perhaps even some of those saying, "I am of Christ," is echoed again and again by those who pride themselves in being disciples of Luther, Calvin, Campbell, or some current religious figure. Virtually every sect and cult of Christendom represents an undue regard for some man or woman whose teachings and interpretations have been in effect canonized and equated with the Scriptures.

7. Division is sinful because it is wantonly wasteful. Time, energy and resources are absorbed by needless duplication. The spectacle of two, three, and often more, partially filled facilities encircling a town square, each burdened with utility bills, office supplies and equipment, insurance, maintenance, salaries, etc., puts a strain on the resources which leaves little left over for missionary and benevolent outreach.

Where do we go from here? Is there no balm in Gilead? Is there no healing for the torn body of Christ—the wounds which we have inflicted even upon ourselves? For we are his body, are we not? Is the great physician helpless to heed the adage to which he himself once gave expression: "Physician, heal thyself," (Luke 4:23). There is.

In Ephesians, chapter four, there is much more said concerning the unity of believers than the mere exhortation to "keep the unity of the Spirit in the bond of peace," (v. 3). In verses 4-6 it is written:

> There is one body, and one Spirit, even as also ye were called in one hope of your calling; one Lord, one faith, one baptism, one God and Father of all who is over all, and through all and in all.

These verses have long been recognized as setting forth the seven pillars which support the portico to Christian unity—recognized, and admired from a distance, but how slow we are to enter therein.

Categorically, the seven pillars of Ephesians 4:4-6 are all inclusive. For example, according to Acts 4:12, there is only one name under heaven that is given among men wherein we must be saved, but that may well be included in the phrase, "there is one Lord." Certainly everything that may be taught as a doctrine "pertaining to life and godliness" is included in the phrase, "there is one faith"—provided of course it is duly set forth in what Jude calls "the faith once and for all delivered to the saints," (Jude 3).

From the Divine perspective the oneness of believers accrues automatically each time a ransomed soul is born into the family of God. When children were born into our household there was never a question as to their family status. Admittedly, situations arose in which it was difficult to keep the family spirit in the bond of peace. But there were substantive factors—commitment, customs, principles, rules, ideals—augmented by filial ties, which held our family together. They still do. The one household has become five, but we are one in the bond of love, and in faith, and hence life-style.

Such is the role of the seven pillars of unity. They provide families, friends and congregations a substantive basis for unity. Camaraderie has its place, but it can be superficial and even nebulous if it is not undergirded and expressed in terms of convictions and commitments which provide substantive unity.

IV. THE SEVEN PILLARS OF UNITY

1. Note the first, there is *one body*. Do you agree? To what degree? This affirmation receives lip service in both evangelical and ecumenical

circles. But is it really believed to be true? Earlier in this volume, we called attention to the fact that the most renowned spokesman for modern evangelicalism, in a widely published work, has gone on record saying:

> The New Testament teaches that while there is actually only one church, there can be any number of local churches formed into various denominations or societies or councils . . . divided along national and theological lines, or according to the temperament of their members.

The New Testament teaches no such thing. Were he speaking simply as an observer of the present spectacle, we would be obliged to agree with him. But he continued to affirm that such is *necessary* and acceptable. He opined that just as we cannot all be content to wear the same style of hat, neither could we be content to belong to the same kind of church. May the day never come when those wearing different hat styles behave like church members and refuse to fellowship those who wear different styles of hats.

To affirm that we all constitute the church no matter what we teach or practice is necessary to the rallying of a divided Christendom (in part at least) to join in a token display of unity in the form of a city-wide crusade. But that is not the degree of unity to which Paul bore witness when he wrote, "there is one body."

2) There is *one Spirit*. That Spirit does not speak with a forked tongue. "God is not the author of confusion, but of peace" (I Cor. 14:33). The apostle John, writing near the close of the apostolic age, warned, "Beloved, believe not every spirit, but prove the spirits whether they be of God." Moreover, he told us how: "We are of God; he that knoweth God heareth us. He who is not of God heareth us not. By this we know the spirit of truth and the spirit of error" (I John 4:1, 6). In the context of those polemic words, the apostle of love branded the gnostic heretics as "antichrists," and declared they were no part of that body of believers who are led by the Spirit of God, (I John 2:18, 19, 4:1-3).

3) There is *one hope*, that hope which is ours in Christ. In view of the fact we have been emphasizing the need of a substantive basis for unity, it is well to recall that the great faith chapter of the Bible opens with the announcement that "Faith is the *substance* (foundation, assurance) of things hoped for" (Heb. 11:1). The word so translated is *hupostasis*, literally, that which *stands under*, as a foundation undergirds and supports a building.

4) There *is one Lord*. The italicizing of the verb in this instance is not a printing error. There *is* one Lord! Of old it was written (and

389

repeated), "The fear of the Lord is the beginning of wisdom" (Prov. 1:7, 9:10; Ps. 111:10; cp. Job 28:28; Ps. 15:33). Few stand in reverence and awe of the Lord today. In fact, the "now generation" seldom stands. They much prefer to loll about in casual (and often scanty) attire, or sway rhythmically as they parrot palsy-walsy, buddy-deity lyrics. The stately hymns of yesteryear which magnified the Lord have been largely scuttled in favor of repetitious subjective mush. Much of it is impromptu, supposedly thereby thusly "given by inspiration."

That is but part of the problem, perchance the middle part. The worst may be yet to come. Suppose we look to the possible antecedents. There are two: (1) A church which has often supplanted obedience by ritual, the bane of the liturgical church, and (2) the evangelical dogma of salvation by faith alone gone to seed. There is little room for the question of Jesus, "Why call ye me, Lord, Lord, and do not the things I say?" (Luke 6:46) if there is nothing one really needs to do either to be saved or remain saved. If even our faith, the lone condition for salvation allowed by popular evangelicalism, is the gift of God, the donees predestined by God's sovereign and immutable election, nothing we do or fail to do really matters.

The Lordship of Christ demands the surrender of self. Void this and one of the most substantive factors leading to a life commitment to the will of God will be sapped of its compulsion and strength.

5) There is *one faith*. Contemporary Christendom pays lip service to this affirmation, but would have it believed that faith may be compared to our solar system. The sun (Son) is the center of the system. The sects of Christendom are akin to the planets which encircle the sun, some nearer thereto, some farther, some far, far away, yet tethered by the sun and enlightened by its rays. Perhaps the analogy could be extended further. Perhaps the splits and spin-offs of the major sects may be likened in turn to the satellites of the several planets.

Such surmisings are a cop-out. The creeds of Christendom do not form an integral system. They are often contradictory. Some are polemic assaults against creedal systems formulated before them. Moreover, other sources of "illumination"(?) are reflected besides the Scriptures. In some cases this is so manifestly so that even the ecumenicists regard such as the Mormons, Christian Scientists, Jehovah's Witnesses, etc., as cults, not just sects. When Paul wrote, "there is one faith" he was referring to something much more specific and uniform in its expression than the creeds of Christendom.

The faith Jude declares to have been "once for all delivered to the saints" (Jude 3) is neither a smorgasbord designed to accommodate finicky and hearty eaters alike, nor is it a sort of salad bar from which the entrees on the menu may be suited to one's appetite and taste.

6) There is *one baptism*. Would I have inserted this into the list if Paul had not done so? I could not be that bold. But neither could I be so audacious as to strike it out. Baptism cannot be downed. It keeps cropping up seemingly everywhere as we peruse the Scriptures. (a) If we speak of the formal preparation for the eminent coming of the kingdom of God, and the dramatic presentation of the Messiah, we are confronted with baptism, (Matt. 3:1-17). (b) If we are to take note of Christ's formal induction into his public ministry, confirmed by the voice of God and the descent of the Holy Spirit upon him, we are confronted with baptism (vs. 13-17). (c) If we take note of his formal and final commission of the apostles, noting the things they were specifically commissioned to do in behalf of believers, we are confronted with baptism, (Matt. 28:18-20, Mark 16:15, 16). (d) If we take note of the role of the Holy Spirit in the inauguration of the church, and the terms which were enunciated (under the direction of the Holy Spirit) for the remission of sins and the gift of the Holy Spirit, we are confronted with baptism (Acts 2:38-41). (e) If we are to consider those institutions of the Gospel which are designed to depict the death, burial and resurrection of Christ, we are confronted with baptism (Rom. 6:3-18). (f) If we are to take note of the only commandment in the Bible ordained to be administered in (or into, Gr. *eis*), the name of the Father and the Son and the Holy Spirit, we are confronted with baptism—a fact that ought not to surprise us since the only time in all recorded history that the three persons of the Trinity were manifested simultaneously was on the occasion of Jesus' baptism, (Matt. 3:16, 17). Finally, but only with a view of limiting the cataloguing of available data to seven particulars, (g) if we are to consider the seven factors which substantiate our oneness in Christ, we are again confronted with baptism, (Eph. 4:5, Cp. I Cor. 12:13). Do you suppose the Holy Spirit is trying to tell us something?

As a contributor to the series of studies being published by College Press under the umbrella title: *What the Bible Says . . .*" attention was caught by a title I observed while browsing in a religious bookstore. Henrietta Mears, in a 688-page paperback, entitled *What the Bible Is All About,* has attempted a chapter-by-chapter summary of the Bible. Can you believe this? In summarizing Romans 6, she never once used the words baptize(d) or baptism. She did not even allude to baptism. The chapters immediately preceding were discussed under the caption:

"How to Be Saved," but chapter six was excluded as though being baptized into Christ's death, buried with him through baptism, and raised to walk in newness of life has nothing to do with salvation. If she is indeed cluing in her readers on "what the Bible is all about," apparently the Bible has nothing to say about baptism that is worth mentioning. One has to be creed-blinded almost beyond hope to "see" nothing about baptism in the most lucid and extensive discourse of the subject in all the Bible. Obviously, the madam's denominational prejudice is showing.

In response to the rejoinder that some of us talk too much about baptism, the question needs to be asked: Which is worse, to talk so much about the subject as to offend those who teach that one may be saved by faith alone, or to belittle the subject, ignore it, or even villify it? Which form of error(?) is more the likely to encourage disobedience of a Divine command commended unto us by Christ's own precept and public example?

Since several different kinds of baptisms are noted in the New Testament, readers will do well to refer back to Lesson Sixteen, Section B.

7. There is one God and Father. At long last we have come to one affirmation the protestant sects can unite upon. And when the rest of the verse is included in the quotation even the papists are inclined to agree: "There is one God and Father who is over all, and through all, and in all."

V. THE DIVINE DESIGN FOR CHRISTIAN UNITY

At the heart of Paul's Ephesian letter is a prayer which serves as an introduction to the discourse on unity which follows. It begins on this wise: "For this cause I bow my knees unto the Father from whom every family in heaven and on earth is named" (Eph. 3:15). Therein is an interesting phrase. What would it take today to 1) denominate and 2) keep in the bond of peace *every* family in even one small community? May I illustrate.

I recall to this day the first church edifice I had occasion to notice. I was a child just entering grade school in rural Idaho. Above the doorway in large letters was the inscription: German Methodist Church. Our nearest neighbors were Germans. I presumed they were Methodists also. They attended church there, sunshine or storm. Our family was neither of Germanic stock or Methodists. We did not seem to belong in that company.

392

I recall another church edifice which claimed my attention. The signboard out in front announced that was a Swedish Lutheran Church. That figured. The countryfolk in that community were mostly Scandinavian dairymen. That signboard also seemed to communicate a society segregated both by race and by creed.

Our next move was to southern California. There an imposing edifice was designated (St. Somebody's) Roman Catholic Church. Those entering that place for masses, funerals, etc. were of obvious Latin extraction.

In those days our family was "unchurched." If asked why, I would likely have replied: "There is no church for us." We did not meet the basic standards which were being communicated at the entrance of virtually every "church."

At age ten a significant thing happened. My parents were invited to a revival at the "Christian Church" in a nearby town. They came, they saw Christ, they were converted—mother by way of renewal of the faith she had embraced as a child, and father by primary obedience, ending years of rebellion against the upbringing in an ultra-strict (non-instrumental) Church of Christ heritage. A year later I was converted, along with my older brother, Don Earl.

Admittedly, that prejudiced me in favor of the Christian church. I loved it. I have devoted the past fifty years of my life to its ministry. My love, however, is not blind. The congregations of the Christian church I have known have all had their "spots and blemishes." My presence among them has added another. But the Christian churches also have a plea that echoes the heart-cry of our Saviour. They have for one of their primary goals the unity of believers. They stand (at least in principle) committed to an unsectarian stance, and a plea for unity in the name that is above every other name, and for a return to apostolic faith and practice.

By the term "unsectarian," as used in this context, is meant that which rightly applies to the *whole* of the church not just some segment (sect or section) of it. By way of illustration:

Fig. 1. represents the world, and the church as it was in the beginning. The tiny dot in the center of the circle represents the church, founded at the crossroads, if not the actual geographical center of the then known world.

Fig. 1

393

Fig. 2 represents the growing church. The X outside the circle is to draw attention to the fact the church is not "out of this world," but in it, else it could not leaven it. Christ prayed not that his disciples should be taken out of the world but that they should be kept from the evil one, (John 17:15, 16).

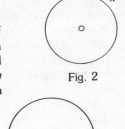

Fig. 2

Fig. 3 is intended to illustrate the fact that as the church grew the world population was growing also. It still is. The tragedy is that the population growth is exceeding by far the growth of the church.

Fig. 3

Fig. 4 consists of two parts. 4A depicts the trend setting in at the church in Corinth. It is intended to illustrate the principle under discussion. In Figs. 2 and 3 there is but one line of demarcation—that

Fig. 4A   Fig. 4B

which separated the church from the world. The church consisted of "the enchristed ones," those in Christ. The world consisted of those outside of Christ. But with the overt outbreak of the sectarian spirit in the church at Corinth the scene changes. Fig. 4A illustrates the potential danger against which Paul warned in no uncertain tones (I Cor. 1:10-13). If the sectarian spirit at work in Corinth were not checked the broken lines of 4A would have become the solid lines of 4B. The church in Corinth might have split into four sects, with at least three of the responsible parties, the Cephasites, the Paulinists and the Apollosians competing with those seeking to be "Christians only."

Fig. 5 is an attempt to illustrate the budding Corinthian catastrophe gone to seed in current denominationalism. Note the line of demarcation between the church and the world is all but obscured. More visible by far are the sectarian lines which separate sect from sect and sub-sects from other sects and sub-sects. As to what percentage of the various sects have their names written in the Book of Life is a moot

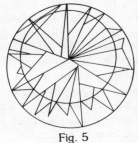

Fig. 5

394

question, beyond our wisdom to discern and our right to judge. We are free only to proclaim what God has promised. What he who alone knows the hearts of men may do beyond what he has covenanted to do belongs to the secret counsel of God. But there can be no disputation of the fact that the sectionizing (sectarianizing) of the church is a formidable barrier to Christian unity.

What then is the Divine design for unity?

At the risk of oversimplifying both the problem and the solution we suggest that the cause and the focus of sectarian lines of separation need to be identified, and avenues of unity laid down within the right of ways reclaimed for a highway to the gates of Zion. Seven suggestions are in order.

1. We need to bow to the authority of the one and only unsectarian figure of the church—Christ, our Lord and Saviour. If the believers in one lone city could not unite behind any one man, not even such illustrious souls as Peter, Paul or Apollos, certainly the church the world over could never be persuaded to unite behind the Roman pontiff, or become followers of Luther, Calvin, Campbell, Joseph Smith, Moon or some other. Note that Paul appealed to all factions at Corinth "in the name of the Lord Jesus Christ," (I Cor. 1:10). That observation leads to another.

2. We need to discard sectarian names in favor of the only name that is given under heaven wherein we must be saved, (Acts 4:12). The thing that betrayed the sectarian spirit of the church at Corinth is the manner in which each faction gloried in the name of their favorite spokesman. Is there any reason to believe Paul would write any differently were he to address directly the sectarian spectacle of our time? Have we learned nothing from history, not even from sacred history?

My father-in-law, C. I. Kenney, was a Transylvania University graduate in the days of the renowned J. W. McGarvey. He enjoyed relating an incident which took place at an inter-denominational conclave in Lexington, Kentucky. As the sessions progressed, one of the speakers, elated by the unexpected camaraderie and unsectarian nature of the gathering, began to wax eloquent. Indicating various personages who shared the platform with him he said, "Dr. (A) is not here as a Baptist. He is here as a Christian. Rev. (B) is not here today as a Congregationalist. He is here as a Christian. Bishop (C) is not here today as a Methodist. He is here as a Christian." One by one, other names were called, their denominational affiliation identified, followed by the phrase attesting the one name in which they were at least for the occasion united. At last, he came to Prof. Loos who had been chosen to represent the Christian churches and churches of Christ at the conclave. By now, the speaker was completely caught up in his rhetoric and awareness of the transcending unity they were enjoying in the name of Christ. "*And*," he said, with voice rising to a crescendo in a final oratorical flourish, "Prof. Loos is not here today as . . . uh, uh . . . (long pause). Folks, I guess Prof. Loos is here today as what he has been all along."

There is one unsectarian name that is given among men. And there is but one name applied to followers of Christ assembled for worship and instruction that automatically calls that name to mind—the name Christian.

3) We need an unsectarian and Divinely authoritative guidebook. Paul appealed to the Corinthian church to "all speak the same thing" (I Cor. 1:10). It is ever true that the Bible plus nothing, minus nothing, makes Christians: unhyphenated and unalloyed.

There was never a Mormon on the face of the earth until Joseph Smith came forth with the *Book of Mormon* some 150 years ago. If, for the sake of unity, we would all accept the Book of Mormon, we would then no longer be united in faith with the saints who have gone before us. We would no longer speak the same thing, we would not be perfected in the same mind and the same judgment, as those who continue steadfastly in the apostles' teaching prior to the advent of the "Joseph-come-lately," self-styled prophet of "The Church of Jesus Christ of the Latter Day Saints." Incidentally, what other kind of saints have been around since the former days passed away and "God in these latter days spoke to us in his Son" (Heb. 1:1, 2)?

4) We need an unsectarian creed. To say this is, in a sense, to repeat ourselves. It has long been a saying among us that any creed which contains more than the Bible contains too much, and any creed that contains less than the Bible contains too little. Technically, that is not true; obviously so in the case of the latter. Multitudes became Christians, some of them exemplary Christians, laying down their lives for Christ, before a single book of the New Testament was written. Only as much of the Divine revelation as is necessary to bring a person to an obedient faith in Jesus Christ and guide him thereafter in righteousness can properly be called that person's creed or confession of faith. We cannot believe what we have never seen nor heard.

It is defensible, however, to say that the one thing we certainly do not need to have thrust upon us is a creed which teaches aught which is not taught in the Scriptures, or which denies something that is taught therein (Rev. 22:18, 19). We have a valid basis for unity in Christ when we speak where the Bible speaks, and as the Bible states it, and are silent where the Bible is silent.

5. To attain and maintain the unity for which Christ prayed, we need an unsectarian model for organizational structure. Through the centuries the church has ever been tempted to model itself after the cultural pattern of the contemporary social and political order. The church revealed in the Scriptures is a theocratic republic, not a dictatorship nor a democracy. Christ is king. The New Testament is the revelation of his will. Guidance and oversight is providentially provided by elders (plural) chosen by the various congregations from among themselves, and by ministers of the Word, called by the Gospel.

Deacons (servants, both male and female) are provided for by Divine example. Almost from the inception of the church, time-consuming details were entrusted to duly qualified persons chosen out of the congregation for the specific task needing attention.

A free-floating, unstructured service devoid of plan or purpose is as foreign to the New Testament order as its antithesis—the vain repetition of a clergy orchestrated ritual. The counsel, "Let all things be done decently and in order" (I Cor. 14:40), was given to a congregation in which individuals were insisting on their right "to do their own thing" in the pretense of being led by the Spirit.

6. If we are to worship the Father in Spirit and in truth we must "prove the spirits whether they are of God," (I John 4:1) by testing both trends and tradition by the apostles doctrine, (I John 4:6). The New Testament does not provide for us any semblance of a proscribed "order of worship." The concept of a regimented agenda for "corporate worship" is a figment of the imagination. It ill behooves any of us to attempt to "freeze history" at any time or place and thereupon bind or loose aught that is not clearly commended or forbidden in the New Testament. To forbid what the New Testament does not prohibit is as sectarian as to demand what the New Testament does not proscribe.

7. Last, but by no means least, we need an unsectarian spirit. Almost immediately prior to Jesus' announcement, "I will build my church," he warned his disciples, saying: "Take heed and beware of the leaven of the Pharisees and of the leaven of the Sadducees," (Matt. 16:6). Take note that he did not warn his disciples against those sects as such. He warned them against the leaven, the mind-set, the sectarian bias which made each sect what they were. Labels change with the

changing times—Pharisees/Sadducees, right wing/left wing, conserva-
tives/liberals, fundamentalists/modernists, non-progressives/digres-
sives, die-hards/free spirits, etc., etc. But the leaven of the Pharisees
and the leaven of the Sadducees, sectarianism of both stripes, continues to get in its insidious work whatever the label in vogue.

Conclusion: Division to the degree that plagues the church has been
long in the making. But the complacency which has appeased the
monstrous evil is being shaken. There is a rising crescendo of irenic
voices being heard. Siren voices will be heard, intermingled among
them. But let us not fail to hear the heart-cry of our Saviour, as he
pled that we might all be one that the world might be won.

THE CHURCH: GROWING BUT DIVIDING
IN THE MIDST OF A GROWING WORLD

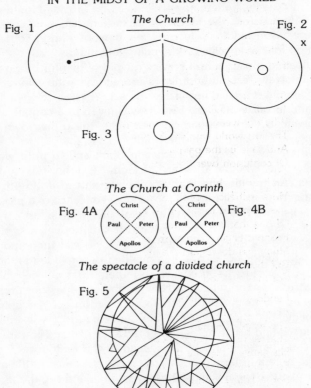

Fig. 1

The Church

Fig. 2

Fig. 3

The Church at Corinth

Fig. 4A   Christ / Paul / Peter / Apollos   Christ / Paul / Peter / Apollos   Fig. 4B

The spectacle of a divided church

Fig. 5

A DIVIDED CHURCH

The world and the devil can chide us
Because of the names that divide us,
And well may they mock and deride us
When party names number two hundred.
One Bible is all the Lord gave us;
One faith all sufficient to save us;
One Lord who redeemed and forgave us:
But what of the two hundred names?

While the cynical world can now revel
And mock and deride with the devil,
It is not all quite on the level.
The Lord never made the two hundred!
He founded one church to redeem us;
Not two hundred such to blaspheme us.
But thus does the world esteem us
With party names over two hundred.

There is naught in a name they tell us,
But party names do make us jealous,
And scores who think they are zealous
Are but zealous for some party name.
Why not wear just the name of the Master?
The lost world would find him the faster
And save us the pain and the disaster
Of confusion over the name.

And creeds, human creeds—how confusing,
More pathetic, indeed, than amusing.
Two hundred to sift for the choosing
Of one that is best suited to me.
I cannot begin to compare them,
Much less do aught to repair them.
But this I can do, I can spare them
For the one God's book holds for me.

I endorse it without alteration;
Accept it without reservation—
The simple Divine revelation
That Jesus the Christ is God's Son.
His name is the one that is given
To bring us to God and to heaven;
For in Him all our sins are forgiven,
Because we confess Him, God's Son.

Men's mouthing of creeds may divide us,
And dogmas confuse and misguide us;
But the Book of all books will guide us
To the oneness in Christ Jesus' name.
We can speak where the Bible has spoken;
Where silent, leave silence unbroken.
One church would then stand as a token
Of Jesus' Divine saving Name.

— C. A. Boulton

PREVIEW—REVIEW QUESTIONS

1. State the burden of Jesus' intercessory prayer.
2. To what degree must we be one to fulfill his prayer request?
3. State three reasons he prayed that we might be one.
4. State the paradox of the New Testament teaching concerning the oneness of the church.
5. State the key to the paradox.
6. State the two facets of unity, and explain the difference between the two.
7. Wherein did the Protestant Reformation fail to keep the unity of the Spirit in the bond of peace?
8. Wherein does the Ecumenical Movement commonly fail in their emphasis upon the need for unity.
9. Distinguish between: a) unity and union, b) unity and uniformity.
10. Define the term denominationalism.
11. What is generally intended to be communicated by the use of various prefixes?
12. Distinguish between non and inter-denominationalism.
13. Compare the linguistic background of the terms, catholic and ecumenical.
14. Distinguish between the linguistic and common usage of the term protestant.
15. Compare the terms reformation and restoration.
16. Cite a text which clearly brands division as sinful.
17. How does division violate the prayer of Christ?
18. How does division hinder the work of evangelism?
19. Wherein does the division of Christendom exceed the ravages of the crucifixion?
20. What principle cited by Jesus makes division a threat to the church?

21. Illustrate via a Biblical example that division exalts man in the stead of Christ.
22. Explain how and why division is wantonly wasteful.
23. List the seven pillars of unity, as cited by Paul.
24. Distinguish between the "lip service" paid to the doctrine of organic unity and the prayer request of Christ.
25. State the principle cited by the apostle John for the proving of the spirits, whether they are of God.
26. State the correlation of faith and hope, according to Heb. 11:1.
27. Note the insidious assault against the Lordship of Christ in popular evangelicalism.
28. Evaluate the popular notion that all "faiths" in the aggregate make up what Paul spoke of as the "one faith."
29. Take note of the various contexts in which the New Testament doctrine of baptism appears.
30. Review question: Since several different kinds of baptism are mentioned in the New Testament, how could Paul say "there is one"?
31. Do the brand names of divided Christendom communicate the oneness of the church and the universality of the Gospel? Explain.
32. Define the terms, sectarian and unsectarian.
33. What is the basic principle that needs to be pursued in the search for an unsectarian faith and practice?
34. State the manner in which the divisions at Corinth provide instruction for those seeking to be non-sectarian.
35. Cite the seven principles suggested by the author as right of ways to be reclaimed for the way to a united church.

26

THE CHURCH'S DIVINELY APPOINTED MISSION

The Great Commission gives to the church its charter, constituting the church a teaching institution whose field is the world and whose commission is to the end of the age (Matt. 28:18-20). The role of the church as a teaching institution is enjoined upon it by a double injunction. There are two words for teach used in Matthew's statement of the Great Commission. The first, *matheteusate*, is commonly rendered "make disciples," except in the older King James Version. The *New King James* has been revised to read "make disciples," a change long overdue. It is not that "teach" is a mistranslation, only that it is not the best translation. The verb, *matheteuo*, and the noun, *mathetes* stem from a root which indicates thought accompanied by corresponding action. Thus the noun is commonly used in the New Testament to denote one who follows someone's teaching, hence an adherent. To disciple is to teach, and may be so translated, but it is to teach with something more in mind than to implant information. It is to teach with a view to commitment.

The second of the two words for teach is *didaskontes*. It is the common word for imparting instruction. While the distinction between the two words used in Matthew 28:19, 20 is not absolute, the first is best suited to the work of evangelism, the second to the task of edification. In evangelism the design is to bring a person to Christ. In edification the intent is to build up one who is in Christ. These two tasks constitute the overriding commission, the business, of the church.

1. Evangelism is the First Task of the Church

The church that is not evangelizing is, at best, in "a holding pattern." The sober truth is that any congregation that remains in that pattern will not long hold onto those it already has. With respect to the charge to evangelize, it is "do or die."

The Field is the World, Matthew 13:38

"The field is the world"—all of it (Matt. 28:18; Mark 16:15), "every nation and tongue and tribe and people" (Rev. 5:9; 7:9; 11:9; 14:6). The latter expression is a Hebraism for the totality of the human race.

The church is "the salt of the earth" and "the light of the world"—the whole of its inhabitants (Matt. 5:13-16). In Acts 1:8 Luke epitomizes the Great Commission, recording Jesus as saying, "Ye shall be my witnesses both in Jerusalem, and in all Judea, and Samaria, and unto the uttermost parts of the earth." Incidentally, that text is the framework, the outline, of Luke's account of the manner in which the apostolic church addressed itself to the Great Commission. Chapters 1-7 revolve around the beginnings of the church in Jerusalém, and in Judea. Chapters 8-11 trace the expansion of the church into Samaria. (Chapter 12 is parenthetical, a flashback to the church in Jerusalem.) Chapters 13ff. trace the expansion of the church far and wide, the beginnings of worldwide evangelism. Peter, addressing the first Gentile converts (Acts 10:34) and Paul (in Acts 17:30, 31) have underscored the fact that the Gospel is worldwide in its scope. No nation is to be denied.

Those persons who are not concerned about the conversion of the unevangelized nations are either ignorant or forgetful of their indebtedness to nations both before and beyond their own time and place. Except for converted pure-blooded Jews (of whom there are few, if any), every one of us represents a race, or races, which were once a mission field to the Christian faith. Paul once spoke of himself as "a debtor to all men" (Rom. 1:14). As Christians, are not we all? In a sense, are we not even the more so? As Gentiles of heterogenous ancestry, we are debtors by reason of our Christian heritage, and we are also debtors by reason of our obligation to share with others what so many others shared to prepare the way for us.

The other side of that coin is the exploitation of the proxy principle. There are persons who can become emotionally and financially involved in foreign missions—perhaps even head up the missions committee of their congregation, but who are disturbed when individuals of obvious third world extraction begin to infiltrate their congregation. I recall the case of two classmates from my seminary days, a couple whose hearts seemed set on going to the Congo as missionaries. Their candidacy had been approved by the United Christian Missionary Society of the Disciples of Christ. But shortly before their graduation, they were notified that for economic reasons the UCMS was obliged to cut back on overseas personnel. No new missionaries would be sent forth in the foreseeable future. They shared their anger and disappointment with the dean of the seminary. He called to their attention that the city of Enid (Oklahoma) had a considerable black sector in which only token evangelism was being done by the Southern Baptists and Methodists. He suggested that since they were working their way through school they ought to consider holding on to their jobs and gain valuable experience by starting a mission to the blacks in Enid. According to Dean Marshall, their indignant response was that they were not about to work with "those dirty . . . (ethnic slur)."

That couple was no doubt of kindred spirit with the lad who upon being asked what he wanted to be when he grew up, responded, "a returned missionary." The field is the world. The world begins next door, and stretches far and wide. Sometimes it begins in our own homes. Anyone moved by a sense of mission to win another person to Christ is a missionary. While it is true that the word missionary stems from a root which is the Latin equivalent of the Greek word from which our apostle has been coined, hence means "one sent," the distance factor is incidental. The purpose of the sending is the important thing. Recall the original commission to the apostles as recorded in Matthew 10:5, 6, to wit:

> These twelve Jesus *sent forth,* and charged them, saying: Go not into any way of the Gentiles, and enter not into any city of the Samaritans; but go rather to the lost sheep of the house of Israel.

The twelve disciples did not become the twelve apostles when their commission was universalized in the Great Commission. They were the "ones sent" (apostles) in the instance of the first commission also.

The Seed of the Kingdom

The field (the soil) is the world; the seed of the kingdom is the Gospel, the good news, the evangel. Evangelism, whether at home or abroad, is accomplished by evangelists proclaiming the evangel. This is a point that is often overlooked by the ecumenicists who put social service ahead of soul salvation on the premise that one cannot give much thought to the things of the Spirit when hungry. But the obverse is the more easily demonstrated. Our affluent society, surfeited with pleasures and creature comforts, is hard to convince they have need of anything save more of what they already have and are enjoying.

One of the current hindrances to world evangelism is the fact that the heathen often confuse Christianity with our western civilization. Once they were reported as saying, "we want your Christ, but not your Christianity"; meaning generally they did not want to become western-ized. Today, a new generation, bribed and plied by first the communist bloc and then the democracies, or both at the same time if they have learned to play the ends against the middle, have been awakened to the possibilities of a more affluent lifestyle. And they like it. To achieve it they will take help from either source, or both. But awareness of spiritual needs often gets lost in the shuffle.

The Gospel is the power of God unto salvation (Rom. 1:16). The first business of the church is the preaching of the Gospel to all the nations (Matt. 28:18; Mark 16:15). It is the mind of Christ, not our culture, which needs to shine forth as a light in the life of every missionary, and every Christian.

The Sowers, Sent Forth to Sow

The field (the soil) is the world; the seed is "the everlasting Gospel to be proclaimed unto all them that dwell upon the earth" (Rev. 14:6), and the sowers are those sent forth to proclaim the Gospel. Who ought they to be? Ideally, every Christian. This is the logical inference to be drawn from the Great Commission as it is stated in Matthew 28:19, 20. The commission reads: "Go ye (the disciples to whom the charge was first given) into all the world and make disciples (adherents—taught and 'caught' by the Gospel), baptizing them (those discipled) into the name of the Father, and of the Son, and of the Holy Spirit, teaching them (those baptized) to observe all things whatsoever I commanded you."

The pronoun "them" (Gr. *autous*) of v. 20 is identical in form, scope, and specific reference to the "autous" (them) of v. 19. The same persons who are to be baptized are the persons who are then to be taught to do all the things their teachers were under commandment to do: 1) go (literally, "having gone"—except for shut-ins and recluses, everyone goes somewhere), 2) make disciples, 3) baptize them, and 4) teach them to go and do likewise. A continuing, recycling chain-reaction process is a built-in feature of the Great Commission. The whole church from its inception to the end of the age is under Divine mandate to fulfill the Great Commission.

Mark this, the commission does not read, "make disciples of *all* the nations, baptize *all* those discipled, but teach only a select *few* to continue the cycle." Making and baptizing disciples is not a restricted ministry, the privilege of a favored few. But at the same time, it is written that when Jesus ascended on high, having led captivity captive, he gave gifts unto men (Eph. 4:8); and included in those gifts is the role of evangelists.

What has just been noted is not contradictory. It is rather precautionary. Jesus well knew that what is "everybody's business" tends to become "nobody's business," unless somebody is specifically assigned to that business. But even if that were not so in this instance; even if every person evangelized, whether a farmer, bookkeeper, housewife, traveling salesman, or whatever, were to do the work of an evangelist whenever opportunity came, that would not make the role of specialized full-time evangelists unnecessary. Whether those who pioneer for Christ among hitherto untouched tribes and tongues and people are called missionaries or evangelists is academic.

The Holy Spirit said to the church at Antioch: "Separate unto me Barnabas and Saul for the work whereunto I have called them" (Acts 13:2). The work to which they were ceremoniously sent forth was much the same as the work which they were already doing. But it differed in one important respect. It took them into population centers where the Gospel had never before been taken. They became thereby itinerant workers. But that is not when they became evangelists.

Years afterwards, Timothy, who aforetime had been a traveling companion of Paul, but who was engaged in a resident ministry in Ephesus at the time Paul addressed two letters to him, was exhorted: "Do the work of an evangelist, fulfill thy ministry" (II Tim. 4:5). Timothy was not thereby being chided and commanded to pack up and get moving. There is nothing intrinsic in the term evangelist which demands that one so called be an itinerant preacher.

The work of evangelism is the first task of the church. Home evangelism and foreign evangelism are not options. The home field and foreign field are the twofold loci of the church's evangelistic responsibility.

From the inception of the Christian era Christ "gave some to be evangelists" on a full-time basis. He still does so. But the truism stands: It will take the whole church teaching the whole Gospel to evangelize the whole world. There comes to mind some lines from a rallying song which was often sung in the opening exercises of the Bible school hour in the days when the Bible school was more widely used as an evangelistic arm of the church:

If to Christ our Lord and King
Men redeemed we strive to bring,
In just one way may this be done:
We must win them one by one.

If you will bring the one next to you
And I will bring the one next to me,
In all kinds of weather
We will all work together
And see what can be done.

So, you bring the one next to you,
And I'll bring the one next to me
And in no time at all
We will win them all.
So win them, win them, one by one.

2. *The Work of Spiritual Nurture*

The work of spiritual nurture begins anew every time the discipling process brings forth a newly baptized babe in Christ. It is only consummated (if ever) when every child of God within the congregation's potential influence has become a full-grown Christian. It therefore bears repeating: The Great Commission gives to the church its charter, constituting the church a teaching institution whose field is the world and whose commission is to the end of time.

Were every human being on earth brought to an obedient faith in the Lord Jesus Christ, the Great Commission would not yet be fulfilled. It is therefore written that Christ not only gave some to be apostles, and some, prophets, and some evangelists, but he also gave some to be pastors and teachers (Eph. 4:11). The verses which follow tell us why:

> for the perfecting of the saints unto the work of ministering, unto the building up of the body of Christ: till we all attain unto the unity of the faith, and of the knowledge of the son of God, unto a fullgrown man, unto the measure of the stature of the fulness of Christ: that we may be no longer children, tossed to and fro, carried about by every wind of doctrine, by the sleight of men, in craftiness, after the wiles of error; but speaking truth in love, may grow up in all things into him, who is the head, even Christ; from whom all the body, fitly framed and knit together through that which every joint supplieth, according to the working in due measure of each several part, maketh the increase of the body unto the building up of itself in love (Eph. 4:12-16).

408

The Goal of the Whole Christian Enterprise

What is the goal of the whole Christian enterprise, collectively and individually? To get us all to heaven (particularly one's self, speaking individually)? So it is commonly supposed. Through the years the foregoing question has been posed to hundreds of students. Almost invariably they have responded thusly.

What then is the goal of the Christian life? This is not just an academic question. It can seriously affect our lifestyle. In fact, it does. If one's personal goal as a Christian is simply to get to heaven and thereby escape the alternative (going to hell), there is an ever present temptation to do only what is necessary to "get by." This is best epitomized by the response of an elder who for the first time was forced to grapple with the doctrine of conditional immortality. "If the unsaved at some point in the age to come may be annihilated, why become a Christian?" he asked, "And why bother to try to persuade anyone else to become a Christian?"

How do you suppose such an attitude comes across to Christ? What heartache it must cause him. If the only reason one becomes a Christian is to escape suffering endless torment in hell; if the privations and struggles of the Christian life are but the lesser of two evils; if one's heart's desire is not to be like Christ, and be with Christ; then what fellowship, what rapport with Christ could such a one have with Christ even if "we all get to heaven" in that state of mind?

Suppose at Christ's coming he were to ask each of us where we would prefer to spend eternity. Presuming each of us would answer, "in heaven," suppose he would then ask, "Why there?" Were one to answer, "We really don't have much choice. Apparently it is either heaven or hell. That brings it down to a choice between the company and the climate. I've got a lot of friends who are going to hell. We've had some great times together. Some of them have been my idols. But I am a weakling when it comes to suffering, so I am opting for heaven."

If that be our goal, it is doubtful we shall ever attain it. "All This and Heaven Too" is a hope or a promise of the script writers of Hollywood, not the Holy Scriptures given us by God.

Heaven Is Not Our Goal—It Is Our Destination

The Christian's goal is not heaven. Heaven is our destination. Each spring, for more than thirty years, following the close of the spring semester I have gone fishing in the Canadian wilderness. My destination, generally, is a chain of lakes which form a principal tributary of the

English River of northern Ontario. But those sparkling lakes are not my goal. My goal is to catch a fish so large I will not even be tempted to lie about it. To be more serious, my goal is respite from the pressures of a busy teaching and speaking schedule; enjoyment of the breath-taking beauty of the nearly unspoiled wilderness; the fellowship and devotions we enjoy each evening about the campfire; and the thrill of wrestling with trophy-sized northern pike, and enjoying my share of being the one fortunate enough to land the biggest. The locale, my destination, is but a means to those desired ends. I know of no other place all of them can be so fully realized.

Likewise, heaven is not my goal. It is our promised destination. It is there that we who love Christ and have striven to do his will and to be like him shall achieve at last what we can only strive after in this present world. There, and only there, will we escape the lusts of the flesh, the lust of the eyes, and the vain glory of this world (I John 2:16). Only in heaven, stripped of "the body of our humiliation" and re-clothed in bodies "like unto his glorious body" (Phil. 3:21) shall we enjoy the fullness of the promise: "We shall be like him, for we shall see him as he is" (I John 3:2b). Thus it is written: "Every one that has this hope set on him, purifieth himself, even as he is pure" (v. 3).

The Goal of the Christian Life Restated

Paul's phrasing of the goal of the Christian life is expressly stated in the text which has already been cited (Eph. 4:12-16). There, amplified and illuminated by an illustrative analogy, Paul tells us plainly the purpose toward which every appointed office (function) of the church is designed and is to be directed. "He (Christ) gave some to be apostles, some prophets, some evangelists, and some pastors and teachers" (Eph. 4:11). Why? Condensed in a few words, "for the perfecting (Gr. *katartismon*—rendering fit, suitable for service) of the saints unto the work of ministering, unto the building up of the body of Christ . . . unto a fullgrown (Gr. *teleion*, "mature, complete") man, unto the measure of the stature of the fulness of Christ" (Eph. 4:12, 13b).

This is in complete harmony with what Jesus stated in his sermon on the mount: "Be ye perfect (Gr. *teleioi*) even as your father in heaven is perfect" (Matt. 5:48). The Greek word which appears in both of the texts cited above, and commonly rendered perfect, does not primarily mean faultless in the sense of moral perfection, as is commonly sup-posed, though it is broad enough in its scope to include that idea. The root meaning of the term relates to the *end*, that is, the design or purpose for which a process is instituted. A newborn baby is pronounced

410

perfect by the attending physician if it is born whole, very much alive, well-proportioned; and all the basic reflexes essential for ready adaptation to life outside the womb are observable and functioning. Never mind the fact that the newly born infant is as ignorant as a newborn calf and considerably more helpless and fragile. The umbilical cord and other accessories to life in the womb have accomplished all they were Divinely designed to do. The baby is therefore perfect in the sense of being whole, complete, a finished product of the prenatal state and apparatus. But unless that baby is properly fed and clothed and exercised, it will not become a "perfect" child, or adolescent, or teenager, or mature man or woman.

THE THREE ESSENTIALS OF GROWTH

There are three essentials of growth: proper food, proper environmental conditions, and proper exercise/activity. Note the repetition of the adjective in the foregoing phrases.

Proper Food—An Essential to Life, Health, and Growth

The proper food for one form of life could prove deadly if eaten by others. Buzzards and maggots thrive on putrefaction. As Christians we need to feed our minds on the Word of God. We need the bread of heaven as well as the bread of the oven. In his temptation in the wilderness Jesus recalled the words of Moses: "Man shall not live by bread alone but by every word that proceedeth from the mouth of God" (Matt. 4:4, cp. Deut. 8:3). Do you suppose he meant that? How long has it been since you read the Scriptures through, from Genesis to Revelation? Have you ever read the whole Bible? Have you ever read the entire New Testament? Or even one of the Gospels?

Along with proper food we need proper eating habits. To gorge oneself one day and then starve oneself for days afterwards is not conducive to health. We need to read the Scriptures 1) systematically and carefully. We will grow thereby in knowledge. We need to read them also 2) sincerely and prayerfully. It is thus that we grow in grace (cp. II Peter 3:18).

Paul commended Timothy on the fact that from a babe he had known the sacred Scriptures which are able to make one wise unto salvation (II Tim. 3:15). But he also charged him to give diligence (to study) to present himself approved unto God, a workman that needeth not to be ashamed, handling aright the word of truth (II Tim. 2:15).

The Corinthians were rebuked that they had remained as babes, still feeding on the milk of the Word when they ought to have been ready

411

for the meat of the Word (I Cor. 3:2). The writer of the epistle to the Hebrews was equally caustic when he wrote:

When, by reason of time, ye ought to be teachers, you have need again that some one teach you the rudiments of the first principles of the oracles of God: and are become such as have need of milk, and not of solid food. For every one that partaketh of milk is without experience of the word of righteousness; for he is a babe. But solid food is for full-grown men, even those who by reason of use have their senses exercised (literally, "gymnasticized") to discern good and evil (Heb. 5:12-14).

Exercise Thyself Unto Godliness

Exercise, participation in a variety of Christian activities, is an essential to spiritual growth, health, and life. Paul told Timothy to engage in spiritual gymnastics; noting that bodily exercise is profitable for a little (quite a little, we might add), but godliness is even more profitable, "having the promise of the life that now is, and of that which is to come" (see I Tim. 4:7b, 8). The Greek word commonly translated "exercise" is *gumnazo*, from whence is derived our word gymnasium.

Paul was a Christian activist. Healthy, growing, zestful Christians always are. Even shut-ins who find some way of expressing and sharing their faith continue to thrive spiritually though their bodies may be wasting away. During his imprisonment Paul wrote letters, received visitors, and apparently made inroads for Christ "throughout the whole praetorian guard" and even in "Caesar's household." (See Phil. 1:13 and 4:22.)

Physically, unused muscles tend to atrophy. Neglected skills and talents diminish. An idle brain has been called "the devil's workshop." Idleness in spiritual service may lead to doubt. Recall the case of John, the baptist, who stood fearlessly before King Herod and pronounced the judgment of God upon his wickedness. But that same John, the forerunner of Christ who boldly declared Jesus to be the long-awaited Messiah, "the lamb of God that taketh away the sin of the world" (John 1:29), when cast into prison and forced into inactivity, found his faith wavering. The time came when he sent his disciples to Jesus, asking: "Art thou he that cometh or must we look for another?" (Matt. 11:3).

Recall the parable of the ejected unclean spirit who returned to find the house from which he was cast out empty, swept, and garnished—clean, but empty! He proceeded to round up seven other spirits even more evil than himself and took occupancy of that house. "And the last state of that man," whose house (life) had been cleansed, became "worse than the first" (Matt. 12:43-45). Once saved, always saved? Saved by faith only? "Ye did not so learn Christ!" (Eph. 4:20).

Nature abhors a vacuum. Wherever a vacuum is created, nature rushes in to fill it. This is also true in the spiritual world. A new convert cannot survive if cleansed only. One cannot turn from using the name of God and his Son as handy curse words to no mention of them, not even in prayer. One cannot turn from evil companionships to no companionship. One cannot turn from reading filth and falsehood to reading nothing. One cannot turn from frequenting bars and theaters to going nowhere. Oh, one can do so. It does happen. But we mean to say one cannot do so and experience Christian growth. Many a sincere convert has been lost again, becoming as a sow that has been washed returning to the mire, and as a dog returning to his own vomit (II Peter 2:22). Taking his cue from Jesus in the parable cited above, Peter says of such persons, "the last state is become worse with them than the first" (v. 21).

The church is under obligation to guide new converts into activities and associations which will fill the void that is left when the task of spiritual housecleaning has been undertaken. We are as responsible for the nurture and care of babes in Christ as parents and older siblings are when a new baby is born into the home.

Desires are awakened in children by observing what others are doing. They become aware of their potentialities, of their possibilities, through observing their role models. It is no less so of the children of God. New converts soon observe that a perfunctory attendance at the Sunday morning worship service is the extent of the involvement of the greater part of the church family in visible Christian activity. Even of the leaders of the church this is often so. What they see being done (or not done) speaks more loudly to them than what they are told should be done. Proper activities in which to engage and the example of role models thusly engaged are essential to Christian growth.

God's Environmental Protection Agency

The church is God's environmental protection agency. Every form of life requires an environment suited to its need. The proper habitat for a porpoise is not suited to a person. Astronauts are obliged to carry the earth's atmosphere with them as they are projected into outer space. This is artificially maintained by elaborate means.

As a nation we are becoming increasingly conscious of air pollution. Industrial and power companies are now obliged to spend millions of dollars in efforts to reverse the trend that has made the very air we

413

breathe and the water we drink life threatening. It is the church's business to create and/or restore a favorable environment for the soul. The wanton pollution of the soul's atmosphere by the big industries—the entertainment media, the press, manufacturers, and merchandisers—combined with changing educational and political philosophies are forcing the church into a life-death struggle.

Like the air which we breathe, our spiritual atmosphere is made up of three basic elements—praise, meditation, and fellowship.

1) Praise is the heart of all true worship. Worship is not just something done in a "worship service." Worship *is* service—service to God, that is. Paul, in Romans 12:2, uses one of the several Greek words translated "worship" (*latreuo*) to so inform us. Our English word is derived from an anglo-saxon word, *worthscipe,* meaning "worth-ship." Whatsoever we ascribe "worth" to, supreme worth, becomes our God. Thus Paul could rightly say, "covetousness is idolatry" (Col. 3:5).

We repeatedly praise those things and persons which we count to be of high worth. We are most comfortable with others who share our value system. We attempt to "evangelize" our associates who do not share some facets of our value system. "Out of the abundance of the heart the mouth speaketh" (Matt. 12:34). Love that is not expressed is not long possessed. The praise of God and of Christ is essential to spiritual growth.

2) With praise we must combine meditation. Meditation is the spring from which praise flows. Praise is but a froth or a frill unless it is the overflowing of a well spring of contemplation upon the mercies and the glories of God. Well has the poet written:

> This is my Father's world,
> And to my listening ears,
> All nature sings and 'round me rings
> The music of the spheres.
>
> This is my Father's world.
> I rest me in the thought
> Of rocks and trees, of skies and seas,
> His hand the wonders wrought.
>
> This is my Father's world.
> The birds their carols raise,
> The morning light, the lilies white,
> Declare their Maker's praise.
>
> This is my Father's world.
> He shines in all that's fair.
> In the rustling grass I hear Him pass.
> He speaks to me everywhere.

That hymn reflects the mind of Christ. He wove the threads of the world about him into the rich tapestry of his sermons and parables of the providence and power of God. He lived and moved in an atmosphere of God-consciousness. Meditation is the well spring of praise.

3) Fellowship is the third essential element which makes up the atmosphere in which the soul of a Christian can best thrive. Nature should teach us that. Birds of a feather flock together. Like not only begets like; it attracts, nurtures, and protects like. We betray what and whom we really like by our association choices. Thus it is written: "Let us consider one another, to provoke (Gr. *paroxusmon*, stimulate, incite) unto love and good works, not forsaking our own assembling together, but exhorting (one another) and so much more, as you see the day approaching" (Heb. 10:24, 25). Tradition holds that the Roman world was given to exclaim concerning the early church, "Behold how the Christians love one another." Lovers long for each other when absent, and seize every opportunity to be together and share with one another.

The Guide to the Goal

The guide to the goal of the Christian life is the Bible, particularly the New Testament. The New Covenant Scriptures provide not so much a book of rules to govern conduct but a set of ideals (preeminently modeled by Christ) to engender character. Conduct is what we do. Character is what we are. If we are what we ought to be, we will do what we ought to do. (The converse of that is not equally true, but it sometimes helps.) "Keep thy heart with all diligence, for out of it are the issues of life" (Prov. 4:23).

Under the old Covenant God presented fleshly Israel with a set of rules by which they were to conduct themselves. But they soon devised ways and means of keeping the letter of the law while voiding the spirit of the law. In his sermon on the mount, Jesus dealt with the spirit behind the law, closing that sector of his sermon with the text out of which our present discussion has arisen: "Ye therefore shall be (imperative future) perfect (Gr. *teleoi*, mature) as your father in heaven is!" (Matt. 5:48).

This is not to say there is no place for letter of the law instruction and rebuke of evil in the context of the Christian faith. (See II Tim. 3:16, 17; 4:2; cp. Rom. 1:18-32; I Cor., virtually throughout; Gal. 5:16-21; Eph. 4:17—5:18; etc.) Chastening and rebuke are not, however, to be the focal center of "instruction which is in righteousness."

Teaching concerning Christian character building tends to polarize. On the one hand it can become so generalized as to be void of specifics.

415

On the other hand the Christian life is sometimes made to appear as an array of prohibitions. The symbol of the Christian faith is not a moral minus sign. The plus benefits of bearing Christ's cross should be preeminent. I once heard of a sailor who felt as though the chaplain's sermon on the ten commandments had flayed him right to the bone. But toward the afternoon a happy thought came to him. He had never made a graven image. Having missed the point of the chaplain's application of that particular commandment, the pangs of guilt began to subside. At least there was one commandment he had not broken, at least not outwardly.

Christian righteousness is not measured simply by compiling a list of bad things we do not do. The familiar parody, "I don't smoke, and I don't chew, and I don't go with boys (girls) who do" could be said of a fence post. "Except (our) righteousness exceed the righteousness of the scribes and Pharisees (we) shall in no wise enter into the kingdom of heaven" (Matt. 5:20).

On the other hand much of today's preaching is so generalized in its teaching concerning sin that sin loses any sense of specificity. The individual members of the flourishing family of Sin(s) have "first names," as does each of us. Besides four distinguishable sub-families, over one gross of specific sins are named outright in the Scriptures.

Categorical Listing of Sins

The New Testament contains several categorical lists of sins. They may be catalogued under seven headings: 1) Sins bearing direct reference to God, 2) Sins which root in human pride, 3) Other sins of the heart, 4) Sins which involve perversion or abuse of the sex drive, 5) Other sins of the flesh, 6) Sins against society, other than sex abuse and perversion, and 7) General terms. The following texts contain listings of specific sins: Romans 1:18-32; I Corinthians 6:9, 10; Galatians 5:19-21; Ephesians 4:17-19, 25-31; 5:2-5; I Timothy 1:9, 10; II Timothy 3:2-8; Titus 3:3, 9, 10; Revelation 21:8; 22:15.

Biblical Definitions of Sins

The two words most commonly translated "sin" are the Hebrew word *chatah* and the Greek word *hamartia*. Primarily they denote "a missing"; more specifically, "missing the mark." It is commonly noted that the etymological origin of the words is to be found in the context of archery. In ancient times the target was not a "bullseye" surrounded by concentric rings, making up in the aggregate a target large enough to accommodate even fledgling archers. It was rather a peeled willow wand scarcely larger (if any) than the shaft of the arrows that were directed toward the mark. With such a mark before them, the archers either hit the mark, or they missed it (hemarton—"sinned"). There was no such thing as a "near miss," at least it did not register. If the arrow missed the wand by a mere fraction of an inch, it went on by to fall to earth somewhere beyond.

In the context of the Christian faith, to sin is to miss the mark of the perfect and singular example we have in Christ. Narrow is the way, the "mark." There is none that does not miss the mark of our high calling in Christ Jesus to some degree.

There are four sub-divisions of sin. 1) Unrighteousness. John affirms "all unrighteousness (Gr. *adikia*) is sin" (I John 5:17). That stands to reason. If it is not right, it is wrong. The negative prefix affixed to the term for righteousness is used in this text.

2) In I John 3:4, John states: "Sin is lawlessness" (Gr. *anomia*). Here the word used describes sin in a more sinister fashion. Sin is that which is un/not lawful. A sinner is therefore an outlaw. One is certainly so if the sin is willful. Such is the core of the outlaw mentality.

3) James declares, "He that knoweth to do good and doeth it not, to him it is sin" (James 4:17). The neglect of known good is sinful, because it is an insight into one's value system. It is possible, of course, to neglect to do one thing that is good in order to do that which contributes to the greater good. But in that case, the one could not rightly be called "neglected." That is not the context in which James is speaking. He is not talking about one who leaves a beggar with an empty outstretched hand to run and snatch to safety a toddler that has wandered into a busy street. He is talking about the sins of deliberate omission.

4) Paul, in Romans 14:23, declares, "That which is not of faith is sin." This is the sin against conscience. The thing which is done may not of itself be wrong. It may even, of itself, be a proper thing to do. But if it is done against one's better judgment, if it violates one's sense of right or wrong, it can impair one's moral fiber. It can weaken the voice of conscience. It can blunt the stabbing of a sense of guilt.

Our Conscience Is Not Our Guide

It needs to be noted that "our conscience is *not* our guide" as it is commonly supposed and said to be. It is not a voice within us telling

417

us what is right and what is wrong. Consider the example of the apostle Paul. In Acts 23:2 we find him declaring: "I have lived before God in all good conscience until this day." Did he mean to say he presided at the stoning of Stephen and laid waste the church in all good conscience? Indeed he did. How could he? Because his judgment was that the followers of Jesus were enemies of God who would destroy the law that had been given through Moses. Being so persuaded, and being zealous for the law, his judgment was that he ought to oppose the sect of the Nazarene in every way open to him. And he did. And his conscience commended him for it. One's conscience does that. It commends doing what we sincerely believe is the thing to do. Later Paul had an experience which completely reversed his judgment, and hence his actions. What once he judged should be opposed with all his ability and resources, he thereafter judged should be promoted with all his ability and resources. At the stoning of Stephen his conscience said in effect, "Bravo, Paul you are God's warrior, fighting the good fight of the faith. Keep it up." His conscience spoke to him the same thing as he came down to his life's closing having by then given more than thirty years to the service of Christ.

That is the reason we need to search the Scriptures daily to see what things are so. Our conscience is not our guide. At best, if we have not blunted it or seared it as with a hot iron, our conscience is our goad. (Cp. Acts 26:14.) Our judgment determines what we think is right or wrong. But our judgment is faulty, being influenced by what we read, what we are told, and what we see. Only from the Scriptures can we come to know that which is right in God's sight.

"Give diligence to present thyself approved unto God, a workman that needeth not to be ashamed, handling aright the Word of Truth" (II Tim. 2:15). In a day when the church is torn by division and suffering reproach, some of it in part deserved considering its present state (to which sad state each of us has contributed at least one spot, wrinkle, or blemish), be it recalled that Christ foresaw all this. Yet, it is written:

> Christ loved the church and gave himself up for it; that he might sanctify it, having cleansed it with the washing of water with the word, that he might present the church to himself a glorious church, not having spot or wrinkle or any such thing, but that it should be holy and without blemish (Eph. 5:25-27).

If we are to have the mind of Christ, if we are to have the approval of Christ, if we are to be workmen that need not to be ashamed, if we are to have "boldness and be unashamed before him at his coming"

418

(I John 2:28); what the Bible says about the church, and what he commissioned his church to do, we must be found believing and doing at his coming. Awake! Arise! On with the task! It is getting late!

PREVIEW—REVIEW QUESTIONS

1. Complete the sentence: "The Great Commission gives to the church . . ." (Locate Bk., Ch., Vs., the textual data.)
2. Distinguish between the two Greek words translated "teach" in the King James Version.
3. State the first business of the church.
4. State the second task of the church which immediately ensues as the first begins to produce results.
5. How big is the field assigned the church? Document your answer.
6. Precisely, what is the seed to be sown? Document.
7. Who are to be the sowers? Was provision made for a) exceptions? b) specialists? Document.
8. Cite a text where the second task of the church is elaborated upon, and explained via an analogy.
9. State the true goal of the whole Christian enterprise.
10. If heaven is not our goal, what is the function or purpose served by heaven?
11. State the three essentials of growth.
12. Note the Biblical provision for each of the three.
13. State the three elements which constitute a proper environment for Christian growth.
14. Identify the true guide to the goal of the Christian life.
15. Comment on the common error that one should "let one's conscience be one's guide."
16. If that is not the role of conscience, state the true role it is designed to serve.
17. What can hinder the conscience from its designed task?
18. State the basic meaning of the Hebrew and Greek words most commonly translated "sin."
19. State and distinguish between John's two definitions of sin.
20. Explain the circumstance or state James defines as sin.
21. Relate Romans 15:23 to the role of the conscience as previously noted.
22. Note a text which particularly sets forth the "mind of Christ" with respect to the church.

APPENDIX

A Third Look at the Baptism of the Holy Spirit

The use of too familiar terms may lead to unwarranted conclusions.

There are two principal, but opposing, views on the subject of the baptism of the Holy Spirit. The "Pentecostal" position is that the baptism of the Holy Spirit, as credentialized by the speaking in tongues, was the normative experience of the apostolic church, hence the mark of apostolicity and restoration of the true church in the latter days. A verse (Joel 2:23) taken from the same chapter of Joel that Peter quoted on the day of Pentecost is commonly cited as proof of their position. Therein it is written: "Be glad then, ye children of Zion, and rejoice in Jehovah your God: for he giveth you the former rain in just measure (lit., in righteousness), and he causeth to come down for you the rain, the former rain and the latter rain." The phrase, "the former rain and the latter rain," is interpreted as promising that an outpouring of miraculous spiritual gifts would mark both the first years of the church and its last.

The position that has become traditional with our own "Restoration" movement denies that the baptism of the Holy Spirit, as credentialized by the speaking in tongues, or otherwise, was ever the norm of the church, much less that it is to be the distinguishing mark of a restored church. Our brethren, generally, have taken the position that the baptism of the Holy Spirit was of limited promise both in time and distribution. It was completely and finally fulfilled almost from the outset of the gospel age. The fulfillment is said to have been accomplished representatively. The baptism of the apostles in the Holy Spirit is said to have fulfilled the promise on behalf of the Jews and the baptism of the household of Cornelius is said to have done the same on behalf of the Gentiles.

Those who are of the latter persuasion likewise cite Joel to support their position. The expression, "I will pour forth of my spirit upon all flesh" is interpreted as referring to the two divisions of the human race, Jew and Gentiles, *through chosen representatives,* and was thus fulfilled in two episodes—Pentecost, and at the induction of the Gentiles into the church via the conversion of the Gentile household of Cornelius. Those so persuaded find it necessary, however, to crack the thenceforth closed door a bit (just once!) to credentialize Saul of Tarsus for the apostleship. For he both professed and demonstrated himself to be "not a whit behind the very chiefest apostles," (II Cor. 11:5).

Recently, some among those of the "faith only" persuasion have attempted to accommodate the many texts which link baptism with

420

salvation, even the means thereto, by affirming that such texts as Acts 2:38; 22:16; Mark 16:16; Galatians 3:27; etc., etc., refer to Holy Spirit baptism. They would have it believed that unless water is specifically mentioned, as in the case of John's baptism and the baptism of the Ethiopian Eunuch, the baptism of the Holy Spirit is to be inferred. In this they are half right, as we shall demonstrate later, but a half-truth is worse than a lie.

In the "faith only" reconstruction of the Biblical doctrine of baptism the revisionists avoid addressing themselves to the phenomena that accompanied the baptism in the Holy Spirit on the two occasions which are indisputably so identified. Their focus is on finding an escape hatch from the New Testament doctrine of baptism for remission of sins. If the repeated New Testament linkage of baptism with salvation may be interpreted as referring to Holy Spirit baptism, versus baptism in water, then the dogma of salvation by faith alone can be proclaimed with less and less respect for what Paul calls "the obedience of faith" (See Rom. 1:5; 16:26; cp. 6:16-18).

It is time, therefore, that we take a serious "third look" at what the New Testament teaches concerning this subject. I am persuaded neither the Pentecostal "restorationist" position nor our own "two-episode" theory squares with what the New Testament teaches concerning this important subject.

Stereotyped "loaded" terms need to be reassessed

In order that we may take a third look at the subject with a lesser degree of bias, let us lay aside the sterotyped "loaded" terms of the past and try to find some new forms of expression that are not immediately defined controversially as soon as they are mentioned.

The discussion of spiritual gifts has long been categorized under such headings as: 1) The baptismal gift of the Holy Spirit (or simply, the baptism of the Holy Spirit), 2) The spiritual gifts (plural) of the Holy Spirit (or the "extraordinary" or "miraculous" gifts of the Holy Spirit) and 3) *the* gift (singular) of the Holy Spirit; *and in that order downward.* The latter has also been commonly designated as the "ordinary" gift of the Holy Spirit, or less disparagingly as "the indwelling presence" of the Holy Spirit.

Those of the non-Pentecostal persuasion have espoused the position that 1) the twelve apostles (Matthias included) received the baptism of the Holy Spirit on the day of Pentecost for the duration of their apostleship, and 2) Cornelius and his household received the baptismal gift, but on a limited basis. That is, for them the gift was a) but an affair of the moment, and b) included no more than the power to speak in tongues on that solitary occasion. How then could Peter say the Holy Spirit "fell on them, even as on us at the beginning" and speak of it as "the like gift"? (See Acts 11:15-17). Is the baptism of the Holy Spirit to be equated with speaking in tongues, as some would have us believe? And if so, how account for the fact that when the apostles received the baptism of the Holy Spirit they were empowered to do so much more? Incidentally, it is not recorded that the apostles ever again so spake as they did on the day of Pentecost, although Paul, the late-comer to the apostolic office, implies he could and did, (I Cor. 14:18).

The case of Cornelius and his household presents a problem to both of the entrenched positions. If theirs indeed was a like gift, that is a gift like that which was received by the twelve apostles "at the beginning," how is it that they received only one of the gifts which Paul lists in I Corinthians 12:8-10 (and that only for a moment, relatively speaking, at least of the record)? And how does all this square with the prophecy of Joel?

If none of the approximately one hundred and twenty brethren who participated in the choosing of Matthias (Acts 1:15), except for the twelve apostles, (cp. 1:26) received the baptism of the Holy Spirit in behalf of the Jewish sector of the human race, that virtually eliminates womankind from the gift; at least "in the beginning," and insofar as the Jews are concerned. Yet, Joel himself interpreted the expression "upon all flesh" as relating to both sons and daughters, servants and handmaids, old men and young (Joel 2:28, 29). The language says nothing about the gift being given on a restrictive basis—racially, and that only representatively, a handful in either case fulfilling the quota for the whole of the human race.

And that is not the end of the problem. The context in which the New Testament predictions of the forthcoming baptism in the Holy Spirit, administered by the Messiah (particularly as phrased in the fuller recording of the promise as found in Matthew 3:9-12 and Luke 3:8, 9) do not jibe with the two-episode theory of the baptism of the Holy Spirit. Two baptisms are there spoken of. They are spoken of in the language of universality, not representation. Together, the two baptisms, the baptism in the Holy Spirit and the baptism in fire, encompass the whole of the human race. Except for the forced interpretation of the baptism of the Holy Spirit and fire as being two facets of the same thing, as in extremist Pentecostal theology, the "baptism in fire is commonly recognized as referring to the destruction (or endless burning) of the whole of the unsaved in the lake of fire. How then may the other baptism spoken of, the baptism in the Holy Spirit, be restricted to a handful of Jews and a household of Gentiles, and be limited as well to the onset of the gospel age?

As an alternative to the traditional terminology, may I suggest three descriptive terms which I have found helpful in conducting a restudy: 1) The Apostolic or Unique gift of the Holy Spirit, 2) The Assisting or Utilitarian gift(s) of the Holy Spirit, and 3) the Abiding or Universal gift of the Holy Spirit.

The Apostolic (Unique) Gift

That the apostles had a unique, unequaled, bestowal of the Holy Spirit is admitted by all but the most radical of theorists. How are we to account for the clearly demonstrated apostolic powers and prerogatives? To say they were baptized in the Holy Spirit (which of course they were) is not of itself enough. So was the household of Cornelius. What prerogatives did they thereafter exercise? Upon whom did anyone of them lay their hands and impart thereby the gift of tongues, or some other specialized spiritual gift or power? What portion of the New Testament Scriptures have we received through some one of them? Apart from receiving a credentializing sign, needed to attest to the fact that "to the Gentiles also God hath granted repentance unto life" (Acts 11:18), what else accrued? One thing of record: Peter forthwith challenged the six deep-dyed segregationist Jewish brethren he had wisely, and providentially, brought with him: "Can any man forbid the water, that these should not be baptized, who have received the Holy Spirit as well as we?" (Acts 10:47). Fortunately there had not risen an ancient counterpart of the anti-baptism evangelicalism of our time, thus "he commanded them to be baptized in the name of (by the authority of) Jesus Christ" (v. 48, cp. Matt. 28:18-20).

One possible explanation of the uniqueness of the apostolic gift of the Holy Spirit may be found in the intriguing implications of John 20:22, 23. Following his resurrection Jesus *"breathed* on them, and said, Receive ye the Holy Spirit: whose soever sins ye forgive, they are forgiven unto them; whose soever sins ye retain, they are retained." This passage has but one parallel. At the first creation Jehovah breathed upon the body which he had formed of the ground and "man became a living soul" (Gen. 2:7), the progenitor of the whole of the human race. On the threshold of "the new creation" (II Cor. 5:17) the parent stock from which the church was to stem was breathed upon by its creator. This could mean that the apostles were thereby prepared for a greater receptivity of the Holy Spirit than has been the experience of all others.

The Assisting (Utilitarian) Gifts

Concerning those powers generally classified as the special (or specialized) spiritual gifts, I call attention to the fact they had a definite pragmatic, utilitarian function. They were neither a sign of, nor a reward for, advanced spiritual attainment. The Corinthian church is witness to that fact. According to Paul (I Cor. 1:7) the church at Corinth was second to none in respect to spiritual gifts but they exhibited no evidence of high spiritual attainment. Moreover, Paul affirms that the moral manifestations of the Spirit which are "grown," as distinguished from the miraculous gifts, which were bestowed, are greater and more to be desired. One of the moral gifts alone, love, Paul declares to be more excellent than any or all of the spectacular gifts of which some among them were prone to boast.

Why then were the miraculous gifts given? They were useful. They were of three classes, and served three functions. They consisted of gifts of knowledge, providing special information, gifts of power, pro-viding confirmation, and gifts of labor, providing administration. Witness the necessity for such gifts in the instance of such a church as that at Philippi. The Philippian church represented the first fruits of Paul's labors in Europe. Of the record it consisted of a traveling business woman from Thyatira, possibly a Greek slave girl from whom he cast a spirit of divination, and a local jailor, plus the "household" of the jailor and of Lydia (a company of women in the instance of Lydia and a group unspecified in number and gender in respect to the jailor). Upon Paul's release from prison, possibly the same morning the jailor and his house-hold were converted, Paul was persuaded by the magistrates to leave town, or at least soon thereafter. In doing so he left behind an infant church, of heterogenous makeup, a solitary Christian colony in the midst of a populous pagan city. To the best of our knowledge it was the only company of Christians in all Macedonia (Greece).

How was that church to be sustained? To our knowledge not one book of the New Testament had yet been written. There were no publishing houses from which to order Christain literature. There were no Bible colleges from which they could obtain even a student preacher.

This situation, repeated again and again as Paul established new congregations from place to place and moved on, was the occasion for the imparting of the specialized spiritual gifts. The situation was not always as precipitous and dramatic. He sometimes tarried longer. On occasion converts were made from among the patrons of Jewish synagogues, and even from among the elders thereof, but in all cases they were needing confirmed information and administration. Through the laying on of the apostles' hands (Acts 8:18) specialized spiritual gifts were distributed in lieu of 1) the continuing presence of an inspired apostle, or 2) the possession of the yet to be written New Covenant Scriptures.

Today we receive the necessary information from the confirmed word of the completed canon of the Holy Scriptures (see Heb. 2:1-4, noting the verb tenses, and the order and the channel of revelation succinctly stated). Administration is provided for new churches in our time by leaders developed in sponsoring congregations. The need for apostles and prophets (personally present), miracle workers, healers, discerners of spirits, tongue speakers and interpreters of tongues, has long since been outgrown. "But now abideth faith, hope, love." These, "the greater gifts" (I Cor. 12:31, Ch. 13) are the gifts to be desired. But these, being the fruit of the Holy Spirit, are not "zapped" upon us. They have to be grown, and that takes time. In this day of "instant" everything, many would prefer it to be otherwise.

The Abiding (Universal) Gift

It was a sad day when the abiding, universal gift of the Holy Spirit came to be called the "ordinary" gift. Technically, that which is not unusual, but of general experience, observation or distribution, may be correctly so called. But the term comes across as being somewhat depreciatory when applied to a gift of such consequence as the indwelling presence of the Spirit of God (Rom. 8:11; I Cor. 3:16). A gift of God which, working together with the quickening power latent in the Word of God, and one's desire to be led of the Spirit to be true to the Scriptures in all that one says or does, is far from being "ordinary," no matter how often it is observed to be at work in the hearts of humankind. It is true that we "grow in the grace and in the knowledge of our Lord and Saviour Jesus Christ," (II Peter 3:18).

In view of the fact that "the Spirit of him (God) that raised up Jesus from the dead" is said to be "dwelling" (Gr. enoikountos, lit., "inhoused") in us, (Rom. 8:11; I Cor. 3:16), the gift of the Holy Spirit promised to repentant, baptized believers (Acts 2:38, cp. 5:32) may well be called "the indwelling gift (or presence) of the Holy Spirit." The same might also very well be called "*the Spirit of Adoption*" (whereby we cry, "Abba, Father," His spirit bearing witness with our spirits that we are children of God, Rom. 8:14-16), cp. Galatians 4:4, 7; I John 3:24; 4:13; Acts 2:38; 5:32; Ephesians 3:16.

The Baptism of (in) the Holy Spirit

The term baptism of (in) the Holy Spirit is nowhere used in the Scriptures, but the verbal phrase, "baptize in (the) Holy Spirit" is used seven times. In five of the usages the expression is contained in a promise. In the other two texts it appears in the context of an historical flashback. (See *Matt. 3:11*; Mark 1:8; *Luke 3:16*; John 1:5; Acts 1:5; and Acts 11:16; I Cor. 12:13.) The italicized references are especially pertinent to the present discussion in that 1) they contain also the phrase, "and fire," and 2) the context in both cases (as distinguished from the other texts cited) includes specific mention and dire warning of the judgment and destiny of the wicked. To overlook this fact, as both the self-styled "Pentecostals" and the two-episode theorists uniformly do, is to miss an important clue to the meaning of what is being said.

Note the implications of the fuller text of John's words, as recorded by Matthew 3:7-12 and Luke 3:15-17, as compared to Mark 1:7, 8, John 1:32, 33, and Acts 1:5. The added phrase "and (in) fire" is found only in Matthew's and Luke's accounts, and it is significant that it is in their accounts that the words of John are couched in the context of his warning to the Pharisees of the fiery judgment that awaits the corrupt and impenitent; of whom they were set forth as "Exhibit A," so to speak.

Three important contrasts or comparisons are drawn. 1) All the penitent believers were presenting themselves for baptism "for the remission of sins" (Mark 1:4) whereas all the self-righteous, hence impenitent (See Luke 7:29, 30) refused to be baptized of John (Matt. 3:7-12; Luke 3:15-17). 2) All those who brought forth fruit worthy of repentance were counted proper subjects of the baptism of John, "a baptism of repentance for (Gr. *eis*, cp. Acts 2:38) the remission of sins." These are compared to trees which bring forth good fruit. Such trees are pruned, cultivated, preserved, that they may bring forth more fruit. Compare Jesus' parable of the vine and the branches, John

426

15:1-7. In contrast, "every tree that bringeth not forth good fruit is hewn down and cast into the fire, Matthew 3:10b; Luke 3:9. 3) The wheat, the desired fruitage of the sowing, the "harvest," is gathered into the garners, whereas the chaff is burned with unquenchable fire, Matthew 3:12.

The baptism of the Holy Spirit and the baptism of fire are obviously two different baptisms administered by Christ, for two different classes of persons. Together they are universal. To be not a participant in the one is to be assuredly a participant in the other.

Fire is mentioned three times in the two accounts in which the judgment of the wicked is included in the context. 1) The fire that shall consume the unfruitful trees is certainly the fire of the consuming judgment. 2) The fire that is said to likewise consume the chaff, the residue of the grain harvest, is likewise undeniably the fire of consuming judgment. 3) What then is the fire that is mentioned in the midst of the context? That too is the fire of judgment, not a secondary phenomenon attending the baptism of the Holy Spirit on the day of Pentecost. There was neither wind nor fire on that day, only a sound and sight that is said to have been "like as of" wind and fire (Acts 2:2, 3).

The baptism of fire spoken of by John the baptist is the same fire of which the apostle Paul forewarns us in II Thessalonians 1:7-10, as he informs us that at the revelation of Jesus Christ from heaven, with the angels of his power "in flaming fire he will render vengeance upon them that know not God, and to them that *obey not* the Gospel of our Lord Jesus." These, Paul declares, "shall suffer punishment, (even) eternal destruction from the face of the Lord and the glory of his might" (II Thess. 1:7-10).

If the promise of Joel, repeated by Peter, that in the latter days (as distinguished from the former days, the Jewish age) God would pour forth his spirit upon all flesh, without respect to age, sex, or caste was actually fulfilled for all time by two small representative groups of human beings—twelve Jews in Jerusalem and a household of Gentiles in Caesarea; and if the prediction of John the baptist, though couched in the language of universality, inclusive of both the penitent and impenitent, is likewise to be interpreted so restrictively (insofar as the baptism in the Holy Spirit is concerned), what then are the implications as to the baptism of fire for the wicked? Will that too be fulfilled, representatively, by a handful of heathen who know not God, and a handful of impenitents who "obey not the Gospel"? The one conjecture is as reasonable, or rather unreasonable, as the other.

The following chart, depicting the prophecy of John the baptist, as recorded by Matthew and underscored by Luke, graphically sets forth the implications of what John said:

"He (Christ) shall baptize you" (Matt. 3:11b) in:

Elements	(✔) Check	Recipients
The Holy Spirit	( ) Apostles & Household of Cornelius	
	( ) All saved persons	
Fire (3:10)	( ) A selected few "corrupt" trees	
	( ) All trees not bearing good fruit	
Fire (3:11)	( ) A selected few impenitent persons	
	( ) All impenitent persons	
Fire (3:12)	( ) A forkful or so of chaff	
	( ) All the chaff	

Obviously, John was not suggesting only a few of the wicked shall suffer the judgment of the unquenchable fires of hell. We ask therefore, if the two-episode theory of the baptism of the Holy Spirit be allowed to stand, are we then to assume that John was meaning to say to the throngs at the Jordan, "I indeed baptize in water as many as bring forth evidence of repentance, but he that comes after me will be much more selective than I am. He will baptize in the Holy Spirit only a dozen of all the seed of Abraham, plus one household of Gentiles to show he is no respecter of persons, at least not insofar as race is concerned"? What think ye?

I categorically challenge and openly deny the validity of the two-episode theory of the baptism of the Holy Spirit. The two episodes commonly supposed to *fulfill* (fill-full) the promise thereof are alike in only two respects: 1) Christ is the baptizer (as only he can be) and 2) the immediate credentializing sign was the same in each case, and for an obvious reason. Since it was the gift of tongues which credentialized the preachers on Pentecost on behalf of their audience, Jesus chose the same sign to credentialize the audience on behalf of the preacher at the time appointed for the opening of the doors to the Gentiles. Peter called attention to this fact when he was obliged to defend himself before the brethren at Jerusalem. Fortunately he had the six brethren who accompanied him as supporting witnesses. The telling effect is expressed as follows: "Then to the Gentiles also God hath granted repentance unto life" (Acts 11:18).

Comparison of Phenomenal Terms

The prophecy of Joel, as renewed in the New Testament, provides further insight into the interpretation of the promise stated as receiving at least partial fulfillment with the "coming" of the Holy Spirit upon the apostles on the day of Pentecost. Joel stated that the Holy Spirit would be "poured out." Luke records that the sound which accompanied the event "came from heaven," the sound thereof filled the house, and the apostles "were all filled with Holy Spirit, and began to speak with other tongues as the Spirit gave them utterance" (Acts 2:4). When the tongues phenomenon was repeated at the household of Cornelius the Holy Spirit is said to have "fallen on all them that heard the Word" (the preaching of Peter), Acts 10:44. It was on the latter occasion that the promise of Joel is identified with the promise of "the baptism of the Holy Spirit," and equated with both episodes, providing at least a tentative basis for the two-episode hypothesis.

Obviously we have in this datum an entirely different application or meaning of the word baptize than that which is intrinsic in the etymology of the term. Since the root meaning and common New Testament usage of the term is to dip how can the outpouring/falling of the Holy Spirit be called "baptism"? The answer is found in the figurative usage of the term. The act itself is a dipping, but the interim result of the act is an overwhelming of the person or thing immersed. Thus the suffering and anguish with which Jesus was to be engulfed was spoken of by him as a "baptism." See Matthew 20:22, 23 (KJV); Mark 10:38, 39; Luke 12:50. By the same token, to be baptized in the Holy Spirit is to be overwhelmed by the Holy Spirit. This is the usage that Paul makes of the figure of speech when he affirms: "In one Spirit are we all baptized into one body, whether Jews or Greeks, whether bond or free, and were all made to drink of one Spirit" (I Cor. 12:13). Heresy? A verse to be explained away, some way? Only by those locked in on the two-episode hypothesis.

When the Divine intent of the baptism (engulfing) is to produce an immediate and miraculous credential, in the form of a sign to those beholding, the Holy Spirit is said to "fall" or "come upon" the persons empowered thereby. (This is in keeping with Old Testament expressions describing the special endowment of chosen vessels by the visitation of "the Spirit of God." See Judg. 14:6; 15:14; I Sam. 10:10; 11:6; 19:27. Cp. Acts 2:1-4; 8:15, 16; 10:47, 48; 19:7).

Generally speaking, when the Holy Spirit is said to have fallen or come upon someone the immediate result was often a "for the occasion" affair, that is, of limited duration, and extra-ordinary in effect. In contrast, when the Holy Spirit is said to indwell the recipient the effect is extensive in duration and results in a process of spiritual growth and fruitage.

Question: If the metaphorical usage of baptism denotes an over-whelming, how can the mere indwelling of the Holy Spirit be called "baptism in the Holy Spirit"? Answer: There is no such thing as a *mere* indwelling of the Holy Spirit. The presence of the Holy Spirit, whether within or upon, is no *mere* thing. Never! If God chooses to work patiently and gradually in the human heart to effect a process of growth leading to the production of the fruits of the Spirit, His *modus operandi* is through the indwelling gift of the Holy Spirit. Such growth and fruitage is not attainable by "the natural man." Only if one counts the ability to perform on occasion eye-popping spectacular feats more important and more to be desired than spiritual growth and fruitage could such a one be minded to speak of the indwelling presence of the Holy Spirit as something *mere*. But what a perversion of values that is.

Are We Teaching Two Baptisms, Contrary to Ephesians 4:5?

When we speak of the Baptism of the Holy Spirit as an overwhelming of a surrendered human spirit, a state to be sought and attained by all believers, are we teaching two baptisms—one of the water and one of the Spirit, in contradiction of Ephesians 4:5? This is a common objection to the position taken herein. No. There are not two baptisms from which we are to choose or to which we are to submit. There is one baptism with two facets. There is the physical aspect consisting of the immersion of the body in water—an outward visible manifestation of the surrender of the human spirit to the Spirit of God. This is a part of what Paul calls "the obedience of faith," and "the obedience from the heart to that form of doctrine delivered us" (Rom. 1:5; 6:17). To the defiant, disobedient "mind of the flesh" this is a demeaning, debasing command. In any case it accomplishes nothing, spiritually speaking, unless it is an expression of an inward state consisting of the submission of the human spirit to the will and Spirit of God.

John states, "There are three who bear witness, the Spirit, and the water, and the blood: and the three agree in one," (I John 5:8). The very order in which the three are said to bear their concerted witness is important. Unless it is the Spirit that leads one to the water one is not cleansed by the blood. Except we "draw near (the throne of grace) with a true heart, in the fullness of faith" we may have the body washed with pure water, but there will be no sprinkling of the heart from an evil conscience by the blood of Christ. Christian baptism is not just the putting away (symbolically) of the filth of the flesh, but "the answer of a good conscience towards God" (Heb. 10:22; I Peter 3:21).

But does not the Scripture refer to only two episodes constituting the baptism of the Holy Spirit? On the surface, yes. But by the same token one could contend that only the Roman and Colossian Christians were "buried with Christ in baptism." It is readily granted that only two accounts of "baptizing" in the Holy Spirit are spoken of in so many words. But actually neither of those happenings is so identified at the time the two events occurred. Instead it is recorded that the Holy Spirit was "poured out" upon them. It was not until Peter found himself obliged to justify his participation in the Caesarean episode that the descent of the Holy Spirit on that occasion, and on Pentecost, was identified as the baptism of the Holy Spirit. Were it not for the bigotry and prejudice of the "brethren back home" it is likely neither of those occasions would ever have been so identified. What then would the two-episode theorists have done for proof texts?

But did not Peter speak of the Caesarean episode as having only one counterpart—the Pentecost episode? No, he did not even imply that, much less did he say that. For one thing, as we have already noted, the phenomena exhibited were alike in only one particular. Otherwise they differed greatly. On Pentecost it was the preachers who spoke with tongues, at Caesarea it was the auditors. At Pentecost the recipients had already been baptized in water "for the remission of sins" (Mark 1:3; Matt. 3:11). At Caesarea the recipients were baptized in water afterwards (Acts 10:47, 48). Moreover, as we previously pointed out, the extent of spiritual empowerment, both in endowment and duration, can in no way be demonstrated as equal. Not even the one point of similarity, the speaking in tongues, could have been demonstrated as dramatically at Caesarea as it was on Pentecost. There were not "Jews from every nation under heaven, hearing the household of Cornelius all speaking in the "back home" dialect of each one who heard.

Why then did Peter select Pentecost for his point of comparison? Because at Pentecost the phenomenon visited upon the recipients was convincing to the Jews who heard. At Caesarea it served the self same purpose. (See Acts 11:18, and recall the reluctance of Peter to go there in the first place.)

Comparison with Other Recorded Episodes

While we are on the topic of comparative episodes a question arises. How may we conclude the Samaritans of Acts 8 and the twelve brethren of Acts 19 did not receive the baptism of the Holy Spirit? The same descriptive language is used in each case, and the same phenomenon was displayed in the latter case. The fact is, that aside from the phenomenon of tongues, every significant phrase associated with the baptism of the Holy Spirit on Pentecost and at Caesarea is applied also to other episodes in the book of Acts and in the larger context of the New Testament to the church universally.

Is the Holy Spirit said to have been "poured out" upon the apostles? It was (Acts 2:17, 18, 33). And Titus 3:5, 6 informs us that by his mercy he has "saved us, through the washing of regeneration and *renewing of the Holy Spirit which he poured out upon us richly*, through Jesus Christ our Saviour."

Were the apostles said to have been filled with the Holy Spirit when they received the baptism of the Holy Spirit? They were indeed (Acts 2:4). The same thing is said of the whole church in Acts 4:31. It is also said of Saul of Tarsus (Acts 9:17). The fact is John the baptist is said to have been filled with the Holy Spirit from his mother's womb, (Luke 1:15). Moreover, his mother, Elizabeth (v. 41) and his father, Zacharias (v. 67) were also said to have been filled with the Holy Spirit. Such disclosure is a bit disconcerting to those who have been persuaded that the Holy Spirit showed up on earth as a virtual stranger on the day of Pentecost. (I was taught that, and taught it myself—a victim of the "I thought you checked it" syndrome). And in Ephesians 5:16 we are commanded to "be filled with the Spirit."

Is the Holy Spirit said to have fallen on the household of Cornelius? Definitely (Acts 10:44); and by inference the same could be said of the apostles (cp. v. 47, 11:15, 17). The same is strongly implied concerning the Samaritans (Acts 8:15-17) and the twelve brethren at Ephesus (Acts 19:6).

Are Cornelius and his household said to have "received" the Holy Spirit, the same being later described as the "gift" of the Holy Spirit? Yes, indeed (Acts 10:47, 11:17). This is the very same language that is used concerning the promise which we claim for ourselves on the basis of Acts 2:38; 5:32.

There remains one more question along the same line, though a step removed. Do we not insist that to be born of water (John 3:5) means to be baptized in water? Why then does not the term joined with it by the conjunction *and* communicate the fact we are baptized in the Spirit? Does not I Corinthians 12:13 unequivocably inform us that "in one Spirit we are all baptized into one body"? We bristle when those of the faith-only persuasion seek to wring the *water* out of John 3:5, and insist that despite the fact the language in the passage is metaphorical it is to be taken at face value. Consistency demands that we recognize the fact that Christian baptism has two facets, human and Divine. Christ baptizes in the one Spirit those who yield themselves to him as servants of righteousness in the baptism of water. Together, they constitute the "one baptism" of Ephesians 4:5.

Whereunto will this thing lead, or grow?

The fear that gripped the hearts and blinded the eyes of the captains of the temple and the chief priests (Acts 5:24) poses a problem to ourselves also. It was certainly so with me as this study began to lead in a direction I was at first unready to go. In presenting the foregoing considerations I am almost invariably asked: "Does not such a position give aid and comfort to the (so-called) "charismatics"? Is it not, at least in part, a capitulation to the Pentecostals? Far from it. The position taken herein tends to disarm them. It upsets their strategy. It undermines the areas in which they counted themselves the most unassailable.

Prior to my arrival at the position set forth in this study every encounter with the neo-Corinthian glossolalists and old-line Pentecostals developed into an eye-ball to eye-ball confrontation, with more heat than light marking the exchange. Today I feel unthreatened by their challenge and generally manage to wring some concessions from those at both extremes.

On one hand a careful analysis of the Corinthian catastrophe, viewed in the light of Paul's appraisal and recommendations, demonstrates the fact that the gifts of the miraculous order in which the Corinthians gloried were 1) not a mark of spiritual maturity nor of Divine favor,

2) they were a cause of dissension then, as now, and would not likely contribute to attaining or maintaining of "the spirit of unity in the bond of peace," and 3) tongues, apparently the most oft-claimed gift, then as now, caused more harm than good, if indeed the gift contributed anything to the good of the church as a whole.

On the other hand it can be demonstrated that the overwhelming (baptism) of the Holy Spirit was manifested in the form of moral gifts as well as miraculous, and it was the moral manifestation of the presence of the Holy Spirit that drew Paul's recommendation and praise.

It was a sad day when we concluded, on the basis of the implications of the two-episode theory, that the gift of tongues is *the* sign of the baptism of the Holy Spirit. Having so conceded we were then forced to contend that the baptism of the Holy Spirit was but a temporary and limited phenomenon in order to deny the validity of such claims today. Committed to the same basic error Pentecostals and their imitators are forced to convince themselves that their gibberish is the gift of tongues in order to assure themselves they have received the baptism of the Holy Spirit. The fault in either case is with the major premise.

This is nothing new. From the text of I Corinthians 12-14 it is evident that the "gift of tongues" was the "gift" most sought after, counterfeited and claimed—then, as now. And it was the gift that the inspired apostle most belittled. Were it genuine in the instance of every claimant, even the troublemakers, would Paul have dared to so disparage a "gift from God"? Generally speaking, what Paul did in dealing with the subject, was to use the debate technique of conceding a point in order to make a point.

In One Spirit Were We All Baptized into One Body

Paul's startling announcement in I Corinthians 12:13 is not to be explained away. It is to be understood in its proper light and demonstrated, and indeed it can be. He used the word baptized in its metaphorical sense, as Jesus did when speaking of "the baptism of suffering." See Mark 10:38, 39. A football team is said to receive its "baptism" when the forward wall of the opposing team, play after play, rolls over them like a tidal wave. A soldier is said to receive "the baptism of fire" when he is caught up in the midst of battle with shot and shell raining down upon him on every side. We receive the baptism of the Holy Spirit when we yield ourselves body, soul, and spirit to the Spirit of God. What is accomplished in us when we are thus "overwhelmed" depends on the Divine purpose God seeks to work through us.

434

If I should suddenly find myself speaking in language I had never studied, that would be an action beyond my spirit to effectuate. Should that happen, and that is precisely what happened to the apostles on the day of Pentecost, I would hesitate not at all to claim the baptism of the Holy Spirit. But is there no other sign? Is that the best or most God would have one do?

Suppose I should be found loving as Christ loved, loving those who hate me and despitefully use me. Do you think that is my natural spirit? Then you do not know me very well. Suppose in the midst of trial and tribulation my soul were at peace, serene, fully trusting. That is not my natural spirit either. I am inclined to be like the lady who told her preacher that when the Lord gave her tribulation she was supposed to tribulate. Were I to exhibit amid every circumstance of life the perfect fruitage of the Holy Spirit—love, joy, peace, longsuffering, kindness, goodness, faithfulness, meekness, self control—(Paul did! See Phil. 4:10-13, 18a), there could be but one accounting: The baptism of the Holy Spirit.

Conclusion

A matter of some technical import bears on this subject. There are two Greek words commonly transliterated *baptism*: baptismos (pl., mois) and baptisma. The latter is the form most often used in the New Testament. In fact it is used only in the New Testament and later literature contingent upon the New Testament. In contrast, *baptismos* (mois) abounds in the literature of the era. It is used in the literature of the pagan cults, Jewish sects and in secular literature. It is used in the New Testament only in Mark 7:4, (8, KJV) Heb. 6:2, 9:10. In each of those texts it is used of "divers(e) washings," the repetitive rituals of the Mosaic law. When used outside the New Testament, as indicated above, it likewise refers to repetitive ritual ablutions. It is never used of the baptism of John nor of Christian baptism; neither of the water nor of the Spirit.

Noted scholars such as L. H. Cremer, George Milligan, J. Moulton, G. Abbott-Smith, call attention to the fact that the difference between the two words lies in the meaning of the suffixes. These play an important role in the Greek language in forming and determining the meaning of new words.

The suffix *ma* is used to denote a state of being, as of the mind. The suffix *mos* simply denotes physical action. Thus *baptisma* implies commitment. It is a once-for-all event, the effect of which is from thence onward. *Baptismos* describes an action of a moment, the kind of action that is repeatable in the experience of the same persons, and generally was repeated, to the point of being repetitious, hence its usage in Mark 7:4; Heb. 6:2; 9:10.

Not so with Christian baptism (*baptisma*). The outward, viewable, physical aspect, like *baptismos*, is a momentary act but the state of mind, the commitment which *baptisma* dramatizes, like the atoning work of Christ on Calvary is a once-for-all time commitment. See Heb. 9:24-28, 7:26, 27.

Baptisma is the verb form that was coined and used uniformly by the inspired penmen of the New Testament to describe both facets of Christian baptism—1) the surrender of our body to the engulfing, overwhelming water in a visual dramatization of Christian baptism as a "baptism of repentance for the remission of sins" (Acts 2:38, cp. Mark 1:4); being a "baptism into death" (dying to sin, once for all, as Christ so died for our sins, Rom. 6:3-18) and 2) the surrender of our "inner man" (our spirit) to receive the immersion in the Holy Spirit that we may thenceforth be "led of the Spirit," thus manifested as children of God. (See Rom. 8:1-17, particularly vs. 14, 16.)

Such is the Divine design and the New Testament ideal. But the dichotomy Paul candidly discusses in Romans 8 (see also Gal. 5) is a problem with which we continue to contend. "The flesh (indeed) lusteth against the Spirit and the Spirit against the flesh; for these are (indeed) contrary one to the other" (Gal. 5:17). No wonder Paul once cried out in agony of spirit: "O wretched man that I am, who shall deliver me out of the body of this death?" (Rom. 7:24). Romans 8, the chapter which follows, was written to encourage us with the hope that he found in the Spirit of Christ.

Admittedly, the state which baptism denotes is not constantly manifest in us. But we too find the courage and the strength to fight on. Nations which have overwhelmed and conquered their adversaries have lost many a skirmish and even a few battles in the interim. According to Divine promise this flesh, our outward man will perish, "but the inward man is renewed day by day" (II Cor. 4:16). At Christ's coming, this body which is the seat and avenue through which temptation assails the spirit shall be changed. "He shall fashion anew the body of our humiliation, that it may be conformed to the body of his glory" (Phil. 3:21).

"The hour cometh in which all that are in the tombs shall hear his voice, and shall come forth, they that have done good unto the resurrection of life, and they that have done evil unto the resurrection of judgment" (John 5:28, 29). Then shall come to pass *forevermore* the saying that is written: "He, Christ shall baptize you (one and all, both the good and evil) in the Holy Spirit, and in fire."

Such shall be the consummation of that state we entered when the love of Christ constrained us to surrender our spirits to God, that we "might be ·strengthened with power through his Spirit in the inward man" (Eph. 3:16). Thus strengthened we began the task of bringing under control the outward man. In token thereof we yielded our bodies for burial in baptism, and to God, to become "instruments of righteousness unto sanctification" (Rom. 6:19). When our spirits stopped even our very breathing, when we closed our eyes as in death, and surrendered ourselves to be buried in the waters of baptism, we first entered the state that shall be perfected and perpetuated in the second resurrection. Meanwhile we do well to pray, in the words Christ taught his disciples to pray: "Thy kingdom come, thy will be done, as in heaven, so on earth," yea, *in us*—"that the word of God be not blasphemed" (Matt. 6:10; Titus 2:5b).

Index of Scriptures

444

450

Index of Subjects

453